THE CATHARS

Texts written with the collaboration of:
Julie Roux
Historical advisor:
Anne Brenon
Translated by:
Barbara Jachowicz-Davoust

S U M

Christ in majesty, Toulouse

The Cité

M A R Y

Arques

Régine Tower and Cabaret

Soldier

arcassonne

1

HERESY

1

DOGMA AND HERESIES

After the apostles' generation, the Christian Church expanded rapidly. Depending on the places where it was established, varying interpretations of Christianity appeared. Refuting heretical ideas, in the 2nd century the Church Fathers laid the bases of theology whose dogmas were defined at the great Councils of the 4th and 5th centuries. Towards the year 1000, heresy was again on the agenda in Bulgaria, Greece, Saxony, Champagne, Burgundy and Perigord. Burning at the stake took place. In the 12th century, besides Pierre of Bruys, Henri of Le Mans, or Valdès of Lyon, there were other heretics who attempted to live according to evangelical ideals. Bernard of Clairvaux discovered them in Occitania, and, in the Rhineland, the Abbot of Schönau invented the name *cathars* to describe them.

Hadrian's temple in Ephesus

Antoninus's baths in Carthage

DETERMINING CHRISTIAN DOGMA

By the end of the first century A.D., although the first generation of apostles had died, Christianity had been established thanks to Paul's travels and the action of anonymous missionaries in most of the great cities of the Mediterranean East: Jerusalem and Caesarea in Palestine, in Tyre and Antioch of Syria, Salamis and Paphos on the island of Cyprus, at Ephesus, Philippi and Thessaloniki in Macedonia, as well as Athens, Corinth and Alexandria. In the West, where only Rome seems to have been affected in the first century, Christian communities have been attested in Lyon and probably existed in Autun by the following century. In the course of this second century, Christianity developed along the North African coast starting from Carthage. In the East, after the destruction of the Temple and the capture of Jerusalem by the Romans in 70, the Judeo-Christians emigrated to Pella in Transjordan. Already present in the large coastal cities, the new religion spread eastwards and inland, reaching Dura Europos in Persia. During the 3rd century, Christianity expanded rapidly and overflowed its previous, essentially urban, limits. From Alexandria, it reached the rural areas of Egypt, notably Fayum. Tolerated by the first Sassanids, it progressed in Persia. In Syria and in Asia Minor, and particularly in the provinces of Cappadocia and Pontus, it spread in rural areas. At the beginning of the 4th century, Christianity was adopted as the state religion in the Kingdom of Armenia. During this same period in the West, Christian communities have been attested in northern Italy and in Sicily, in the Balkan provinces, south-eastern Gaul and southern Spain. Each of these early ecclesiastical organizations, from the Greek *ekklêsia*, assembly, or churches, developed an arrangement setting up, beside the college of presbyters-episcopies –from the Greek *presbyteroi* "ancients" and *episcopoi* "surveillants"– charged with the spiritual and liturgical functions, deacons who were in charge of material life, social and charitable services (or social work...). In the 2nd and 3rd centuries, a single bishop, defined as the apostles' successor, was elected by the faithful to be the head of each large urban community. Ordained by his peers by the laying on of hands, the bishop in turn ordained priests and deacons. He was responsible for small local communities run by priests. Baptism, the ritual marking belonging to the Christian community, consisted of being immersed three times in running water, followed by the laying on of hands and unction with oil. It was preceded by a long period of instruction, the catechumen, at the beginning of which the candidate received the Christian "symbol", that is, the formula for the confession of the faith. The community gathered every Sunday in order to celebrate the communion or Eucharist, the central rite of Christianity that commemorates the last supper of Jesus Christ, his death and his redemptive resurrection.

But the integration of Christians into the Roman world was not accomplished without difficulties. Those who advocated the separation between religion and politics and refused to honour the gods of the city, to swear an oath to the divine emperor, who spread subver-

Reference Dates	
The burning of Rome. Nero's persecution of Christians.	64
• Domitian's reign and persecutions. • Preaching by Simon the Magus, allegedly the first Gnostic.	81-96
Ignatius of Antioch meets the first attested Docetae.	≃ 110
Excommunication of Marcion.	144
Irenaeus becomes Bishop of Lyon.	177
Tertullian of Carthage, an adversary of Gnosticism, joins Montanism.	207
Excommunication of Sabellius.	220
Beginning of Mani's preaching.	242
Death of Origen of Alexandria.	≃ 250
Deposition of Paul of Samosata.	268
Edict of Milan. Emperor Constantine proclaims freedom of worship for the different religions.	313
First ecumenical Council of Nicaea. Condemnation of Arius.	325
• Christianity becomes the Empire's official religion. • Second ecumenical Council of Constantinople.	381
Beheading of Priscillian.	385
Baptism of the future Bishop Augustine of Hippo.	387
Banishment of the Patriarch of Constantinople, Nestorius.	431
Third ecumenical Council of Chalcedon.	451
Deposition of the last Western Roman Emperor.	476
Baptism of Clovis.	498
Beginning of the iconoclastic crisis in the Byzantine Empire.	726
Council of Aachen: Charlemagne has the *Filioque* incorporated into the symbol of Nicaea.	809
Schism between Catholics and Orthodox.	1054

Constantine, church in Cappadocia

SYMBOL OF FAITH

··

T he drawing of a fish is one of the very first Christian symbols. The word *ichtus*, fish in Greek, is in fact an acronym for an expression meaning "Jesus Christ Son of God the Saviour".

Fish, Byzantine church in Tabgha

sive messages, questioned a system based on slavery, and exalted temperance and virginity were marginalized, strangers in a Roman society held together by activities they condemned (banquets, circuses, etc.). They were rapidly slandered, even accused of eating babies covered in flour. After the great fire of Rome in July 64, Nero, who was looking for someone onto whom he could divert suspicion, found the perfect scapegoats. The imperial persecutions of 64 A.D. were the first in a long series, the most murderous of which took place during the second half of the 3rd century. At that moment, faced with the barbarian peoples' unexpected and devastating breakthrough of the borders of the empire, the emperor, the symbolic link between Rome and its protective gods, made the imperial cult obligatory. However, in 313, through the Edict of Milan, Constantine, master of the Western Empire since his victory over his rival, Maxentius, –a victory he owed, according to his Christian biographers, to the help of Christ– proclaimed freedom of religion for the persecuted. With the exception of Julian the Apostate (362-363), all the following emperors were Christians. With the privileges accorded by the political powers, the Church became a great property owner. In the cities, bishops became important and powerful personalities. Exempted from paying taxes, elected by the clergy from among local worthies, often with imperial approval, the bishops obtained judicial and administrative positions that went beyond a strictly religious framework. At the head of a hierarchy that distinguished between superior clerics –priests and deacons, and minor ones– lectors, deaconesses and exorcists, bishops ran complete structures of social work, organizing the distribution of food and clothing, building orphanages, hospices and hospitals in the suburbs of towns. The bishops of the same region –the ecclesiastical province– gathered together under the authority of the bishop of the principal city, called the metropolitus. The metropoliti of Rome, Constantinople, Alexandria and Antioch had precedence over the others and had the title of patriarchs.

However, in a bitter repetition of history, new coercive measures were adopted by the imperial powers, this time directed against the followers of traditional religions like Judaism or paganism, or against "heretics" such as Gnostics or Manichaeans of the Christian religion. This was supposed to lead to the triumph of an *orthodoxy* proclaimed to be the Empire's official religion by Theodosius 1st in 381. The expression of this Christian orthodoxy, in other words that which had been decided as being the right opinion of God, the right doctrine as opposed to *heresy*, i.e., another "choice" (*hairesis* in Greek) and very quickly, the wrong choice, that of false doctrine, happened in a fairly progressive manner. During the 1st century, Christianity appeared much more as a way of existence, an appeal to live in the footsteps of Jesus Christ resurrected, sent by the Father to save humanity and allow it to be sanctified by having the Holy Spirit descend on it, rather than as a dogmatic religion. However, in the 2nd century, at a time when direct witnesses of the "Son of Man" were no longer there to guarantee the authenticity of his message, to defend him from his detractors or to answer the questions of new converts, the Christian communities felt the need to define and

MANICHAEISM

Manichaeism takes its name from its founder, Mani, who in Greek texts was called *Manikhaios*, "Mani the Living". The son of a Parthian prince named Pattig, of the Arsacide dynasty, Mani was born in April, 216, in northern Babylonia, in the region of Selecia-Ctesiphon. After experiencing a vision, his father had converted to an aesthetic ideal, and Mani entered with him into a Baptist sect. At the age of twelve, he received his first revelations about the eternal combat between Light and Darkness. When Mani was twenty-four, other revelations caused him to break away from his original community and to proclaim himself the supreme apostle of Light and of salvation, the ultimate continuity of Zoroaster, Buddha and Jesus. A first journey took him to India. On his return to Persia in about 242, the Sassanid sovereign Shapur 1st (241-272) gave him permission to preach his new religion. Spreading throughout the Sassanid empire, this religion coexisted with Mazdeisme. Within a few years, Manichaeism spread through

Iran, India and Syria. Allegedly, Mani even went to Tibet and to China, and also entrusted the mission of propagating his doctrine to his disciples Adda, Thomas and Hermas. The doctrine arrived in Egypt at the end of the 260's. However, contested by the priests of traditional Mazdeism, Mani was arrested by a successor of Shapur 1st, Bahram II, and put to death in 277. Mani presented himself as the prophet of a new religion, the heir of all previous religions. Simultaneously inspired by Judeo-Christian Gnosticism and Iranian Zoroastrianism, Manichaeism solved the problem of evil by professing an absolute dualism. It affirmed the existence of two co-eternal principles, equal in strength but radically opposed: Light and Darkness, Good and Evil, with matter being fundamentally evil. Manichaeism preached a theory about the regular appearance of prophets, both saviours and saved, cast into Darkness and then brought up into the Light. As its final prophet, Mani claimed to possess all the gifts previously transmitted by the

Justinian

prophetic spirit. After the death of its founder, Manichaeism spread from China to North Africa, but was persecuted in the Roman Empire starting in 302. In the 6th century, it was the object of severe repression under Justin 1st (519-527) and Justinian 1st (527-565).

Bas-relief at Temple of Bel, Palmyra in Syria

The Four Gospels

THE DOCETAE

The Bishop of Antioch, Ignatius, who died about 110, was the first to denounce what he called Docetism. Arrested during the reign of Trajan (98-117) for publicly preaching the Christian faith, Ignatius was taken to Rome under escort to undergo martyrdom. As he crossed the cities of Asia Minor, he nevertheless continued to propagate his faith in Jesus Christ, God made Man, who had died and resurrected. It was then that he came into conflict with certain Christians for whom the divinity of Christ could not be reconciled with his human condition. In their opinion, the body he took on was simply an appearance, and he himself did not really suffer on the cross. To mock them, Ignatius threw the argument back at them: even they existed only in appearance, thinking Christ suffered only in appearance. They are therefore *Docetae*, from the Greek *dokein*, to seem or appear.

strictly organize their beliefs. At a time too when, through contact with the different milieus and diverse cultures that welcomed it, differing interpretations of this message –Gnosticism, Marcionism or Montanism, for example– began to be elaborated by those thinkers whom the Church recognized as its "Fathers". This Christian theology progressively defined its doctrine as coming from texts claiming to be the authentic, apostolic tradition, and ended up imposing its own orthodoxy during the great Councils of the 4th and 5th centuries, rejecting any interpretation of Christianity henceforth judged as being deviant, or heretical. Thus, wishing to defend their religion against the hostility met within the Empire, Apologists, such as Justin of Rome (martyred in about 165), introduced elements into the newly-forming Christian theology to make it comprehensible to cultured pagans. They took ideas inherited from Greek philosophy, in particular the Stoics, which they used to define their Christology starting with the Gospels of John. Since all eternity, God has carried within him his *Logos*, that is, the creative principle, organizer of the world and of History; "begotten" for creation, this *Logos* was subsequently incarnated in Jesus Christ, in order to save Man damaged by sin and to restore God's initial purpose. In his *Adversus Haereses*, a five-volume treatise offering a vigorous refutation of Gnostic theses based on the theme of unity, Irenaeus of Lyon provided a synthesis representative of this doctrinal development of the 2nd century. It was simultaneously linked to disproving "heresies" and to the contribution of Greek philosophy. To the dualism proposed by the Gnostics or Marcion, distinguishing a creative God, or Demiurge, from the veritable and transcendent God, or Saviour, Irenaeus opposed a unique God, emphasizing the unity of His work, beginning with the creation of Adam, fettered by sin and the Fall, but saved, renewed and completed by Christ. Similarly, to their Docetism, in other words their purely spiritual concept of the nature of Christ, denying his physical, carnal reality, he opposed the theme of the unity of Christ, at the same time God and man, *Logos* incarnate, the "Word made flesh". Nevertheless, the problem of the relations between God, "the all-powerful Father" and Jesus Christ, "His only Son", as it is expressed by the symbol of the apostles at the beginning of the 3rd century, was far from being resolved. On the contrary, it fanned the flames of controversy. Indeed, how was it possible to conceive of the existence of two divine beings within a monotheistic religion, claiming the Old Testament as its authority? In opposition to the Christology of the *Logos* that they willingly accused of ditheism, the Adoptionists and the Patripassianists, both strictly monotheistic, or Monarchian, provided a response. Preached in Rome towards the end of the 2nd century by Theodore of Byzantium, Adoptionism said Jesus was a mere man, chosen for his merits and adopted by God, who brought the Spirit down upon him during his baptism in the Jordan River. Although condemned, this doctrine was revived once again in Rome, between 230 and 250 by Artemon, and again in a different form in Antioch between 260 and 270 by the very controversial Bishop of that city, Paul of Samosata, who was deposed in 268. As for Patripassianism, preached for the first time in Smyrna by Noetum at the end of the 2nd century, it

MARCION

B orn in about 85 in Sinope, in Pontus on the Black Sea, Marcion was the son of a bishop. He reached Rome but, upon his excommunication in 144, he decided to found his own church. He died in about 160, after founding communities all around the Mediterranean. Marcion wished to preach the message of the Gospels in all its purity. According to him, the God of love, Father of Christ, was not the irascible God of the Old Testament. The latter was simply the Demiurge creator of the world, the judge who wrote the Law. Unlike the Gnostics, Marcion denied that man contained any part of the God of love, but was created "in the image and resemblance" of that Demiurge. It was through sheer goodness that the Father sent his Son to Earth, in order to show men his mercy and to allow them to live without fear, by doing good. The Son only took on a human appearance and, crucified, went down into hell to announce the resurrection of souls. Marcion preached a strict form of asceticism, a renouncing of matter –the substance of this world– and its temptations. He was the author of a first neo-testamentary canon, which he gathered by correcting certain writings, thereby providing a scriptural basis for his theology.

Christ's Descent into Hell

THE GNOSTICS

Born at the eastern end of the Mediterranean at the end of the 1st century A.D., Gnosticism developed during the 2nd and 3rd centuries within different systems and in as many sects, scattered all around the Mediterranean basin, from Iran as far as Gaul. In general, the Christian authors who battled against them, such as Irenaeus of Lyon in his *Against Heresies*, called Simon the Magus the first Gnostic. Inspired by classical philosophy and oriental religions, Gnosticism found its most favourable ground in Egypt, the native land of Carpocrates, Basilides, Isidore or Valentinius –the great figures of Christian Gnosticism. In 1945, in Nag' Hammadi, Upper Egypt, a sealed jar was discovered. It contained a veritable Gnostic "library", with about fifty Coptic texts, among them The Apocryphon of John, the Gospel according to Thomas, The Gospel of Truth, or the Apocalypse of James. Gnosticism took its name from the knowledge –*gnosis* in Greek– that its followers searched for as the only path to salvation. Gnostic teaching was characterized by the transmission of a mythical tale. The Syrio-Egyptian myths claimed that at the beginning there was the *Pleroma*, a universe of perfection, unity and light, over which the real God reigned, surrounded by *aeons*. But one of the *aeons* begot the Demiurge, the creator of this world of division, change and death. The Syrian movements, however, supposed the initial coexistence of two opposed substances –those of Good and Evil– which mixed together and provoked the creation of the sensible world. The purpose of these always complex myths was to account for the destiny of the spirit –*pneuma*– of man, the spark of light originally located in the celestial, spiritual and light world, but who tragically fell to earth during the creation and was locked in a sensitive body. The God of the *Pleroma* –often assimilated into the God of the Gospels, in opposition to the Demiurge of Genesis and the Old Testament– sent Jesus on Earth to teach spirits how to free themselves from the prison of their flesh. Being spiritual, the Saviour only took on a human appearance, since the divine could not associate with matter. Hence, Basilides taught that it was Simon of Cyrene, and not Christ, who was crucified. Becoming aware of the divine spark living inside him, and of his condition of being *foreign* in this life, the Gnostic tried to liberate himself of matter in order to reach true life. According to the Gnostic systems, the universe created by the Demiurge consisted of seven, twelve, or even three hundred and sixty-five concentric circles, corresponding to as many worlds separating the Darkness, in other words the world on Earth, from the Light or *Pleroma*. A guarantee of salvation, the spirit's path from Darkness towards Light appeared above all as an interior ascension toward spiritual perfection. It was characterized by a flight from the world and a set of ritual and continent practices. Depending on their degree of knowledge, Gnostic followers were divided into three groups: material or believers (*hulikos*), animate or auditors (*psukhikos*) and spiritual or chosen (*pneumatikos*). The latter, keepers of the saving gnosis, were the spiritual chiefs of the Gnostic sects.

Temple of Baal Shamin in Palmyra

PAUL OF SAMOSATA

....

A native of Samosata in Syria, Paul, a high-level civil servant in the administration of Queen Zenobia (266-272), was also the Bishop of Antioch. However, his worldly life-style and his doctrine, close to Adoptionism, aroused discontent and several councils were called starting in 264. The council held in Antioch in 268 managed to depose him after a debate opposing Paul and the priest, Malchion. Although he was relieved of his duties, Paul refused to leave the ecclesiastical buildings. He was removed by force, once Antioch was returned to Roman administration after Aurelian's capture of Palmyra in 272. Paul of Samosata's disciples created a sect that was still in existence at the time of the Council of Nicaea in 325.

taught that the Son was just another name, another manifestation of the Father. Noetum was condemned by the priests of Smyrna, but Patripassianism was introduced to Rome with the preaching of Epigonus, and was then taken up by a certain Sabellius. After his excommunication in Rome in about 220, Sabellius continued to spread his beliefs throughout Libya and Egypt, where they developed under the name of Sabellianism. In fact, although the Roman episcopal hierarchy rejected the Adoptionist doctrine that denied the divine nature of Christ, as it condemned Patripassianism for not distinguishing the Father from the Son, it had not clearly expressed its own position. Nonetheless, the controversy gave the Fathers of the Church the opportunity to develop and deepen their own theses. Hence, in Africa at the transition from the 2nd to the 3rd century, Tertullian of Carthage (c. 155-c.255), the first theologian to write in the Latin language, arrived at the affirmation of a divine unity distributed among three *persons* –the Father, the Son, and the Holy Spirit– who were numerically distinct, each *person* of this *trinity* being God because they consisted of the same and unique divine substance. At the same time in the East, the Christology of the *Logos* developed through the thinkers of the Alexandrian school, such as Clement (c.180-before 215), and especially Origen (c.185-c.250), whose work, although it ended with a gnosis, exercised considerable influence over 3rd and 4th century theologians in the field of doctrine as well as in biblical exegesis. However, though the symbol of Caesarea at the end of the 3rd century expressed a belief in "a single

God" and in "Jesus Christ, *Logos* of God", the question of the status of this *Logos* remained fairly ill-defined. And it was only the controversy created around this subject by the priest Arius, who in about 318-320 in Alexandria supported Subordinationist theses, that caused Emperor Constantine to intervene and call for the first ecumenical council in Nicaea in 325. The orthodox position was defined there. Eager to preserve the monotheism inherited from the Old Testament, Arius in fact claimed that the Son was inferior and posterior to God. According to him, the absolute mark of divinity was not only being non-created, but also being non-begotten. Begotten by the will of God, the Son could therefore not be entirely God. Arius was excommunicated by the Bishop of Alexandria a first time in 320-321, then had anathema pronounced against him in 325 by the Council of Nicaea. The council established that divinity did not have to be associated with the concept of begetting and imposed as a dogma of the faith the belief in "a single Lord Jesus Christ, Son of God [...], the true God born of the true God, begotten but not created, consubstantial [*homoousios*] with the father". But most of the eastern bishops present in Nicaea, with Eusebius of Caesarea (263-339) at their head, accepted only reluctantly the term of *homoousios* –consubstantiality– a non-Scriptural term most certainly proposed by western bishops, who were perhaps unaware that it had already been used by Paul of Samosata, whose doctrine had been condemned. Therefore, after the death of Constantine in 337, gathered together in a general synod by Emperor Constantius II (337-361) in 341, the eastern bishops decided to adopt a symbol strictly based on quotations from the Scriptures, which defined the Son as "the only God begotten by Him who made everything, begotten by the father before all the centuries, True God from True God, all from all, unique of the unique, perfect of perfect, King of King, lord of lord, living *Logos* [...], adequate image of divinity, of substance, of will, of the power and the glory of the father, the first-born of all creation, who at the beginning was in God, *Logos* of God according to the Gospels". But by deleting from their creed this criterion of orthodoxy constituted by the term *homoousios*, the bishops of the East in fact re-opened the debate. And while in Antioch Aetius and then Eunomius took up and even radicalized Arius's theses, a third party, approved by Emperor Constantius II, professed a milder Arianism, claiming the unicity and solitude of God the Father, the subordination of his Son, but also an undefined similarity between the Father and the Son. Ratified by two councils in 359-360, of western bishops in Rimini and eastern bishops in Selecia, this Arian creed was adopted as official Christianity. It was with this same Arian creed that Bishop Ulfila (311-383) evangelized the Goths, and which was adopted by most of the Germanic peoples before they invaded the Roman Empire. But meanwhile, the situation had changed and the Nicene orthodoxy had finally triumphed, though not without long and passionate discussions between the various Churches of the East and West. The second ecumenical council gathered at Constantinople in 381 by Theodosius 1st (379-395) definitively settled the Trinitarian doctrine by completing the Nicene Creed with the affirmation of the divinity of the Spirit that "proceeds from the

Byzantine street in Caesarea

ROMAN OR BYZANTINE?

....

The name *Byzantine Empire* was given to the *Roman Empire of the East* only in the 19th century. It was due to the fact that in 330, Emperor Constantine chose the site of former Byzantium to build his new capital city, Constantinople.

Mosaic of Christ, Saint Sophia

Father and is adored and glorified together with the Father and the Son". However, the theological investigations were far from over. The problem of the humanity of Christ, emphasized by the Arians in order to stress the inferiority of the Logos, reappeared at the beginning of the 5th century. Indeed, what about the nature –*physis* in Greek– of Jesus Christ, at the same time God and man? The Monophysites of Alexandria, with Bishop Cyril at their head, who insisted on the subordination of Christ's human nature to his divine nature, were opposed by the Dyophysites of Antioch, among them Nestorius, a former Syrian monk who was elected Patriarch of Constantinople in April 428. Finally, to put an end to the controversy, in 451, Marcian, the emperor of the East, imposed the dogmatic compromise, "the union of the two natures, with no confusion nor division, in the person of Christ". But the Monophysites of Egypt, the Coptic Church, and of Syria remained faithful to their belief, and their religious divergence took on a definite political aspect. Within the context of opposition to the Empire, it allowed them to assert themselves against the dominant Greek culture. Abandoned to the Arian Germanic peoples after 476, the Christian West was divided into several independent kingdoms. Clovis, King of the Franks, was the first, in 498, to accept the Catholic faith, a gesture which gave him the support of the local bishops and facilitated his conquests. The Visigoths converted in 589 and the Lombards followed during the second half of the 7th century.

The Trinity, reredos, Rigaud Museum

NESTORIUS

M aking a precise distinction between Christ's human and divine properties, the Patriarch of Constantinople, Nestorius, was opposed to the habit of calling Mary, the *Mother of God*, preferring the title of *Mother of Christ*, mother of the man Jesus. Accused of dividing Christ, he was deposed by the Council of Ephesus in 431 and exiled to Petra, then to a Libyan oasis, where he died in 451.

Baptism of Clovis, gallery of kings, façade of Notre Dame in Reims

The Virgin, fresco in Göreme

SAINT AUGUSTINE

Augustine was born in Tagaste in Numidia in 364 of a pagan father and a Christian mother. He studied in Tagaste and Madaura, then in Carthage, a cosmopolitan city where he met the woman with whom he had a son, Adeodatus, in 372. Preoccupied by the problem of evil, Augustine joined the Manichaeans in 373. As a professor of rhetoric in Tagaste, then in Carthage, he obtained a teaching position in Rome in 383, before moving to Milan. His reading of Plotinus and the preaching of the Bishop of Milan, Ambrosius, were at the origin of his conversion to Christianity in 386. Baptized at Easter 387, Augustine renounced worldly life and returned to Tagaste, where he created a small, monastic community. Becoming Bishop of Hippo in 396, he was soon known as the principal authority of the Christian West. He fought Manichaeism, Donatism, and Pelagianism, which was opposed to his doctrine of grace and predestination. Of his immense written work, the most outstanding are the autobiographical book, *Confessions*, the *Treatise on the Trinity*, and *The City of God*, which analyzed the relations between the Church and temporal powers. Augustine died in 430, in a Hippo besieged by Vandals.

St Augustine, Rabastens church

PRISCILLIAN

Since they had become Christians after the conversion of Constantine, Roman emperors progressively adopted coercive measures against heretics. First, their meetings were forbidden, then their goods confiscated, and finally, they were excluded from public positions. In 381, it was forbidden for Manichaeans to inherit goods, to bear witness or to start court proceedings. In 405, the same measures were applied to the Donatists of North Africa. In his Code, Emperor Justinian (527-565) reinforced all these laws, excluding heretics from the public services, from the practice of law or teaching, forbidding them from testifying against a Catholic or from inheriting anything. However, the death sentence for heresy, although it was to become common practice in the West during the 11th century, was only rarely applied in Late Antiquity. Priscillian, the Bishop of Ávila, was the first and last known heretic to be condemned to death by beheading in Trier, in 385. A secular, educated Spaniard from a wealthy Christian family, Priscillian began to preach in about 370-375. Condemning the clergy's licentious lifestyle, he opposed it with strict asceticism, encouraged by a negative concept of the material world. Partially founded on the reading of apocryphal texts and understanding astrological influences, his preaching rapidly became popular in Galicia, the Asturias, Lusitania and as far as Boetica. The bishops Hydatius of Merida and Ithacius of Ossonuba were the first to oppose Priscillianism, which was condemned on their authority at the Council of Zaragoza in 380. However, Priscillian, whose doctrine was spreading in southern Gaul, received the support of the bishops Instantius and Salvian, who even consecrated him Bishop of Ávila. But Ithacius and Hydatius convinced Emperor Gratian to ratify a decree against Manichaeism, in fact aimed at Priscillianism. Under threat, Priscillian escaped to Italy where he vainly solicited help from Ambrosius, Bishop of Milan, and Damasus, Bishop of Rome. He nonetheless managed to have Gratian's decree annulled. However, taking advantage of the accession of the usurper Maximus (383), Ithacius went to Trier, the imperial residence, where he obtained the condemnation of Priscillian and the calling of a council in Bordeaux. In 384, the council declared Priscillianism to be a heresy and deposed Instantius. Having refused to appear before the council, Priscillian went to Trier to plead his cause directly to the emperor. But a new council, attended by Ambrosius of Milan and Martin of Tours, confirmed the condemnation of Bordeaux. It was then, at the demand of Hydatius and Ithacius, that the Bishop of Ávila and his friends were called to appear before the prefect of the tribunal for accusations of breach of morals and magical practices. After being tortured, Priscillian was beheaded in Trier in 385, along with one of his disciples, despite the opposition of Ambrosius and Martin of Tours. Brought back to Spain, the bodies of the two men were buried and raised to the status of martyrs. Though condemned by the Councils of Toledo in 396 and 400, Priscillianism remained active in Northern Spain, especially in Galicia, until the end of the 5th century.

EAST AND WEST

The rivalry between the patriarchates of Rome and Constantinople appeared at the end of the 4th century, when the Byzantine patriarch began to claim a primacy that had heretofore been granted to the Bishop of Rome. During the 4th c., decision-making power within the Church was collegial, belonging to episcopal synods or councils. However, ever since the Council of Nicaea had promoted the great cities of Rome, Alexandria, Antioch and Jerusalem to patriarchates, their bishops were listened to more attentively. In particular, the Bishop of Rome was the only one who was allowed to use the name *Pope* starting in the 5th c. and he enjoyed unrivalled prestige. This power derived from the political importance of the Empire's traditional capital, but also from the fact that Rome had been the site of the preaching and martyrdom of two of the principal apostles, Peter and Paul. At the end of the 4th century, the idea gained ground in the West that, as Peter's successor, the Pope alone should preside over the government of the universal Church, and that this was according to the will of Christ. "You are Peter and on this rock I will build my Church." But the patriarch of Constantinople, the new capital chosen by Emperor Constantine in 330, had also acquired a certain authority. Because of the importance of his city, the residence of a Christian emperor who called and presided over the great ecclesiastical councils, in 451 at Chalcedon the patriarch obtained the same prerogatives as his Roman colleague, to the great displeasure of the latter. After the upheaval of the first wave of invasions, the fall of Rome (476), and the constitution of new barbarian kingdoms in the West, a much diminished Roman, or Byzantine, Empire remained in the East. The popes, whose city was recaptured from the Ostrogoths by the Byzantines in 554, had remained faithful to the emperor, who had the final

say over their nomination. But in these troubled times, the links between Rome and Constantinople grew looser and the papacy acquired greater autonomy. Latin was imposed as the language of the liturgy in Rome, where hardly anybody still spoke Greek. Furthermore, the Empire was busy defending its lands in the Balkans, invaded by Slavs in the 6th century, as well as in Mesopotamia, Syria and Egypt, first coveted by the Persians in the 7th century, then by the Arabs. The Empire could thus no longer defend its Italian possessions, abandoned during Lombard raids after 569. So in Rome, popes such as Gregory the Great (590-604) acted as real heads of state and organized the city's defence. At the same time, the patriarchs of Constantinople acquired greater importance in the East after the patriarchates of Antioch, Jerusalem and Alexandria had passed under Muslim domination. In 692, the patriarch of Constantinople was named primate of the whole East, just as the Pope was recognized as primate of all the West, by the Council of Quinisexte. Several canons of the council – never ratified by the papacy – were evidence of the differences between Roman and Byzantine traditions. An example was canon 13, which disapproved of the ecclesiastical celibacy accepted in Rome. In the East, married men living with their wives were regularly ordained to the priesthood, and this had been the custom since apostolic times. Then in the 8th century, the accession to the imperial throne of the Isaurian dynasty (717-802) and the beginning of the iconoclastic crisis – from the Greek *eikon*, image, and *klazein*, to shatter – made relations between Byzantium and the Roman papacy deteriorate. In 726, Emperor Leon III (717-741), for reasons that were never made clear, began propaganda hostile to icons. In 730, invoking the Law of Moses and the condemnation of idolatry, he forbade

all representation of Jesus Christ, his mother and the saints, calling for the destruction of their icons. During the reign of his son and successor, Constantine V Copronymus (741-775), iconoclastic doctrine was defined more fully at the Council of Hiereia (754), and violent persecution was organized against iconodules (image worshippers), particularly monks. Although the Council of Nicaea II, called in 787 by Empress Irene (780-790) re-established the cult of images, iconoclasm was once again proclaimed during the reign of Emperor Leon V the Armenian (813-820). It was not definitively abolished until the council called in Constantinople by Empress Theodora, on March 11, 843. Ever since 730, the Roman popes had been opposed to the iconoclastic measures. Quick to respond, in 732 Leon III amputated the Roman patriarchate of the Byzantine territories in southern Italy and in Illyria and placed them in the jurisdiction of the patriarchate of Constantinople. Under these conditions, Pope Gregory III (731-741) could not count on imperial aid when the Lombards attempted to unify Italy under their authority and threatened Rome in 739. He thus turned to the mayor of the palace, Charles Martel, the great victor of Poitiers in 732, to whom he promised to refuse all allegiance to the Byzantine emperor. But Martel, allied to the Lombards against the Arabs, refused to intervene. However, his son, Pepin the Short, elected King of the Franks and anointed, according to the biblical concept of kings chosen by God, in Soissons in 752, sealed the alliance between the papacy and the young Carolingian dynasty. Also in 751, the Lombard King Aistulf captured Ravenna, thus dangerously threatening the Duchy of Rome. Pope Stephen II (752-757) undertook to cross the Alps in the middle of winter, meeting the Carolingian king in Ponthion on

January 6, 754, and obtaining his help. Named "Patricius" of the Romans, Pepin and both his sons, Carloman and Charles, were anointed a second time at Saint Denis by the pontiff, who played a decisive role in the accession to royalty from then on. With two victorious campaigns, in 755 and 756, Pepin recaptured from the Lombards 22 towns located in the exarchate of Ravenna, Emilia and Pentapoli. Instead of returning them to the Byzantine emperor, he entrusted them to Peter's successor through a deed of perpetual donation, thereby beginning the constitution of an independent state whose temporal sovereign was the Pope. Another famous false document produced about this time was intended to legitimize the papacy's temporal powers. According to the *Donation of Constantine*, before leaving for the East, Constantine allegedly entrusted Pope Sylvester 1st (314-335) with the government of Rome and all the western territories of the Roman Empire. Becoming Pepin's sole heir at his brother's death in 771, Charlemagne (771-814) came to power. Through his wars of conquest, he managed to make himself the master of nearly the entire western territories, in which he carried out missionary activity that was intense, and sometimes strong-armed, particularly in Saxony. In 774, responding to the call of Pope Hadrian 1st (772-775), he captured Pavia, the Lombards' capital, deposed King Desiderius, and assumed the title of "King of the Franks and the Lombards". In 796, his armies razed the Avars' (Huns) *ring* between the Tisza and Danube Rivers, and sent in Christian missionaries. In Spain, after the failure of Zaragoza in 778, after 785 his son Louis led several victorious offensives in the north-east of the former *Tarraconensis* province, capturing Gerona and Urgell in 785, and Barcelona in 801. Done in the name of Christ, the *dilatation imperii*, territorial expansion, took place

simultaneously with *dilatation christanitatis*, the expansion of Christendom. Beyond ethnic divisions, it was baptism that united Charlemagne's subjects under his authority. Spread throughout the entire kingdom by *missi dominici*, the Carolingian capitularies were charged with providing fairer justice, training clergy, monastic discipline and the instruction of laymen. They also imposed baptism on the newborn, Sunday rest and attendance at mass, religious marriage ceremonies, communion and confession three times a year. *Rex et sacerdos*, king and priest following the example of the *basileus*, Charlemagne did not hesitate to interfere in questions of orthodoxy. He charged Alcuin with revising the *Vulgate* and approved the *Libri carolini*, which took position against the Byzantine theologians. In 794, he convoked a council in Frankfurt, where the conclusions of the Council of Nicaea II (787) were vigorously condemned, with the Greeks being falsely accused of adoring images. Furthermore, the Adoptianist theses of Elipand, Archbishop of Toledo, introduced into Septimania by Bishop Felix of Urgell, were declared heretical. Glorified as a "new Augustus" reigning in his "new Rome", i.e., in Aachen, at Christmas 800, Charlemagne received the imperial crown from the hands of Pope Leo III at Saint Peter's in Rome. The Byzantine emperors took a long time before accepting the coronation of an outsider, especially a *Barbarian*. But in 812, after years of struggle, the *basileus* Michael 1st (811-813) recognized Charlemagne and abandoned all of Italy to him, except Veneto and Dalmatia. However, the political and religious rupture between the Frankish empire, linked to the papacy, and the heirs of the old Roman Empire was reaffirmed over the course of the 9th, 10th and 11th centuries. Already old, religious dissensions between the Greek

and Latin worlds hardened after 807 over the controversy of the *Filioque*. Attested already in the 4th century in the writings of Ambrosius, adopted by the Visigoths at the Council of Toledo in 589, the mention of the *Filioque*, according to which the Spirit proceeds "from the Father and *the Son*" –"a *Patre Filioque*"– had spread throughout the western liturgy during the 6th and 7th centuries. Meanwhile, Greek theologians had remained faithful to the creed of Constantinople (381), according to which the Spirit proceeded only from the Father. The quarrel broke out in 807 when the Latin monks of a monastery in Jerusalem, accusing the Byzantines of heresy for reciting their creed without the *Filioque*, called for Charlemagne to intercede. He did so at the Council of Aachen in 809, and had the *Filioque* officially incorporated into the symbol of Constantinople. The schism between the two patriarchates was not consummated until the 11th century, after an incident that appeared unimportant to its contemporaries. In 1053, the Byzantine Emperor Constantine IX Monomachus allied with Pope Leo IX (1047-1054) against the Norman invaders who were threatening the Byzantine possessions of southern Italy. In March, 1054, a pontifical mission left Rome to re-establish the ecclesiastical union between the two patriarchates. But the interview between the papal legates and the patriarch Michael Kerularios went badly. The debate covered Byzantine liturgical customs contested by the Latins, such as clerical marriage, using ordinary bread for communion, the refusal to adopt the *Filioque* in the Nicene-Constantinople creed... Eventually, the legates excommunicated the patriarch, and he responded by excommunicating them a few days later. The separation between the Church of Rome and the orthodox patriarchates had been sealed.

The abbey basilica in Saint Benoît sur Loire

ROMANESQUE CHRISTENDOM

After having disappeared since Antiquity, the accusation of heresy reappeared around the year 1000. Referring to the treatises of the Fathers of the Church, chroniclers gave the name Manichaeans to the protesters thirsting for evangelism, who suddenly appeared as the Roman Church was in crisis and was itself looking to return to the purity of its origins.

The Church in the Year 1000

By the year 1000, the Church had somewhat turned away from its primary functions. Donations had provided it with wealth comparable to that of a temporal lord; it was an integral part of government power in the Ottonian Empire, or else immersed in feudal society. With the installation of the first feudal age, which followed the break-up of the Carolingian Empire, princes, dukes and, soon, local lords, all-powerful on their lands after seizing royal prerogatives, appropriated ecclesiastical lands and unscrupulously took advantage of episcopal and pastoral positions, or those linked to abbeys. Hence it was not rare for a prince to name a close relative to head a diocese, without worrying about their aptitude to carry out the role of bishop or archbishop. Other powerful dukes or princes accumulated the positions of lay abbots, setting up their family in a monastery and taking for themselves the income destined for the community, which was entrusted to a prior. Nearly all the churches were private on the parish level. Whether they demanded a right of patronage if their ancestors had founded the church, or the church had been given to them as a fief, the lords did not hesitate to take most of, if not all, the parish's revenues. They named their freed serfs as priests in charge of chapels, although their religious instruction and culture were often rudimentary. Within this context of excessive secularization, of osmosis between aristocrats and clergy, it was clear that religious vocations were hardly taken into account and, at all levels of the hierarchy, non-residence and nicolaism, that is, marriage or public cohabitation of the clergy, sometimes leading to hereditary attribution of their positions, were common practice. Similarly, simony, or the selling of ecclesiastical positions or spiritual goods (sacraments) for sums of money, material presents or protection, was denounced by reformers. Because it was also clear that neither the entire priesthood nor all the laypeople had suddenly fallen into disgrace. Many were convinced of the need for reform, and these ideas were first of all advocated in the monasteries. An example is the rise of the reforming abbey of Cluny, founded in Burgundy on September 11, 909 (or 910), at the initiative of Guillaume III, Duke of Aquitaine and Count of Mâcon. In its founding charter, Guillaume left the community free to elect its abbot and renounced all rights over the establishment, placing it directly under the protection of the pope. Freed from the yoke of secular authority, the first abbot, Bernon (909/910–926), restored monastic asceticism through the strict application of the

DUKES, COUNTS, KINGS, POPES AND EMPERORS

After the reign of Louis the Pious (814-840), by the Treaty of Verdun in 843 his sons divided up his empire into three kingdoms: Lewis the German acquired the lands east of the Rhine River –Saxony and southern Bavaria; Lothar obtained territories stretching from the Mediterranean to the North Sea, with their western border set by the valleys of the Rhone, Saone, Meuse and Escaut Rivers; lastly, Charles the Bald got the lands west of this border. Following other divisions, Charlemagne's empire was fleetingly reunited under Charles the Fat (881-888) but this ended with his death, and the crowns of the West Frankish kingdom, Germany, Burgundy, Italy and Provence became elective positions. Disputed by Carolingians and Robertians throughout the entire 10th century, the crown of the West Frankish kingdom fell to a Robertian, Hugues Capet, elected in Senlis and anointed in Noyon in 987. Although the Capetian dynasty managed to establish itself despite the elective principle, its royal authority was exercised over a relatively small area, between Senlis and Orléans, the capital of Robert the Pious (996-1031). Several dozen aristocratic families descended from high-level functionaries of the Carolingian administration had monopolized the *honores* originally granted to them as their own, hereditary possessions. They reigned over vast principalities, sometimes raised to duchies or marquisates. In the North, the counties of Flanders, Champagne, Blois and Anjou, and the duchies of Normandy, Burgundy and Brittany, rivalled the Capetian domains. The south was divided between the enormous Duchy of Aquitaine, the County of Toulouse and the Duchy of Gascony. Beyond the Pyrenees Mountains, the Catalonian counties of the former Carolingian Marches of Spain had become independent in 985. Other counties, often in the hands of urban bishoprics, were linked to these great territories. The kingdom of Germany was divided into five great principalities –Lotharingia (later Lorraine), Saxony, Swabia, Bavaria and Franconia– each under the authority of a duke. Elected by these dukes, Otto 1st (936-973) succeeded his father, the Duke of Saxony, Henry I the Fowler (912-936), as the King of Germany. Crowned in Aachen, Otto presented himself as the heir to the Carolingian tradition. Wishing to restore his authority, he placed members of his family at the head of the great duchies, and invested clerics –abbots or bishops whose nomination he controlled– with important public positions. Attempting further expansion, he provided a new impetus for the evangelization of the Slavs, and created marches on the Elbe River, where monasteries and bishoprics were founded. In 937, he subjugated the kingdom of Burgundy.

Through his marriage with Adelaide, the widow of the Italian monarch Lotar, he had himself elected King of Italy in Pavia in 951. His victory in Lechfeld near Augsburg in 955 put an end to incursions by Hungarian horsemen and con-

Charlemagne

ferred great prestige on him. Therefore, on February 2, 962, during an expedition to Italy, Otto was crowned emperor by Pope John XII. At his death in 973, he had no difficulty imposing his son Otto II (973-983) as successor. With the restoration of the Holy Roman Empire, pontifical elections, which had been subjected to the whims of the Roman aristocracy throughout the tenth century, passed under the exclusive control of the emperors. They knew how to make effective choices, for example, Otto III (983-1002) who gave the pontifical tiara to a man considered among the most brilliant thinkers in the 11th century West, his former tutor, the monk Gerbert of Aurillac, Archbishop of Reims and Ravenna, who became Pope under the name Sylvester II.

Neonian baptistery, Ravenna

Crypt of St Benigne in Dijon

Benedictine rule reviewed by Benedict of Aniane, which gave a large place to the celebration of holy offices. During the abbacy of Odon (927–942), Pope John XI (931-935) entrusted the abbey with the privilege of reforming any monastery whose lay abbot requested it, and to accept monks whose abbot refused to be reformed. Cluny soon acquired a certain renown, which was enhanced further by the acquisition of the relics of Saints Peter and Paul in 981 during the abbacy of Maïeul (948-994). Finally, under Abbot Odilon (994-1049) in 998, Pope Gregory V (996-999) granted the abbey the right of exemption, removing it from any episcopal supervision. In 1024, John XIX (1024-1032) extended this privilege to all Cluniac monks "wherever they are", thus signing the birth certificate of the *Ecclesia cluniacensis*. This became an enormous network of abbeys and priories depending on the Burgundy mother abbey, covering "with a white mantle of churches", according to the words of the monk Raoul Glaber, "the world […] shaking off the rags of its old age", an image of the West becoming Christendom. In this way, during the 10th and 11th centuries, the ultimate state of spiritual perfection was represented by these men of Cluny, Saint Benigne, Saint Gall, Monte Cassino, Fleury sur Loire, Marmoutier, Gorze, Saint Victor or Lerins, whose entire lives, dedicated to prayer and the glorifying of God, were lived in chastity and asceticism, far from the secular world, behind the perfect enclosure of the cloisters, gardens reflecting a celestial order where Romanesque art flourished. The vitality and the will to reform of the lay clergy were expressed through the

RAOUL GLABER

Raoul, known as *Glaber* i.e., the bald, was born in Burgundy about 985, probably the son of a cleric. At the age of twelve, his uncle sent him to an abbey, most likely Saint Germain of Auxerre. He was expelled a short time later because of his presumptuousness, according to his own account. However, he was accepted in another monastery because of his literary talent. The same thing happened, and Raoul became a monk at Saint Léger of Champeaux, in La Réôme. His meeting with William of Volpiano, abbot of La Réôme until 1002, then of Saint Benigne in Dijon, was a turning point in Raoul's life. The latter most certainly accompanied the famous abbot to Italy between 1026 and 1028. He also wrote a biography about him. In 1031, the dying William charged his friend with finishing his principal but uncompleted work, *Histories*. Staying at Cluny with Abbot Odilon, at Saint Pierre of Bèze, and at Saint Germain of Auxerre, the abbey of his young days, Raoul remained faithful to this friendly request. And until his death in 1037, he worked on the account of "facts and marvels that happened before and after the millennium of the incarnation of the Saviour".

Lérins Monastery

Detail of church in Toulouges

THE SUNDAY OF TOULOUGES

···

The initiative of the Truce of God can be ascribed to the son of the Count of Cerdagne, Oliba, Abbot of Saint Michel of Cuxa and of Ripoll, who was also the bishop of Vich starting in 1019. Wishing to put a halt to the violence and exactions of aristocratic, Catalonian lords, he called for synods of peace, in the style of those of Aquitaine, in the dioceses of Elne and Vich. But Oliba added his own original touch. Hence, the synod over which he presided at Toulouges near Elne in 1027 decreed, besides measures forbidding knights from attacking clerics and unarmed laymen, and from violating churches and houses, that "no inhabitant [should attack] his enemy between the ninth hour of Saturday and the first hour of Monday, each one honouring Sunday as agreed." Six years later, in 1033, in his own diocese of Vich, Oliba started the Truce of God, in addition to Sunday, during the liturgical periods of Christmas, Easter and Pentecost.

Gregorian reforms of the 11th century, but also through the councils of peace that started at the end of the 10th century. Although these were times of feudal wars, the councils were called by bishops wishing to establish ideals of peace and social harmony, within which everyone –whether belonging to the class of the *oratores*, those who pray, the *bellatores*, those who combat, or the *laboratores*, those who work– would honour his condition and be useful to the others. The peasant was to carry out his role of producing and feeding; the knight would assure defence, and the cleric, guarantor of the moral order, was to pray and intercede with God. More practically, the councils of peace aimed at stopping the exactions of knights and assuring the protection of *inermes* civilians, clerics or peasants "without arms". The first councils took place in southern France, in Aquitaine. In 989, the Archbishop of Bordeaux called a council at Charroux, near Saint Sauveur Monastery, in the presence of the province's bishops, gathering together lay lords and the crowds who had come to see the holy relics exhibited for the occasion. Four canons were decreed. The first called anathema on knights who defiled churches; the second, on those who stole goods from the poor; the third, on those who struck clerics; and the fourth, on prelates guilty of nicolaism. At the end of the meeting, before the people gathered there, the warlords swore a solemn oath on the relics to respect the council's canons. Other similar councils were organized in about 990 by the Archbishop of Narbonne, and in 993/994 by the Bishop of Le Puy. Supported by Cluny starting in the second decade of the 11th century, the Peace of God was followed by the Truce of God, which imposed stopping combat at certain moments of the week and of the liturgical year. The Truce of God first appeared at the assembly of Toulouges, in the Roussillon area, in 1027. All warring activity was forbidden on Sundays. The Great Council called in Arles by the city's archbishop in 1041 forbade combat between Christians from Wednesday evening until Monday morning, to commemorate the holy days of Holy Week, as well as during liturgical periods.

Tower and chapterhouse in Charroux

POWER AND SOCIETY IN THE WEST FRANKISH KINGDOM IN 1000

At the dawn of the 11th century, the Capetian kingdom was composed of a multitude of principalities nearly independent of royal power. The princes holding them were descended from old Carolingian aristocratic families. In the course of the 10th century, these families had taken over the *honores* –in other words, public positions attached to the usufruct of property– earlier granted by Carolingian sovereigns. Starting in about 950, princely authority began to run into trouble and the principalities broke up to the advantage of local counts who freed themselves from the prince's authority, taking over rights originally held by the monarch, such as the right of judgement, punishment and constraint. The rupture of political structures and the dispersal of authority continued at the beginning of the 11th century, when viscounts or provosts –former representatives of the count's power– or attorneys –charged with defending ecclesiastical goods–or even simple freeholders– landowners who did not depend on a lord, took over the ban on lands around the castles that had been entrusted to them or that they had built themselves. This was the beginning of "banal seigniories" in the 11th century. Having at his disposal nearly total power over those living in his jurisdiction, in order to defend his lands the lord surrounded himself with a troop of horsemen. After the 1030's, granted a fief in exchange for an oath of fidelity, these *milites* increased the numbers of the nobiliary classes through the link between a lord and his vassals. Furthermore, the peasantry who, until about 950, lived in scattered settlements, gathered willingly or not around the lord's castle to obtain his protection. In this

way, between 950 and 1050 the first fortified villages appeared –the *castella* in Northern Italy and the Occitanian *castra*. Exploited, burdened by the lords' levying, victims of the violence of private wars, the peasantry nevertheless lived in improving conditions by the year 1000. The warming climate, favourable for food-production, especially cereals, produced better har-

vests, reducing the number of great famines although shortages continued. Besides the mastery of iron and fire, greater mastery of animal energy, thanks to the frontal yoke and the hitching collar, helped in working the land. Hydraulic mills spread throughout the countryside, and irrigation techniques inherited from the Muslims became common in the

Mediterranean countries. Great works of drainage and improvement in river traffic, as well as land reclamation through polders in Flanders and the Netherlands, were undertaken. These factors all helped to increase agricultural production that was the basis for the double phenomenon of demographic and economic development. This development was accompanied by an urban rebirth, beginning

Threshing wheat, fresco in royal pantheon of San Isidoro, Leon

in the north-west of the Capetian kingdom, where commercial towns served by ports, most often built around an abbey or a castle, like Bruges, Ghent or Douai, expanded rapidly. In the south, cities like Montpellier or Marseille, took advantage of the resumption of maritime trade with Africa and especially with the East after the year 1000.

Vertus church

ADHEMAR OF CHABANNES

....

Descending from a younger branch of high nobility in the Limoges area, Adhemar was born in Chabannes, thirty kilometres from Limoges, in about 988. When he was very young, his parents sent him to Saint Cybard Monastery in Angoulême. However, he pursued his studies at Saint Martial's Abbey in Limoges where, on a famous stormy night in 1010, Christ sobbing on his cross in the sky, flooding the town with his tears, appeared to Adhemar. After his studies were over, Adhemar returned to Saint Cybard, became a priest and carried out intense activity in the scriptorium –gathering texts, copying, composing and publishing. In 1025, he began his *Historia* in three volumes, tracing the history of the Franks from their origins until the beginning of the 11th century. In 1028, he began to eagerly defend his contested thesis about the apostolate of Saint Martial. He created a file, even having recourse to counterfeiting, that he offered to Saint Martial's Abbey. In 1030, he went on a pilgrimage to the Holy Land and died in Jerusalem four years later. He left behind over a thousand autographed folios, including editions of texts, copies, sermons, chronicles, poems, musical notations, calculations and various texts, some of them even illustrated in his own hand.

The Heretics of the Year 1000

Nevertheless, along with the will for reform and the restoration of morals expressed by the regular and lay Church, a will that would flourish during the second half of the 11th century during the high point of the Gregorian reform at the dawn of the second millennium, there were other faithful, probably concerned with their salvation and wishing to lead an authentic, Christian life. However, their words and writings took the path of dissidence and are known only piecemeal, deformed by the pens of those denouncing them. They were thus called "Manichaean heretics", "messengers of the Antichrist", adorers of the devil, guilty of ritual orgies and spreading their harmful, erring ways through the ashes of sacrificed newborn babies. In his *Histories*, completed in 1048, the monk Raoul Glaber recounts that, "towards the end of the year 1000", a certain Leutard, a humble peasant from the village of Vertus in Champagne, a man until then, "healthy in mind and religious", suddenly sent away his wife "using the pretext of the Gospels", destroyed the crucifix in his church, then began to preach the Gospels himself, opposing his words to "the teaching of the masters", and claiming to whomever would listen that nothing justified the payment of tithes. Glaber specified that this sudden change in behaviour came after a swarm of bees sneakily entered poor Leutard's body through his backside while he was asleep, and came out through his mouth "with a terrifying humming [...] ordering him to carry out actions that were humanly impossible". The story was not unlike one about a man native to the Berry area who, after being attacked in a wasteland by a cloud of flies, was possessed by the Devil who bestowed on him prophetic gifts, an anecdote told by Gregory of Tours (c.538-c.594) in his *History of the Franks*. However it happened, the Bishop of Châlons-en-Champagne, Gibuin, "a man of vast culture", when informed of Leutard's behaviour, had him appear before his court. Leutard tried to justify himself by invoking Holy Scripture, but "he did not know it well", Raoul tells us. Therefore, since he was an ignorant madman, he was convicted of heresy. In despair, Leutard committed suicide by throwing himself into a well, a tragic ending which only confirmed for his accusers his belonging to demonic powers. "At the same time," still according to Raoul, "a similar evil happened in Ravenna", where a certain Vilgard, "passionate about the study of grammar", was condemned by the bishop of his city for having taught "theories contrary to holy dogma". "There are in Italy many zealots of this pernicious dogma", continued Raoul. They "perished by the sword or by fire", although some took refuge in Spain. Then sometime around the year 1017, Adhemar of Chabannes mentioned in his *Chronicle* the presence in Aquitaine of "Manichaeans who are seducing the people", "denying baptisms, the cross and the entire holy doctrine", "are abstaining from food, look like monks and pretend to be chaste, but between themselves abandon themselves to lust". And he concluded by saying that "these were the messengers of the Antichrist, who estranged many people from the true faith". At least four distinct sources –the *Life of Gauzlin* by André de Fleury, Raoul Glaber's *Histories*, the *Chronicle* of Adhemar of Chabannes, and the essay of the

THE GREGORIAN REFORM

Reforming the lay clergy, begun during the papacy of Leon IX (1048-1054), was continued by Pope Gregory VII (1073-1085), hence giving it its name. It was not finished until the early decades of the 12th century. This Gregorian reform aimed above all at re-establishing morale and discipline within a Church in crisis, in a state of dissolution caused by the feudal system. The reformist popes wanted to work at eradicating simony and nicolaism, which were calling into question the validity of the sacraments. They thus decided to make ecclesiastical celibacy obligatory and, above all, to free the Church from all secular power. This emancipation from the supervision of the lords, kings or emperors, according to the reformers a *sine qua non* condition of re-establishing morality,

had to start at the top. In 1059, a decree of Pope Nicholas II entrusted pontifical elections to the cardinals alone, whereas until then they had been under the exclusive control of the Holy Roman Emperor. Those who received the title of cardinal were the bishops geographically close to Rome (Tusculum, Ostia, etc.), the curates of the city's main churches, and the city's deacons. Together they formed the College of Cardinals, whose role was electing the pope. Nicholas's successors attempted to break up secular investiture by reserving the elections of bishops and abbots for cathedral or monastical chapters. The measures were at the origin of the investiture quarrel between the papacy and secular power, and particularly imperial power, a quarrel envenomed during

the papacy of Gregory VII. In 1075, Pope Gregory VII promulgated his *Dictatus papae* affirming pontifical pre-eminence and power. Placing himself above not only bishops but also princes and kings that he intended to excommunicate and depose at will, the pope presented himself as the unique and universal head of the church and of Christian society, by virtue of the very will of Jesus Christ. Emperor Henry IV attempted to respond to the affirmation of this theocratic ideal by having Gregory VII deposed by the Assembly of Worms in January, 1076. However, excommunicated by the pontiff, the emperor was forced to humble himself at Canossa, in January, 1077. Finally, a compromise was signed in Worms in 1122: the spiritual investiture by the crosier and the ring of bishops and abbots was henceforward reserved for the metropolitan. As for the emperor, he would carry out the investiture by the sceptre, conferring the royal rights attached to the ecclesiastic ministry. At the level of local churches, the papacy's primacy and interference were visible through the sending of legates, at first occasional, but later permanent. These legates enjoyed nearly absolute power over the bishops and presided over nearly all the provincial councils. The Gregorian reform appears as a hierarchical reorganization of the structures of the Western Church. It was an opportunity to affirm the primacy of the Roman papacy, which was at the origin of the schism with the Eastern Church. This primacy was also affirmed at the level of the society of the faithful, whose life was subsequently regulated by clerics —marriage became a sacrament, penitent pilgrimages developed, and so on.

Church dignitaries, detail on tomb of Doña Urraca, Cañas

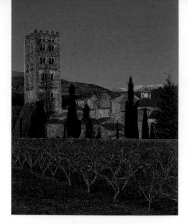

Saint Michel de Cuxa

ABBOT OLIBA

O liba, to whom the monk John wrote about the canons of Orléans, was the abbot of Saint Michel de Cuxa, in the Catalonian Conflent. He held this position from 1008 to 1046. This brother of Guifre, Count of Cerdagne, was also Abbot of Ripoll and, starting in 1019, Bishop of Vich. An active man, he organized the Synod of Toulouges, which inaugurated the Truce of God in Roussillon county and the bishopric of Elne. Under his authority, new work was begun in Cuxa abbey church, building an ambulatory around the choir and, at the western end, two round superposed chapels –one dedicated to the Trinity and one to the Crib.

Capital in Saint Michel de Cuxa

monk Paul in the cartulary of the Holy Father of Chartres– told the dark tale of the canons of Orléans, burnt at the stake after being accused of heresy on the orders of King Robert the Pious in December 1022. According to Raoul, it was a woman who had come from Italy who "infected [...] with the venom of her perversity" the clerics of Orléans, but Adhemar claimed that they "had been taken advantage of by a peasant who claimed he had magical powers and who carried on him powder made of dead children, and of which he could quickly make a Manichaean if he could share it with someone". Denounced by a priest from Rouen, or, according to other versions, arrested thanks to a relative of the Duke of Normandy Richard II, Lord Arfast, who had been charged with infiltrating the sect, the heretical canons appeared before a court of bishops, presided over by King Robert, in Holy Cross Church in Orléans. At the head of the accused was Étienne, the first chaplain, and Lisoie, the confessor of Queen Constance. Both of them were most respected and wise clerics, known for the rectitude of their morals, but were called on to confess their beliefs. "They said", wrote Paul the monk, "that Christ was not born of the Virgin, that he had not suffered for man and that he was not dead, that he had not really been placed in a tomb, and that he was not resurrected. They added that baptism does not wash away crimes, that there is no sacrament of the body and blood of Christ in the priest's consecration, and that praying to martyred saints and confessors served no purpose." Raoul continued that, "they affirmed that heaven and earth, as we see them, have always existed in this way, with no initial author. [...] They raved and barked like dogs. [...]Like the Epicurean heretics, [...] they believed that we risked no compensatory vengeance if we throw ourselves into pleasures." André de Fleury reported that, "according to them, marriage did not need any benediction, but that anyone could take a wife when he wanted. For them, there is no bishop who can ordain a priest through the existing liturgy, because he does not have the gift of the Holy Spirit. They claimed to have a mother similar to the one of the Son of God." Therefore, as Docetae questioning the humanity of Jesus Christ, denying divine creation, and rejecting the authority of the Roman Catholic Church and its sacraments (the Eucharist, baptism, penitence, ordination), the canons of Orléans also refused the cult of sainthood, which was highly developed at the beginning of the 11th century, with the rapid expansion of the worship of relics and pilgrimages. And like the late Leutard, the canons also seemed to encourage chastity, by refusing marriage, and asceticism, in other words to disdain matter and flesh because, according to another source, a letter from a monk called John to Abbot Oliba, they abstained from eating meat and fat "as though they were impure things". Instead of the "false official doctrine", they substituted that of the Holy Spirit "which taught the deeper meaning and real truth of the Scriptures", reported the knight Arfast. They also had their own sacrament, the "gift of the Holy Spirit" through "the laying on of their hands, which washes away all sin", as well as their blessed bread, that they called "celestial food". But the double agent Arfast and the monk Paul with him, in all likelihood influenced by the writings of Tertullian, had pierced the secret of its horrible composition. "On

Holy Cross Cathedral in Orléans

Infanticide, fresco in San Isidoro

THE FALSE APOSTLES OF PERIGORD

I n Perigord, a circular letter from the monk Philibert sounded the alarm. "A new heresy has been born in this world [...] preached by pseudo-apostles [...]. It is said they lead an apostolic life. They do not eat meat, they do not drink wine, or else in moderation [...]. They genuflect hundreds of times. They do not accept money and, when they happen to have some, they give it away with propriety. But [...] they say alms are nothing and that one should receive nothing [...]. They hold that the mass is of no use and teach that one should not receive communion, but only pieces of blessed bread. They claim that singing in the church is pure vanity [...]. They adore neither the cross nor statues of the Lord and prevent as much as possible others from adoring. [...] They have bound numerous persons in this heresy: not only laymen who have abandoned all their belongings, but also clerics, priests, monks and nuns [...]."

some nights, they gathered in their usual house. [...] They recited the names of demons like a litany. And suddenly they saw a demon coming down among them, taking the appearance of an animal. Hardly had this vision appeared, they turned out the lights, and each one took her who was nearest at hand and abused her, [...] mother, sister or nun, it did not matter. [...] If a child was born from this horrible copulation, then eight days later they made a great bonfire in the middle between them and [...] the child was burnt [...]. The ashes were gathered up and kept with the same veneration that the Christian religion dedicates to the body of Christ. They gave it as a viaticum to the ill as they were about to die." The same accusations of infanticide had been made in 192 A.D. and had led to the martyrdom of the Christians of Lyon. And King Robert condemned the satanic prelates to be burnt alive, and ordered the stake to be set up at the gates of the city. Coming out of the church, Queen Constance, revolted by such shamefulness, "ripped out the eye of her former confessor with a stick she held in her hand", which did not prevent the thirteen or fourteen condemned men, on their way to be tortured, from "boasting that they were not afraid", and even, "walking ahead of those who were dragging them towards the fire" and "abandoning themselves to it freely". For the first time since the Late Empire, a secular power had taken charge of sending men accused of heresy to the stake. But the Orléans affair, on December 25, 1022, was just the beginning. If Adhemar of Chabannes could be believed, at the same time heresy was also being repressed in Toulouse and other "Manichaeans" were appearing "in various parts of the West" perverting "men and women". Meanwhile in Perigord, the monk Erbert denounced the existence of "pseudo-apostles". In northern France, during his stay in Arras in 1025, Bishop Gerard of Cambrai was informed of the existence in that city of a group of heretics "putting forward a kind of *justice*", assuring "that one was justified by it alone, and there was in the Church no other sacrament through which one would reach salvation." The suspects were arrested and underwent interrogation, and were most likely tortured for three

La Roque Saint Christophe in the Vézère valley of Perigord

days before appearing before the synod called by Gerard in Saint Mary's Church in Arras. Questioned about their faith, they confessed to having "listened to a certain Gondulfe, a man of Italy" and having been "instructed by him in the precepts of the Gospels and the apostles". But according to them, their *law* and their *discipline* were not contrary to the precepts of the Gospel, nor to the Acts and Epistles of the apostles. They consisted in "leaving the world, to curb the concupiscence of the flesh, to live by working with one's hands, to do no harm to anyone, to be charitable to all". This was all that counted, baptism being "of no use at all" because "the bad life of those officiating could not bring salvation to the baptized" and that in truth "the vices which were renounced on the baptismal font were perpetrated in life", finally "that will and faith [...] could in no manner concern a newborn who did not want it and did not remember it, who knew nothing of faith, salvation and the help that it brings [...]". After listening to them, Bishop Gerard refuted their statements by making a very elaborate profession of faith, respecting all the rules and in Latin, to which the accused reacted by showing "signs of a certain repentance", and were then invited to accept it. However, since they did not understand Latin very well, the sermon and condemnation had to be translated into the common language, which the accused finally approved and marked with a cross. Furthermore, a letter attached to the acts of this synod, written during the same period by Bishop Gerard, reproached one bishop R., probably Roger, Bishop of Châlons (1008-1042) and hence successor of Bishop Gibuin who had confounded Leutard, for having released "unscathed, like innocents", "harmful men, bewitched by the spirit of error" and whom he suspected of being at the origin of the deviance of the Arras heretics. A few years later, at a date traditionally given as 1028, heresy was discovered in the Piedmont area of Italy, but this time, like in Orléans, it was dealt with at the stake. The story was told by Raoul Glaber: "There was in Lombardy [...] a castle called Monforte, inhabited by numerous men among the most noble of this people. All were affected by heresy to the point that they would have preferred an atrocious death rather than to return to the faith of Jesus Christ Our Lord. They worshipped idols, in the manner of the pagans, and like the Jews, they attempted to offer them inept sacrifices. Not only Manfred, the wisest of marquesses, but also his brother Aldric, Bishop of the town of Alba, and whose diocese included the above-mentioned castle, as well as the other bishops of the surrounding areas, had attacked them on several occasions, even capturing some of them. Unable to tear them away from their madness, they delivered them to the fire." There followed the story of a heretical chatelaine from Monforte who allegedly came, accompanied by demons all dressed in black, to visit and lay her hands on a ill person in a neighbouring castle. But once the chatelaine had left, the demonic beings stayed behind at the bedside of the patient, to whom revelations were made about the accession of the Holy Roman Emperor Conrad and Emperor Michael IV of Constantinople. The Milanese writer Landulf the Elder, at the beginning of the 12th century, seemed to be better informed about the beliefs of the heretics of Monforte. His tale presented the Archbishop of Milan, Aribert (1018-1045), who during a

St Vaast, Arras Museum

THE CITY AND BOROUGH OF ARRAS

In 52 B.C., Commius, King of the Atrebates, had to give in when faced with the Romans settling on his land. Caesar installed his winter quarters at *Nemetocena* in 51 B.C. This place has been identified as *Nemetacum*, future Arras, a town located on Baudimond Hill, between Amiens and Thérouanne. During the Late Empire, it was known for its cloth. About 500, Arras became the seat of a bishopric, with Saint Vaast as its first bishop. In 658, Saint Aubert founded an abbey on Madeleine Hill to the west of the town. St Vaast's relics were brought to the abbey, which was placed under his patronage. A town developed around the abbey and specialized in making cloth, then high-warp tapestry starting in the 14th century. A great centre of the Carolingian renaissance, Saint Vaast Abbey is known for its rich library and the quality of the illuminated works in its scriptorium. Reformed by its abbots Richard of Saint-Vanne (1009-1018) and Ledouin (1018-1040), the abbey was reputed for the intense activity of its scriptorium and, until the end of the Middle Ages, remained one of the wealthiest and most prestigious monastic establishments. The abbey was totally rebuilt in the 18th century.

stay in Turin "heard about a heresy [...] which had formed in a castle located above a place called Monforte". Upon being questioned, the head of the sect, a man called Gerard, confessed to the archbishop that he and his disciples advocated virginity, and for married people, "perpetual chastity", the wife being to the husband "like a mother or a sister", that they never ate meat, but devoted themselves "continually to fasting and prayer" so that not an hour went by "without prayer". He said they put all their goods in common, that they confessed to the Father, the Son and the Holy Spirit, adopted the Old and the New Testaments, but as Docetae they defined Christ as "the Spirit sensually born of the Virgin Mary, that is, born from the Holy Scriptures". Consequently, they refused transubstantiation, the mystery of the Eucharist that transformed bread and wine into the flesh and blood of Christ. Furthermore, they believed they were "bound and loosed by those who had the power of binding and loosing", or in other words, by their own clergy. And they accepted as their pontiff "not the one in Rome, but another who visited every day [their] brothers scattered throughout the world". Having listened to him, Aribert soon had the other noble occupants of the castle of Monforte arrested, and among them was the countess herself. He had them

Triptych of the Eucharist, detail

Saint Sophia, Istanbul

taken to Milan where "he suffered for long days with priests [...] in the desire to make them return to the Catholic faith". But it appeared that their presence provoked trouble in the city of Milan, "the secular rulers of the city", in their haste to be finished with it, "lit a gigantic fire on one side, and raised the cross of the Lord on the other". Then, "against the wishes of Aribert", they imposed on the heretics, who as Docetae refused the cult of the cross, "either to adore the cross after having rejected all heresy", or else "to go into the fire to be burnt alive". And although several of them abjured their faith, "many of them, putting their hands in front of their faces, went into the flames", concluded Landulf. Finally, to end these evocations of the return of heresy during the 11th century, mention should be made of the group of peasants excommunicated by the

THE HUNT FOR HERETICS

In the course of the 11th century, the Roman Church gathered behind its pontiff appeared ever more intransigent and exclusive in its pretension of ruling the universal Church and all of society. The Roman clergy frequently made use of accusations of heresy. In the excommunication bull of the Patriarch of Constantinople, Michael I Cerularius, placed on the altar of Saint Sophia Church in front of the congregation during the schism of 1054, the papal legates of Leon IX expressed themselves in the following terms: "As far as Michael is concerned, he who is given the abusive title of patriarch, and the partisans of his errors, they spread the germs of heresy with abundance. Indeed, like the Simoniacs, they sell the gift of God...; like the Nicolaists, they authorize and support marriage of ministers of the holy altar...; like the Pneumatomacs and the Theumacs, they have suppressed from the symbol the procession of the Holy Spirit from the Son; like the Manichaeans, they declare, among others, that fermented bread is animate...; and letting their hair and beards grow, they refuse communion to those who cut their hair and, according to the prescriptions of the Roman Church, shave their beards..."

Saint Paul baptizing the first Christians by laying on his hands, Tokali Kilise fresco in Göreme

Bishop of Châlons in 1048. "They followed the perverted dogma of the Manichaeans […] claiming […] to give the Holy Spirit through a sacrilegious laying on of the hands, […] abhorring marriage and avoiding the eating of meat, saying that it was impious to kill any animal." Worse still was the fate of men arrested in 1052 at Goslar in Saxony, who were excommunicated then hanged on the order of Emperor Henry III (1017-1056). They had been convicted of Manichaeism for refusing to kill a chicken.

Through so many sources and various stories, caricatures, grotesque anecdotes, stereotypes, or more solemn and serious accounts, what should we think of those "Manichaean heretics"? It is a preconceived, unequivocal term that was used to describe a reality that was multiple. These "heretics" appeared in the West shortly before the year 1000 and during the first half of the eleventh century. They included men and women, clerics and laymen originating in all classes of society from the lowest to the aristocracy, illiterate or educated. They were reported all over France –in the south around Toulouse, Aquitaine or Perigord; further north, in Orléans, in Champagne in the diocese of Châlons, and as far north as Arras. They were also present in Saxony, in northern Italy, and perhaps in Spain. But within the obscure reports concerning them, a similarity of theme emerges, despite the numerous shadings. Their opposition was aimed at the hierarchy and authority of the Roman Catholic Church, which they considered perverted. Therefore, instead of masses celebrated and sacraments delivered by priests who were openly unworthy of doing

Relic of the Virgin's veil

St James Matamoros

BEATUS OF LIEBANA

I n a *Hispania* that had become
Muslim in 711, Christian
resistance had begun to organize
very early in the north, in the remote
mountains of the Cantabrian
cordillera. Beatus was a monk in
Liebana monastery, in the valley of
the Deva. It was he who was credited
with claiming that the Iberian
peninsula had been evangelized by
James the Greater, the future
Matamoros. He was one of the
forces behind this early resistance.
Probably originally from one of the
great centres of Visigothic culture,
such as Sevilla, Cordoba, Toledo
or Merida, like so many others
Beatus had fled from the emirate
of Al Andalus to the harsh regions
of the north. In 776, he wrote the
first version of his famous
Commentary on the Apocalypse, which
was very successful. In an apocalypse
that carried hope, Beatus and his
fellow Christians foresaw their
future victory against the Beast
–seen as Islam, contemptible
Babylon– Cordoba, and the false
prophet –Mohammed. For over
four centuries, the *Commentary* was
ceaselessly recopied and illuminated
by Mozarab or Romanesque artists.
Thirty-three copies of this *Beatus*,
dated from the 10th century to the
1200's, have survived through the
ages to our own time.

so, instead of idolatrous, superstitious cults of saints and their relics,
the heretics simply preferred direct access to neo-testamentary texts,
out of which they wished to obtain the only "justice", and the only discipline of life that were beneficial. These were very close to the spiritual ideals of their time, as incarnated by Cluny or later by Citeaux,
preaching chastity, fasting, poverty and prayer. Of course, this refusal
of the flesh and of matter, this strict asceticism, indicated "dualistic"
or "Manichaean" tendencies. But were these tendencies not also
characteristic of the Romanesque period which saw the development
of monasticism, which was also the period of the copying and illumi-
nating of the *Commentaries on the Apocalypse* by Beatus of Liebana, illus-
trating the last combat and final victory of the Lamb over the Beast,
before the Last Judgement? Did not the heretics of the year 1000 represent the religious demands, the evangelical hopes of the men and
women of their time, who were no longer satisfied with the framework imposed by the Roman Catholic Church? However, among
some of them, there appeared also theological reflections and practices peculiar to those whom their adversaries, starting in the 12th
century, called *Cathars*: as Docetae, the heretics of Orléans, Perigord
or Monforte refused the human nature of Jesus Christ and hence the
Eucharist, for which they substituted the simple sharing of blessed
bread. They seemed to have their own clergy, "capable of binding or
loosing", and their own sacrament. Through the laying on of hands,
the canons of Orléans baptized by the Spirit and conferred ordination. The first demonstrations of the Christianity of Good Men were
therefore visible among some of these "heretics of the year 1000" at a
time when Bogomil religiosity was spreading in the Greek world,
appearing in many respects as an eastern sister of Catharism.

St John falls at the foot of the Angel, *Apocalypse,* **Beatus of Liebana**

THE BOGOMILS

Bogomilism appeared in Bulgaria during the reign of King Peter (927-969), as attested in the anti-heretical treatise written by a priest called Cosmas in 970. This Christian, dualist religiosity, in all points similar to that of the future Western Cathars, was preached by a certain Bogomil. His Bulgarian name meant *loved by God*, and it was subsequently given to his successors. Bogomil found followers throughout the entire Bulgarian kingdom, from Preslav near the Black Sea, to Okhrida in Macedonia, recruited particularly among ordinary people. The Bogomils abstained from meat and wine, refused marriage, lived by praying, fasting and working with their hands. Advocating evangelical poverty, they denounced the powerful, rich boyars on their estates, and condemned the unworthy lives of clerics. At the beginning of the 11th century, the sect was denounced by a monk called Euthymius, from Peribleptos Monastery in Constantinople. Euthymius claimed the Bogomils were present as wandering preachers in towns and countryside of western Asia Minor, especially around Smyrna, and more generally in the areas of Opsikion, of Thracians and Cibyrrheotes. In these regions they were called Phoundagiagites, that is, *carriers of a beggar's bag*, in reference to their habits of mendicant friars. They themselves simply used the name Apostles. In her *Alexiade*, a chronicle of the reign of her father, Emperor Alexis I (1081-1118), Anne Comnenius in turn evokes the austere Bogomils, wearing black coats and hoods, against whom a first campaign of persecution was launched at the beginning of the 12th century. After his arrest, the principal sectary of the Bogomils of Constantinople, a doctor named Basil, appeared before Alexis I. His testimony was taken down by Euthymius Zigadenus, another monk from Peribleptos. The Bogomils practiced baptism by the Spirit, by placing the Gospels of John and then the hands above the head of the applicant. Paternoster was their main prayer. They were divided into three groups: the *auditors* or catechumen; the *believers* or baptized; and finally, the *elect*, men or women members of the clergy. Emperor Alexis had many of them arrested, even among notables of the city. Those who refused to abjure their faith spent the rest of their lives in prison. Basil was publicly burnt, around 1100, in the hippodrome of the imperial capital, thus being the first victim to die at the stake for crimes of heresy in the Byzantine Empire. Anne Comnenius also mentioned the presence of Bogomils in the region of Philippopolis (Thrace) in 1114. New waves of repression against Bogomilism took place under Manuel I Comnenius (1143-1180), and in about 1165, one of his councillors, Hugo Ethrien from Pisa, wrote a treatise against the "Patarins" of the Hellespont, advising the emperor to burn them or to have a black *theta* marked on their foreheads. At the time, there existed in the East five Bogomil Churches, as attested by the Bogomil Bishop Nicetas in 1167, who had come to confirm the structure of the Cathar Churches in Languedoc at the Council of Saint Felix. There was a Church in Romania, in the region of Constantinople, of which he himself was bishop; another in Dragovitia, in the north of Macedonia, including the towns of Okhrida and Salonika; that of Melenguia in the Peloponnesus; the Church of Bulgaria; and finally, that of Dalmatia, on the eastern shore of the Adriatic Sea. There existed two orders in the Bogomil Church, by filiation of the sacraments: the order called "absolute dualists", perhaps linked to the Church of Dragovitia; and that of "moderate dualists", attached to the Bulgarian Church. Nazario, eldest son of the Cathar Church of Concorezzo, thus received in 1190 from the eldest son of the Church of Bulgaria, the apocryphal *Interrogatio Johannis*, a reference text for theologians of "moderate dualism". Writing in 1250, Rainier Sacconi, a former dignitary of the Cathar Church of Concorezzo who became an inquisitor, mentioned the presence of six Bogomil Churches: that of Slavonia, that is Bosnia; that of the Latins in Constantinople, started after the conquest of the city by Crusaders in 1204; that of the Greeks of Constantinople, heir of Nicetas; that of Philadelphia, now Alakheir, in the heart of Asia Minor; the Bulgarian church, and finally, that of Dragovitia. According to Rainier, the two latter Churches were at the origin of all the others. Pursued elsewhere, the Bogomils took advantage of the remarkable tolerance of the Bosnian bans, starting during the reign of Kulin (1180-1204). At the beginning of the 14th century, the *djed*, or Bishop of the Bosnian Bogomil Church, played an essential role in the affairs of state, mediating the relations between the sovereign and his vassals, managing diplomatic relations with Ragusa. Bogomilism disappeared from Bosnia with the Turkish invasion of 1463. Funerary stele of Bosnian Bogomil dignitaries dating from the early 15th century are on exhibit at the National Museum in Sarajevo.

Urban II preaching the crusade at Clermont in the presence of Philippe I, King of France, Chronicle of Saint Denis

Daniel in the lions' den, capital in La Sauve Majeure

Robert of Molesme's crosier

GOOD CHRISTIANS CALLED CATHARS

Eager to restore its authority in the face of the dissident movements that "teemed in Gaul" in the middle of the 11th century, according to the Church's own terms at the Council of Reims in 1049, presided over by Pope Leon IX (1048-1054), the Church proclaimed the excommunication of "heretics, [...] along with those who receive gifts or a service from them, or who give them [...] support or defence." Several years later, in 1056, another council convened in Toulouse by Pope Victor II renewed the condemnation, excommunicating heretics and their "accomplices" in the widest sense, in other words, "those who have any relations with them [...] other than with the purpose of bringing them back to the Catholic faith." However, during the second half of the 11th century, religious authorities were busy reforming the Church by fighting against the corruption and loose morals of its clergy, preaching crusades, and also affirming the supreme authority of the pope over emperors and kings. They therefore did not appear to be preoccupied by the struggle against heresy. It is true that there was the doctrine of Berenger (c.1000-1088), a canon at Saint Martin's of Tours and director of the cathedral school, who rejected the real presence of Christ in the Eucharist host. Berenger was condemned a first time in 1050 during a council in Rome; then, humiliated and forced to throw his writings into the fire during another Roman synod in 1059, he renounced his beliefs. But there was no more talk of the heretical communities mentioned earlier by Raoul Glaber in Champagne, Artois or Italy, by Adhemar of Chabannes in Aquitaine, or by the monk Erbert in Perigord, among many others. Had they simply been forgotten, or had they disappeared? In fact, the new "heretics" denounced by the prelates of the Gregorian reform were indeed those –Simoniac or Nicolaist clergy– who had been incriminated by the heretics at the beginning of the century, considering them unworthy of delivering the sacraments. Hence, by the end of the 11th century, "the heretics' ideas were in power" according to Jean Duvernoy. In Milan, the Patarini rebelling against corrupt clergy received support from Pope Stephen IX (1057-1058). In Cambrai, Pope Gregory VII (1073-1085) placed Bishop Gerard II under an interdict, as well as paying his respects to the martyrdom of a certain Ramihrd of Esquerchin, who had been convicted of heresy and burnt alive a short time previously on the orders of this same bishop, Gerard II, for denying the validity of sacraments given by the local clergy whom he considered guilty of simony. This was a period of great renewal of the apostolic model and of eremitical asceticism. To go away, leaving everything behind, to live in the footsteps of Jesus and his apostles, to compel oneself to poverty and rough asceticism – this was the ideal of Stephen, who settled in Grandmont in 1074; of Geraud, founder of La Sauve Majeur in 1079, and of so many others who were beatified, canonized or simply remained anonymous. Reconciling eremitism and coenobitism could be the definition of the path taken by Robert of Molesme, the founder of Citeaux in

Kitchen of Fontevrault Abbey

ROBERT OF ARBRISSEL

T he son of the parish priest of Arbrissel in the Rennes diocese, and of Orguende, a poor woman, Robert was born in 1045. After succeeding his father in his position at the church, Robert decided to go and study in Paris. There he joined the Gregorian reform movement to the extent that he returned to Rennes to combat nicolaism. Faced with the clergy's hostility, he left Rennes in 1093 and pursued his studies in Angers. His spiritual quest led him to become a hermit in Craon Forest. For his disciples, he founded an abbey of regular canons at La Roe. In 1096, Robert met Pope Urban II on his return from Clermont. The Pope gave him the title of "sower of the divine Word" and assigned him to go and preach. Barefoot, dressed in rags, surrounded by male and female disciples, Robert preached in towns and villages against the clergy's vices, often provoking clerical indignation. In 1101, he created four monastic establishments at Fontevrault and entrusted their responsibility to an abbess: Saint John for men, Saint Lazarus for lepers, the Great Monastery for noble women and Madeleine for repentant prostitutes. Hermit Robert died in Orsan in 1115, in the course of one last journey.

1098, and before him, of John Gualbert in Vallombrosa (1039). Clerics, monks, ordinary laymen become hermits, some aiming for pure contemplation, like Bruno who settled in the Chartreuse in 1084. Others, like Robert of Arbrissel, the founder of Fontevrault in 1099, and his friend Vital of Savigny, or again Bernard of Tiron, emphasized preaching. But starting in the first decades of the 12th century, once the great wind of reform had ceased blowing, there were the disappointments of those who felt their hopes had not been fulfilled. The ostentatious wealth of the Church and its prelates had remained the same, and the goods rapidly acquired by the new orders issuing out of the reform were shocking when compared to the apostolic poverty preached by their founders. Certainly, the Church had freed itself from secular supervision, had taken on a hierarchical organization, and a renewed monastic spirituality had flourished in the 11th century. But what about the aspirations of the most humble, of simple villagers, of their appetite for evangelism that had existed a century earlier? Hence, at the beginning of the 12th century, the "heretics" were to reappear and become more numerous than ever before. In the south of France, Pierre of Bruys († before 1140) and Henry the Monk, (†c. 1145), new hirsute vagrants in the line of Robert of Arbrissel, but in their case heretics held in contempt by the Church, preached the Gospels and poverty, in opposition to the corrupt clergy. Between 1110 and 1115, a certain Tanchelm raised crowds in Bruges and Antwerp in Flanders, in the Brabant at Louvain, and in the

Canal in Bruges

PIERRE OF BRUYS

A dedicating letter in *Contra Petrobrusianos*, an anti-heretical treatise written during the years 1139-1140 by Peter the Venerable, Abbot of Cluny (1122-1156), is the only document supplying precise information about Pierre of Bruys. The famous heresiarch was perhaps a parish priest in a village of the High Alps before he decided to spend his time spreading his ideas. These ideas were resumed in five points by the abbot of Cluny: the refusal of baptism for infants, because only faith can save and a small child is not conscious enough to believe; rejection of places of worship, since the Church is not a stone building but a spiritual reality; a horror of the cross, the instrument with which Jesus Christ was tortured; the stupidity of the Eucharist, because transubstantiation took place only once – during the Last Supper; the pointlessness of funeral practices (offerings, masses, alms), since men could not hope for anything more than they had received while living. Although he advocated an internalized faith, Pierre of Bruys's preaching was nonetheless violent (profaned churches, altars tipped over, crosses burnt). It was very successful in Provence, then spread through Languedoc and Gascony. Pierre of Bruys probably died near Saint Gilles, between 1132 and 1139, thrown by indignant faithful onto a bonfire of crosses that he himself had lit. Features similar to those of Pierre's teachings, although expressed less radically, were expressed by Henri of Le Mans.

Detail of Saint Gilles Abbey Church

THE PATARIA

The *Pataria* was a religious movement started in Milan during the second half of the 12th century. Led by the deacon, Arialdo, and the priest, Landolfo, it attacked the wealth and vices of the traditional clergy, to which it opposed the ideal of evangelical poverty. Using the method of "liturgical strikes", i.e. refusing the sacraments delivered by Simoniac and Nicolaist clergy, members devoted themselves to preaching and provoking street protests. Followed by many poor people –the name *Patarins* adopted by their adversaries meant "those in rags"– the *Pataria* crystallized Milanese social and political divisions. At the end of 1056, violent clashes took place between Patarins and traditionalists, grouped around the nobility and Archbishop Guido da Velate, named by the emperor. The deacon Arialdo was excommunicated, but his followers went to Rome to see Pope Stephen IX, who sent a mission of legates to Milan to uphold the Patarin cause. A new pontifical mission, led by Petrus Damiani during the winter of 1059-1060, decided to re-ordain all the corrupt clerics.

However, many Milanese soon revolted against the Patarins, whom they considered guilty of weakening the traditions of the Ambrosian Church and favouring Roman interference. Arialdo was assassinated in 1067. A third papal mission from Alexander II tried to quell the unrest. But the conflict continued, embittered by the quarrel over investitures. In 1071, Emperor Henry IV invested Archbishop Gotofredo da Castiglione. On their side, the Patarins led by Erlembaldo, brother of the late Arialdo, elected Attone. In 1075, Erlembaldo too was assassinated. Reconciliation did not take place until 1096, when the emperor and Archbishop Anselmo da Rho submitted to Pope Urban II. A ceremonious burial was provided for the body of Erlembaldo by the pontiff and the Milanese archbishop. Though it was present in other Italian cities like Piacenza, Cremona or Florence, it was in Milan that the *Pataria* had the greatest influence. A radical wing of the movement was probably at the origin of the evangelical and pauperist demands of the 12th century, in particular those of Arnold of Brescia.

Florence

ARNOLD OF BRESCIA

....

Born in about 1090 in Brescia, Arnold left Italy in 1115 for France, where he studied under Pierre Abelard. On his return to Brescia in 1119, he became a regular canon. When political troubles broke out in his city, he joined the emperor's partisans in the struggle against the Pope. Denouncing ecclesiastical property-holding, advocating ideals of evangelical poverty for clerics, Arnold was condemned at the Second Lateran Council of 1139 by Pope Innocent II. Forced into exile, he went to Paris where he taught theology to poor students on Montagne Sainte Geneviève. Faithful to his friend and master, he remained at Abelard's side during the Synod of Sens in 1140. They were both condemned to monastic enclosure. Taking refuge in Switzerland, Arnold spent time in Zurich and perhaps in Constance, whose bishop had been warned by Bernard of Clairvaux about the danger represented by the canon of Brescia's preaching to laymen. However, Arnold repudiated his opinions in Viterbo in 1145, before Pope Eugene III. Sent on a penitential pilgrimage to Rome, in 1146 he entered a city in great political turmoil. Taking the head of a republican communal movement, he started to preach whenever possible against clerical worldliness. He endowed the city with a senate and an equestrian order, and confined the clergy and the papacy to spiritual affairs. In 1152, Pope Eugene III and the Holy Roman Emperor Frederick I allied against the Romans, who refused to hand over Arnold, excommunicated by Adrian IV. But in 1155, the pontiff placed Rome under an interdiction. Deprived of religious services, the *cives* surrendered. Arrested in June 1155, Arnold of Brescia was perhaps hanged before his body was delivered to the flames. His ashes were scattered in the Tiber River so that no relics would be available for popular worship.

Netherlands in the region of Utrecht. He too criticized the ecclesiastical hierarchy, denouncing the greed of the clergy and denying the Eucharist's validity. He was arrested by the Archbishop of Cologne before being killed by a priest annoyed by Tanchelm's words, probably in 1115. In Rome, Arnold of Brescia, revolted by the worldliness of the Church's high dignitaries, raised the people against Pope Eugene III (1145-1153) in 1146. But at the side of these fiery preachers, from the very beginning of the century, there were entire communities, structured and perfectly integrated into social life, and which, although they did not attract attention with showy acts or words, rejected the Roman Church's authority and its sacraments, all the while claiming to obey the most authentic, apostolic tradition. For example, in the Soissons area in about 1114, two men, Clement and his brother Ebrard, born in Bucy le Long, were arrested as the principal members of a heretical sect that, according to the terms of Abbot Guibert of Nogent sous Coucy as he related the facts in his autobiography, "does not defend its dogma publicly, but propagates it by continual whispering". Interrogated by Bishop Lisiard of Soissons, the two accused, who fluently quoted the Gospels, were condemned to the judgement of exorcised water before being thrown into the fire by a furious public, along with two other heretics from Dormans. Abbot Guibard presented Clement and Ebrard as "yokels who claim to live the life of apostles and spend all their time only reading their Acts". As Docetae, the members of their community denied the Eucharist. They also

Castel Sant'Angelo

rejected baptism for small children, the sacrament of marriage, lived in chastity and abstained from any food produced by copulation. It would appear that these heretics, said by Guibert to be "spread throughout the entire Latin world", were allowed a certain amount of tolerance by Clement, Count of Soissons. Five years later, on July 8, 1119, the council held in Toulouse, presided by Pope Calixtus II (1119-1124), in its Canon III condemned "those who, feigning the appearance of a religious order, condemn the sacrament of the body and blood of Christ, the baptism of infants, the priesthood, other legitimate orders, and the bonds of marriage." Temporal powers were given the order to pursue them, and anathema was cast upon those lords who tolerated, protected or defended them. Heretics corresponding exactly to the descriptions of the Council of Toulouse were arrested in Liège in 1135. Narrowly escaping being stoned by the crowds, all but three of them managed to get away. Of those captured, one was burnt alive, the two others preferred to abjure their faith. In 1139, the Second Lateran Council renewed the condemnations of the Toulouse Council of 1119, and demanded the support of temporal authorities in the struggle against heresy. Around 1143, Evervin, Provost of the Premonstrants of Steinfeld in the Rhineland, addressed a letter to Bernard of Clairvaux. In it he described his perplexity on the subject of the heretics recently arrested near Cologne. Judged in his presence before the city's archbishop, the wretches perished by being burnt alive at the initiative of the crowd, according to the

Bishop Notger's evangelistary

DEATH AT THE STAKE

The burning at the stake of 1022, when the heretical canons of Orléans perished on orders from the King, was the first of its kind in France. Was Robert the Pious influenced by the Germanic custom of burning witches? Whatever its precedent, starting in 1022, although no law on the subject had been passed, burning at the stake became the death penalty sanctioning heresy. Not only was it a particularly atrocious way to put someone to death, but in a period when heresy was easily considered as an illness, a cancer, and most often even a contagious illness, like leprosy or the plague, fire appeared as a hygienic measure, one of cleanliness. Furthermore, from the Christian point of view, reducing the heretic to ashes was to condemn him to eternal damnation, depriving him of bodily resurrection on Judgement Day. Emperor Frederick II sanctioned this practice in his anti-heresy laws of 1224 and 1232, which provided for death at the stake for heretics, but only at the demand of ecclesiastical authorities. In documents of the Inquisition, this demand was expressed in the terms of *relinquere judicio saeculari* or *animadversio debita*.

The Stake, miniature in the Great Chronicle of Saint Denis

41

Angels in paradise, Brioude church

PURGATORY

I n the beyond, purgatory is the intermediary place between paradise and hell, destined for the incompletely purified souls of sinners. There they atone for their sins before they can reach paradise. This notion was allegedly born in monastic milieus that had become specialized in saying prayers for the dead. It spread during the 12th century through scholastic teaching, then in the 13th century through the mendicant orders. In one of his sermons, Bernard of Clairvaux (1090-1153) speaks of it in the following terms: "There are three places where, according to their varying merits, the souls of the dead are received: hell, purgatory, heaven. In hell, the ungodly; in purgatory, those who need purification; in heaven, the perfect. Those who are in hell cannot be redeemed (…). Those who are in purgatory are waiting for redemption, first of all tormented by raging fire, severe cold or by another form of torture. Those who are in heaven enjoy the sight of God (…). Since the former cannot be redeemed and the latter have no need of redemption, it remains that our compassion should go to the second, to whom we have been attached by human connections."

cleric. However, "they enter into the fire, bear the torment not only with patience, but even with joy", wrote Evervin, an eyewitness who was left with a lasting impression of such sacrifice. And he questioned the great abbot of Clairvaux, "Where can these sons of the Devil find, in their heresy, courage similar to that which the power of faith in Christ inspires in the truly religious?" As for the heresy itself, it consisted above all in living according to apostolic precepts. The arrested heretics –who called themselves the *poor of Christ* or *apostles*– had their own "bishop", according to the evidence of Evervin of Steinfeld. Confronting an assembly of clerics, this bishop and his companion "defended their heresy with the words of Jesus Christ and his apostles", wrote the Premonstrant, who then directly transcribed their words. "We, the poor of Christ, […] like the sheep in the midst of wolves (Matt. 10, 16), we suffer from persecution with the apostles and martyrs; however we lived a very holy and very strict life, in fasting and in abstinence, spending day and night in praying and working, looking to take out of this work only that which is necessary for life." Evervin specified that they abstained from milk and its derived products, as well as all that was produced by copulation; that they held baptism in vain, condemned marriage and in general, "all the observances of the Church that are not founded on the teachings of Christ and the apostles", notably the cult of the saints, the belief in purgatory and funerary practices. In their evidence, the heretics talked of three degrees organizing the members of their community: the *auditors*, or lay faithful; the *elected*, or members of the clergy, and in an intermediate stage between the two, the *believers*, whose status could be compared with that of novices. Like the canons of Orléans or the heretics of Perigord a century earlier, their sacrament consisted of baptism "in the fire and the Spirit" by the laying on of hands. It had a double value. As an initiatory ritual marking the entrance into the religion, it was administered to those *auditors* who wished to become *believers*. Administered to *believers* at the end of their noviciate, it entrusted them with the power to baptize and ordain in their turn. This clergy was characterized by total integration of both men and women in the believers and the elected. And last of all, every day at the table, the elected blessed bread and wine in commemoration of the Last Supper, a ritual which was a reminder of paleo-Christian banquets. Conscious of belonging to a greater whole, not only in space and number, but also in history and time, these Rhineland *apostles* claimed to be "a great multitude spread throughout nearly the entire world." And according to them again, their religion remained hidden in the West "since the time of the martyrs", but "was maintained in Greece and in other lands". Indeed, "[they] and their fathers, in the line of the apostles, remained in the grace of Christ and will stay [there] until the end of centuries." The heretic community dismantled in Cologne in 1143 was thus part of a veritable counter-Church, claiming to belong to the most authentic apostolic tradition. And through the perspective of history, the presence in the West of similar communities has not been contradicted. On the contrary, those presented in Evervin's letter to Saint Bernard, those heretical *apostles* or *poor of Christ* are evidence of the existence in the Rhineland during the 12th century of people similar to others, known as *Albigensians* or *Cathars*, whom the Roman Catholic Church destined for total extinction. In 1143, in response to Evervin's letter, the abbot of Clairvaux in his sermons 65 and 66 on the *Canticle of Canticles*, called these heretics, whose hypocritical asceticism and clandestinity he denounced, "little foxes who spoil the vineyards" that have to be captured and, according to him, "to be restrained by the sword, rather than be allowed to lead others into heresy. Anyone who punishes a wrong-doer in righteous wrath is a servant of God." The Cistercian abbot seemed to have other information about the heretics and put forward the notion that they were numerous among "weavers and their wives". In 1145, heretics answering the description in Evervin's letter were arrested in Liège. They nearly perished at the stake lit by the crowd, but on this occasion the clergy was opposed to their death. The canons of Liège who related the events in a letter addressed to Pope Lucius II (1144-1145), specified that the heresy had spread as far as their city from the locality of Mont Aimé in Champagne. In this same year of 1145, Bernard of Clairvaux, obsessed about a monk called Henry preaching with impunity in the Languedoc area despite being the object of a condemnation at the Council of Pisa in 1135 in Bernard's presence, decided to go to the area in person in order to contradict Henry's heretical sermons. He announced his arrival to the Count of Toulouse, Alphonse-Jourdain, in a letter denouncing the "strange monster" preaching on his land without being dis-

Baptistery, cathedral and leaning tower, Pisa

HENRY THE MONK

M ost likely a Benedictine monk, Henry left his monastery in about 1110 to wander and preach. In 1116, he arrived in Le Mans, where Bishop Hildebert, about to leave for Rome, allowed Henry to stay. But on his return, the bishop found the people of Le Mans rebelling against the local clergy. Expelled from the city, Henry reached Poitiers, then preached in Bordeaux, before being arrested by the Archbishop of Arles in 1134. Preferring "to obey God rather than man", he advocated poverty, love of one's fellow man, denounced the Church's wealth and clerical unworthiness that called the validity of sacraments into question. Some of his ideas –the uselessness of funeral practices, sacred buildings, infant baptism– are similar to those of Pierre of Bruys, whom he may have met. Brought in 1135 before a synod in Pisa, in which Bernard of Clairvaux and Peter the Venerable participated, Henry appeared to retract his words, and even agreed to join the Cistercians at Clairvaux. Did he do so? In any case, by 1136 in Toulouse, he had recommenced his reprehensible activities. His success, and his evident impunity, encouraged Bernard of Clairvaux to come to Languedoc in 1145. At this point, any trace of Henry disappeared. The "apostate" monk and "scholar", a "predatory wolf" in Bernard's terms, in some ways a precursor of the Waldensians, may have been arrested by the Bishop of Toulouse in 1145 and perhaps finished his days in the city's jails.

Wolf, Kastoria church

BERNARD OF CLAIRVAUX

B ernard was born about 1090 at
the castle of Fontaine lès Dijon.
His father was a knight and his
mother a descendant of nobility
allied to powerful families of
Champagne and Burgundy. Destined
for the clergy, Bernard received a
solid literary education at the canons'
in Châtillon sur Seine. In 1112, he
convinced thirty of his relatives to
follow him to the New Monastery of
Citeaux, where they were welcomed
by the abbot Stephen Harding.
In 1115, Harding sent Bernard to
found a monastery near Troyes,
in Champagne. This was Clairvaux,
where Bernard was to hold the
position of abbot his entire life,
dedicating himself to the monastery's
development so well that, at his death
in 1153, of the 345 monasteries
in his Order, 167 of them depended
on Clairvaux. Following a
disagreement with Cluny in 1124,
Bernard, a spokesman not only for
Citeaux but also for Church reform,
was sought out by political and
religious officials to intervene as a
mediator during episcopal and abbey
elections. In 1128, he participated
in the Council of Troyes where the
Templar Order's statutes were
decided. Bernard himself composed
In Praise of the New Knighthood for
the Templars. In 1130, during the
Anaclet schism, Bernard took the
side of Pope Innocent II, whom he
imposed after eight years of struggle
and many journeys. He participated
in the theological controversies
around Pierre of Bruys, Henry of
Lausanne, as well as Arnold of
Brescia and Pierre Abelard, whom
he had condemned at the Synod
of Sens in 1140. After his mission
in Languedoc and the failure of
the crusade he had preached at
Vézelay in 1146, Bernard retired
to Clairvaux with the satisfaction
of seeing one of his monks become
Pope under the name Eugene III
in 1145. Bernard died in 1153,
leaving a large quantity of
correspondence and sermons such
as those on the *Canticle of Canticles*.

turbed. But the abbot of Clairvaux was far from realizing what he
would actually discover – the completely accepted and well-estab-
lished presence on these Occitanian lands of other heretics, similar
to those *foxes* burnt in Cologne, or the *weavers* of his sermons.
Accompanied by the Bishop of Chartres and a pontifical legate,
Albert the Cardinal-Bishop of Ostia, Bernard started his mission in
Bordeaux in May, 1145. Travelling through Poitiers, Périgueux,
Sarlat, Tulle, Cahors, Toulouse, Verfeil and Saint Paul Cap de
Joux, Bernard ended his journey in Albi on June 29, 1145. In a letter addressed to the chapter of Clairvaux, Bernard's secretary,
Geoffroy of Auxerre, travelling with him, related what had happened in Toulouse. There, "[Bernard] was received with quite a lot
of devotion […] This city in fact had few people favourable to the
heretic [Henry]. […] But as for those who were favourable to [the
weavers' heresy, here called Arians], they were very numerous, and
among them the greatest notables of this city. Shortly before our
arrival, they had won over one of the wealthiest personalities of the
city and his wife, to the extent that they had retired, leaving behind
their fortune and a very young son, to a locality full of heretics,
from which they could not be brought back by any arguments of
their close relations." Bernard called Henry the Monk and the
principal Arian sect leaders to appear before him for a public ver-
bal joust. But nobody came. The abbot therefore left to preach in
the area, "in the little castles that [Henry] had won over". "The
people listened willingly", related Geoffroy, "but we found a few
obstinate knights […] who hated clerics and enjoyed Henry's
jokes." Then came the events of Verfeil. Guillaume of Puylaurens,
in his *Chronicle*, told how the local church, where Bernard was rant-
ing in one of his acerbic, virulent sermons against the *little foxes*,
gradually emptied of its listeners, the notables at first, soon imi-
tated by the common people. But that was not enough to discour-
age the Cistercian abbot, who followed the crowd outside and continued his harangue in a public place. Therefore, as resolved not to
listen as Bernard was to continue his sermon, the local worthies
went home, making such a noise slamming their doors that it was
impossible for the abbot to continue. Since he was unable to continue, Bernard used his gift of repartee, cursing the town with a
pun on the town's name, "*Vert/feuil* (green leaf), may God dry it
up!" as he left the little town. The abbot had further difficulties in
store for him. The inhabitants of Albi, not just content with being
"contaminated", according to Geoffroy of Auxerre, "more than all
the others in the area with heresy", provided an unusual welcome
to the legate, Albert, who had preceded the rest of the delegation
by two days. They sat on donkeys, banging on tambourines and
calling out mockingly. "And when the bells rang to call people to a
solemn mass," wrote Geoffroy, "barely thirty turned up." Receiving
a better welcome in the city of Albi, Bernard was also more successful in his preaching on June 29th. He then returned to his
Burgundy retreat, from which the new Pope Eugene III (1145-
1153), a former monk from Clairvaux, was soon to call him and
charge him with preaching the second crusade in Vézelay, in
March 1146. It is thus obvious that "weavers" or "Arians" were

GOD WILLS IT

In 1144, the Franks lost Edessa and Pope Eugene III asked Bernard of Clairvaux to urge princes and lords to start on a second crusade. The confrontation between a Christian West and a Muslim East dated from the

Bernard of Clairvaux preaching the second crusade

year 711, when seven thousand Berbers crossed the strait separating Africa from Europe, which would receive the name Gibraltar, Jebel Tariq, after the governor of Tangier who led the expedition. Muslim troops invaded the Iberian peninsula, then moved north over the Pyrenees mountains before being defeated by

Lions Courtyard, Alhambra, Granada

Charles Martel at Poitiers in 732. But Christian resistance began to organize right after the battle of Covadonga in 722, starting the *Reconquista* that would finally emerge victorious in 1492, with the fall of the Kingdom of Granada. The Italian peninsula too was invaded by Arabs from Tunisia who, in the middle of the 9th century, invested Sicily and Sardinia. In 846, Rome and its Saint Peter's Basilica suffered from their raids and looting. In 848, Bari was occupied; in 856, Taranto suffered the same fate. Although Emperor Louis II recaptured both cities on the Adriatic Sea in the 9th century, it was not until the 11th century that the Normans managed to expel them from Sicily and the Pisans and Genoese drove them out of Sardinia. The papacy intervened in 1063. At the request of Pope Alexander II, two French barons, Eble of Roucy and Guy-Geoffroi, Duke of Aquitaine, helped provide some impetus for the *Reconquista*: the Christians recaptured Coimbra in 1064 and Toledo in 1085. However, it was Pope Urban II who gave substance to the idea of a crusade that was springing up. On November 27, 1095, in Clermont-Ferrand, he

launched his call for the delivery of the Holy Sepulchre and for the defence and protection of Christians in the East who were living under the Muslim yoke, but also for the protection of pilgrims on their way to Jerusalem. Until that time, confrontations between Christians and Muslims had retained a rather political character, especially for the former. It was a question of defending or reconquering national territory. Urban II united Christendom in a single combat for a sacred cause. To one holy war, the *jihad*, was opposed another holy war, a crusade. Even though kings and the emperor remained cautious, an enormous mystical movement responded to the call. It joined knights and barons, but also common people thanks to preachers like Peter the Hermit or Gauthier Sans, who relayed the Pope's call among them. Everyone became a crusader, sewing a material cross onto their clothes. In 1100, to maintain the energy of this movement, Urban II's successor, Paschal II, delivered the first indulgences for those who became crusaders. The mystical inspiration remained more or less present in the various crusades that took place over several centuries, but it was sometimes seriously blurred with the idea of conquest and colonization. After Urban II, several popes called for crusades. But the designated enemies could change. Hence, Innocent III called for a crusade against the Albigensians in 1208. In 1305, Clement V wanted a crusade to eradicate the Dolcinian danger. Pontifical power used the weapon of crusades for a very temporal cause when, in 1282, Clement IV called for a crusade against Pierre III of Aragon who had just recaptured Sicily from Charles of Anjou.

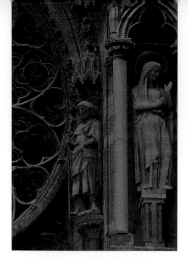

Reims Cathedral

ÉON DE L'ÉTOILE

....

A descendent of petty nobility, Eon or rather Eudes, gathered his disciples in Brittany's Broceliande Forest starting in 1142. His message, tinged with apocalyptic influences, lay within the framework of 12th century contentions against the Church. Eudes rebaptized his followers with apostles' and angels' names, and claimed to be the Messiah of the Church of Latter Days, come to judge the living and the dead. His own nickname, *de l'étoile* (of a star) came from the passage of Halley's Comet in 1145. From the forest, he and his band pillaged churches and monasteries, using or redistributing the loot. Eudes found recruits among peasants suffering from the return of famine, and more generally among society's outcasts. Widespread in Brittany and later in Aquitaine, Eudes and his disciples were at first tolerated by lords wronged by the Gregorian reform, but were quite rapidly persecuted. Arrested, the chief appeared before the Council of Reims in 1148. Judged insane, he was imprisoned and died shortly afterwards. In the diocese of Saint Malo, Bishop Jean of Châtillon (1143-1163) pursued Eudes' followers, some of whom died at the stake. In 1206, Innocent III denounced the persistence of the movement in the dioceses of Nantes, Rennes and Saint Malo.

numerous in Toulouse, Albi and the neighbouring *castra*. Before 1150, Hervé, a monk from Bourdieu in the Indre region, also mentioned their large numbers in the area around Agen, to the extent that the term *Agenais* was used to designate these heretics during the second half of the 12th century. Alarmed by the situation, Pope Eugene III took measures during the Great Council, or *concilium generale*, convoked in Reims in February 1148. With the Pope presiding, over four hundred French, Italian, German, English and Spanish clerics, abbots, bishops and clerical scholars gathered. The council condemned the heretics and placed the territories of their "protectors" under interdiction. These were numerous in the lands of Gascony, as Bernard of Clairvaux was able to see for himself, but also in Provence. The assembly did not hesitate to call on secular powers and to have the Breton heretic Éon de l'Étoile thrown into irons for looting and burning monasteries, even though, in all probability, he was insane. In any case, his disciples were not spared and were condemned to die by being burnt at the stake. About nine years later, in October 1157, another council was organized in Reims, presided over by Archbishop Samson. The first canon was entitled *De piphilis*, i.e. *About the Piphles*, the name given to heretics in Flanders. Although the meaning of the term remains uncertain, it was certainly pejorative. It was most likely a synonym of *piffre*, a glutton, unless it was derived from the German *Pfeifer*, or reed-pipe player. With this term, Archbishop Samson condemned the members of the "very wicked sect of the Manichaeans who hid among the poor and who, under the veil of religion, work at undermining the faith of the humble, a sect spread by despicable *weavers* fleeing from place to place, often changing name and dragging with them women plunged into sin." The council prescribed well-defined secular punishment for the *Piphles*, from confiscation of their belongings, to marking with a hot iron, and expulsion from the town to life imprisonment, or even death, for the "leaders" of the sect. Hence, repression was organized, and the lugubrious march towards the Inquisition was set in motion. Samson's successor as the Archbishop of Reims, Henry, the brother of King Louis VII of France, zealously undertook the cleansing of the territories in his jurisdiction of all Piphles. In 1162, he went to Flanders and had several burghers arrested. The latter were put on trial before Pope Alexander III (1159-1181) in person, who was exiled in Tours at the time. In a letter to the pontiff, King Louis VII himself recommended severity against the heretics arrested by his brother, whom he called *Publicans*, perhaps referring to the publicans in the Gospels –often associated with pagans or sinners– tax collectors who were charged with collecting customs duties and particularly detested by the people because of their application of arbitrarily high tariffs. Meanwhile, in May 1162, Pope Alexander III had presided over a council in Montpellier during which the condemnations of the councils of Toulouse in 1119, Lateran in 1139, and Reims in 1148 and 1157 were renewed, aimed at heretics and lords guilty of not carrying out repression against them, contrary to the orders of the Church. In May 1163, the pontiff presided over another council in Tours, where the problem of heresy spreading

Saint Cecile's Cathedral in Albi

Saint Bernard

THE FOX AND THE VINE

I n his sixty-fifth sermon on the
Canticle of Canticles, commenting
the verse "Catch us the foxes,
the little foxes that spoil the vines.
Because our vine has flowered."
(*Cant.* II, 15), Bernard of Clairvaux
assimilated the proto-Cathar
heretics to foxes. He wrote:
"As far as his life and moral
conduct are concerned he harms
no-one, distresses no-one, does
not set himself above anyone.
His face is pale from fasting,
he does not eat the bread of
idleness, he supports himself
with the labour of his hands.
Where is your fox now? We had
him in our power a moment ago.
How has he slipped from our
hands? How did he disappear so
suddenly? We must go after him,
dig him out. By his fruits we shall
know him; and certainly spoilt
vines point to a fox. Wives have
left their husbands, and husbands
their wives, to join these people.
Clerks and priests, young and old,
have left their people and their
churches, and all, smooth-cheeked
and bearded, are to be found there
among weavers and their women.
Is this not great havoc? Is this not
the work of foxes?"

secretly but very rapidly "like a cancer" was taken up. This was the case in the south of France. The southern lords were charged with arresting the heretics living on their lands and confiscating their goods. The faithful were to abstain from all relations, even commercial ones, with them. Anathema was cast on the lords who sheltered heretics and tolerated them. Henceforth, southern prelates took it upon themselves to carry out enquiries in order to flush them out. Shortly after 1163, in Germany, the Benedictine abbot Eckbert of Schönau wrote a series of sermons dedicated to Rainald of Dassel (1156-1167), Chancellor of Emperor Frederick I Barbarossa. The sermons were directed against heretics that "Flanders called *Piphles*, France, *Weavers*", and he, Eckbert, called *Cathars*. This latter term, which was to become well-known especially starting in the 19th century, was allegedly created derisively from a double etymology: the popular name from the Latin *cattus* or *catier* in the French language used in northern France (*langue d'oïl*) for sorcerers who adored cats; and the scholarly word of *catharistes*, taken from the Greek *Katharos*, meaning "pure", and which had been used as a name for a Manichaean sect during Antiquity. Between 1138 and 1154, while he was still a canon in Bonn, Eckbert had been confronted with these *Cathars*, whose beliefs he had carefully taken down in writing in order to better refute them. And in 1163, when five *Cathars*, probably coming from Flanders and who worked as weavers, were arrested in a barn near Bonn, the Archbishop of Cologne called on Eckbert with the intention of confronting them. Brought before the tribunal, the heretics persisted in their faith and were condemned to being burnt alive on August 5, 1163. Among them was an *archicathar* –in Eckbert's term– as well as a young girl who, far from renouncing her faith at the sight of the torture, threw herself into the flames. A short while later, Eckbert had to repress heresy in Mainz, from which he had forty *Cathars* expelled before another stake was lit in Bonn, destroying another *archicathar* and his companions. Eckbert knew more about their religion than the provost Evervin of Steinfeld had in 1143. To the characteristics already mentioned by the Premonstran monk, the Benedictine abbot added the notion of dualism. The *Cathars* preached "that human souls are fallen spirits, fallen into the celestial kingdom during creation; locked into bodies of flesh, they can nonetheless find salvation through works, but only if they belong to the sect," wrote Eckbert. And he continued that for them, "there are two creators [...], one good and the other evil, that is to say, God and the Devil."

Hence, in 1163, the heretical enemy had been designated. Whether they were Bernard of Clairvaux's *little foxes*, the *apostles of Satan* of Evervin of Steinfeld, passing through the *weavers* of Burgundy, the *Arians* or *Agenais* in southern France, *Piphles*, *Manichaeans* or *Publicans* of Flanders, or even the *Cathars* of the Rhineland, they were all part of the same reality, belonged to the same Church which was not that of Rome, but that of men and women whose spiritual and religious aspirations were the continuation of those of the heretics of the year 1000, who had simply called themselves *apostles* or *the poor of Christ*.

Detail of tympanum of the Last Judgement, Conques Abbey Church

Detail of tympanum of the Last Judgement, Notre Dame de Paris

2

THE CATHARS

Called *Publicans* (or *Paulicians*) in Champagne, *Bulgarians* in Burgundy, *Piphles* in Flanders, *Cathars* or *Luciferians* in the Rhineland, *Patarini* in Italy, *Arians* in Languedoc –all these heretics that the papacy covered with opprobrium called themselves *Apostles* or *Good Christians*. Present in the four corners of Europe and as far away as Asia Minor, they claimed to belong to God's true church, inherited from the apostles. A Church legitimized by receiving the Holy Spirit, transmitted through the sacrament of *consolament*, a Church whose clergy observed evangelical precepts and offered a dualistic interpretation of the Gospels. Hounded in northern Europe, the *Good Christians* were especially well established and tolerated in Bosnia, in the Ghibelline cities of Italy and, also, in Languedoc.

Page of a Cathar ritual written in Occitan

GLEISA DE DIO

Although its origin might lie in one of the very first Christian communities from before the period of the great dogmatic councils of the 4th and 5th centuries, Catharism was nonetheless deeply rooted in the spirituality of medieval Roman Christendom. Fundamentally Christian, the Cathars suggested a dualistic reading of the New Testament, which led them into Docetism and hence into elaborating their own cosmogony with its strong whiff of Gnosticism. In any case, they presented themselves as the descendants of the first Church of the apostles, as the authentic *Gleisa de Dio* that they opposed to the "false" pontifical Roman Catholic Church. In fact, as an organized, structured and hierarchical church with its own sacraments, the *Gleisa de Dio* appeared in the Languedoc of the 12th and 13th centuries as a true dissident counter-church. Within its structure, there was a body of clergy, composed of Good Christians, both male and female, or *Bons Hommes* and *Bonnes Femmes*, who had received the *consolament*, and a body of faithful, called believers or *credentes*. Chosen and ordained from among the Good Christians to be the head of a bishopric, the bishop was helped by two coadjutors, his *filius major* and *filius minor*. If he should die, he was replaced by the *filius major*, the *filius minor* then became *major*, and a new *filius minor* was elected among the Good Christians. Ordained by the bishop, the wandering deacons were allocated a territory on which they were supposed to preach, visit religious houses and *console*. The sacrament of *consolament*, the only Cathar sacrament, infused the *consoling* Holy Spirit that Jesus Christ had brought down onto the heads of his disciples on the day of Pentecost, through the double laying on of the New Testament and the hands above the head of the candidate. This *consolament* fulfilled multiple purposes: a spiritual baptism administered to voluntary adult or adolescent believers or *credentes*, it marked their entrance into the Cathar Church after a probationary period; a sacrament of penance or of reconciliation, unbinding the receiver from his or her sins, and it could be renewed in case the receiver sinned again; a sacrament of ordination, it consecrated entrance into religious and communal life and conferred on each *Bon Homme* and *Bonne Femme* who received it the right to preach and transmit it in their turn. It was also used to ordain members of the hierarchy, consecrating bishops, *filii* and deacons. And finally, as a sacrament of salvation, sealing the mystical marriage between the soul and the spirit, it played a role of extreme unction for the sick, ensuring a good end for the dying. Every believer who wished to receive the *consolament* that would make him a Good Christian had to be a novice for at least one year in one of the houses of the Bons Hommes if he were male, or the Bonnes Femmes if she were female. At the end of this noviciate, during which he participated in community life and received religious instruction, he received the tradition of the Holy Orison, a ceremony conferring the right to recite the Paternoster, Catharism's fundamental prayer. A simple believer was not allowed to say it, nor address God directly, but had to ask one of the Good Christians to do it for him. This was why, upon meeting Good Christians, the *credens* or believer greeted them

CHRISTIAN DUALISM

"Satan said to them: I will put you in the soil of oblivion where you will forget what you said and possessed in Sion! And then he made them tunics, in other words bodies of the soil of oblivion…"
Jacques Authié, sermon quotation

Cathar theology was the result of a dualistic reading of the New Testament, attempting to resolve the problem of the origin of evil. "Every good tree produces good fruit, but an ill tree produces bad fruit. A good tree cannot bear bad fruit." (Matt. 7, 17-18), preached the Good Christians. This world, a victim of suffering, violence, injustice and death, cannot be a product of the eternal God of justice, love and mercy, as was testified by Jesus Christ who said, "My kingdom is not of this world." (John 18, 36). The Cathars accepted two opposing and contrary creations: this material world that the terrible Yahve of the Old Testament created in his image and of which Satan (or the Demiurge) is the Prince; and the Kingdom of the Father, knowing nothing of Evil, a spiritual kingdom of light, where Good reigns for all eternity. Using the Judeo-Christian myth of the fallen angels, the Bogomils and Cathars –both called "mitigated dualists"– attributed the creation of the material world to Lucifer, the angel "who carried light" and invented evil by rebelling against God. Expelled from the celestial home with his accomplices, other angels that he had convinced, Lucifer became the demiurge who created material beings and things out of the four elements created by God. According to those theories, he enclosed the fallen angels in the bodies of men, hence giving them a celestial soul, unless, incapable of completely carrying out his project, he had called upon God who sent two angels to help him. However, Lucifer kept them as prisoners, locking one in the body of Eve, the other in the body of Adam. These angels or primordial souls subsequently reproduced at the same time as the bodies, through traducianism. It is thus that every man contained a parcel of divinity, although it was blemished by original sin, the result of the former complicity between the angels and Lucifer. But within a strictly dualist perspective, the demiurge angel responsible for this bad creation was simply the creature of a superior God, creator of the elements, who would therefore be indirectly at the origin of the material world and of evil. Hence, although the Garatists of Concorezzo continued to profess this "mitigated dualism", the other Cathar theologians radicalized their theses starting at the end of the 12th century in order to make the loving God of the Gospels innocent of creating evil. This theory of "absolute dualism" was theorized in the most accomplished manner by John of Lugio, the Albanist Bishop of Desenzano, in his *Book of Two Principles* of 1230. Taking the path of Aristotle's logic, he postulated the existence of two principles that were fundamentally opposed and independent at the origin of the two creations: Good, the principle of being and of the eternal, and Evil, the principle of the temporary and of non-being, of nothingness. During primordial times, the product of the evil principle, Satan, the dragon of the Apocalypse, tried to attack the kingdom of Good. Vanquished by the Archangel Michael, he was thrown to earth with his legions but, sweeping the sky with his tail, he brought a third of the celestial stars with him in his downfall (*Apoc.* 12, 3-9). Cathars preached more specifically that a third of celestial souls were thrown to earth, leaving behind them in the sky their luminous bodies and their holy spirits. Locked by Satan in their "tunics of skin", they were kept in exile by the baleful power of oblivion. Eternal, but forgetful of their divine origin, at the death of each of their prisons of flesh they were thus blindly reincarnated in a new body. However, unable to abandon them, the Father sent his Son, Jesus, to bring them the means of salvation. Jesus took on a human appearance, and through his teachings awakened them, reminding them of their homeland; through baptism, he brought down onto them the Holy Spirit, the sum of all the holy celestial spirits, in order that, once reunited, souls and spirits would regain the Kingdom of the Father and re-enter their luminous bodies. Thus following Christ and the apostles, the Cathar Good Christians awakened souls by preaching the Gospels. The Cathar Bible consisted of only the New Testament (Gospels, Acts, Epistles and Apocalypse). Baptizing "in the holy Spirit and fire" (Matt.3, 11), they saved souls by breaking the cycle of their reincorporations. Their theology contained no eucharist. It was true that Jesus Christ had been persecuted, just as they were persecuted by the Church of Rome. But his body was only appearance, not physical reality, since the Son was immaterial, like the Father in his kingdom. Similarly, there was no Last Judgement and no Hell. But they waited for the day when all divine souls, good and equal among themselves, re-entered the eternal kingdom. And this transitory material world, an emanation of the evil principle, would disappear.

with the *meliorament*– he bent his knee three times, each time accompanying the gesture with a request for benediction and intercession, with the final demand made in the following terms: "Good Christians, pray to God for me, that he will make me into a Good Christian and lead me to a good end." In Languedoc before persecution began, the power of conferring the *consolament* of ordination, the guarantee of apostolic succession, had been reserved for the bishops and their *filii*. The postulant, male or female, was accompanied to the bishop's by the superior –an elder or prior– from the house where his noviciate had taken place. The ceremony took place publicly before an audience of *credentes* and Good Christians. Before receiving the *consolament*, the postulant promised to follow the evangelical precepts of the Rule of Justice and Truth. This rule required observance of a strict, ascetic dietary regimen, excluding meat, eggs, milk, dairy products and cheese. Fish, oil, bread, fruit and vegetables were allowed during the week, except on Mondays, Wednesdays and Fridays which were days of fasting with only bread and water. Three forty-day fasts –preceding Easter, Pentecost and Christmas– punctuated the liturgical year. During these periods, the Good Christian could consume, besides bread and water, a few fruits and vegetables, except on the first and last weeks of the fast and the usual three weekdays. At mealtimes, always taken in common, the Good Christian observed the Holy Orison ritual of bread, in commemoration of the Last Supper. The elder or prior of the community blessed the bread, then shared it out among those present. For the Docetai Good Christians, there was no transubstantiation; the bread was simply the symbol of holy manna, to be distributed like the Gospels. Observance of absolute chastity, forbidding all contact with a person of the opposite sex, even to the extent of refusing to sit beside someone of the opposite sex, was the second requirement of the Rule of Justice and Truth. It also required that the postulant live by working with his hands, never to swear an oath, nor blaspheme, lie, judge, steal nor kill, not even an animal. Henceforward, he or she would live in a community or be accompanied by a coreligionist –the *socius*, and would say the ritual prayers– the Paternoster, Adoremus and Thanksgiving –at regular hours of the day or night. Finally, the postulant made the vow of never abandoning his Order, even at the cost of martyrdom. Once these engagements undertaken, he was ordained by the laying on of hands and of the Holy Scriptures, making him a Good Christian. The ceremony concluded with the kiss of peace or *caretas*, between Good Christians and believers of the same sex. Serious breaches of the rule were punished by loss of the *consolament*, and all lapses required penance. The latter was imposed by the deacon during his weekly visit to the community. Bowing low before him, the Good Christians took part in a general public confession called *servici* or *aparelhament*. Not only a veritable regular clergy, the Good Christians were also clever preachers. A convent without enclosure, their house was open to all, anyone could come and listen to the preaching, share the blessed bread, or simply visit a relation. As for the Bons Hommes, they were free to go out and wander along the roads from village to village, in pairs, with a bible at their belts to support their preaching of the Gospels.

Two apostles, Montceaux l'Étoile

ENDURA ET CONVENENZA

The *endura*, or fast of the dying, has been falsely interpreted as a hunger strike intended to lead to suicide. In fact, since the patient had received the *consolament* of the ending, like all Good Christian he or she was supposed to observe the Rule of Justice and Truth. He was to abstain from eating meat, practice the ritual fasts and recite the Paternoster before meals or have it recited by another Good Christian. If he broke his fast, he had to be re-consoled in order to have a proper death. In Languedoc before persecution, the dying person was carried to the nearest religious house. There, he was helped by a Good Christian who accompanied him until his final hour. But during the persecutions, the fleeing Good Christians could not watch over the consoled dying who, if they were too weak to recite the Paternoster, had to await their return to eat. In these conditions, it was difficult to regain one's strength. As for the *Convenenza* requested by the knights of Montsegur, it was an agreement with the Cathar Church to administer the *consolament* to them at their death, even in the case of their wounds preventing them from speaking and reciting the Paternoster.

Saint Jean des Vignes in Soissons

In All Corners of Europe

The angel Gabriel, Reims Cathedral

In the medieval West, the history of Catharism is best known in Languedoc. However, Cathars had existed under various names ever since the 12th century in Flanders, Champagne and Burgundy, as well as in Germany, England, Italy and Spain. It is nonetheless true that often the memory of the churches and bishoprics they had founded was contained in the ashes of the fires lit by their adversaries, because neither the *Publicans* of Champagne or Burgundy, nor the *Piphles* of Flanders, persecuted as they were, could resist the zeal of Robert le Bougre, the first Inquisitor sent onto Capetian lands. In Germany and the Rhineland, the regrettably well-known legate, Conrad, was cruelly efficient, and in England, King Henry II showed himself to be pitiless. But the Cathars, chased out of northern Europe, Catalonia and Languedoc, found refuge in Patarin Italy, where the Inquisition was under control until 1268.

The Publicans of Champagne

The first sign of heresy around the year 1000, with the unfortunate Lieutard, took place in the region of Vertus/Montwimer (Mont Aimé), south-west of Châlons-en-Champagne. This was the same region that the canons of Liège, in their letter to Pope Lucius in 1145, considered as the original heartland of Catharism in the north of the Capetian kingdom. In 1114, two proto-Cathar preachers, Clement and Ebrard, natives of Bucy-le-Long, perished, with other believers from the village of Dormans, at the stake lit in Soissons. In 1157, the Archbishop of Reims, Samson, ratified a series of penalties against the *Piphles*: confiscation of their goods, branding with a hot iron, and expulsion for believers; imprisonment for life, or even death, for the leaders. His successor, Archbishop Henry, the brother of King Louis VII of France, pursued the heretics zealously. Another stake was lit in Reims in 1180, at the time of Samson's third succes-

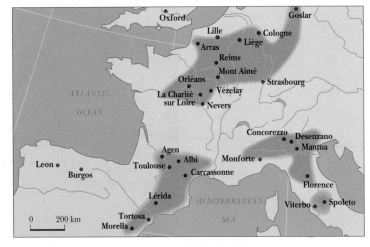

The establishment of Catharism in Europe

Abbey church, La Charité sur Loire

ROBERT LE BOUGRE

A Cathar monk, Robert left the Capetian kingdom for Italy in about 1215. He was a perfect in Milan for around twenty years. Returning to the ranks of orthodoxy in 1234-1235, he entered a Dominican convent, perhaps in Lombardy or in Besançon, France. At this time, Pope Gregory IX (1227-1241) delegated him as an inquisitor charged with pursuing the Cathar heresy in the north of what is now France. According to the chronicler, Aubry of Trois Fontaines, the turncoat Robert, familiar with the habits and customs of Catharism, was capable of recognizing heretics simply from their gestures and way of talking. In fact, Cathar monks, who had vowed never to lie, most often expressed themselves in the conditional tense. Furthermore, they observed such strict chastity that they refused to sit on the same bench as a person of the opposite sex. Robert began his heretic hunting in Burgundy, at La Charité sur Loire and Autun. Then stakes were lit in Flanders, the Soissons region and in Champagne. But he was overly fierce and his mission was interrupted when he was disgraced, shortly after 1236. Robert ended his days in prison.

Thibault IV, Count of Champagne, window in Chartres Cathedral

sor, Guillaume , who was another brother of King Louis VII. One of the victims this time was discovered to be a young woman who an English cleric had found to be in the service of the Archbishop, Gervase of Tilbury. It was because of her fierce opposition to his advances that her death warrant had been signed. Before such chastity, the lord of Tilbury had been persuaded that, "she was of the very impious sect of the Publicans, which was everywhere hunted down and wiped out, but particularly by Phillip, Count of Flanders, who punished them mercilessly with justified cruelty," wrote the Cistercian Raoul, Abbot of Coggeshall, relating the story. A short time later, in 1200, according to the evidence of two other Cistercians, Cesarius of Heisterbach and Aubry of Trois-Fontaines, eight Cathars, or *populicani*, five men and three women, were burnt in Troyes. In 1204, heretics were once again arrested in Braine, between Soissons and Reims. Judged in the presence of the Archbishop of Reims, and the Count and Countess of Champagne, they were burnt alive soon afterwards. "There was among them a painter who was very famous throughout France," related the *Anonymous Chronicle of Laon*. In 1234, in Châlons, a shearer named Arnolin perished at the stake. During this period, repression was becoming harsher in Burgundy, Flanders and the north of what is now France, led by the new pontifical delegate, Robert le Bougre. Robert's stakes were lit first of all in Burgundy and Flanders, then in the regions of Soissons and Champagne, continuing the path set by the Archbishop of Reims. However, the inquisitor's excesses brought on his disgrace and, although he escaped the fate of his German counterpart, Conrad of Marburg, assassinated in 1233, he was nonetheless condemned to life in prison in 1236. Heresy in Champagne was mentioned for the last time in 1239, on the very hill of Mont Aimé where it had originated. The week before May 13, 1239, a grand assembly of bishops and prelates from the north of France was held there. Among the members was the Dominican inquisitor Étienne of Bourbon. At the end of the synod, a great bonfire of heretics was lit, in the presence of the Count of Champagne –King of Navarre since 1234– his barons, and an enormous crowd. The Cistercian Aubry of Trois Fontaines who was there, talked of "a huge holocaust pleasing to the Lord" of one hundred and eighty-three "Bulgars". He also reported that their master and chief, called an *archbishop*, originally from Morains, told them in a loud voice, "You will all be saved, being absolved by my hands." Some historians see this Cathar *archbishop* from Morains –probably coming from the village of Morains le Petit, not far from Montwimer– as the Bishop of the Cathar Church in France, one of whose predecessors had been present at the Council of Saint Felix in 1167. After the bloody repression of Mont Aimé, the surviving members of the Cathar Church in France may have emigrated to Verona, in Italy. In any case, about 1270 in Sirmione on Lake Garda, a "bishop of France", Guillaume Peter of Verona, was mentioned as being with Cathar bishops of Lombardy and from the Toulouse area. Guillaume was arrested in 1289 and transferred to France on orders from the Pope but his fate is unknown.

Lake of Garda

Mont Aimé

The hill of Mont Aimé (once also called Montwimer) forms a kind of natural *oppidum* southwest of the town of Châlons-en-Champagne. It was known by the canons of Liège in 1145 as being the original home of Piphles, Publicans, Bougres and other Weavers from the north of France. In any case, it was there that the history of Champagne's Catharism ended tragically in 1239. Not far away lay the village of Morains le Petit, residence of the Cathar Bishop of Champagne, who may have been a dignitary of the Cathar Church of France. The Cistercian monk Aubry of Trois Fontaines related the legend according to which the hill had been haunted by Manichaean heretics since the 5th century. Mont Aimé took its name from a certain *Wildomar*, a bandit who had been converted to Manichaeism by Fortunatus, the adversary of Saint Augustine (354-430). And, "since that time, this harmful seed of Canaan had never been lacking around the Mount, in the nearby villages," claimed Aubry. Was it to disinfect the area that Blanche of Navarre, the regent of Champagne, had a castle built there at the beginning of the 13th century, but whose sole foundations remain today?

View from Mont Aimé hill

Nave in Vézelay Basilica

POOR BUGGERS

....

The word *bougre* or bugger, from the low Latin *bulgarus*, Bulgarian, took on a pejorative connotation quite early in the Middle Ages. It was used to denote a usurer and/or a heretic and/or a sodomite, all at the same time. In other words, it was a catchall term, used for those categories of people that the Church condemned and cast opprobrium on starting in the 11th century.

Nevers

The Bulgars of Burgundy

In about 1167, nine "Publican" heretics were arrested in the town clustered around the abbey of Vezelay. The abbot sent a letter requesting advice to Thomas à Becket, the Archbishop of Canterbury, and the latter told him to hand them over to the secular powers. For at least two months, the accused were imprisoned separately and interrogated by various prelates. They were finally convicted of heresy and condemned to death at the stake by the archbishops of Lyon and Narbonne, the Bishop of Nevers, the abbot of Vezelay, "and other very wise men in great numbers", reported Hugues of Poitiers. However, two of the accused, having renounced their faith, were subjected to an ordeal by water to test their good faith and hence escape the death penalty. The seven others perished in the flames at a stake lit in the valley of Ecouan, not far from the "inspired hill", on April 10, 1167. In 1198, following a complaint by the Bishop of Auxerre, Hugues of Noyers, concerning heretics who refused to answer his summons, an enquiry was started. Soon, a certain Bernard, dean of the cathedral chapter in Nevers, was accused, and along with him, Raynald, abbot of the regular canons of Saint Martin's in Nevers. Both were suspended from their duties by a synod called in Sens, then sent to Rome to be heard by Pope Innocent III. Finally, convicted of being an "Origenist", Abbot Raynald finished his days in prison. As for Bernard, he was freed after making an oath of purgation. Another cleric from Nevers, Guillaume, a canon and archdeacon, was also pursued but managed to escape. His maternal uncle, the knight Evrard of Châteauneuf, was not as lucky; he died burnt alive on orders of the Count of Nevers in 1201, after a synod held in Paris, which also pronounced the condemnation of his nephew. However, the nephew had taken refuge in Languedoc, where he took the name of Thierry. He found protection under the Lord of Servian, the son-in-law of the Cathar perfect Blanche of Laurac. According to Pierre of Les Vaux de Cernay, in 1026 within the walls of the *castrum* of Servian, this same Guillaume-Thierry participated in a theological debate against Diego of Osma and Friar Dominic, both of whom were supported by the legate Pierre of Castelnau and Brother Raoul of Fontfroide Monastery. However, in the meantime, persecution had swept down on the Cathars of Burgundy. In the words of Robert of Auxerre, Bishop Hugues of Noyers, who died in 1206, "is applying himself hard to reduce the heretics that are called Bulgars [...]. Most of them are deprived of their belongings, some are banished and others burnt." He also specified that "in the town called La Charité sur Loire, very rich men, who had become noticeable for their heresy, [...] were cut off from the Church and delivered to the secular powers". This latter affair provoked the intervention of Pope Innocent III because the wealthy men in question had complained about their bishop's behaviour to the Cardinal-Legate Pierre of Saint Marcel. A few years later, in 1211, the same pontiff, called on by the Bishop of Langres, ordered the opening of an enquiry into a certain Guillaume, canon of Langres and the parish priest of Mussy sur

Vézelay Hill

Temple of Janus, Autun

Seine in the Aube, who was suspected of heresy. When the enquiry had no results, the Pope renewed it in April, 1213. However, Guillaume presented himself spontaneously at the pontifical tribunal, explaining that he had not appeared before the Burgundian bishops because, "in this country the zeal of the faithful against those accused of heresy is such that not only obvious heretics are burnt, but also those suspected". In fact, Guillaume had three brothers, two of whom were burnt for heresy. The third, the knight Colin of Auxerre, bailiff of the Count of Nevers, was pursued twenty years later. In January 1233, Pope Gregory IX opened an enquiry about the bailiff. As a lord reputed to be a heretic, Colin was the accomplice of the Count of Nevers in his exactions against ecclesiastical property. His brother, Guillaume, the former canon and priest, had emigrated to Milan, where he associated with heretics. In June of the same year, 1233, Gregory IX sent a delegation of Preaching Friars from the convent of Besançon to fight heresy in Burgundy. The friars were rapidly joined by the regrettably well-known friar Robert. A former Cathar in Milan, Robert, known as le Bougre, the Bulgar or Bugger, had perhaps met the former canon Guillaume there. He was in any case well-informed about the heretics in Burgundy. His action began in La Charité sur Loire where stakes were lit immediately, putting to death even those who denied. Those who adjured their faith had to humiliate themselves by wearing straps and yokes around their necks. Other fires were lit, especially in Autun, before Robert went to Flanders to continue his exactions.

La Charité sur Loire

The Piphles in Flanders

Heresy first appeared in Flanders during the 11th century, in Arras, where heretics were arrested in 1025. At the beginning of the 12th century, Tanchelm roused the people of Bruges and Antwerp. According to the *Chronicle* of Saint André des Champs of Cambrai, in 1130 there remained in the region numerous disciples of Ramihrd, burnt alive for heresy in the second half of the 11th century by Bishop Gerard II of Cambrai. "Of [Ramihrd's] sect, many remain in certain castles, and as they earn money through their profession of weavers, they are called by that name," related the Cambrai chronicle. At the Council of Reims in 1157, Archbishop Samson, of whom the bishops of Cambrai and Arras were the suffragans, issued a series of penalties against these *Weavers* or *Tesserants*, also called *Piphles*. In 1162, Archbishop Henry, Samson's successor arrested *Publicans* in Flanders. The Archbishop of Reims struck again in Arras in 1172. A cleric named Robert, who had expressed doubt about the Eucharist, was convicted of heresy and sent to the stake. In 1182, following measures taken by Pope Alexander III at the Lateran Council of 1179, the new Archbishop of Reims, Guillaume of Champagne, uncle of King Philip Augustus, organized an expedition to Flanders with the help of its count, Philip of Alsace. It was directed against those "enemies of peace and faith", *routiers* and heretics. In Arras, where four heretics had already been summoned by the bishop, the archbishop proceeded with the arrest, upon denunciation, of a large

Side aisle in Reims Cathedral

The Last Supper, first Eucharist

ORDEALS

Derived from the Anglo-Saxon word *ordal* that in German gave *Urteil*, the term ordeal meant the judgement of God. The custom of invoking divine intervention during a physical test imposed on the accused in order to prove his innocence or guilt has been attested in barbarian legislation. The innocence of the accused was proved if he or she survived the test more or less unharmed: being plunged into icy cold or boiling water, a red-hot iron placed on a part of the body. Guaranteed by the clergy by virtue of the belief in the immanent justice of God, the ordeal, accompanied by liturgical pomp, was a common practice in the High Middle Ages. It was applied either to the accused alone, who was subjected to a physical test, or to both parties, who then had recourse to a judicial duel. Even though Pope Calixtus II still prescribed ordeals at the 1119 Council of Reims for all accused other than the military, God's judgement was contested starting in the 12th century. In 1215, the Fourth Lateran Council forbade the clergy from participating in ordeals, condemned by Pope Honorius III (1216-1227). Ordeals were abolished in France by King Louis IX in 1258.

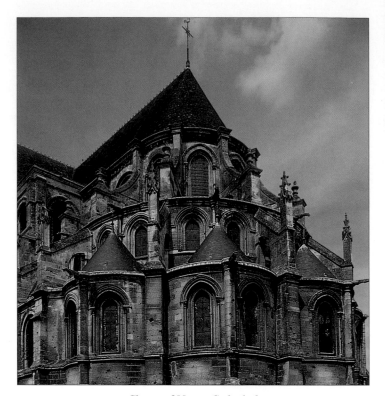

Chevet of Noyon Cathedral

Saudémont angel, Arras

range of people: nobles, commoners, peasants, young girls, widows, married women. Many of them died at the stake, with the clergy and civil authorities sharing out their belongings. Some, having renounced their faith, managed to save themselves by supporting ordeals by water or fire (hot irons). This was the case of twelve heretics arrested in Ypres who, after renunciation, were released after they submitted to the hot irons. Their heresy, which rejected infants' baptism and the Eucharist, consisted of believing that "all eternal things were created by God, but [corrupt and material things] were created by Lucibel," reported Guillaume of Nangis. Heretics were once again burnt in Cambrai in 1217, according to Cesarius of Heisterbach. In 1235, Robert le Bougre inflamed the region with his fiery stakes, eradicating heresy from Flanders. According to the *Rhyming Chronicle* of the poet Philippe Mousket, originally from Tournai and contemporary with the events, the inquisitor was escorted by the king's serjeants and assisted by the Archbishop of Reims and the bishops of Tournai, Arras and Noyon. He came through Peronne, Cambrai, Douai, Lille, Ascq, Leers and Toufflers, putting to death the heretics called *bougres* or *catiers*. The latter term, in the *langue d'oil*, was used for sorcerers who adored cats. It had already been used by Eckbert of Schönau in 1163 as one of the roots for his term *Cathar*. According to the English Benedictine Monk, Matthew Paris, in two months Robert had fifty people burnt. Aubry of Trois Fontaines talked of twenty heretics burnt in Cambrai, and thirty-one in Douai and its surroundings.

Péronne Castle

Notre Dame Church in Douai

One of Hildegarde's visions

HILDEGARD OF BINGEN

....

Born into a family of petty nobles in Hesse, Hildegard (1098-1179) was dedicated to God at the age of eight. She lived with a recluse subject to the Rule of Saint Benedict in a cell beside a monastery. Hildegard took the veil when she was fifteen. She was elected abbess in 1136 and in 1150, founded Saint Rupert's Monastery in Bingen. By this time, her fame had spread beyond the Holy Roman Empire. Not only was Hildegard an efficient abbess, from the age of three she had been having visions that she wrote down in her *Scivias* starting in 1146. Her texts were approved by Pope Eugene III and Bernard of Clairvaux in 1147. A talented writer, she composed two other visionary books –the *Book of Life's Merits* and *The Book of Divine Works*– telling the story of salvation, the Creation and the Apocalypse. A committed prophetess, Hildegard travelled around Germany after 1158, preaching against the Cathars but also criticizing clerical vice. She left voluminous correspondence, addressed to popes, bishops, monks or simple laymen, but also to Emperor Frederick I Barbarossa, who she condemned. The first woman to sign a musical composition, she was also the author of a medical treatise and another on natural history.

The Luciferians of Germany and the Rhineland

It would appear that Cathars were particularly well established in the Rhineland. In 1130-1135, heretics were arrested and burnt in Liège, a suffragan bishopric of Cologne. In Cologne itself, a stake was lit in 1143, according to the testimony of Evervin of Steinfeld. New arrests took place in Liège in 1145. Eckbert, a canon in Bonn before becoming abbot of Schönau, mentioned several successive waves of repression of heresy in Bonn, Mainz and Cologne, between about 1154 and 1164. During the years 1163-1164, Hildegard, the famous abbess of Bingen, warned the Rhineland prelates during a sermon in Cologne cathedral. She said that men "with pale faces", "with shaven heads", dressed "in cheap capes of faded colours" had been "seduced and sent by the Devil" in order to join with secular leaders to denounce the unworthy morals of some members of the clergy. These men of "calm and placid morals", continued the nun, "did not like greed, have no money and in private practiced such abstinence that it would be difficult to reproach them in any way. But the devil is with them...". During another preaching journey to Mainz in 1167, the abbess renewed her warnings against "heretics and Sadduceans, [who] deny the very holy humanity of Christ and the holiness of his body and his blood that are presented in the offering of bread and wine...". In the heart of the Empire, the highest secular authorities, in the person of the emperor himself, did not

Tower of Great Saint Martin and the Cathedral, Cologne

St Martin's Cathedral in Mainz

Column-statues of St Peter and St Mary's Cathedral, Cologne

PUBLICANS IN ENGLAND

Towards the end of 1165, "a bit more than thirty *publicani*" were arrested and appeared before an episcopal synod called in Oxford by King Henry II Plantagenet. Having come to England from Germany, these *weavers* had managed to convert only one old woman, who recanted the heresy as soon as the community was discovered. Facing the prelates, the spokesman, Gerard, spoke against baptism, marriage, the eucharist and the Church of Rome. When the clerics threatened him with punishment, he answered by citing the *Beatitudes* (Matt.5, 10): "Blessed are those persecuted for righteousness' sake, for theirs is the kingdom of heaven." Condemned by the council and given over to secular justice, the heretics underwent an exemplary fate following Henry II's wishes: "their foreheads branded with red-hot irons, […] their leader must undergo the disgrace of two brandings, on the forehead and the chin. Their clothes are cut to the waist, and with much beating they are chased out of the city in the merciless cold. Nobody showed the least pity and they died of distress." Shortly afterwards, in 1166, Henry II issued the first secular legislation against heresy. He forbade "anyone, in England, to receive in his house, on his lands or on any property of his jurisdiction, whomever from this sect whose members were branded with the iron and excommunicated in Oxford. And whoever receives them shall be at the mercy of the King, and the house in which they stayed will be taken out of the village and burnt." In 1190, the presence of heretics was noted in the province of York. And finally, in 1210, a year after the start of the crusade against the Albigensians, according to the *Chronicle* of the mayors and viscounts of the city, an Albigensian was allegedly burnt in London, although nothing is known of the story.

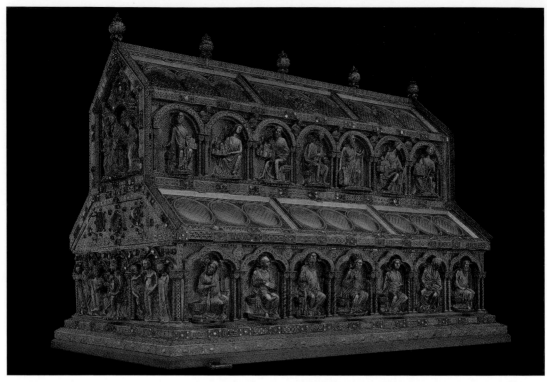

Reliquary of the Three Kings, St Peter and St Mary's Cathedral in Cologne

hesitate to give their support to the Church in the struggle against heresy. Hence, in 1184, the decretal *Ad abolendam* of the Council of Verona was signed jointly by Pope Lucius III and Emperor Frederick I Barbarossa (1155-1190). In 1211, a stake was lit in Strasbourg and ten Cathars perished. In November 1220, on the occasion of his imperial coronation by Pope Honorius III (1216-1227), Frederick II agreed to support the pontifical struggle. Resuming the equivalence between heresy and the crime of lese-majesty, he promulgated a series of laws against heretics. Ten years later, in 1230, Pope Gregory IX sent all the German archbishops a series of decrees that were to be proclaimed from their pulpits every month. In these decrees, the pontiff reiterated the anti-heretic measures of the Fourth Lateran Council, to which were added the measures adopted at the Toulouse Council of 1229: incitement to denunciation, death at the stake for heretics who were *pertinaces* or *relapsi*, wearing the cross or prison for those who abjured. Three years earlier, in June 1227, Pope Gregory IX had charged Conrad of Marburg with the struggle against heretics in Germany. Starting in 1231, Conrad, the first inquisitor delegated by the papacy, enjoyed nearly unlimited powers. He was able to use excommunication, interdiction or calling on secular authorities. His fanaticism and the many stakes lit soon caused general indignation. But his assassination by his enemies in 1233 was unfortunately not enough to slow the development of the Inquisition.

PILGRIMAGE TO COLOGNE

The Three Kings, who were guided by the star from Arabia to the nativity crib in Bethlehem, were allegedly baptized by Saint Thomas. They spread the word of the Gospels and their relics, discovered in Saba, were brought to Constantinople. During the 4th century they were given to Milan, which in turn donated them to Cologne in 1164. Kept in a remarkable reliquary, made by goldsmiths from the area of the Rhine and Meuse Rivers at the end of the 12th century, the relics were placed in the city's new Gothic cathedral, built starting in 1248. In the 14th century, Cologne had become a major centre for penitential pilgrimages imposed on heretics by the Inquisition.

REPRESSION CODIFIED

The papacy provided the anti-heretic struggle with its first codification with the decretal *Ad abolendam*, signed in Verona in 1184 by Pope Lucius III and Emperor Frederick I Barbarossa. Any arrested heretic, if he accepted to renounce his faith in public and usually after being scourged and being excommunicated by the Church, would have his goods confiscated and be banned from the Holy Roman Empire. If he did not repent, or if he relapsed, he was to be immediately handed over to secular justice. In 1199, Pope Innocent III (1198-1216) completed the definition of heresy in canon law with the bull *Vergentis in Senium* addressed to the clergy in Viterbo. In it, heresy was assimilated into the crime of lese-majesty, usually sanctioned by the death penalty in the measures of Roman law. But in this case, it was even more serious, consisting as it did divine lese-majesty. The penalties of confiscation of goods, exclusion from public offices and of disinheritance for heretics were thus fully legitimized. The Fourth Lateran Council convoked by the pontiff in 1215

San Zeno Maggiore Church in Verona

strengthened the measures of 1184. Secular sovereigns who protected heresy were more severely condemned. A bishop was to make two annual visits to the concerned regions of his diocese; he was to make, under threat of excommunication, the inhabitants swear to denounce those on whom the slightest suspicion of heresy rested. Hence, an enquiry

could be started on the basis of a simple rumour, the *mala fama*. In 1229, under Pope Gregory IX (1227-1241), the Council of Toulouse ratified eighteen measures systemizing the methods to be used against heresy: in each city or commune, the archbishop was to choose a small group of sworn men, a priest and two or three laymen, charged with discovering heretics. Once found, the latter were denounced to the bishop who pronounced their punishment, which was carried out by bailiffs. Death by fire sanctioned the *pertinaces*, the "obstinate" who did not want to recant, as well as the *relapsi*, those who had already been condemned for heresy and recanted previously but had fallen back into error. Those who recanted through fear of death were imprisoned by the bishop. Those who recanted through conviction were condemned to wearing a cross sewn on their clothes, as well as temporary exclusion from their town. And finally, every inhabitant was obliged to swear an oath of orthodoxy and to denounce heresy.

St John of Lateran Basilica

CONRAD OF MARBURG

Born between 1180 and 1190, probably in Marburg, Conrad was a priest and perhaps a Premonstrant canon. Educated and erudite, known for his strict asceticism, he had a university degree that may have been obtained in Paris and gave him the title of *magister*. He appeared on the public scene in Germany in 1213 as a talented preacher for the crusades. The Landgrave of Thuringia, Louis IV, made Conrad famous starting in 1225-1226 by making him the confessor of his wife, the future saint, Elizabeth, aged 18, the daughter of King Andrew II of Hungary. Conrad directed the couple's life towards asceticism and poverty. During this period of the rise of the new mendicant orders, Elizabeth stood out by her sense of charity and she multiplied good works in favour of the poor. In 1227, when the Landgrave died in Brindisi from the consequences of the epidemic that decimated Frederick II's crusader troops and thus delayed the emperor's departure for the Holy Land, incidentally provoking his excommunication by the new Pope Gregory IX, Conrad became Elizabeth's true spiritual adviser. Elizabeth refused to remarry and decided to leave her in-laws and the castle of Wartburg so that she could dedicate her life to serving the ill and lepers. Accompanied by her servants, she retired to an old house near Eisenach, then in 1228 she moved to Marburg, where she founded a hospital under the patronage of Saint Francis of Assisi. Living in complete self-denial, Elizabeth spent the rest of her short life in the service of the neediest. It would, however, appear that her spiritual adviser was excessively severe in his relation with her, even to the extent of cruelty. Not only did Conrad insist that she leave behind her three children, but also that she send away her devoted servants. The future inquisitor chose another servant to replace them, one who was hostile to his mistress and even beat her on Conrad's orders. When she died of exhaustion on November 19, 1231, as a consequence of excessive fasting and mortification, Elizabeth was only twenty-four years old. Conrad rushed to carry out the measures needed for her canonization, which was pronounced by Pope Gregory IX in 1235. In 1236, in the presence of Emperor Frederick II, the saint's bones were ceremoniously transferred to the church built for her in Marburg by the Teutonic Knights. However, Conrad did not attend the ceremony because he had died in the meantime, the victim of assassination in 1233. Besides his position as a confessor, since 1227 he had been carrying on certain activities that earned him fatal animosity. Since the departure for Brindisi of the Landgrave, Conrad had had at his disposal the right of patronage of the earnings and prebends of Thuringia. In June 1227, within the framework of reforming German clergy, Pope Gregory IX invested him with the title of *monasterium in Alemania visitator*, but also charged him with pursuing heresy and denouncing any heretic to the episcopal tribunal. In 1231, the pope sent Conrad important procurations concerning the anti-heretic struggle, making Conrad totally independent of episcopal authorities. He was granted the right of autonomous jurisdiction, that of delegating certain elements of the procedure, of calling on the secular arm of justice, and finally, of excommunicating and placing an interdict on the protectors of heresy. In 1231, Conrad had thus become the first anti-heretic judge delegated by the pope, in other words, the first inquisitor. And although, very shortly afterwards, the pontiff delegated two other inquisitorial judges to Germany, the Dominican prior Burkhard of Ratisbonne and his confrere Theodoric, it was Conrad who left the darkest recollections in the annals of German persecution of heretics. It is certain that at his beginnings, the confessor of the future Saint Elizabeth was highly regarded by the episcopal clergy, and both the Archbishop of Mainz and the Archbishop of Trier did not hesitate to support him in his struggle against those he called the "Luciferians" in his reports to Pope Gregory IX. According to Conrad, the Rhineland Cathars were the members of a diabolical sect, adoring Lucifer and organizing ritual orgies; they ran three schools in Trier, where, in fact, a stake had already been lit in 1231. To fight these Cathar-Luciferians, in 1231 Conrad appointed two sub-delegates, in accordance with the pontifical procurations. One was a Dominican named Conrad Dorso, the other a layman called John the Blind, one-eyed and one-armed, described in the annals of Worms as a "scoundrel". This was the opening in the south and west of Germany of a vicious campaign of persecution of heretics, whether they had confessed or were simply suspected. The chronicle of the Dominicans in Erfurt resumed the facts: "In the year of the Lord 1232, a perfidious heresy showed itself in Germany after having bred secretly for a long time. This is why several heretics in the Rhine region, and innumerable others elsewhere were examined by Master Conrad of Marburg, in the name of the apostolic authority and burnt after secular condemnation. Four were burnt in Erfurt on May 5th, in the presence of this same Conrad." In that same year, a stake was lit in Strasbourg, on which died Frederick König and Henry Guldin, two of the wealthiest and most influential burghers of the city. In the Rhineland, the Counts of Arnsberg, Solms and Sayn, neighbours of Cologne, were harassed by Conrad. This leads us to suppose that, like in the south of France, the aristocracy tolerated the heretics. Conrad's methods soon provoked criticism by his contemporaries, even those who had supported him at the beginning. In 1234, after Conrad's assassination, Archbishop Siegfried III of Mainz denounced Conrad's methods to the pope, Gregory IX, even though the latter continued to allow them: general encouragement of denunciation, "of brother against brother, of wife against husband, of the lord against the servant…"; the abandon of regular procedures of accusation for the new procedures of the Inquisition; of an enquiry against the heretic being started even in the absence of a complaint or findings of an offence, the inquisitor and his helpers taking over gathering "witnesses" thanks to denunciation; setting up summary trials, disregarding the most basic rights of defence of the accused, with death as the penalty for all those convicted of heresy by the inquisitor; even those who denied being heretics were imprisoned in such terrible conditions that they finally confessed to anything Conrad demanded, for example "having greeted with the kiss of peace a toad, a cat, a pale man and similar incredible creatures". Starting in 1233, Siegfried of Mainz, alone at first but later supported by the archbishops of Trier and Cologne, notified Conrad of his displeasure with the inquisitor's methods. In vain. Conrad even started proceedings against several members of the Rhineland nobility, among them the powerful Count of Sayn. However, the count managed to obtain a regular trial instead of the inquisitorial procedure whose issue was always fatal.

Conrad of Marburg

With Conrad as the accuser, the trial took place in Mainz on July 25, 1233, in the presence of King Henry VII. But Conrad's witnesses either refuted their evidence, or else were eliminated by the defence as being mortal enemies of the accused. The count's beliefs were publicly declared as orthodox by the Archbishop of Trier and he was acquitted. As for the other apparently highly-placed people whom Conrad had accused of heresy, since they did not bother coming to the trial Conrad decided to set the population on a crusade against them, despite opposition from the Rhineland's archbishops. These were the circumstances surrounding the assassination of the inquisitor of Marburg

on July 30, 1200. His friend, the Bishop of Hildesheim, called the men of Saxony and Thuringia on a crusade against heresy. Meanwhile, after the trial in Mainz, King Henry VII and the archbishops of the Rhineland charged a canon from Spire with going to Rome to obtain the Pope's opinion about Conrad's methods. But the pontiff pronounced no condemnation and, on the contrary, showed great indignation when he learned of the assassination of his inquisitorial delegate. However in Germany, at the Diet of Frankfurt, gathered in February 1234 under the presidency of King Henry, the supporters of the late Conrad did not manage to get their way against the adversaries of his methods. One of the latter even suggested exhuming his body and burning it at the stake. The Count of Sayn repeatedly professed his orthodox faith. The Count of Solms, previously convicted of heresy by Conrad, declared having confessed to the inquisitor because he was afraid of the stake and was freed. Fifty other men who had admitted heresy to Conrad just before his death and been shorn also appeared before the Diet. Six of them had been present during the inquisitor's assassination. All were treated with leniency: they were admitted to purgation and, as a penance, Pope Gregory decided to send them to swell the ranks of Christian troops in the Holy Land. As for the inquisitor's two henchmen, they died within a short time of each other: Conrad Dorso was murdered in Strasbourg, and John the Blind was hanged near Friedberg. Conrad was buried near Elizabeth in Marburg's Spitalkirche, then his bones were transferred, like those of the saint, into the town's new Saint Elizabeth's Church in 1235. It was said that miracles often took place on their tombs. Afterwards, other sources were silent about Catharism in Germany.

The Patarini of Italy

According to the sources, heresy in its widest accepted meaning first appeared in Italy, in the Piedmont. Heretics discovered at the castle of Monforte died at the stake in Turin in 1028. Starting in the 12th century, several movements advocating the ideals of evangelical purity appeared in Italy. Among them were the *Humiliated* of Lombardy, the *Poor Catholics* of Durand of Huesca, the *Poor Reconciled* of Bernard Prim, not to mention the major figure of Saint Francis of Assisi (1181-1226). In some places there were also Cathars, occasionally called *Patarini*. This latter term was derived from *Pataria*, a dissident religious movement born in Milan during the second half of the 11th century. The Milanese Pataria, which denounced abuse by the traditional clergy –simony and nicolaism– received the support of Pope Stephen IX (1057-1058) within the context of the Gregorian reform. But the movement also reached the cities of Piacenza, Cremona and Florence, where it was repressed. It was therefore the old term of Patarini, with its pejorative connotations in cities other than Milan, that was used for Italian Cathars during the 13th century. The existence of an authentic Italian Cathar Church was attested starting in the second half of the 12th century. A certain Marco of Concorezzo, near Milan, was at its head. A French notary described him as a former gravedigger converted to Catharism. Marco gained disciples in Lombardy, the Marches of Treviso and in Tuscany. During his pastoral journey in the West in about 1167, Nicetas, the Bogomil Bishop of Constantinople, stayed with him in Milan before travelling to Languedoc in his company. At the Cathar "council" of Saint Felix, Marco was ordained Bishop of Lombardy. However, at his death his successors did not manage to agree among themselves and, at the beginning of the 13th century, the Italian Cathar Church split into six obediences: the Church of Concorezzo, near Milan and Marco's heir, regrouped around a certain Garatto, hence giving the name of *garatenses* to its members. Rainier Sacconi, who had been one of them for seventeen years before becoming a Dominican inquisitor, wrote in his *Summa* of 1250 that, at the time he had been a Cathar, the Bishop of his Church had been Nazarius, in contact with the Bulgarian Bogomil Church, and of which he possessed writings called the *Secret Last Supper* or *Interrogatio Johannis*. For its doctrine, the Church of Concorezzo professed a "mitigated dualism", contrary to the Cathar Church of Desenzano, on the shores of Lake Garda, that followed "absolute dualism". The Church of Desenzano had been founded by John the Handsome who claimed to belong to the Bogomil Church of Dragovitia. This latter region corresponds to a Greek Orthodox, later Bulgarian, bishopric that no longer exists but used to be located in the area known as Thrace, near Salonika. The Cathars of Desenzano were called *Albanenses*, after Albano, their bishop in the years around 1200. At the time of Rainier Sacconi, their bishop was named Belesmanza. His *filius major* and successor, John of Lugio from Bergamo, was the presumed author of *The Book of Two Principles*, in answer to which was written the work, unfortunately

Bargello Palace, Florence

The Ponte Vecchio in Florence

THE BOOKSELLER OF SPOLETO

S poleto stands on a hill on the left bank of the Tessino, which is crossed by the Ponte delle Torri, dating from the 14th century. On Corso Mazzini, the shelves in the Casa del Libro contain a few books on Catharism and other southern heresies. And, noting his customer's interest in the subject, the bookseller adds that, in the 13th century, the Cathars of Spoleto lived in a neighbourhood in the south of the town, today occupied by the square called Piazza San Domenico.

The Ponte dei Torri in Spoleto

Catharist Writings

Cathar Bible

A Cathar bible written in early 13th century Occitan language is preserved in Lyon. It consists of the complete New Testament.

The Secret Supper

Composed at the turn of the 11th and 12th centuries, this Bogomil apocrypha of Slavic origin presents the dialogue between the apostle John and Jesus Christ, hence its title *Interrogatio Johannis*, during a secret Last Supper. The great myths of "mitigated dualism" are mentioned: the fall of the angels, the creation of the world and man, the coming of Christ. The Cathar Bishop of Concorezzo owned a copy, brought from Bulgaria in 1190.

The Book of Two Principles

A short version of this polemical, theological treatise, probably written in the early 13th century by John of Lugio, *filius major* of the Desenzano Church, is kept in Florence. The author based himself on the Scriptures and Aristotle and used scholastics to demonstrate the existence of two distinct and co-eternal principles and theorize "absolute dualism".

Anonymous Cathar Treatise

This is a collection of commented quotations from the scriptures, for the pastoral use of Christian Dualism, recopied and criticized in the *Contra Manichaeos* attributed to Durand of Huesca (about 1220).

The Rituals of Lyon and Florence

One of these was copied in Occitan from the Lyon Bible, the other in Latin from the *Book of Two Principles*. These fragmentary rituals describe Cathar liturgical practices (*consolament, servici*, etc).

The Dublin Ritual

Copied in Occitan after 1375, this fragment consists of the *Treatise of the Church of God*, a bishop's sermon to a postulant.

lost, of Didier, *filius major* and successor of Bishop Nazarius of Concorezzo. A third Cathar Church was located in Lombardy, in Mantua-Bagnolo, founded by a certain Calojani, and whose members were called *Bagnolenses*. It was linked to another Balkan Church, that of Slavonia, just like the Cathar Church of Vicenza and the Marches of Treviso, founded by Nicholas, in Veneto. In Tuscany, the Cathar Church of Florence, founded by the Bishop Peter, and whose creed was close to that of the *Albanenses*, had three theological schools in Poggibonsi, Pian di Cascia and Pontassieve. And lastly, the members of the Cathar Church of the valley of Spoleto, doctrinally close to the Florentines, were numerous in the cities of Orvieto and Viterbo. The presence of Cathars was also attested in southern Italy, in Calabria, where Joachim of Flore (c.1132-1202) fought against them. Italian Cathars were also established in the cities of northern and central Italy –Milan, Vicenza, Ferrara, Treviso, Bologna and Verona– all places where stakes were to be lit by the Inquisition, as well as in the villages nearby. Within the same city, it was not unusual to meet heretics of different obediences, simple believers or even perfects, and they would sometimes gather in one of the *domus patarinorum*, such as the one that existed in the heart of Vicenza, in the quarter of Santo Stefano, until the Dominicans replaced it with the Church of Santa Corona. Similarly, Verona had its *domus catharorum*, Modena its *molendina patarinorum* –its mill of Patarini, or even Rimini with its *fossa patara*. In Bologna, the last heretics arrested lived in the quar-

Orvieto

THE CATHARS OF ORVIETO

A ccording to Master John, canon of the cathedral and author of the *Vita de Pietro Parenzo*, the Cathar heresy developed in Orvieto during the bishop's absence in 1198 through the preaching of a certain Peter the Lombard. It is true that, at the time, religious and political opposition were rapidly entangled and Orvieto, located in the heart of the Papal State, was struggling against papal ambitions. Orvieto rose up and in 1199 Innocent III sent a Roman noble, Pietro Parenzo, to re-establish order. Parenzo was killed, and for Master John, who considered him a martyr, there was no doubt that a heretic was to blame. In any case, not knowing the *Rule of Justice and Truth* of the Good Christians, the canon also wrote that the Cathars confiscated the goods of Catholics, expelled them from the town or even put Catholics to death. A strange reversal of roles.

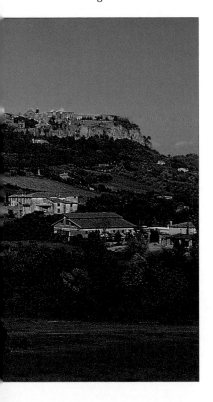

GUELPHS AND GHIBELLINES

The terms *guelph* and *ghibelline* spread through Italy around 1240. They were a reflection of the major division in political life in the north and centre of the country. This opposed the supporters of the papacy –the Guelphs– and those of the emperor –the Ghilbellines. Both terms had their root in Germany. Welf or Guelf was the name of the lineage of the Dukes of Bavaria, enemies of the Dukes of Swabia, the Hohenstaufen family from which the emperors Frederick I Barbarossa (1122-1190) and Frederick II (1220-1250) descended. In 1209, Pope Innocent III (1198-1216), the regent of the young king of Sicily Frederick II, crowned as Emperor the Welf Otto of Brunswick, who had earlier been exiled by Barbarossa. The term Ghibelline came from the name of the castle of the Hohenstaufen, *Waiblingen*, used as a war cry by the imperial forces. As an alliance with the papacy against the Hohenstaufen, Guelphism became rooted in the struggle between empire and the religious authorities. The development of Guelphism in Italy dated from the reign of Frederick I. During the Diet of Roncaglia in 1158, Barbarossa expressed his will to re-establish his authority over the cities of Lombardy, which had given themselves autonomous political organizations during the 11th and 12th centuries. The cities replied by forming the Lombard League in 1167. The league was supported by Pope Alexander III (1159-1181), to whom the emperor opposed two anti-popes, Victor IV in 1159, and Paschal III in 1164. In 1176, Frederick I gave in when faced with the communal troops at the battle of Legnano. One year later, in Venice, he signed a peace treaty with Alexander III, and, with the Peace of Constance,

confirmed the cities' autonomy in 1183. But the conflict broke out again starting in 1220, when the King of Sicily, Frederick II, was crowned Emperor. The master of southern Italy, Frederick II wanted to restore his authority over the north and the centre. He came into conflict with the cities, which recreated their league in 1226 and allied with the Pope, Gregory IX (1227-1241). Pontifical troops invaded Apulia in 1229 but, beaten, Gregory IX agreed to the Peace of San Germano in 1230. In 1237, the emperor defeated the troops of the Lombard League in Cortenuova, though without managing to completely break the cities' resistance. Within the cities, the dominant families were to splinter: the Guelphs were anti-imperialist; the Ghilbellines advocated good relations with Frederick II. This antagonism was in fact added to much older conflicts of interest, between rival families and between rival cities. Most of them underwent successive domination by both factions. The death of Frederick II in 1250 was a blow to the Ghibellines of the north. However, Manfred, the emperor's illegitimate son, usurped the throne of Sicily in 1258 and continued his father's policies. This was when the papacy called on Charles of Anjou who invaded southern Italy. He got rid of Manfred and Conradin, the last of the Hohenstaufen, before extending his influence over Lombardy, Tuscany and even Rome. From this time on, the terms Guelph and Ghibelline lost their significance. When Pope Gregory X (1271-1276) opposed Charles's imperialism, the Guelph party fell apart. Hostile to the French Angevins, Ghibellinism revived during the Italian incursions of Emperors Henry VII (1310-1313) and Louis of Bavaria (1327-1330).

A NOBLE FLORENTINE

"O'er better waves to speed her rapid course/The light bark of my genius lifts the sail,/Well pleas'd to leave so cruel sea behind;/ And of that second region will I sing, In which the human spirit from sinful blot Is purg'd,/ and for ascent to Heaven prepares."

Divine Comedy, Purgatory, I. 1-6

Dante Alighieri was born in 1265 in Florence, into a noble family. He grew up during the struggles between the Guelphs, supporters of the pontifical cause, and the Ghilbellines, partisans of the emperor. In 1266, Florence, which had been Ghibelline for five years, passed into Guelph hands. The Guelph faction then divided into moderate Whites and Blacks, ardent supporters of the papacy. Dante was less than nine years old when he met his future and eternal love, the eight-year old Beatrice Portinari, the daughter of a Florentine worthy. Dante's mother had died before 1275, and he was pursuing his studies of law and philosophy when Beatrice married a banker in 1287. The *gentilissima* died three years later. Dante found a remedy for his unhappiness in the study of philosophy, which he defined in his *Convivio* written about 1304 as, "the happiness that is acquired in contemplating truth". He also attended classes in rhetoric given by Brunetto Latini and, between 1291 and 1295, Dante elaborated *Vita Nova*, a selection and commentary on poems written in the common language celebrating his love for Beatrice, hence inaugurating the "gentle new style " at the origin of his generation's lyrical poetry. In 1292, he married Gemma Donati, from a

Guelph family. In 1295, a new law allowing nobles who had been excluded from Florentine public life to participate in it again on condition that they register in a professional corporation. This was intended to make

Dante, Piazza dei Signori, Verona

them give up their rank. Registered as a poet in the corporation of doctors, apothecaries and booksellers, Dante, a White Guelph, joined in the city's political life. Elected to a position as a prior in 1300, he attempted to calm the conflict between the Whites and the Blacks by proscribing the leaders of the two factions. In 1301, he was sent to Pope Boniface VIII, who kept Dante at his side and called for the intervention in Florence of Charles of Valois in order to re-establish the Blacks. Banished from his city in 1302, condemned to death at the stake if he should be captured on Florentine territory, Dante, betrayed, had to go into exile. Henceforth, he would harbour vehement feelings against the Roman Ccuria, which he expressed in

his *Divine Comedy*. Wandering from city to town, Dante took the side of Emperor Henry VII and, in 1311, he composed his *De monarchia* in which he argued for the separation of Church and State. Guided by Revelations, the pontiff's role was to lead human beings to eternal life; the emperor was to lead humans to temporal happiness, according to the teachings of philosophy. But Dante interrupted his writing of the treatises to dedicate himself to composing the *Comedy* that posterity was to call "Divine" and whose title in fact defines a genre less noble than tragedy according to contemporary literary categories. Dante worked on this long poem, consisting of a hundred cantos and 14,229 verses, throughout his years of exile and until his death in Ravenna in 1321. The *Comedy* relates the allegorical voyage of the poet in the beyond, a path of liberation and salvation that leads, thanks to the intercession of Beatrice, to a vision of God. Lost "in the middle of the path of life", in the dark forest of sin, in the fictional year 1300, Dante makes a journey into hell and purgatory, led by Virgil, the emblem of philosophy and classical poetry, then into paradise, guided by Beatrice, the symbol of love and new poetry. In these three kingdoms, Dante meets historical personalities whose destinies sometimes touched on the history of Catharism. Among them were popes Innocent III and Honorius III (Canto XI 92-99), the "*Gascon*" Clement V and the "*Cahorsin*" John XXII (Canto XXVIII, 58), Bishop Foulque of Toulouse (Can. IX, 94), Saint Dominic (Can. X, 95) and Saint Bernard (Can. XXXXI and XXXIII) or Fra Dolcino de Novara (Enf. XXVIII, 56).

Lamberti Tower, Verona

ter called San Martino dell'Aposa, among the workshops of the curriers and leatherworkers. In fact, heresy concerned all social classes: tradesmen, artisans, innkeepers, judges or notaries, and even members of the nobility. For example, the two Cathar bishops of Concorezzo, Nazarius and Didier, were the protégés of the Lord of Giussano, Roberto Pacta. After their deaths, they were both buried within the walls of his castle at Gattedo. And that was where inquisitors came in 1254 to dig up their heretical bodies in order to burn them. The followers of Catharism were even present in community governments. Hence, in Vicenza, the dominant da Romano, Gallo or da Colle families all included heretics among their members. The papacy soon became alarmed at the situation and, in 1173, Florence was placed under an interdict "because of the Patarini". In 1200, Pope Innocent III threatened to deprive Viterbo of its bishopric if the city continued to favour Catharism. In accordance with the wishes of the papacy, Emperor Frederick II made a point of persecuting heresy immediately after his accession in 1220, and assimilated heresy into the crime of lese-majesty. In 1124, the Hohenstaufen emperor promulgated a special law for Lombardy, seriously increasing the severity of the anti-heretic measures of his 1220 coronation law. All heretics would henceforward have their tongues slit –for blasphemy– and would perish by fire. However, starting in 1227, the struggle between the religious authorities and the empire, briskly reignited between Pope Gregory IX and Frederick II, soon changed the situation of Italian Cathars. The conflict had all of Italy as its theatre and influenced the political situation in the cities of the north and centre of the country, where Cathars were particularly well established. Cities were divided between *Guelphs*, on the side of the papacy, and *Ghibellines*, who supported the emperor. And from then on, Emperor Frederick II did not hesitate to reserve much better treatment for those heretics attacked by his principal enemy. In the words of André Vauchez, the Cathars thus became his "objective allies" against the pontiff. These troubles noticeably slowed the instauration of the Inquisition, created by Gregory IX in 1231 in Italy, where his inquisitors could not operate in Ghibelline cities. And although repression was sometimes fierce in 1232, although stakes were lit in cities where Guelphs had taken over, such as Milan, Treviso or Vicenza, the situation was nonetheless far from that in Languedoc. Hence, within the walls of their Ghibelline cities, Italian Cathars, joined by their Languedoc brothers fleeing persecution, enjoyed a relative respite. But it was not to last beyond the death of Frederick II in 1250. The brother of the French King Saint Louis, Charles 1st of Anjou (1227-1285), coming to the aid of the papacy and investing Sicily in 1264, helped the papacy to get rid of Manfred (1232-1266), Frederick II's illegitimate son, and of Emperor Conradin (1252-1268), the last of the Hohenstaufen. The Inquisition was then free to act. Like Robert le Bougre in the north of the Capetian kingdom, the most persistent Italian inquisitors were themselves former Cathars who converted, like the Dominican Peter of Verona, assassinated near Milan in 1252 and canonized the following year.

PETER OF VERONA

B orn about 1200 into a heretic family of Verona, Peter studied law at the University of Bologna. He soon recanted his faith, converted and entered the Dominican Order. In 1233-1234, he created in Milan confraternities to hunt down Cathars and put pressure on authorities to apply the anti-heretical measures issued by the papacy. In 1244, he created similar confraternities with the same purpose in Florence. During the height of the struggle between Frederick II and Pope Innocent IV, Peter's preaching roused the Guelph cities of Romagna and the March of Ancona. As the prior of the convent in Como, Peter was first named inquisitor in Cremona, then he became head inquisitor in the diocese of Milan in 1251. Leading a ceaseless preaching campaign on the lands under his jurisdiction, vigorously repressing heresy, he was assassinated by his adversaries in 1252, between Como and Milan. Canonized by Pope Innocent IV a year after his death, under the name Peter the Martyr, his cult was spread by the Preachers. Before 1265, his name was included in the *Golden Legend* (Lives of the Saints) of Jacobus de Voragine.

Cathars in the Iberian Peninsula

Luke, the Bishop of Tuy in Galicia from 1239 to 1249, was the author of an anti-heretical polemical work, whose subject was the Cathars observed in Leon between 1209 and 1236, while he had been a canon in that city. These Cathars had allegedly been in Montclus, a castle that no longer exists, in Sobrarbo, in about 1230. Although this information remains uncertain, a letter from Pope Gregory IX dated 1236 attested that Ferdinand III, King of Castile and Leon (1217-1252) had issued a series of penalties against heresy and had applied them in Palencia. Another pontifical letter dated 1238 attested the presence of Cathars in Burgos in 1232. Accounts about Catalonia are more precise. According to the acts of the "Council" of Saint Felix (1167), the limits of the Cathar bishopric in the Toulouse area extended as far as Lerida, in Spain. Catharism seems to have developed in the mountainous eastern regions of the county of Barcelona –Andorra, Cerdagne, Castelbon, Urgell, Cardona– in the heart of noble families neighbouring or allied with the Counts of Foix. Thus, in 1202, the future Count of Foix Roger-Bernard II, nephew of the famous perfect, Esclarmonde, and son of Countess Philippa, who retired to Dun in 1206 to be head of a house of perfects, married Ermessinde, daughter of Viscount Arnaud of Castelbon. It is true that in 1214, a year after the battle of Muret, Lord Raymond of Josa, in the Sierra of Cadi, recanted –only for a while– his Catharism before the legate Peter of Benevento, who had come to have the young James 1st (1213-1276) recognized by Aragon's nobility. However, in Mirepoix in 1221, Guilhabert of Castres, a Cathar Bishop of the Toulouse area, and Raymond Agulher, deacon of Sabarthès, met Viscount Arnaud of Castelbon and Roger of Comminges, Count of Pallars and Viscount of Couserans, probably with the intention of organizing the settlement of Cathar refugees from Languedoc in the highlands of Catalonia. It was in 1224 in Castelbon that Viscountess Ermessinde and Tiborg, the wife of Raymond of Josa, listened to the preaching of Cathar perfects in the company of Dias of Deyme, a lady from the Toulouse area. In 1234, Isarn of Castillon, one of the lords of Mirepoix, died in Castelbon where he had come to be consoled, in the presence of Raymond Sans de Rabat, another lord of Mirepoix. In 1226, at the Cathar "council" in Pieusse, a regular deacon, Peter of Corona from the Toulousain Church, was named for Catalonia. Through Quié of Sabarthès, he left to preach in Josa, Cervera, Berga, where the perfect Arnaud of Bretos lived, close to the mountains of Ciurana, and also in Lerida. But in 1237, the synod convoked in Lerida by the Bishop of Urgell opened the door to the Inquisition. Later on, the bodies of the relapsed Raymond of Josa in 1258, and the bodies of Arnaud of Castelbon and his daughter Ermessinde, in 1269, were exhumed and burnt. Meanwhile, the Catalonian Cathars who were able to went into exile in Italy, like those of Languedoc. The Catalan deacon Philip, called Cathala, went to live in Cremona (1262), then in Pavia until 1277. He was ordained *filius major* of Bernard Olive, exiled Bishop of the Toulousain, and probably managed to escape the stake in Verona in 1278.

Cape Finisterra in Galicia

HERETICS OF THE CAMINO

Although some repentant heretics were condemned to carry out the pilgrimage to Santiago de Compostela as penance for their sins, others used the *via Tolosana* linking Northern Italy and the Pyrenees, via Provence and the Languedoc, for other purposes. Pursued, they took on the pilgrims' bag and staff, wore the cloak and passed incognito among the other pilgrims. It was perhaps in this way, through the *Camino francés*, that Catharism reached Castile, Leon and Galicia. In any case, it was against "the members of the sect of the [Piedmont] heretic Dolcino, who falsely called themselves Apostles of Christ [...] and who, fleeing their country [...] passed into Spain", that the Toulouse inquisitor Bernard Gui warned the Spanish clergy in a letter dated 1316. The Archbishop of Compostela replied that he had arrested "in Compostela and in various other regions [...] people who appeared to be soiled with this perversity."

The White Virgin of Villalcázar de Sirga

The mountains of Ciurana

Roads to Compostela

With the help of a star lit by Providence in the sky of Galicia, the tomb of the apostle James the Greater was found at the beginning of the 9th century. Tradition held that he had been the evangelist of Spain. He had died as a martyr in Jerusalem, beheaded on orders of King Herod Agrippa in 64 A.D. According to legend, his body had been taken by his disciples and placed in a boat that took seven days to reach the shores of Galicia, where the body was buried. Starting in the 11th century, the pilgrimage to Santiago de Compostella –the *Campus stellae* or field of the star– developed rapidly. Coming from all over Europe, pilgrims followed one of the four main routes that, leaving from Paris, Vézelay, Arles or Puy en Velay, crossed France and, once in Spain, joined together to form the *Camino francés*. During the 13th century, James the Greater became the *Matamoros*, the champion of the Christian *Reconquista* of the Iberian peninsula from the Muslims of al Andalus. Compostela became one of the "major pilgrimages" imposed as a penance by the Inquisition on repentant heretics. A tale relates the miracle of a Cathar perfect who, after renouncing heresy, had to make the pilgrimage carrying a heavy staff weighing twenty-four pounds. Walking along the *camino* with difficulty, he stopped one day to pray to the Virgin of the church in Villalcázar de Sirga. At that moment, his staff broke as a sign that his sins were forgiven and he could continue more lightly on his way to Santiago de Compostela. But in an irony of history, a hypothesis put forward in the early 20th century and renewed by contemporary historians is that the relics worshipped in Compostela since the 9th century are in fact those of Priscillian of Ávila, condemned to death for heresy and beheaded in 385.

Verfeil

LAND OF THE ALBIGENSIANS

Walls of St Felix Lauragais

....

The emergence of feudal lords' rights and jurisdictions (châtellenies), characterized by large, private fortresses, and the setting up of a rural "seigniorial order" starting in the 10th century, was accompanied by the clustering of men and their habitat. Through constraints or providing benefits, the lord attracted peasant families and rural tradesmen, who built their houses around his castle. Agricultural land was developed around this clustered and fortified housing, structured around the castle, a church and a cemetery, the whole usually built on a hill. This phenomenon, which could also be the result of developing new arable lands, was called *incastellamento* in northern and central Italy. It was to be found all over the Mediterranean area. The word *castrum*, in a wider sense, could evoke any fortified place and can thus be translated as "fortress". But in southern France, it was particularly used to describe a fortified village. The organization of these *castra* varied according to their history and the layout of the land. Sometimes the houses stood around the castle in concentric circles; elsewhere, they were aligned along parallel streets linking the castle to the fortified gate in the walls.

During the first decades of the 11th century, the presence of "Manichaeans" was denounced in Perigord, as well as in Toulouse where, according to Adhemar of Chabannes, a stake was lit in 1022. However, this stake was the only one recorded in these lands favoured by the Cathar religion until the beginning of the Albigensian Crusade in 1209. Catharism was well established in Languedoc by the first half of the 12th century. But unlike the northern areas where it remained clandestine, here Catharism developed in full view of everyone, under the protection of the local nobility living in the fortified towns of the areas around Albi and Toulouse. This was the first nobility won over by Cathar ideology. Hence, according to Elie Griffe, the feudal *castrum* called Castelnaudary in 1118, or *Castel nou d'Ari*, surely must have sheltered among its inhabitants some of those Cathar heretics called disciples of Arius in southern France. These were the same Arians condemned by the Council of Toulouse in 1119. In 1145, Bernard of Clairvaux noticed how tolerated they were, and how perfectly integrated into the society and life of the *castra* in the Toulousain region, such as the fortified towns of Verfeil or Saint Paul Cap de Joux where, from the top of the castle keep, the seigniorial class watched over a community of merchants, shopkeepers and peasants. Elsewhere, in the north of France, in the Rhineland, Burgundy, Champagne and Flanders, the *Piphles*, *Weavers*, *Publicans* or other *Cathars* were arrested, forced to recant, and most often handed over to secular authorities and doomed to death at the stake, once they had been subjected to the ordeal of water or fire. In those regions, the ecclesiastical authorities allied with the secular powers, applying the measures of the Councils of Toulouse (1119), the Lateran (1139), Reims (1148) or Tours (1163) to repress heresy, following the examples of the Archbishop of Reims or the Count of Flanders, the pope or the emperor. But the Arians of the regions surrounding Albi, Toulouse and Agen –like their Patarin brothers in the Ghibelline communities in northern Italy after them– enjoyed an amazing amount of tolerance by secular authorities. They were allowed to preach with impunity and safety on the roads of Languedoc, gather in their house-workshops open to all, or even publicly compare their theses and interpretations of the New Testament with those of orthodoxy. Thus, in 1165 in Lombers, in the Trencavel Viscounty of Albi, the Cathar bishop of the Albigensian area, most probably the one named Sicard Cellerier, publicly opposed the prelates of the Catholic Church in the presence of Raymond Trencavel and of Constance, Countess of Toulouse. About two years later, in 1167, it was once again publicly and in complete security that Sicard Cellerier and the chief representatives of the Cathar Churches of Languedoc gathered in Saint Felix, on the border between the areas of Toulouse and Albi. There they met Robert of Epernon, the Cathar Bishop of France, in other words, of the regions of Champagne and Burgundy; the future Cathar Bishop of Italy, Mark, from Lombardy; and Nicetas, the Bishop of the Bogomil Church of Constantinople. By this date, the Cathar bishopric of the Albigensian

some claims over the County of Toulouse because of a distant marriage, in 1094, between Philippa, grand-daughter of the Count of Toulouse, Raymond of Saint Gilles (1080-1105) and Guillaume IX (1071-1127), Eleanor's grandfather. In 1159, Toulouse was besieged by Henry II Plantagenet (1154-1189) who, allied to the Count of Barcelona, soon marched on Cahors. And after the Catalano-Aragonese coalition was re-formed in 1181, in 1188 Henry II's rebellious son and Eleanor's favourite, Richard the Lionheart, led an expedition into the Quercy and captured seventeen Toulousain fortresses, including Moissac and Cahors. The backdrop was the struggle between Capetians and Plantagenets, transposed to the Provencal conflict re-ignited in 1166, that opposed the Count of Toulouse, vassal of the King of the Franks, and the Count of Barcelona and Provence, the ally of the Plantagenets. In 1154, Raymond V strengthened his ties with his suzerain Louis VII by marrying Constance, the sister of the Capetian King. Within this context, alliances were established and cancelled, while the country was devastated by ceaseless wars opposing the counts of Toulouse and the dukes of Aquitaine and the kings of Aragon, but also, starting in 1142, their former Trencavel vassals and allies. Although the Trencavels were at first in conflict about Carcassonne with the counts of Barcelona, they eventually joined the Catalano-Aragonese side. The Count of Toulouse Raymond V (1148-1194) tried to improve his dangerous situation in 1171 by giving the hand of his daughter, Azalais, to Roger II Trencavel. But the conflict over Provence did not calm down until the turn of the 13th century, when the Count of Toulouse Raymond VI (1194-1222) got married for a fifth time in 1200, on this occasion to the sister of Pedro II of Aragon.

Furthermore, in the towns of Languedoc, the knightly nobility henceforward had to deal with the emergence of a new power –the urban consuls who were recruited principally from among the merchant middle class, which was becoming richer through the development of trade and import and export. Thus, by the end of 12th century, the citizens of Toulouse were represented by a consulate

Gemelled windows in the house of Azalais in Burlats

THE CONSULS

S tarting in the 11th century, the lords in the cities of southern France surrounded themselves with councillors from the merchant bourgeoisie in order to provide the urban administration with their political and economic experience. The consulates were born out of the emancipation of these councillors, with their freedom of action at the head of municipalities negotiated with the lords. Beziers and Narbonne had consulates before 1130, Avignon in 1129, Arles in 1131, Montpellier in 1141, Nîmes in 1144, and Toulouse before 1152. Chosen from among the notables, the consuls controlled municipal life, exercised civil and sometimes penal justice, defended the town's economic interests. In theory, their decisions remained subordinate to the lord's approval. However, in Toulouse the municipality enjoyed remarkable freedom. The existence of a consulate in Toulouse was mentioned for the first time in 1152. It was composed of twelve consuls. In 1176, these consuls were divided equally between inhabitants of the borough and the city. Probably elected, there were twenty-four Toulouse consuls in 1180, twelve representing the borough, and the twelve others, the city. Their assembly, the *Capitol* or Chapter, was assisted by a common council composed of the members of all the notable families. The wide jurisdiction of the Toulouse consuls extended over civil justice as well as nearly all criminal justice. Of course, the consuls took charge of municipal administration, public works, and the urban militia. Towards the end of the 12th century, to hold their Chapter they had a Common House built at the limits between the borough and the city. The consuls of Toulouse were called *Capitouls* –the abbreviation of "lords of the *Capitol*– starting in 1220.

Saint Trophime Cloister in Arles

The Torrazzo Tower in Cremona

Rue Croix Baragnon, Toulouse

THE CONTADO

....

During the 12th century, the free communes of northern and central Italy extended their authority over the nearby countryside, where they could find provisions, troops, labour, and could raise taxes. The Italian word *contado*, from the Latin *comitatus*, "county", designated this rural territory depending on a commune. The *contado*, which could correspond to a diocese in its maximum extension, also permitted control over commercial arteries. Hence it was a source of rivalry between adjoining communes: Genoa and Lucca were opposed to Pisa; Bologna to Modena; Milan to Pavia and Cremona; Florence to Siena and Pistoia. These wars of influence provoked armed conflict but were also expressed artistically. Indeed, each commune tried to attract prestigious artists to decorate its churches, convents or the abbeys of its *contado*.

of twenty-four notables or *capitouls*. Intermediaries between the count's authority and the population, their assembly –the Chapter or *Capitol*– enjoyed widespread administrative and judicial powers. And although Toulouse remained greatly attached to its counts at the end of the 12th century, it was nonetheless becoming a truly independent republic. The city even had its own militia. As for the notables of Toulouse, they exercised their authority over the seigniories of the surrounding countryside –Lanta, Launaguet– which could at that time be compared to the *contado* of the communes in northern and central Italy.

And it was in the *contado* of Toulouse, as well as in the most contested areas in the struggle between the Trencavel and Raymondine dynasties, that Catharism found its best allies. This was the area in which a kind of political void had developed, and it was rapidly filled by the independent nobility mentioned above, that of Laurac, Fanjeaux, Saverdun, Mirepoix and Puylaurens.

This southern petty nobility, scattered into vast familial clans, shared with the counts and viscounts their taste for courtly pleasures, hunting, tournaments, and the poetry of troubadours. Geoffroy of Auxerre, Bernard of Clairvaux's secretary presented this petty nobility in 1145 as being deeply anticlerical, and not so much for religious reasons but, he said, for the "greed" of the clergy. During this first half of the 12th century, it indeed seemed that several economic patterns were not unrelated to the sympathy shown the Cathar Church by the knights of the Languedoc *castra*. They had been impoverished by the breaking-up of their property among brothers, cousins and distant cousins because of the lack of birthright laws. At a time when the prelates of the Gregorian reform, especially in the Toulouse and Carcassès regions, ordered them to return the parish tithes that had been usurped throughout the 11th century, the reticent lords of Languedoc were eager to listen to, and willing to open the gates of their towns to the preachers of the Cathar Bons Hommes. Did these preachers not denounce the wealth and greed of the established Church, whose "priests and clerics [...] extort and take the tithes

The Tournament, a painting by Jean-Paul Laurens

and premises from the people, on things for which they have not worked," according to the words of a believer from Ax les Thermes before the Bishop of Pamiers, Jacques Fournier?

In fact, since the Cathars openly showed their detachment for worldly possessions, they never owned large properties such as fields or vine-yards, unlike wealthy ecclesiastics whose riches often rivalled those of feudal lords. The Cathar Bons Hommes never demanded tithes or taxes from their faithful, and in the spirit of the apostolic model, they worked with their hands to earn a living. They were thus able to open their house-workshops in complete peace in the streets of the towns of Languedoc. And during these times of war when, despite attempts at peace in the 11th century, banditry and exactions by *routiers* were common, the wandering Cathar preachers were able to count on the armed protection of knights, who granted them a *guidage* or safe-con-duct in return for payment. But the Cathar Church also possessed other trumps that could conquer the hearts of the petty nobility in the *castra*. In these lands where the *langue d'oc* was characteristic of the language and culture, the Good Christians based their preaching on an exegesis of the New Testament translated into the vernacular tongue, the language of the troubadours, –their *cansos*, their *tensos* and their *planhs*. Open to discussion, these Good Christians left every-one free to come to them and, through the openness of their house-workshops, free to observe to what extent they strictly conformed their way of living to the Gospels. When the final hour came, was it not therefore more fitting that the *bellator* entrusted them, rather

Routiers sacking a city

HERESY AND COURTESY

In the early 13th century, Catharism and courtesy existed side by side in Languedoc. The knight Raymond, one of the lords of the small castle of Miraval in Cabardès and a famous troubadour, lived at the turn of the 12th and 13th centuries. His uncle, or cousin, Gaucelm, was a perfect in Cabaret and Gaucelm's mother was also a perfect. The troubadour had several protectors: the young Raymond Roger Trencavel, the provost of Carcassonne Pierre-Roger of Cabaret, Olivier of Saissac, and especially, Count Raymond VI of Toulouse, referred to under the *senhal*, or pseudonym, of Audiart, which was also the poet's *senhal*. The Church pronounced anathema against all these protectors and started a crusade in 1209 on the pretext that they supported heretics. But before 1209, only Love directed the pen of Miraval who sang, under the *senhal* of Mais d'Amic –"*Plus qu'Amie*", more than a friend– of a lady of Cabaret, perhaps Loba, the lady-wolf of Cabardès, daughter of Lobat of Pennautier. Another troubadour, Peire Vidal, approached Loba, whose name meant wolf, dressed in a wolf-skin. He also sang of the blonde Azalais of Boissezon, wife of the Lord of Lombers, a rather venal lady who left Raymond for a more profitable match. There is no doubt that neither Loba nor Azalais, regular visitors at the courts of Cabaret or Lombers, were Cathar believers, not in itself evidence of irreproachability. In 1212, after the capture of Montegut by Montfort, Raymond, who had lost Miraval, called in an ultimate poem on King Pedro II of Aragon to retake the country from the French. "Then ladies and lovers will regain their lost delights!" exclaimed the poet. Because courtesy needed peace and freedom. But after the defeat of Muret in 1213, courtesy and heresy would both be uprooted from Languedoc.

THE GREAT LYRIC POETRY OF THE TROUBADOURS

An art of the court, the lyric poetry of the troubadours was born in Languedoc during the first half of the 12th century. Starting in 1150 it spread into most of the western countries. Whether they were called *Minnesänger* in the Germanic countries, *troubadours* in Languedoc or *trouveres* in northern France, the name given to the courtly lyric poets expresses the intrinsically musical nature of their poetry, a literary composition that was always accompanied by a melody. *Troubadour* and *trouvere* come from the Latin *tropare*, "to compose tropes". In the medieval West, a trope described a literary and musical work grafted onto a liturgical chant. The German *Minnesänger* –from *Minne* "courtly love", and *singen*, "to sing"– also referred to chants. In fact, the Occitan word *canso*, "song" or "*chanson*" in French, designates the troubadours' works. Alas, of the surviving 2,500 12th and 13th century cansos, only one out of ten retains its musical accompaniment. No rhythmic information is marked on the remaining scores. The composer obviously left the interpreter free to quantify the beat, and to modulate his *canso* at each performance. It was in Poitou and the Limousin around 1100 that this poetry appeared with all its originality with respect to previous tradition. Eleven songs remain from the first known troubadour, the Duke of Aquitaine Guillaume IX (1071-1127), whose court lived in Poitiers. His vassal, the Limousin Viscount Eble of Ventadour also composed. Then the art of lyric poetry spread throughout the entire south-west: Jaufre Rudel was prince of Blaye, and the wandering poets Cercamon and Marcabru, of humble origin, were from Gascony. Troubadour poetry

flourished between 1160 and 1210, with its greatest representatives Bernard Marti, Bernard of Ventadour, the Toulouse burghers Peire Vidal, Guiraut of Bornehl, the future Bishop of Toulouse Folquet of Marseille, the canon Pierre Cardenal, the knight

Portable organ player, Puivert

Raymond of Miraval, and many others, among whom were several *trabairitz*, or women troubadours, such as the Countess of Die or Lady Na Castelloza. However, starting in 1209, the Albigensian crusade caused a rupture from which Languedoc lyrical poetry would never fully recover. Faced with the disappearance or impoverishing of the seigniorial courts, some of the troubadours left for Spain or Italy; others moved to urban settlements. Religious and political themes then acquired greater importance. As courtly poetry, the troubadours' lyric poetry had evoked themes linked to the life taking place at court. As a spokesman for a seigniorial clan, the poet sang of the feudal lord's trials and tribulations, the blows and misfortunes of the suzerain-patron. However, it was above all their love poetry that provided the troubadours with their literary fortunes. Singing of his passionate love, whether real or fictitious, his *fin'amor* –where fin',

"distilled" was perhaps a part of the vocabulary of alchemy– the poet spoke of his desire for the unnamed pleasure that only a Lady could provide him with, and whose future or already refused possession would engender *joi* –a term evoking both joy and *jeu*, amusement or play. The inexorable distance separating the poet from the object of his desire created a poem that expressed his pleasure as well as his sadness, his hopes and fears, in a characteristic poetical language, originally constituted from the dialects spoken between Limoges and Toulouse. Several styles defined the form of the poem: the *trabar leu* was a simple style without any stylistic devices; the *trabar ric* emphasized ringing tones, and finally the *trabar clus*, where the poets played with oppositions, was based on obscure metaphors and hermetic meanings. A *canso* was composed in four or eight stanzas –or *coblas*– of identical length or metre, and ended with a *tornado* equal to half the *cobla*, which addressed the person to whom it was dedicated. However, in the *descart* (discord), all the stanzas were different. The *sirventes* was a satiric or polemical *canso*, most often composed with political intentions. Finally, the *planh* was a *canso* in which the poet lamented the death of a patron or the death of a beloved. Adapted into the *langue d'oil* (spoken in northern France) in 1160, courtly lyric poetry developed in strength and brilliance north of the Loire from the 12th to the 14th centuries. Purer and clearer, the troubadours' poetry avoided the *trabar clus*. Starting in 1230, it developed religious themes, especially about the Virgin Mary, and established itself among the prosperous bourgeoisie in the cities of the north, like Arras.

The hill of Montségur

than anyone else, with the salvation of his soul? And after the end of the subtle games of the *fin'amor*, after the end of the troubadours looking for *joi*, many noble ladies, often wives, mothers or widows, found answers to their deepest longings in the manner the Cathars lived their faith. In lands where convents of nuns were sorely lacking, the Cathar house, a convent without enclosure within the walls of a town, offered them the possibility of living an authentically religious life. The Cathar house was also used as a school, ensuring the religious training of future Bons Hommes or Bonnes Femmes. Its workshop provided the community's subsistence; and as a hospice it welcomed wandering perfects, the needy or the dying who wished to die a good death. On becoming a widow, Blanche of Laurac, the mother of four daughters and a son, retired to a Cather house with her youngest girl, Mabilia. In Mas Saintes Puelles, Dame Garsende, a widow and mother of the five co-lords of the Mas, with her daughter, Gailharda, opened a house for perfects where her grandsons, Jourdain of the Mas and Jourdain of Quiders, grew up. They were the future "faydits", defenders of Montsegur. Hence, true Cathar lineages formed around these mothers who became Good Christians.

Vassals joining Catharism soon led to their suzerains doing so, and by the end of the 12th century, the entire nobiliary society of Languedoc had been affected. Although Raymond V remained a Catholic, the letter that he sent in 1177 to the Chapter General of Citeaux and indirectly too to the King of France, within the framework of the conflict opposing him and the Plantagenets with the Catalonians, was unequivocal. "The greatest nobles of my lands are already affected by the evil of infidelity, taking with them a great multitude of people who have abandoned their faith", wrote the Count. The greatest nobles, starting with Viscount Roger Trencavel, who held the Catholic Bishop of Albi prisoner under the guard of his seneschal of the Albigeois, Guillaume Peyre de Brens, whose family was Cathar. The greatest nobles like the Count of Foix, Raymond-Roger, whose wife Philippa became a perfect in Dun and

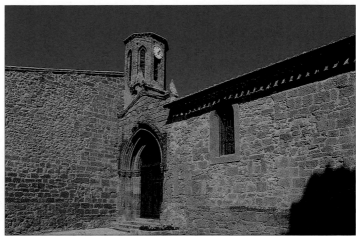

The church in Mas Saintes Puelles

whose sister, Escarmonde, was ordained a perfect in his presence at Fanjeaux in 1204. The greatest nobles like Raymond VI who, unlike his father, showed complete tolerance towards the heretics.

Perfectly integrated into the society of their time and fully participating in the development of its economy, the Cathars were weavers, leatherworkers, carpenters or tailors, working and trading with scrupulous honesty, perhaps selling the fruits of their labour at fairs and markets in local towns. Contrary to the theologians of the Catholic Church, it would appear that they did not condemn the practice of lending money with interest, an additional advantage in making the merchant class aware of their religion. And for the rich nobles of the Toulouse bourgeoisie, was not adhering to Catharism a way of rising into the ranks of the aristocratic classes? After the nobility, the merchant classes were won over, and soon artisans and peasants were also attracted by the exemplary lives led by men and women often ordained before their very eyes, openly living their religion and preaching, in their own language, words of equality, unencumbered by Roman Catholic liturgy and its interminable Latin litanies. They in turn became Cathar believers or Bons Hommes.

Fur merchants

A GRUESOME SCENE

While the Cathar heresy was establishing its roots in Languedoc, relations between Occitan princes and the clergy were tense and often marred by incidents. At the death of Roger II Trencavel in 1194, his son Raymond-Roger, aged nine, succeeded him. He was under the guardianship of Bertrand of Saissac until 1199. Pons Amiel, the abbot of Saint Mary's of Alet, died in 1197. The abbey's monks elected Bernard of Saint Ferreol, the abbot of Saint Polycarpe's monastery attached to Alet, to succeed him. However this choice did not please the guardian of the young viscount. Bertrand went to Alet, had the new abbot placed in irons, organized a new election presided by the corpse of Pons Amiel which he had exhumed. His candidate, a certain Bozom, was elected but after causing the abbey's ruin, he was degraded by the Council of Le Puy in 1222. Construction on the abbey was started at the end of the 11th century, on the site of a Carolingian foundation. In 1318, Pope John XXII raised the abbey seat of Alet to a bishopric. The abbey was destroyed in 1577, during the religious struggles that tore the Razès apart from 1573 to 1596. All that remains is a magnificent ruin whose ochre stones are lit up by the sunshine.

Saint Polycarpe

The chevet of Alet Abbey Church

2

REPRESSION

1

THE AFFAIR OF PEACE AND FAITH

Councils and synods defined the penalties incurred by "enemies of peace and faith", represented by the Cathars and the lords tolerating or even protecting them. Dominic, joining the pontifical legates sent to Languedoc, chose to confront them on their own ground. But after the murder of the legate Pierre of Castelnau, the barons of northern France obeyed Pope Innocent III's call for a crusade, and they attacked Occitan lands. By 1209, Simon de Montfort was master of Carcassonne before capturing Toulouse in 1215. But *paratge* (nobility of blood and soul) moved the Raymonds of Saint Gilles, who freed the lands of the South. Another crusade led by the French King Louis VIII led to the surrender of Raymond VII and the signing of the Treaty of Paris in 1229.

Fontfroide Abbey

FROM ANATHEMA TO THE CRUSADE

On April 11, 1162, Pope Alexander III arrived in Maguelone near Montpellier. Here he was welcomed by Raymond V, Count of Toulouse; Raymond Trencavel, Viscount of Béziers, Albi and Carcassonne; and Ermengarde, Viscountess of Narbonne. A first council was held in Montpellier on May 17, 1162, and one year and two days later, on May 19, 1163, the Council of Tours began.

Councils and Conferences

For the seventeen cardinals, one hundred and twenty-four bishops and four hundred and fourteen abbots participating in the Council of Tours, the ultimate goal was the re-establishment of pontifical authority, which had been seriously shaken by Emperor Frederick I Barbarossa's support of the anti-Pope Octavian. But, at the request of the prelates from the Midi (Southern France), a canon was dedicated to the heresy that was spreading throughout their dioceses "in the manner of a canker". The text called on clerics to be vigilant and defined the methods to be used in the struggle against heresy: anathema was to be pronounced against those who provided the heretics with shelter; the duty of lords whose fiefs were concerned was to arrest them and confiscate their property; the faithful must forbid all relations, even commercial ones, with heretics; and above all, to flush out the heretics the canon prescribed the use of investigations when denunciation was not sufficient.

In 1165, Guillaume, the Bishop of Albi, organized a conference in Lombers, located in the south of his bishopric. This step was taken within the framework of the measures decided by the synod of Tours. He wanted at the same time to identify the heretics, prove their errors and bring the local lords to abandon their support for them. The choice of the *castrum* of Lombers was not fortuitous, since the town contained many heretics. Raymond Trencavel, Constance, the wife of Raymond V and sister of the King of France, Louis VII, attended the conference along with Sicard of Lautrec and Isarn of Dourgne, who had come as neighbours. Several prelates had also answered the invitation: Pons of Assas, the archbishop of Narbonne named by Alexander III at the Council of Montpellier in 1162, the bishops of Lodève, Toulouse, Agde and Nîmes, and eight abbots, including those of Fontfroide, Saint Pons and Saint Guilhem le Désert. The Bishop of Lodève, the former abbot of Aniane, led the debates. The heretics, led by one named Olivier, were interrogated. They contested the authority of the Old Testament, accepting only the Epistles and the Gospels. They refused to make a general statement about their faith and avoided the question of baptizing infants; they claimed that a layman, just as well as a cleric, could carry out the eucharistic consecration. They evoked Saint Paul in support of their argument that, in marriage, man and woman joined together for lust and fornication. They remained evasive on the sacrament of penitence and only claimed that the sick could confess to whomever they wished, clergy or layman. The sentence was pronounced: "I,

Reference Dates	
Council of Tours	1163
Conference of Lombers	1165
Cathar "council" in Saint Felix	1167
Mission in Languedoc by the pontifical legate Peter of Pavia	1178
Third Lateran Concil	1179
Pre-crusade in Languedoc by pontifical legate Henri of Marcy	1181
Saladin captures Jerusalem	1187
• Deaths of Raymond V of Toulouse and of Roger Trencavel • Council of Lerida	1194
• Election of Pope Innocent III • Rainier and Guy are named pontifical legates • Anti-heretical edicts issued in Gerona	1198
Legation of Pierre of Castelnau	1203
• Marriage of Raymond VI and Eleonore, sister of Pedro II of Aragon • Pleading in Carcassonne in the presence of Pedro II of Aragon • Arnaud-Amaury is named pontifical legate	1204
• Cathar "council" in Mirepoix • Nomination of Foulque as Bishop of Toulouse • Beginning of preaching in Languedoc by Dominic and Diego	1206
• Foundation of Prouille Monastery by Dominic • Theological disputation in Montréal • Contradictory debate in Pamiers	1207
• January 14: murder of Pierre of Castelnau • March 10: Innocent III calls for a crusade • March 28: Innocent III designates Arnaud-Amaury as the spiritual leader of the crusade	1208
• Beginning of June: the host meets in Burgundy, Nivernais and Lyon regions • June 18: reconciliation of Raymond VI with the Church at Saint Gilles	1209

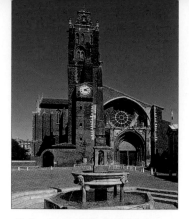

St Stephen's Cathedral, Toulouse

ARAN FOR AGEN

···

T he question of whether the document relating the Cathar gathering at Saint Felix in 1167 is authentic has been raised. The document was published for the first time by Guillaume Besse in 1660, in a work entitled *The History of the Dukes, Marquesses and Counts of Narbonne*. This scholar from Carcassonne declared that he had recopied this *notitia* from a document which had been entrusted to him in 1652 by a prebendary of Saint Stephen's Cathedral in Toulouse. In 1933, the canon Louis de Lacger set out to prove that the document was a fake. In 1946, Father Antoine Dondaine rehabilitated Besse's transcription. The main point causing the problem is the mention of the *ecclesia aranensis* as the Cathar Church in Languedoc. In all probability it is an incorrect transcription of *ecclesia agenensis*. Paradoxically, this crude error is evidence of the document's authenticity. In 1968, Yves Doat reintroduced suspicion by contesting the existence of a Cathar Church in Melinguia, cited by Nicetas in the *Notitia*. But after all, the Melingi, a Slavic people in the Peloponnesus, were perhaps affected by Cathar preaching in the 12th century. And Jean Duvernoy, considering that "it does not seem possible that an author in the 17th century could talk about Melinguia", closed the debate and re-established Besse's honour.

Gaucelin, Bishop of Lodève, by order of the Bishop of Albi and his assessors, judge that those who call themselves Bons Hommes are heretics." The conference ended with some confusion because Olivier and his companions refuted the sentence, called the bishop a heretic and then pronounced a completely orthodox declaration of their own faith. But they refused to swear an oath, first of all because it was contrary to the Scriptures and also because, in their opinion, the Bishop of Albi had committed himself not to ask them to do it. The sentence was nonetheless confirmed and the knights of Lombers were invited to "no longer give them support". From then on, the heretics were often called Albigensians.

In May 1167, an important meeting –today often called a council– gathered Cathars in Saint Felix in the heart of the Lauragais and, like Lombers, on lands belonging to Trencavel. Among those present were Nicetas, the leader of the Bogomil Church of Constantinople, Robert of Epernon, the Bishop of the Church of France, Mark, the Bishop of the Church of Lombardy, Sicard Cellerier of the Church of Albi, accompanied by their councils and members of the Churches of Toulouse, Carcassonne and Agen. First of all, the *consolament* was renewed for all the perfects present at the meeting. On this occasion the bishops of the Churches of France, Lombardy and Albi were re-ordained, then Bernard-Raymond, Bishop of the Church of Toulouse; Guiraud Mercier, Bishop of the Church of Carcassonne, and Raymond of Casalis, for Agen were designated and ordained. The re-ordination of bishops already in place makes some historians

THE VISCOUNTY LANDS OF THE TRENCAVELS

Before 1007, Garsinde, the heiress of Viscount Guilhem of Béziers and Agde, married Raymond, Count of Carcassès and Razès. Raymond was one of the three sons of Roger the Old (†1011), Count of Carcassonne-Foix-Couserans. Garsinde and Raymond transmitted their titles to one of their sons, Roger III, who died in about 1066 leaving no heirs. His lands went to his niece Ermengard, who had married the Viscount of Albi and Nîmes, Raymond-Bernard Trencavel in 1060. Fearing that the Count of Foix, Roger 1st, grandson of Roger the Old, was going to claim his rights over Carcassès and Razès, the couple bought powerful protection by selling the two counties to Ramón Berenguer I (1035-1076), the Count of Barcelona. But taking

advantage of a weakening of the Catalonian house, their son, Bernard-Ato Trencavel (†1130) recaptured his hereditary lands in 1082. However, Carcassonne, which supported Ramón-Berenguer III (1096-1031), revolted in 1107 and 1120. Bernard-Ato then allied with Barcelona's rival, the Count of Toulouse, Alphonse-Jourdain, who helped him to take control of the city in 1124. At his death, Bernard-Ato IV shared his properties among his sons: Roger inherited Albi, Carcassès and Razès; Raymond obtained Béziers; Bernard-Ato got Nîmes and Agde. But by 1150, Raymond inherited the lands of his late brother Roger and allied with the Catalonian Ramón-Berenguer IV against Toulouse.

Saint Felix Lauragais

Poitiers

LETTER TO CITEAUX

"The corruption and contagion of this heresy have so prevailed that nearly all those who accept it believe they are paying homage to God. It has caused divisions between husband and wife, father and son. Even those serving the priesthood are depraved by the contagion of heresy; the ancient churches [...] are being abandoned [...]; baptism is being refused; the Eucharist is seen as an abomination, penance is scorned; all of the Church's sacraments are considered as nothing and, what is worse, two principles are even being introduced... As for me, who am armed with two divine swords and who, I admit it, am established to be the avenger and the minister of the wrath of God, when I try to place a limit and an end to such abandoning of the faith, I must confess that I lack the means to accomplish a task of this kind and of this importance: the most noble of my lands have let themselves be corrupted... Since we know that the force of the spiritual sword cannot manage to eradicate such a heresy, it has to be reduced by the material sword. In order to do that, my opinion is that the lord King of France come from your regions, because I think that, by his presence, it will put an end to this great evil."

suppose that at Saint Felix, the Languedoc Churches which had until then been followers of "mitigated dualism" opted for the "absolute dualism" of the Dragovitia Church, but this does not appear in the sources. During this important meeting, the limits between the Churches of Toulouse and Carcassonne were clearly defined by a charter setting out the boundaries, and Nicetas invited the four Languedoc Churches to live in the same harmony as that reigning between the five Churches of Greece, which presupposes that this had not always been the case. This conference appears as evidence of the progress made by the heresy in Languedoc and its desire to develop even further through the establishment of a new organization.

In 1173, the Archbishop of Narbonne, Pons of Assas, in a letter to King Louis VII denouncing the intrigues of Henry II, King of England, raised the question of heresy in rather alarmist terms. "The Catholic faith is immensely affected in our diocese and the boat of the blessed Pierre is receiving such blows from the heretics that it is on the point of being swamped." Several years later, in September 1177, before the meeting of the General Chapter of Citeaux, Raymond V of Toulouse wrote to Alexander, the order's abbot. This was a call for help from one of the greatest lords of Christendom, the grandson of one of the heroes of the first crusade, Raymond IV. The letter showed that he had perfectly understood the situation he described completely, as well as its seriousness. Did he suspect that this same situation contained the seeds of the misfortune of his lands and the extinction of his dynasty less than a century later, to the advantage of the very Capetians on whom he was calling to intervene? On September 21, 1177, thanks to the mediation of the pontifical legate, Peter of Pavia, Cardinal of Saint Chrysogone, Louis VII and Henry II met and sealed a peace treaty. Informed of the contents of Raymond V's letter by the abbot of Citeaux, the King of France suggested that he and the King of England jointly lead a military operation in Languedoc. The abbot of Clairvaux, Henry of Marcy, wrote to Louis VII in April 1178, and told him of his intention of going to southern France to visit the Cistercian abbeys of the Clairvaux lineage, in particular Grandselve, Belleperche, Candeil and Fontfroide. But he gave up his project, just like the Capetians and the Plantagenets gave up theirs. In a missive written to the pope in May, 1178, the abbot of Clairvaux asked him to extend the mandate of Peter of Pavia's legation and to entrust the latter with a mission to Languedoc. This mission was organized with the support of the kings of France and England. The pontifical legate was accompanied by the archbishops of Narbonne and Bourges, the bishops of Poitiers and Bath, and by Henry of Marcy. In Toulouse, the legate and the prelates were not very well received. They nonetheless invited heretics to participate in a debate on "the rule of the true faith". Since there were not many candidates for such a confrontation, the Cistercian abbot noted that "the foxes have been turned into moles". The legate called for denunciation; upon appeal, the clerics, consuls and faithful of the city gave the names of heretics. Among them appeared that of one of the city's wealthy notables, Pierre Maurand. Raymond V sent for Maurand to appear a first time; the abbot of

THE SAINT GILLES DYNASTY

In 781, Charlemagne created the Kingdom of Aquitaine for his three year-old son Louis, with Toulouse as its capital, and entrusted it to his cousin Guillaume of Gellone in 790. When Louis the Pious (†840) succeeded his father at the head of the empire in 814, he ceded Aquitaine to his son Pepin, who died in 838. For a while, Aquitaine fell to Pepin II, the son of the latter, but who appeared sufficiently unruly for the emperor to dispossess him in favour of his second son, Charles, called the Bald, the King of Neustria (western Frankish empire) after the partition of Verdun in 843. But Pepin II, excluded from the partitions, claimed his rights over Aquitaine and revolted against Charles the Bald in 843. This rebellious nephew, captured by his uncle in 852, had, in 840, named the Count of Rouergue, Fredelon, as the head of the County of Toulouse, the most prestigious seat in Aquitaine. In 845, Fredelon chose the side of Charles the Bald, who confirmed him in his position and named his brother Raymond as Count of Quercy. At Fredelon's death in 852, Raymond (†864) succeeded him, but was removed in 863 by Bernard, Marquis of Gothia. However, Bernard's insubordination angered both the king and Pope John VIII, who excommunicated him in 878. A powerful man, the Count of Auvergne, Bernard Plantevelue, took his place at the head of a March of Gothia that included the County of Toulouse. Conscious of his superiority, Plantevelue allowed Eudes, Raymond's son, to settle in Toulouse. Guillaume the Pious succeeded his father Plantevelue, who died in 885. But he let himself be supplanted by the grandson of Eudes of Toulouse, Raymond III Pons, who annexed his lands in 924. Through alliances or arrangements, his

heirs, whose sovereignty already extended over Quercy, Rouergue and the Albigeois, acquired the Duchy of Narbonne and then the County of Saint Gilles further east. The sharing out of the inheritance forced the Raymondine family to split into two branches: that of the Counts of Rouergue who soon captured Nîmes, and that of the Counts of Toulouse and Saint Gilles. The latter progressively extended their sovereignty over most of Languedoc. Williäm Taillefer (†1037) acquired new lands in Provence through his marriage with Emma, daughter of the Count of Arles. His grandson Guillaume IV gave himself the title "Count of Lodève" in a document dated 1079. This Guillaume, Pons's son, died in 1093 leaving a daughter, Philippa. In 1094, she married the Duke of Aquitaine, Guillaume IX, who from then on claimed rights over the county of Toulouse. It was however Raymond IV of Saint Gilles who had succeeded his brother Guillaume in 1088. A first marriage with a daughter from the Provencal house brought him the Comtat Venaissin, as well as rights and privileges in Provence. Then through an inheritance from the younger branch of his family, he acquired Rouergue and the Narbonnais. Raymond IV, who had already fought against the Muslims in Spain in 1087, was one of the first to answer Pope Urban II's call for the first crusade. Entrusting his Languedoc territories to his son Bertrand, in 1096 he left Provence at the head of an army and went overland through Italy, Dalmatia and Greece. In Constantinople, he distinguished himself by refusing to pay homage to the Basileus. In 1098, he played a decisive role in the capture of Antioch but had to cede his place to Bohemond of

Taranto. Similarly, he actively participated in the capture of Jerusalem but stepped aside before Godfrey of Bouillon. Raymond died in 1106 while besieging Tripoli. His third wife, Elvira, daughter of Alfonso VI of Castile-Leon, had followed him to the Holy Land and had given birth to a son there in 1103. This was why he was baptized Alphonse-Jourdain. Arriving in Languedoc, Alphonse was not quite ten years old when he succeeded his half-brother Bertrand in 1112. Having gone to the Holy Land in 1109, Bertrand won renown in taking Tripoli. Married to Faydide of Provence in 1112, Alphonse came up against the Provencal ambitions of the Count of Barcelona, Ramón Berenguer III, husband of Douce, Faydide's sister. The Catalonian count allied with the Duke of Aquitaine, Guillaume IX (†1127) against the Count of Toulouse. Two coalitions formed around the rival lords of southern France. The war subsided in 1125 with the creation of the Marquisate of Provence, a possession of the Saint Gilles, and the County of Provence, which went to the Catalonian count. The conflict began again at the death of Ramón Berenguer III in 1131. From then on, the Count of Toulouse had to confront King Louis VII, the Duke of Aquitaine through his marriage with Eleanor, grand-daughter of Guillaume IX. Alphonse-Jourdain fought in Spain (1134), founded Montauban (1144) and embarked for the second crusade in 1147, but died on his arrival in the Holy Land, having been poisoned. His son Raymond V, who succeeded him in 1148, was one of the last of the dynasty which ended after the death of his grandson Raymond VII (1249) with his great-granddaughter, Jeanne, in 1271.

Steeple, Notre Dame du Taur

Clairvaux interrogated him in the name of the legate. Maurand denied being a heretic but refused to swear an oath, which was the equivalent of a confession. Then Maurand claimed that consecrated bread was not the body of Christ. He was declared a heretic and he was placed in the keeping of Raymond V. He agreed to be reconciled, which was done during a ceremony that took place the next day in the abbey church of Saint Sernin. An enormous crowd watched his entrance into the shrine, bare-chested and barefoot, surrounded by the Bishop of Toulouse and the abbot of Saint Sernin who hit him with birch rods. When he arrived in front of the altar, he prostrated himself before the legate and abjured his heresy. He was condemned to penitence, but did he accomplish it completely? In any case, by 1182 Maurand's name appeared on the list of consuls of Toulouse.

At the time when Peter of Pavia's mission was in Toulouse, the Bishop of Albi, co-lord of the city, was being held hostage by the Seneschal of Albi, Guillaume Peyre de Brens, known for his sympathy towards heresy, and who had been named to the position by Roger Trencavel, the other co-lord of Albi. Roger Trencavel was the son-in-law of Raymond V, having married his daughter Azalais. His position with respect to heresy was not as clear as that of his father-in-law. The pontifical legate sent the Bishop of Bath and the abbot of Clairvaux to Albi. They were accompanied by the Viscount of Turenne and a lord from the Toulousain. Their mission was to obtain the prelate's freedom and to invite Roger Trencavel to be more co-operative in the struggle against heresy. But Trencavel had left the Albigeois and

STRONG PUNISHMENT

A fter having renounced his heretical beliefs, Pierre Maurand had to do penance. He had to leave for Jerusalem within forty days and stay in the service of the poor for three years. Upon his return, his confiscated belongings would be returned to him. Before leaving, he had to go into every church in Toulouse, bare-chested and barefoot, to receive discipline. He promised to return the goods taken from churches, any interest that had been demanded and repair any damage done to the poor. He was also condemned to pay a fine of five hundred pounds to the Count of Toulouse. And lastly, his house in the Rue du Taur was razed except for the ground floor and the tower.

Turenne

The chevet of Saint Sernin's Basilica, Toulouse

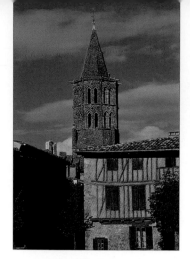

Saint Felix Lauragais

the legate's representatives headed for Castres, where Trencavel's wife, Adelaide, was staying. Many heretics were living in the *castrum* and they were quite indifferent to the preaching of the delegation that joined the viscountess and declared the viscount to be a traitor, a heretic and faithless before excommunicating him. Henry of Marcy left for Clairvaux. The Bishop of Bath then met two heretics, Raymond of Baimiac and Bernard-Raymond. Both had participated in the meeting at Saint Felix, where the latter had been ordained Bishop of the Church of Toulouse. Addressing the prelate, they complained about an edict expelling heretics issued by Raymond V, which had led them to settle in the Albigeois, the fief of a much more understanding Roger Trencavel. They declared themselves ready to appear before the legate on condition that they be allowed to return home, a condition that was promised. They were interrogated in Toulouse, in Saint Stephen's Cathedral. The two heretics, reading from a parchment, made a completely orthodox profession of the faith. They spoke in Occitan but the prelate asked them to speak Latin. They tried to do so, but their mastery of Latin was such that they reverted to the vernacular.

Gargoyles on St Stephen's Cathedral, Toulouse

SAINT STEPHEN'S CATHEDRAL

In the 11th century, Isarn, the Bishop of Toulouse, had had a Romanesque church built on the site of a Paleochristian shrine. A cloister, demolished in the 19th century, abutted onto it. It was under the bishopric of Foulque, before 1211, the date of the first siege of Toulouse by Simon de Montfort, that construction began on the nave in *Raymondine* style. Further work undertaken by Bishop Bertrand of L'Isle Jourdain in 1272 provided the cathedral with a new chancel. But it was only in the 16th century that the two parts of the building were joined together, at the foot of a new steeple and around an enormous pillar.

Peter of Pavia, who had doubts about their sincerity, had the assembly moved to the nearby Church of St James. There the heretics' profession of faith was read aloud and they confirmed it, causing murmurs of perplexity among the audience. The two men were invited to swear an oath. This they refused to do. The legate therefore believed that their refusal was evidence of their heresy, and demanded that they recant before reconciling with the Church. Faced with their refusal, he pronounced a sentence of excommunication and condemned them as Satan's henchmen. Thanks to the safe-conduct negotiated earlier, the two heretics were allowed to return home. It was nonetheless decided that if, within a period of eight days they did not return to orthodoxy, the edict of expulsion of heretics issued by the Count of Toulouse would be carried out against them.

Pope Alexander III called for a council to be held in Rome's Lateran palace in March, 1179. His legate, Peter of Pavia, was supposed to attend but, before arriving in Italy at the beginning of 1179, he was supposed to find a successor for Bernard of Villemur, the Bishop of Toulouse. He considered Henry of Marcy but the abbot refused after writing to both the pope and even to King Louis VII asking that such a position not be given to him. Previously sounded out about becoming the Abbot of Cîteaux, he had also refused that position in December, 1178. The canons of the Toulouse cathedral chapter chose their Bishop in the course of 1179. This was Fulcrand. Henry of Marcy was named Cardinal-Bishop of Albano on March 15, 1179, when the Third Lateran Council had been under way since March 5. A certain number of prelates present at the council, such as the Archbishop of Narbonne, the bishops of Carcassonne, Béziers, Uzès and Maguelonne, besides the former abbot of Clairvaux and Peter of Pavia, were able to knowledgeably discuss the Cathar problem in Languedoc, the object of Canon twenty-seven. This same canon also dealt with the problem of the *routiers* or highwaymen. The clergy at the council also made decisions relating to the Iberian peninsula, then undergoing the *Reconquista*: any Christians helping the Muslims, dealing with them commercially, selling them weapons or working on their ships would be excommunicated. The Church did not deal only with its outside enemies, but attempted to re-establish clerical discipline; another canon requested that the clergy reduce their living expenses and prohibited the selling and accumulation of sacerdotal positions.

The Fenestrelle Tower, Uzès

THE AFFAIR OF PEACE AND FAITH

Starting in 1150-1180 in Western Europe, mercenary fighters appeared at the side of feudal contingents in armies. These mercenaries were called *routiers*, a word derived from the Latin *rupta*, "ruptured, broken", which is also the origin of the medieval word *route*, meaning part of an army. Forming troops consisting of varying numbers, often foot soldiers, the *routiers* were recruited in different social milieus. *Branbacons*, *Germans*, *Hennuyers* (from *Hainaut*), *Catalonians*, *Basques*, *Aragonese*, *Navarrese* –all these terms were used to designate them and geographically define the areas where they were recruited. Extremely efficient on the battlefield but totally ignoring any ethics of chivalry, the *routiers* were feared because of their cruelty, violence and

rapacity. It often happened that the lords for whom they fought let them get their payment off the land. Numerous in the south of France, they appeared as the enemies of the peace the Church had been championing since the end of the 10th century with its institutions of the Peace, and then Truce, of God. The Third Lateran Council assimilated the anathema against the heretics into that against the *routiers*, including the heretics, "enemies of the faith", with the criminal *routiers* "enemies of peace". But paradoxically, the establishment of this "peace" –which in fact attempted to impose, both inside and outside Christendom, a unique vision of the world, of faith and of society– was to lead to the crusade against the Albigensians.

LATERAN III, CANON 27

T he first part of this canon referred to heretics called Cathars or Patarins or Publicans, analyzed their geographical establishment, invited feudal authority to take on its mission of defending the faith and condemning those who supported heresy. The second part concerned the *routiers* who roamed through and devastated Languedoc. The council denounced those who had hired them with the same severity as the heretical agitators. However, those who opposed the *routiers*' exactions were to receive indulgences and the protection of the Church, just like those who made a pilgrimage to the Holy Sepulchre. As for the *routiers* themselves, lords and princes were authorized to act against them, by reducing them to servitude and confiscating their property.

SAINT SERNIN ABBEY CHURCH

"One should also go to worship the body of blessed Sernin, bishop and martyr […] buried in a beautiful site near the city of Toulouse; an immense basilica was built there in his honour."

Aimery Picaud, *The Pilgrim's Guide*

A community of canons was charged with watching over the relics of Saint Sernin kept in the Paleochristian basilica. A first mention of this community's existence appeared in a charter of privileges granted it by Charles the Bald on April 5, 844. During the first half of the 9th century, with the complicity of the canons Saint Sernin's revenue was put at the disposal of the local aristocracy which took charge of distributing ecclesiastical positions. The Gregorian reform was to put an end to these practices. In 1056, a first council was organized in Toulouse by Pope Victor II "to eradicate simoniac heresy". Another in 1060-1061, presided over by Hugo, the pope's legate, attacked the same problems and issued sufficiently weighty spiritual punishment as remedies to re-establish order. Bishop Isarn, elected in 1072, strongly contributed to this renewal and the canons once again returned to their regular life, opting for the Rule of Saint Augustine at the end of the 11th century. The construction of a new collegiate church was undertaken towards 1070. The decision to do so was a necessity; the original shrine could not cope with the growing population of Toulouse and the constant increase in the number of pilgrims who travelled to Santiago de Compostela along the *via Tolosana*. Construction was possible because the Saint Sernin chapter found itself at the head of a very large and growing source of revenue consisting of many churches, from which it received revenue, but also land, houses and shops that it had enfeoffed around the collegiate church and which made up the town. It thus had the necessary financial means to start a building of this size. One man played a particularly important role in the construction of the Romanesque part of the building: Raymond Gayrard. When he became the master builder in 1080, the chevet was nearly completed. He directed the work on the transept, finished in 1096, and the nave, which was nearly completed at his death on July 3, 1118, one year after the collegiate had been raised to being an abbey church. Meanwhile, on May 24, 1096, Pope Urban II had come to consecrate the church and the magnificent altar of Bernard Gilduin, in the presence of Raymond IV of Saint Gilles who was about to leave for the first crusade. After Raymond Gayrard's death, work on the abbey church was interrupted. It was to start again during the second half of the 13th century and continue until the beginning of the 14th century, providing the abbey church with its Gothic elements. However, in the 12th century, a cloister, no longer in existence, flanked the church on its north side. The layout of Saint Sernin Abbey Church, similar to the cathedral in Santiago de Compostela, its contemporary, is that of a pilgrimage church with a nave and transept with side aisles, a choir with an ambulatory that serves the radiating chapels, and a high roof, permitting the placing of galleries. The programme of Romanesque sculptures is particularly rich. Among them, one should mention the two hundred and sixty capitals, the ambulatory's bas-reliefs, including an extraordinary Christ in Majesty, all made by Bernard Gilduin; the tympanum of the Miegeville doorway, framed by portrayals of Saint Peter and Saint James, where the Ascension of Christ is watched by the apostles on the lintel. In the upper crypt, the relic of the True Cross is a work from the second half of the 12th century and that of Saint Sernin dates from the first half of the 13th century. The latter has been preserved, which is not the case of the Gothic reliquary in which the remains of the first Bishop of Toulouse were placed on June 25, 1283, nor its baldaquin, both of which were destroyed in the French Revolution. In 1860 Viollet-le-Duc undertook the restoration of Saint Sernin's, as Prosper Merimée wished in 1845. In attempting to do it well, did the architect go too far? In 1969, a long campaign of "de-restoration" was undertaken, aiming to return the church to the simple beauty imagined and wanted by its builders.

Bas-relief, St Sernin Basilica

Tomb of St Hilarius (detail)

BOUND DESTINIES

S ernin, or Saturnin, the first Bishop of Toulouse, died in 250 during the consulate of Decius and Gratus, a victim of the intolerance of a population barely affected by his preaching. His disciples buried his body discreetly and in 360 one of his successors, Hilarius, found his tomb in the place where Notre Dame du Taur Church now stands. He had a brick vault built overhead and, beside it, a wooden shrine. The cult of Saint Sernin began to develop. At the end of the 4th century, construction began on a basilica about three hundred metres to the north and where his relics were transferred. On February 22, 970, the relics of Saint Hilarius were discovered, in the presence of Garin, Abbot of Cuxa, in an abbey founded at the end of the 8th century on the site of an oratory located south of Carcassonne. It had been dedicated to Sernin by the finder of his remains. The abbey was named for St Hilarius and contained a sarcophagus with his relics. This sarcophagus, sculpted by the Master of Cabestany, bound Sernin and Hilarius together because, with his chisel the artist pictured in marble the arrest, the martyrdom of Sernin attached to an angry bull, the burial by the saint Puelles (2 young girls), and the saint blessing with his hand the executioners and spectators.

Progress of the Heresy

The new Cardinal-Bishop of Albano, Henry of Marcy, was named a pontifical legate in the course of 1179. In early 1180, he went to Citeaux and then continued to Lyon where, in March, he presided over a synod. On July 1, 1181, he was at Lescure, near Albi, before going on to Lavaur, residence of Raymond of Baimiac and Bernard-Raymond, the two heretics whom Peter of Pavia's mission had confronted in 1178, and who, in fact, were never troubled. The two heretic chiefs had even made Lavaur, which Guillaume of Puylaurens called "the synagogue of Satan", the seat of the Cathar Church of Toulouse. Henry of Marcy wanted sanctions to be applied. Troops had been placed at his disposal by Raymond V and Lavaur, the *castrum* of the Lauragais, was besieged. It was Adelaide, Viscountess of Béziers, Albi and Carcassonne, present in Castres three years earlier, who had the city gates opened. After negotiations, Roger Trencavel was forced to deliver the two heretics; his excommunication was then lifted. Raymond of Baimiac and Bernard-Raymond were taken to Le Puy where, on August 15th, a council was held. There, before the legate surrounded by the Archbishop of Auch and the bishops of Cahors and Toulouse, they recognized their errors and abjured their heresy. This conversion was certainly sincere because Guillaume of Puylaurens mentioned that Raymond of Baimiac became a canon at Saint Sernin's in Toulouse, and Bernard-Raymond, a canon at Saint Stephen's Cathedral in the same city.

In September, 1181, the legate returned to Rome where Lucius III had just succeeded Alexander III. In October 1184, the new pope and Emperor Frederick I met in Verona to take anti-heretical measures in that part of northern Italy, where Catharism was well-established. On November 4, in Verona Cathedral, the Pope issued a decretal *Ab abolendam* specifying enquiry procedures, whose principle had been decided in Tours in 1163. Bishops were supposed to systematically visit or have visits made of the parishes in their dioceses; they were invited to request evidence, under oath, from their faithful, denouncing unorthodox behaviour; those suspected of such behaviour would be summoned before an episcopal tribunal which, if they were convicted of heresy or if they refused to swear an oath, would hand them over to the secular authorities.

Pontificates in Rome lasted just a short time. In 1185, Urban III succeeded Lucius III. In 1187, Urban III was replaced by Clement III and, four years later, Celestine III was elected Pope at the age of eighty-five. This relative instability of pontifical power, which was furthermore concerned with events in the Holy Land, where Jerusalem had been recaptured by Saladin on October 2, 1187, and with the often conflicting relations with the Holy Roman Empire, did not favour continuity in anti-heretic policies, even though in 1195 Celestine III sent legates to Montpellier to attend a council reiterating the measures taken at the Lateran in 1179.

In Languedoc, this relative removal of the Holy See from the Cathar problem could only be beneficial to the progress of a heresy which was taking advantage of other favourable circum-

Apostle, St Gilles Abbey Church

OBSTINACY

....

E n 1196, Celestine III reproached Raymond VI with destroying the churches of Saint Gilles Abbey, looting its domains and building a castle the pope ordered razed. If the count did not comply, he would be excommunicated. In 1198, Innocent III removed the sanctions in return for the count's promise to destroy the fortress. Instead, Raymond VI strengthened its defences…

stances. First of all, despite the Lateran measures, the southern lands were in the hands of *routiers*, whose numbers had doubled during the armed conflict that, from 1179 to 1185, opposed Raymond V and Roger Trencavel. The insecurity reigning in the country was hardly propitious for any action by local clergy that was powerless in the face of an organized and dynamic Cathar Church. The regular clergy had problems collecting tithes and sometimes found themselves in extreme material difficulties. After 1180, they also had to deal with the presence of Waldensian preachers in the Lauragais and Carcassès, while some of members of the clergy, even among the most eminent such as Berenger, named Archbishop of Narbonne in 1191, did not display exemplary behaviour. And last of all, with the death of Raymond V in 1194, the orthodox camp lost one of its rare partisans and, in this respect, his son Raymond VI did not promise the same support. Hence, in 1196, Pope Celestine III rose up against the exactions forced on Saint Gilles Abbey by the new Count of Toulouse, whom he excommunicated and to whom he wrote on March 1st: "Although it is with regret and despite ourselves, we have the fervent obligation to renounce the fervent affection that our heart felt for you." On the Trencavel side, many of whose vassals sheltered heretics in their *castra* and castles, when they themselves were not heretics, Roger died in 1194. His nine year-old son Raymond-Roger succeeded him. On January 8, 1198, Celestine III died at the age of ninety-two. His successor was Cardinal Lotario Conti. He took the name Innocent III.

Saint Gilles Abbey Church

THE POOR OF LYON

In 1173, during the Archbishopric of Guichard of Pontigny (1165-1181), a burgher of Lyon decided to convert to the ideal of evangelical poverty after hearing the legend of Saint Alexis. Named the Waldensian, from Vaulx or *Valdesius* in Latin, probably from his place of birth, (Vaulx-en-Velin?), he gave up all his riches. He sold his goods and distributed the money to the poor, returned her dowry to his wife, and placed his daughters in Fontevrault Abbey. Knowing little Latin, he used his last money to have passages from the Scriptures translated into the vernacular or common language. From then on, he preached the Word of God and lived off charity. A text dated 1368 gave his first name as Pierre. Today he is known as Waldes or Valdes. By 1179 he had gathered in Lyon a small fraternity, which paid particular attention to the *Sermon on the Mount*, refused any spilling of blood as well as swearing an oath. In March 1179, the "Waldenses" went to the Lateran Council presided over by Pope Alexander III and presented their Bible. Although some made fun of them, they received permission to preach if they were authorized by their archbishop. The cleric Walter Map, who met them on this occasion, described them thus: "They have no fixed abode, travel two by two, barefoot, dressed in wool, having everything in common like the apostles, nakedly following the naked Christ." In 1180, Waldes appeared at the synod of Lyon, called by Archbishop Guichard, in the presence of the legate Henry of Marcy, Cardinal of Albano, and the Cistercian abbot of Hautecombe, Geoffroy of Auxerre. At the request of the clerics, did Waldes make a profession of the orthodox faith? And was his "word of life" agreed by the legate? Whatever the outcome,

the situation had changed by 1181. The "poor of Lyon" had been banned from the city by Guichard's successor, Archbishop Jean of Bellesmains. Rebelliously, in the name of Peter's famous phrase to the Sanhedrin, "We must obey God rather than men" (Act.5, 29), they decided to "go into all the world and preach the Gospel" (Mark, 16, 15). Going northwards following the valley of the Saône River, they spread throughout Bresse and the County of Burgundy. In the south, their word spread in Provence, Languedoc and Aragon. But in 1184, anathema was declared on them by the Council of Verona, and towards 1190, Bernard, the Premonstrant abbot of Fontcaude, wrote a treatise about them, reproaching their preaching without permission from Rome and for accepting women among them. In 1192, 1197 and 1204, the King of Aragon banished them from his kingdom. Despite the condemnations, and perhaps even the death of their founder before 1202, the Waldensian movement developed. It was present and active in the Lauragais and Quercy areas at the beginning of the 13th century, as witnesses testified later on before the Inquisition. These witnesses were moreover persuaded that "at that time [around 1228], the Church did not pursue the Waldenses". In fact, these Waldenses lived according to apostolic ideals and worked without payment —on church construction sites, in bakeries, in vineyards, as doctors– living on what they were given in return. Of course, they celebrated the Last Supper on Holy Thursday, receiving bread, wine and fish; but they also participated in Holy Offices in Aigues-Vives in the Minervois or Castelnaudary. Tolerated in Montauban, they had their own hospice, schools and cemetery

there. They preached on public squares, unlike the "real" Cathar heretics. The Waldensian scholar Durand of Huesca, or of Osca, was the presumed author of the *Liber antiheresis* against the Cathars. After having confronted the Bishop of Osma and perhaps Dominic in Pamiers in 1207, Durand returned to the Church and founded the order of the Catholic Poor, approved by Innocent III and joined to the Dominican Order in 1254. In Laurac in 1208, another Waldensian, Bernard Prim, confronted the Cathar deacon Isarn, the brother of Bishop Guilhabert of Castres. Bernard reconciled in his turn in 1210, creating the Order of the Reconciled Poor, rapidly attached to the Dominicans as well. But the Cistercian Alan of Lille who composed, from 1190 to 1202, his *De Fide catholica*, gathered several grievances against the Poor of Lyon that had already been alleged against Pierre of Bruys, Henry of Le Mans, and more generally, against all heretics, such as the refusal of sacraments because of clerical unworthiness. In 1214, in Morlhon in Rouergue, shortly before the Lateran Council of 1215 that was to condemn the Waldenses as schismatics and heretics, crusaders burnt a Waldensian community. Systematically pursued by the Inquisition after 1230, the Waldenses resisted. They were still present in Italy at the beginning of the 16th century, but also in Dauphiné and in Provence. Entering the Reformed Church in 1532, they suffered from the same trials as their Protestant brethren. They joined the Ecumenical Council of Geneva as soon as it was created. Today, the Waldensian Church is still alive in various regions of Italy and in the Rio de la Plata in Uruguay. Its annual general synod is held at Torre Pellice in the Piedmont.

San Pau del Camp, Barcelona

CHURCH LAW

....

T he set of provisions and dispositions that govern the Roman Catholic Church compose Canon Law. They specify the rights and duties of the faithful as well as the nature and the role of the jurisdictions charged with supervising their enforcement.

Innocent III Takes Charge

Lotario Conti, the son of the Count of Segni, had studied theology in Paris and canon law in Bologna. At the age of twenty-one, he became a canon at Saint Peter's in Rome; by thirty, he was a cardinal. Becoming Pope Innocent III at the age of thirty-eight, he intended to make the struggle against the Cathar heresy one of the great themes of his pontificate. He had just been elected to the papacy when he received a letter from the Archbishop of Auch informing him "about the canker of heresy that [was] spreading in Gascony and the neighbouring regions". Catalonia had also been affected because in February, 1198, Pedro II of Aragon issued the edicts of Gerona. These edicts reiterated the measures of the Council of Lerida in 1194, ordering heretics to leave the kingdom of Aragon and its vassal territories before Easter on penalty of death and confiscation of property. On April 1st, Pope Innocent III answered the Archbishop of Auch, reminding him of the existing anti-heretical measures and asking him to be vigilant about ecclesiastic benefices being held concurrently, to sanction lying clerics and to make straying monks return to their abbeys. On April 21, the pope addressed a letter with similar requests to the archbishops of Auch, Aix, Embrun, Arles, Vienne, Lyon, Narbonne and Tarragona, as well as to the faithful and the lords of these provinces. The latter were supposed to confiscate the property of heretics and their abettors. Furthermore, the document announced the mission to Languedoc of the two legates, Rainier and

Saint Mary's Cathedral, Officialité Palace and Armagnac Tower, Auch

Fontenay Abbey, daughter of Clairvaux

Sénanque Abbey, daughter of Bonnevaux

The Order of Citeaux

On March 21, 1098, several reformist monks from the abbey of Molesme, with Abbot Robert and Prior Alberic at their head, founded their New Monastery to the south of Dijon, in order to observe the Benedictine Rule in all its original purity and to live in prayer, sacred readings and manual labour. Set in a wooded and swampy place called *Cistels* –old French for rushes– the New Monastery, renamed Citeaux in 1119, obtained the privilege of exemption from Pope Paschal II in 1100. The existence of these monks away from the temptations of the world, rejecting all revenue linked to the possession of curial or seigniorial rights and living only from the product of their work, their spirituality bound to the essential and excluding the superficial –simplicity of clothing, liturgy and furnishings– attracted new recruits. Citeaux developed greatly under the abbacy of Stephen Harding (1109-1133), during which the first five "daughters" were founded: La Ferté (1113), Pontigny (1114), Clairvaux, Morimond (1115), and Bonnevaux (1119). The *Charter of Charity*, elaborated by Stephen Harding and completed over time by several statutes and customs, provided the Order with an original organization: through filiation. Each new abbey possessed its own abbot and remained autonomous, with the immediate father abbot charged with visiting the daughter annually. All the abbots gathered annually at the Citeaux General Chapter. The rapid success of the Cistercian reform was visible in its acquisition of properties, rights and exemptions received from popes, kings or lords. Starting during the abbacy of Bernard of Clairvaux (1115-1153), Cistercians were chosen as bishops, legates or cardinals. One of them even became Pope under the name of Eugene III (1145-1153).

JOACHIM OF FLORA

Joachim was born in Celico, in Calabria, about 1133. A notary at the Norman chancellery in Palermo, he undertook a pilgrimage to the Holy Land in 1156, during which he had his first visions and converted to monasticism. On his return to Sicily, Joachim became a hermit and later a lay friar at the Cistercian monastery of Sambucina, where he remained for a year (1159-1160). He came out to devote himself to being a wandering preacher. However, the Church reserved pastoral duties for its priests so he decided to prepare for the priesthood at the abbey of Corazzo in 1168. In 1178, he was named its abbot. In about 1182-1183, he stayed with the Cistercians at Casamari, the mother abbey of Sambucina, and composed his principal works, the *Book of Concord of the Two Testaments* and a *Commentary on the Apocalypse*. Popes Lucius III and Urban III approved his revelations in 1184 and 1186. His monastery in Corazzo joined the Cistercian family in 1188, but after that time, Joachim came into conflict with the Order. Giving up his post, he founded at Fiore, in Sila, a new Benedictine congregation, placed under the patronage of Saint John the Baptist, and whose statutes were approved by the papacy in 1196. During the last years of Joachim's life, the powerful such as Richard the Lionheart, Henry VI, Empress Constance and Frederick II consulted his presages. But after the election of Innocent III, relations between Joachim and Rome deteriorated. A key figure in the millenarian ideas of the 13th century, Joachim developed a Trinitarian vision of history: the age of the Father, marked by Law, was succeeded by that of the Son, when priests were in control. The age of the Spirit was to start in 1260, when monasticism would triumph. At Joachim's death in 1212, his Order had six abbeys in southern Italy. Some of his ideas were condemned by the Fourth Lateran Council in 1215.

Guy, both of whom were Cistercians. Rainier, one of the first disciples of Joachim of Flora, enjoyed the new pope's confidence and respect. Retained in Spain by another mission, he arrived in Languedoc where Brother Guy had acted alone while waiting for him. But Rainier had to leave for Rome. In 1199, he returned briefly but did not have to deal with an affair concerning Saint Guilhem Abbey, which was entrusted to Pierre of Castelnau, the archdeacon of Maguelone. Rainier retired to the Cistercian abbey of Fossanova. On March 25, 1199, Innocent III issued the decretal of Viterbo ratifying the legality of confiscating the property of heretics and their abettors. In 1200, the pope received a letter, probably from Guilhem of Montpellier, inviting him to intervene. In his answer, the pope informed his correspondent of the nomination of another legate, John of Saint Paul, Cardinal-priest of Saint Prisca, at the side of the pontifical legate to the King of France, Cardinal Octavia, the Bishop of Ostia. John came to Montpellier on November 9 to attend the consecration of a church, but he did not go anywhere in the search for heresy and instead returned to Rome at the beginning of 1201. In the same letter in which he had announced the strengthening of the legation, Innocent III charged that the responsibility for the situation in Languedoc was that of the prelates themselves, and in particular, of Berenger, Archbishop of Narbonne. At the end of 1201, Innocent III wrote to Count Raymond VI, whose excommunication he had rescinded a year previously, to remind him of his obligations in the struggle against heresy. A new legate did not arrive in Languedoc until the autumn of 1203. This was Pierre of Castelnau. The former archdeacon of Maguelone had, in the meantime, become a monk at Fontfroide Abbey. His associate was another monk from the same Cistercian abbey, Brother Raoul. Perre of Castelnau wanted to go to Toulouse and asked the Archbishop of Narbonne, Berenger, and the Bishop of Béziers, Guillaume of Roquessels, to accompany him and Raoul. Both prelates refused. The two legates arrived in Toulouse at the beginning of December. Raymond VI was not there. On December 13, in the presence of Bishop Raymond of Rabastens and the abbot of Saint Sernin, the consuls professed their Catholic faith under oath and obtained the legates' confirmation of their city's privileges. Pierre of Castelnau and Raoul next went to Béziers, where the bishop refused to ask the inhabitants to take an oath. He was suspended from his position by the legates. Believing that events were taking a favourable turn, Innocent III reinforced the legation by adding two preachers on January 24, 1204 –the abbot of Valmagne and a canon from Narbonne.

In this same month of January 1204, in Perpignan, Raymond VI married Eleanor, the sister of Pedro II of Aragon. A few months later, in April, in Millau, the King of Aragon, his brother Alfonso, Count of Provence, and his new brother-in-law, the Count of Toulouse, gathered to sign a mutual defence pact "against any man in the world". Furthermore, Raymond VI lent one hundred and fifty thousand *sous*, in Melgueil money, to Pedro II who gave him the counties of Millau and Gevaudan as security. This money was supposed to help Pedro II pay for his marriage, in June, to Marie of Montpellier, and for his journey to Rome. Through this marriage, Montpellier came under

Saint Guilhem le Désert

The lavatorium in Valmagne Abbey

BERENGER AND THE OTHERS

"…dumb dogs that cannot bark and do not know how to use their voice or a stick to chase away the wolves that devastate the Lord's fold…"
Letter from Innocent III to his legates, May 28, 1204

If Innocent III strengthened his legates' missions, it was because he had understood that if he wanted to implement his policies in Languedoc, he could hardly count on the local prelates who were not very interested in his reforms. A summary of the situation in the early years of the 13th century was not very encouraging. In Carcassonne, Bishop Othon had been in place since 1170. Being very old in 1198, he preferred to make way for his nephew, Berenger, the archdeacon of Saint Nazaire Cathedral. The latter's commitment against heresy had led to his being chased out of the city by its inhabitants. He had been replaced by Bernard-Raymond of Roquefort, from a noble family of the Montagne Noire, an area greatly affected by heresy since his mother and two of his brothers were perfects. The mother, who lived in a heretical community, and the prelate of the orthodox side, at least in principle, were both present at Termes in 1210, the former on the side of the besieged; the latter among the besiegers. In 1211, Bernard-Raymond of Roquefort had to cede his post to Guy, abbot of Les Vaux de Cernay. At the death of Fulcrand, the Bishop of Toulouse, in 1200, his bishopric was materially decayed. His successor, Raymond of Rabastens, the archdeacon of Agen, was elected in questionable conditions. Opposed by another candidate, Raymond Arnaud, Bishop of Comminges, he was suspected of having schemed to win the election. He was eventually deposed for simony and replaced by Foulque in 1206. In 1215, he was at the side of Raymond VI at the Lateran Council. In 1203, Guillaume of Roquessels, Bishop of Béziers, joined the cause against the legates who wanted to make the consuls of Béziers recant. He also refused to accompany them to Toulouse. On February 18, 1205, he was removed from his position by the Pope. As for Berenger, the Archbishop of Narbonne, he managed against all odds to remain, from 1191 to 1212, at the head of his province which was almost entirely affected by heresy. And yet… This illegitimate son of Ramón Berenguer, Count of Barcelona, brother of Alfonso II of Aragon, and uncle of Pedro II, even after being named Archbishop of Narbonne by Pope Celestine III, had retained the abbacy of Montearagón, of which he had become abbot in 1170. His presence at the Lateran Council of 1179, in his position as the Bishop of Lerida, did not prevent him from paying off a *routier* twenty years later to hold the *castra* of Capestang and Cruscades. He completely neglected his province, and even his diocese, since after ten years as archbishop he had still not visited them. He received a gratuity for ordaining the Bishop of Maguelone. His personal life too was far from being exemplary. The Pope ordered an enquiry in November 1200. In May 1203 and January 1204, the Pope asked Berenger to resign, but to no end. On May 28, 1204, Innocent III sent a letter to his legates using extremely virulent terms about the stubborn prelate, telling them to force him to resign his charge. But Berenger appealed and gained some time. On June 6, 1205, the pope ordered him to leave the abbacy of Montearagón, which he finally agreed to do. His nephew, Ferdinand, the brother of Pedro II of Aragon, a professed monk in Poblet, took his place. In May 1207,

The lavatorium in Poblet Abbey

the pontiff gave his legates, Arnaud-Amaury and Navarro, Bishop of Couserans, the power to depose him. Nothing happened, especially since Berenger showed a few signs of good will. In April 1207, he donated the church of Saint Martin in Limoux to Brother Dominic. On July 25, 1209, he went before the crusading troops to present, with Viscount Aimery, the submission of Narbonne. And in 1210, he was present at the siege of Minerve. It was not until 1212 that he was replaced by Arnaud-Amaury. With Foulque in Toulouse, Guy of Les Vaux de Cernay in Carcassonne, and Arnaud-Amaury in Narbonne, Pope Innocent III could finally count on his prelates, a true Cistercian guard.

Aragonese influence. In October, the King of Aragon and his suite went to Rome, where Pedro II was crowned by Innocent III, his suzerain.

In February 1204, Pierre of Castelnau and Brother Raoul went to Carcassonne, where Pedro II was staying at the time. The town contained many Cathars and Waldenses and the two legates organized a sitting, under the aegis of the King of Aragon. A first session brought together Catholics and Waldenses, who were declared heretics at the end of the debates. On the following day, on either side of the King, thirteen Catholics and thirteen Cathars, including Bernard of Simorre, the Bishop of the Cathar Church of Carcassonne, confronted each other. The next day, the Cathars too were declared guilty of heresy. During this operation, Pedro II appeared particularly tolerant with respect to the heretics, since both Cathars and Waldenses left the sessions freely. This incited Innocent III to write to him in June, reminding him of his duty. At the end of May 1204, Innocent III wrote several letters, two of them addressed to his legates. He encouraged them in their work and announced that a new legate was going to join them and, in fact, become the leader of the legation. The leader in question was their Order's abbot, Arnaud-Amaury, a Catalonian, former abbot of Poblet and then of Grandselve, respectively daughter- and mother-abbeys of Fontfroide. He also addressed the Archbishop of Narbonne to announce that he was revoking the dispensation allowing him to hold his position at the same time as the abbacy of Montearagón. And finally, for the first

The cloister in Poblet Abbey

In the Church's Service

Abbot

The head of an abbey

Archbishop (or Metropolitan)

The primary bishop of an ecclesiastical province. He is raised to the rank by the pope, who gives him the *pallium*, a strip of white wool decorated with black crosses.

Canons

Clerics living in a community around a bishop. Their college makes up the cathedral chapter. A canon's revenue is called a prebend.

Cleric

A man of the Church who has been ordained. Although he has not necessarily been ordained, a monk, wearing a tonsure as a sign of his consecrated state, is considered a cleric. There is then a distinction between lay and regular clerics.

Bishop

Spiritual leader of a diocese. He administers the sacrament of confirmation, ordains priests and consecrates churches. He is the suffragan of the archbishop to whose province his diocese belongs.

Legate

An agent on a mission delegated by the pope, sent to a given area for a defined period of time. The legate, *a latere* from the Latin *latus*, side, has the rank of a cardinal.

Oblate

A child entrusted to an abbey or a monastery to become a monk.

Prelate

An ecclesiastical dignitary: cardinal, archbishop, bishop, abbot.

Vidame

A lay lord charged by a prelate with administering revenues due to the authority of this prelate.

FONTFROIDE ABBEY

In 1093, Aimery 1st, Viscount of Narbonne, authorized the settlement of a group of Benedictine monks in a valley in the Corbières range, watered by a torrent called *Fons Frigidus*. In 1144, the community entered into the obedience of Grandselve Abbey. In 1145, during his travels through Languedoc, Bernard of Clairvaux passed through Grandselve, which joined the Cistercian Order by affiliating with Clairvaux. In the following year, Fontfroide in turn adopted the rule of Citeaux and became a daughter of Grandselve. At the request of the Count of Barcelona, Ramón Berenguer IV, Fontfroide spread to Poblet in 1149. In his struggle against the Cathar heresy, Pope Innocent III used the support of the Order of Citeaux. In 1203, he named two of the abbey's monks, Pierre of Castelnau and Raoul, as legates. After the murder of Pierre of Castelnau near Saint Gilles in 1208, the pope called for a crusade against the Albigensians during which the abbey in the Corbières appeared as a stronghold of Catholic orthodoxy. In January 1224, the abbey was repaid for its loyalty to the Montforts. Before leaving Languedoc, Amaury granted it pastures in the Minervois. The abbey's revenues were then very important; it controlled at least thirty granges. In 1297, Arnaud Nouvel, a former monk from Boulbonne, was elected abbot of Fontfroide, which he ran for eleven years. During the spring of 1306, Pope Clement V asked him to temporarily replace Bernard of Castanet, the Bishop of Albi who had been temporarily suspended from his post. In 1308, Arnaud Nouvel, working with the abbot of Saint Papoul, conducted the investigations for the trial of the same bishop. That year, he received the cardinalate purple and, in 1313, intervened in the trial of the Templars. He died in Avignon in 1317, and his body was buried at Fontfroide under the abbey church's main altar. His nephew, Jacques Fournier, was elected abbot of Fontfroide in 1311. In 1317, as the Bishop of Pamiers, he led the tribunal of the episcopal inquisition and conducted the investigations for the last Cathars of Sabarthès, before becoming Pope under the name Benedict XII. The black plague of 1348 arrived in Marseille and reached Fontfroide via Narbonne. Half the community died. Commendam was put in place at Fontfroide in 1476. At the French Revolution, the abbey and its lands became state property. In 1858, the community that Father Barnouin had settled in Sénanque four years earlier, revived Fontfroide. In 1901, the monks went into exile in Spain after the law about associations was passed. They returned and joined the community at Lérins. In the meantime, the abbey had been put up for sale and bought by a family, still the owner today, who undertook restoration work. In a Cistercian abbey, the lay brothers, friars recruited to help the monks with heavy labour, did not live with the monks. They had their own refectory, and this is the first room the visitor to Fontfroide discovers. In the abbey church, their choir was separate from that of the professed monks. They reached it through a passage, while the monks entered through the cloister. Construction of the Gothic cloister in Fontfroide began at the end of the 12th century and was completed in the 14th century. Its eastern gallery communicates with the chapter house, with its capitals decorated with flat leaves, the *cistels* of the Burgundy ponds at the origin of the name Citeaux. The abbey church's doorway is set in the cloister's southern gallery. The church dates from the end of the 12th century; its nave, twenty metres high and covered with a broken barrel vault, is the most ancient part. The stained glass windows were made in the early 20th century following a treatise on making stained glass written in the 12th century by a monk called Theophile. Upstairs, the monks' dormitory is separated from that of the lay brothers, in which one arrives through a walkway running above the northern gallery of the cloister.

The chapter house in Fontfroide Abbey

time, he requested that the King of France intervene in Languedoc and force his vassals of the Midi to become involved in the struggle against heresy. He did not however receive an answer. At the end of 1204, Pierre of Castelnau, who realized that the legation was not making progress, asked the pope to free him from his obligations so that he could return to his abbey of Fontfroide. In a letter dated January 26, 1205, Innocent III refused. On January 16th, he wrote to Philip Augustus, to whom he addressed a new letter on February 7th. In both cases, he repeated his request for intervention, "so that the material sword joins, in this affair, the spiritual sword". As in 1204, the Capetian King did not bother to reply.

A great Cathar "council", attended by six hundred perfects, was held in Mirepoix in 1206. The town itself was largely won over by Cathar ideas and contained fifty heretics' houses. Over one hundred heretical believers have been identified, including one of its co-lords, Pierre-Roger of Mirepoix, and Raymond of Péreille, his cousin. The town's deacon, Raymond Mercier, and the perfect, Raymond Blascou, asked Raymond of Péreille to restore the *castrum* of Montsegur, then in ruins, in order to make it a religious establishment.

SAINT GUILHEM LE DÉSERT

I t was because his legate Rainier was ill that in 1199, Pope Innocent III had appointed Pierre of Castelnau to lead the enquiry about the abbot of Saint Guilhem le Désert, suspected of simony. Set at the exit of the gorges of the Herault River, the abbey had been founded in 804 by Guilhem, a friend of the Goth Witiza, who had taken the name Benedict after retiring to the nearby monastery of Aniane. Before settling into the silence of his modest *cella*, William-Guilhem had been one of Charlemagne's brave knights and had been named Count of Toulouse in 790. He became the legendary hero of the *geste* of William of Orange, the first version of which dates from the middle of the 12th century.

Opening with small arcades in Fontfroide Abbey cloister

Pillar in St Guilhem cloister

Diego and Dominic

In that same year of 1206, orthodoxy in Languedoc was about to receive powerful reinforcements. First of all, on February 5th, Foulque, the former abbot of the Cistercian abbey of Thoronet, succeeded Raymond of Rabastens, dismissed from his post, at the head of the bishopric of Toulouse. Until the end of his bishopric on December 25, 1231, he was to be a zealous defender of orthodoxy in a city and region where Cathars and their defenders were well-established. Subsequently, in June, when the three legates were in Montpellier and Arnaud-Amaury was preparing to return to Citeaux to attend the General Chapter of his Order in September, they accidentally met the Bishop of Osma, Diego of Acebes, and one of his canons, Dominic of Caleruega. Diego and Dominic, returning from a mission in Denmark, had passed through Rome and Citeaux on their way back to Castile in Spain. Montpellier was a stop on their journey home. The two Castilians met the legates, rather demoralized and about to offer their resignations to Rome, who explained the situation and their difficulties. Diego insisted on the importance of preaching and the necessity of confronting adversaries with their own weapons, those of humility, poverty and charity, and advised them to give up all pomp. The three legates, all Cistercians, could only agree with such a move but wished to be supported by some religious authority. The Bishop of Osma offered to provide it and sent his following and carriages on to Osma. So then, he and Dominic accompanied Pierre of Castelnau and Raoul, while Arnaud-Amaury returned to Citeaux. They moved on foot and lived off charity. They left Montpellier at the beginning of July. Their first stop was Servian, whose lord, Etienne of Servian, was the son-in-law of the perfect Blanche of Laurac. Bernard of Simorre, the Bishop of the Cathar church of Carcassonne, and Thierry, the former canon of Nevers, dismissed for heresy, were both in the *castrum*. The discussion between Catholics and Cathars lasted a week and the Catholics slowly turned the situation to their advantage. Pierre of Castelnau's aggressiveness brought on his opponents' enmity. His companions advised him to retreat and he retired for seven months to Villeneuve-lès-Maguelone, near the bishopric where he had been archdeacon. The Catholic preachers went on to Carcassès and Verfeil in the Lauragais, where Diego was confronted by two perfects over questions about the human nature of Jesus Christ and the interpretation of a passage from the Gospel of St John.

At the beginning of 1207, Diego and Dominic stayed in Fanjeaux, in the Lauragais, a stronghold of heresy. At the foot of the *castrum*, in a locality called Prouille, Dominic founded a convent for nuns in an abandoned church granted to him by Foulque, Bishop of Toulouse. The convent soon registered the arrival of Guillaume Claret and her sister, who donated all their property to the new foundation, as well as nineteen women including some who were repentant Cathar perfects. In April, at Cathar request, a theological disputation was organized in Montréal, a *castrum* close to Fanjeaux, and like it, a stronghold of heresy. It lasted two weeks.

St Paul, Maguelone Abbey

MAGUELONE

Before entering the Abbey of Fontfroide and being named legate by Pope Innocent III, Pierre of Castelnau had been a canon and archdeacon in Maguelone. In the 6th century, the seat of a Visigoth bishopric had occupied these basaltic rocks in the heart of ponds separated from the sea by an offshore bar, near the former maritime trading post of Lattara. The Arabs captured it and Charles Martel had to destroy this Saracen enclave. Maguelone then lost its episcopal seat, transferred to Villeneuve-lès-Maguelone, but recovered it in the middle of the 11th century. Construction began on Saint Peter's Cathedral and a new episcopal city, whose stages were carefully described in the 12th century in the *Chronicon Magalonense vetus*. In June 1096, Pope Urban II stayed in Maguelone and proclaimed the church to be "the second after Rome".

HEART AND SOUL

I n the *Paradise* of his *Divine Comedy* Dante evoked the man who had been a troubadour, "these people called me Folquet", he has him say. Indeed, several years before he occupied the bishop's seat in Toulouse, this son of a Genoese merchant, wealthy, married and the father of two children, had composed verses that contained both lyricism and sensuality from 1179 to 1195. About twenty works have been preserved. The poet was appreciated by important people and he frequented Richard the Lionheart and Alfonso VIII of Castile. In 1196, having poured out his feelings, he began to think about the salvation of his soul and entered the Order of Citeaux. He became a monk at the abbey of Our Lady of Thoronet, not far from Lorgues, in the diocese of Fréjus. Construction of the abbey church was underway and the contribution of the new monk's fortune allowed the work to go faster. In 1199, he was elected abbot and, on September 14, 1205, because of this position he participated in the Chapter General of Citeaux, under the leadership of Arnaud-Amaury. Named Bishop of Toulouse, Foulque arrived in the capital of the Saint Gilles on February 5, 1206, and occupied the post until his death. He put all his energy and faith into the struggle against the Cathar heresy and was hence a loyal and devoted assistant of the French side engaged in a merciless struggle against the lords of Languedoc. His mission was difficult and Guillaume of Puylaurens, who lived in the prelate's entourage from 1228 to 1230, wrote as an epitaph: "In the meantime, and as much as he was allowed to do, the bishop never left his charge, putting order in the churches, visiting nearly novice crowds [...]. When he had carried out everything successfully and revived a nearly dead bishopric..., he ended his days at Christmas 1231, God wishing to reward his servant."

The chevet of Thoronet Abbey Church

A window in Thoronet's cloister

Lavatorium in Thoronet's cloister

THE LOST BET OF SAINT DOMINIC

"Go towards the lost sheep of the house of Israel. [...] Freely you have received, freely give. Do not take along any gold or silver [...]; take no bag for the journey, [...], or sandals or a staff. For the worker is worth his keep."
Matthew 10, 5, 9-10.

Dominic was born in 1170 in Caleruega, in Old Castile. His father, Felix Guzmán, was the governor of the city; his mother descended from an old, noble family. Destined for an ecclesiastical career very early in life, Dominic studied theology at the university in Palencia. In about 1195, he was named a canon at the chapter of Osma Cathedral. Ordained a priest at the age of twenty-five, he became a sub-prior in 1201. This was the young and brilliant cleric chosen by Diego, the Bishop of Osma, to accompany him on a missionary journey to Denmark (1203-1205). On their return, passing through the south of France, Diego and Dominic joined their preaching to that of the Cistercian legates against the Cathar heresy. The Castilians opposed the Bons Hommes on their own ground, announcing the Gospels with humility, penance and begging. In the course of the winter of 1206-1207, Dominic founded a convent intended for converted Cathar ladies in the former church of Saint Mary at Prouille, near Fanjeaux. Diego died in this same year of 1207. Dominic then took charge of the preaching, which he organized out of Prouille, then from Toulouse, from 1209 to 1211, with the support of Bishop Foulque. In the meantime, the crusades had attacked

Languedoc, and the papal curia, using a different kind of weapon, developed radical coercive measures against the heretics. Nonetheless, starting in April 1215 in Toulouse, Dominic took the lead of a fraternity of clerics whose mission was "to go out, in evangelical poverty, on foot, dressed as a monk, to preach the evangelical truth". In October 1215, Dominic met Pope Innocent III to ask him to confirm an Order "that would be and would be called preachers". The pontiff agreed on condition that the

Saint Dominic's tomb

Order be attached to a regular tradition. Dominic chose the Rule of Saint Augustine. The Order of the Preaching Friars obtained confirmation from Pope Honorius III in 1216 and 1217. By 1217, Dominic sent the first sixteen friars to preach, study and recruit in Madrid, Paris, Bologna and Rome. He himself also travelled a lot and perhaps met Saint Francis in 1218, at Portioncula near Assisi. In 1220, the Order's first General Chapter was held in Bologna. It had provided itself with original legislation: entirely devoted to preaching the Word of God, the brother must grant a fundamental place to regular study of the Word and to intellectual labour. He had to renounce all revenue and live only from begging. And last of all, each brother participated in the Order's government, electing the convent's prior with his peers; the priors in turn designated their provincial prior, and these provincial priors elected the Order's Master General. At the time of his death in 1221, Dominic left behind a greatly expanding order that already consisted of twenty-five convents. He was lucky enough not to see Pope Gregory IX entrust the preachers with running the tribunals of the Inquisition set up in 1231. Dominic was nonetheless canonized by the same pope in 1234.

Saint Dominic

Diego, Dominic, Raoul and Pierre of Castelnau who had joined them represented the Catholic side; Guilhabert of Castres, who was then living in Fanjeaux and was the future Bishop of the Cathar Church of Toulouse, Pons Jourda, Arnaud Hot and Benoît of Termes, the future Bishop of the Cathar Church of the Razès, provided the arguments for the Cathar side. Knights, including Aimery of Montréal, and inhabitants of the region attended the discussions, refereed by a jury consisting of two nobles and two burghers, who eventually pronounced no judgement. Pierre of Castelnau left his companions, before the end of the debate but shortly afterwards they were backed up by Arnaud-Amaury returning from Citeaux, accompanied by twelve abbots, including Guy of Les Vaux de Cernay, the future Bishop of Carcassonne, and several monks. All these clerics formed small groups and continued their preaching. As for Pierre of Castelnau, he went to Toulouse to inform Raymond VI of his excommunication and to lay an interdiction on his lands. These sanctions were confirmed on May 29, 1207, by Pope Innocent III who, on November 17th, wrote to Philip Augustus for the fourth time to request his intervention in Languedoc. Similar letters were addressed to the barons of France. This time, the King of France responded through the intermediary of the Bishop of Paris, saying that the armed quarrel opposing him and the kingdom of England did not allow him to give a positive answer to his request but that if the pope could convince John Landless to agree to a two-year truce, he could do so.

Saint Dominic's house

A MIRACLE!

In his *Historia Albigensis*, Pierre of Les Vaux de Cernay relates that on the occasion of the theological debate in Montréal, Dominic had written down quotations from various authors that he had used during a debate. He entrusted his manuscript to a heretic so that the latter could note his objections. That evening, the heretic presented the manuscript to his companions who were sitting around the fire. They suggested throwing the writings into the flames and waiting for Divine Judgement: if the manuscript burnt, Dominic would have been wrong; if, on the contrary, it remained intact, they would then convert to his beliefs. But when the manuscript was thrown on the fire, it immediately rose up intact. The experiment was carried out twice more, but always gave the same result. However the miracle did not have the good fortune of pleasing the heretics who "remained in their malevolence" wrote the chronicler. This was in any case a strange miracle since the ordeal by fire was usually carried out by the heretics' enemies, and was totally foreign to the apostles of non-violence called "the enemies of the faith".

The fire miracle at Fanjeaux, detail from *Coronation of the Virgin*, Fra Angelico

Remains of Dun Castle

Lay brothers' room in Clairvaux

After the Montréal conference, Diego and Dominic found themselves quite isolated. At the request of the pope, Arnaud-Amaury had gone to Provence, where he was joined by Pierre of Castelnau who had left Toulouse. The Cistercian abbots and monks slowly regained their abbeys, and Raoul died at the beginning of the summer. Diego decided to return to Osma and Dominic went with him as far as the Pyrenees. They stopped in Pamiers, where the Count of Foix organized a debate between Catholics and Waldenses. The abbot of Saint Antonin de Frédelas and the Count of Foix, whose castle stood on top of the Castella, held joint authority over the town. The count of Foix's wife, as well as one of her sisters, Esclarmonde, were Cathars; another of her sisters was a Waldensian. On the opposing sides of the debate, the Catholic arguments were made by Diego, Dominic, Foulque, Bishop of Toulouse, and Navarre, Bishop of Couserans. Among their opponents were several Cathars but mostly Waldenses led by Durand of Huesca, including Bernard Prim. The mediator was Master Arnaud of Crampagna, a lay cleric from Pamiers who appreciated Waldensianism but who, after the debate, returned to strict orthodoxy, as did many other Waldenses, including Durand of Huesca and Bernard Prim. A year later, Innoncent III conferred the authorization to preach on the new community founded by Durand of Huesca, the Poor Catholics. In about 1195, Durand of Huesca published a *Liber antiheresis*. He was also credited with writing the *Liber contra manicheos* in 1222-1223. From Pamiers, Diego went back to Osma where he died on December 30, 1207. As for Dominic, he returned to the Lauragais to take care of his foundation in Prouille to which, in April 1207, the Archbishop of Narbonne had donated Saint Martin's Church in Limoux. Berenger, on his return from Rome where he had met the pope, had many reasons to hope for forgiveness. Dominic also continued to preach. There are few sources for this period of his life, but one can imagine that his task must have been difficult in these lands largely won over by heresy. Perhaps he had even lost his temper and thrown the terrible premonitory expression at his detractors, "There where it is not worth a blessing, it is worth a stave."

THE FEMININE CONDITION

The contradictory debate that, in 1207, opposed Catholics and Waldenses was held in the castle near Pamiers of Raymond-Roger, Count of Foix. The count's sister, Esclarmonde, was a Cathar perfect, as was his wife Philippa, who ran a house in Dun, between Pamiers and Mirepoix. During the discussion, Philippa intervened on the side of the heretics. One of Dominic's disciples, Étienne of Metz, retorted, "Madam, go and spin your distaff. It is not up to you to speak in a debate of this kind."

On the Banks of the Rhone

At the beginning of January 1208, a meeting was organized in Saint Gilles between Raymond VI and Pierre of Castelnau. The Count was hoping to have lifted the excommunication fulminated against him by the latter several months previously. The meeting between the two men was stormy, with Raymond VI refusing the legate's demands and allegedly even threatening him with death. Pierre of Castelnau and his suite left Saint Gilles and spent the night on the banks of the Rhone River. The next day, January 14, 1208, they were preparing to cross the river when one of the Count of Toulouse's men attacked Pierre from behind, piercing him with his spear. Before dying, the legate addressed his murderer, "May God forgive you as I have forgiven you." This, at least, was how the event was related by Pope Innocent III himself in the papal bull dated March 10, 1208, sent to the archbishops of Narbonne, Arles, Embrun, Aix and Vienne, as well as to the King of France and his barons. "Forward, soldiers of Christ!" With this expression Innocent III invited the king and his lords to intervene militarily in Languedoc. On information from Arnaud-Amaury, the pope named Count Raymond VI as the instigator of the assassination. In a document extensively repeated by Pierre of Les Vaux de Cernay in his *Historia Albigensis,* the pope pronounced anathema against Raymond VI, as well as the murderer and his accomplices, delivered his vassals from their oath of fealty, exposed his lands "as booty" "subject to the rights of the principal lord", promised the "knights of Christ" and "the courageous recruits of the Christian army" who undertook to participate in this crusade on Christian lands "the remission of their sins." However, the pope gave Raymond VI a chance to make amends. "He must devote all his strength to expelling the heretics and quickly adhere to a fraternal peace," and the pope added, "It is above all because his guilt was established on these two points that the ecclesiastical censure was pronounced against him." Was the murder of Pierre of Castelnau simply a pretext?

This time, Philip Augustus sent a letter to Innocent III explaining his refusal, or at least, setting the conditions under which he would intervene. The war opposing him and the Plantagenets would have to have a truce, and the campaign in the Midi would have to be paid for by the clergy and laymen. Furthermore, the King of France expressed serious doubts about the judicial basis for such an operation and wrote, speaking about the Count of Toulouse, "We have learned from eminent and educated men that you do not have the right to behave in this way as long as you have not condemned him as a heretic. And if he were to be condemned, you would have to inform us and ask us to expose his lands because he obtained them from us."

Arnaud-Amaury left Rome. Through a bull dated March 28, the pope had conferred full authority on him and named Navarre, Bishop of Couserans, and Hugo, Bishop of Riez, to his side. On his way through Citeaux, he met the Duke of Burgundy and the Count of Nevers. Both were ready to join the crusade but wanted

Weapons

Anathema

Formula of curses or imprecations used against enemies of the faith and the excommunicated, swearing them to eternal damnation.

Excommunication

Exclusion of a Catholic from the community of the faithful by an ecclesiastical authority. Although baptism is in no case questioned, the excommunication can be major, that is, total; or minor, with just the forfeiting of sacraments.

Indulgence

Deferring or cancelling penance the faithful has incurred in the beyond. It is decided by an ecclesiastical authority. After the Fourth Lateran Council of 1215, indulgences could be granted *post mortem.*

Interdiction

A punishment in church law, at the disposal of popes and bishops, depriving a territory or city of all religious life.

Suspense

Church law sanction preventing a cleric from administering the sacraments.

GRIEVANCES AGAINST RAYMOND VI

Several grievances against Raymond VI were at the origin of his excommunication, pronounced by Innocent III in 1207. He was reproached with maintaining Aragonese *routiers* who devastated the ecclesiastical province of Arles, of entrusting public positions to Jews, of transforming churches into fortresses, of having collected unjustified tolls, of expelling the Bishop of Carpentras, of violating the peace, especially in the conflict opposing him and the Lord of les Baux for the control of Marseille, of having destroyed the vineyards of the Abbey of Candeil, of protecting heresy and refusing to act severely against it. In his bull dated March 10, 1208, the pope furthermore accused the Count of Toulouse of being the instigator of the murder of his legate Pierre of Castelnau. It must be emphasized that the count's responsibility in the matter was far from being proved. Isolated and with no other recourse, he had to *go to Canossa*. While waiting for the act of reconciliation on June 18, 1209, in Saint Gilles, several days earlier in Valence, Raymond VI had to pledge seven of his castles: Oppède, Mornas, Beaumes, Roquemaure, Fourques, Montferrand and Largentière. If he did not keep his promises, they would purely and simply be confiscated.

Oppède le Vieux

Montferrand Castle

Mornas Castle

The keep at Châlus

the approval of the King of France. The king gave it to them in May, but limited the number of knights each of them could take to five hundred, but then went back on his decision. Innocent III wrote again in early November to the king and the prelates of the kingdom. He confirmed his promise of indulgences and brought up the question of money because he realized that it was the sticking point. Every crusader would be given a moratorium on his debts for the time he wore the crusader's cross, and the population would have to pay ten percent of their earnings to finance the crusade, copying in this the request the Archbishop of Sens made of his faithful. The Count of Toulouse, Raymond VI, too was busy at the end of 1208. He had met his nephew, the twenty-three year-old Raymond-Roger Trencavel, Viscount of Béziers, Albi and Carcassonne, to form a common front but the disagreement of one of the parties, it is not known which one, led to nothing. The count went to Aubenas to offer his submission to Arnaud-Amaury, who sent him to the pope. He then sent an embassy to Innocent III. It consisted of the Archbishop of Auch, the former Bishop of Toulouse, Raymond of Rabastens, and of Pierre Barrau, Prior of the Hospitallers of Saint John. They informed the Holy Father of Raymond VI's good intentions but also of his complaints about Arnaud-Amaury's behaviour and his wish to be provided with another legate to negotiate with. Innocent III accepted this final request and named Milon as legate, with Tedisio, a canon from Genoa, as his assistant. He did nonetheless tell Tedisio, who was his secretary, to consult with Arnaud-Amaury all the time.

On February 3, 1209, the pope wrote to Philip Augustus for the sixth time, asking him to lead the crusade or to entrust the command of the crusading army to his son or another man of his choice. At the end of March, Milon and Tedisio joined Arnaud-Amaury in Auxerre from where they requested an audience with Philip Augustus who was holding an assembly with his great vassals at Villeneuve sur Yonne, south of Sens. They wanted to give him a new letter from the pope. Once again, the king refused to intervene because "he had two great lions on his flank: Otto, the so-called emperor, and John Landless." He did however authorize his vassals to take the cross. While preparations for the crusade were being made, Milan and Tedisio called Raymond VI to Valence. The interview took place during the first two weeks of June. His excommunication would be lifted if he promised to obey the Church, repair any wrongs he had caused and make amends. Raymond VI agreed and had to provide seven castles as pledges. The public act of reconciliation was held in Saint Gilles on June 18. There, barefoot and bare-chested, the Count of Toulouse appeared before the doorway of the church, where Milon waited for him surrounded by the archbishops of Auch, Arles and Aix and nineteen bishops. He swore an oath on a host and the saints' relics presented to him by the prelates. The preamble of the sermon was a reminder of the motives for Raymond's excommunication and the text ended with his agreement. Any failure to comply would lead to a new excommunication for the count, an interdiction placed on his lands, the confiscation of the castles he had

PHILIP AUGUSTUS

Born in 1165 in the month of August, hence his nickname, Philip Augustus became King of France in 1180. Richard the Lionheart, the son of Henry II and Eleanor of Aquitaine, received Philip's support against his father, the King of England, whom he succeeded in 1189. Philip Augustus, Richard the Lionheart and Frederick I Barbarossa left for the third crusade in 1189. The King of France soon returned home. On his return in 1193, Richard was taken prisoner by Emperor Henry VI. Philip Augustus, who had a pact with John Landless, Richard's brother, did all he could to prevent his being freed. Richard, released for a ransom, inflicted a defeat on the French at Courcelles, but died at Châlus in 1199. Philip Augustus then turned on John Landless, whose continental possessions he confiscated in 1202. In 1214, at Bouvines, he was victorious over the Anglo-German coalition and enlarged the royal domain before becoming interested in the south of France. He died in 1223, leaving his kingdom "in the hands of a woman and children". Six years later, with the Treaty of Paris, conditions were met for Languedoc to be joined to the Kingdom of France. This woman and children, one of whom was Louis VIII, were obviously worthy of the great King Philip Augustus.

pledged, and the freeing of his vassals from their oath of fealty. Sixteen vassals swore an oath and the consuls of Saint Gilles acted as guarantors for Raymond VI. Then the legate placed his stole around the count's neck and led him into the nave of the church while whipping him with birch-rods. The crowd was so dense that Raymond VI had to leave through the crypt and pass in front of Pierre of Castelnau's tomb. Guillaume of Puylaurens noted, "A just judgement of God! He was forced to show respect to the corpse of the one who, alive, had suffered from his contempt." Two days later, Raymond VI asked to take the cross and placed himself at the disposal of the crusader army when it arrived on his lands which, in this way, would be under the protection of the Holy See. It was well played by the Count of Toulouse but, at the time that he made that decision, the machine of war was already moving forward.

The army had gathered in Burgundy, in the Nivernais and the Lyonnais. Under the command of Arnaud-Amaury, the crusaders followed the Rhone valley along the river's left bank, their weapons and equipment having been loaded on boats. The troops were ill-assorted and colourful: there were prelates and clerics, lords of all ranks, knights, foot soldiers, nobles' servants –squires and valets, assorted hangers-on, as well as many common people– peasants, tradesmen and merchants hoping for indulgences. It is also most likely that there were *routiers* or bandits. There were probably close to fifty thousand men.

Overlooking the Rhone Valley, Crussol Castle

Judas' kiss, doorway in Saint Gilles Abbey Church

The crypt in Saint Gilles Abbey Church

The Abbey of Saint Gilles

On June 18, 1209, Raymond VI suffered great humiliation at Saint Gilles, the very cradle of his dynasty, and a few steps away from his castle. Legend has it that in the 7th century, Gilles left Greece on a boat that Providence brought to the shores of the French Camargue. The hermit's solitude was barely troubled by visits from a young deer, killed during a hunt by the Visigoth King, Wamba. In compensation, the king ceded Gilles lands on which to build an abbey. In 721, Gilles died and his tomb became the object of pilgrimages. The hermit's relics were kept in a monastery founded in the 7th century and dedicated to the apostles Peter and Paul. In 1077, the abbey was affiliated with Cluny and construction of a new abbey church was undertaken. The altar in the new shrine was consecrated by Pope Urban II in 1096. At the beginning of the 12th century, conflict between the monks and the Count of Toulouse brought a temporary halt to construction. The often tense relations between the counts and the abbey hindered progress in the work. In 1136, Pierre of Bruys was burnt at a stake placed before the abbey. The sculpture programme, a major masterpiece of Romanesque art, covering the three doorways in the abbey church's façade, was carried out by several artists from 1140 to 1160. In 1154, indulgences were granted to pilgrims going to Saint Gilles, and the pilgrimage developed rapidly. The ancient Regordane Way, crossing the Massif Central and the Cévennes, took the name Saint Gilles Way and the abbey became a stage on the *via Tolosana* leading to Santiago de Compostela. Remains of the Romanesque abbey church include the triple doorway, the crypt and the famous 12th century spiral staircase, which remains a model for stone-carvers of the *Compagnons du Devoir*.

Casseneuil

CRUSADERS IN CHRISTIAN LANDS

At the beginning of the month of June 1209, while the crusaders from the north were making their final preparations before moving down the Rhone Valley, while Raymond VI was getting ready to meet Milon in Valence, another crusading army led by the Archbishop of Bordeaux was gathering in the Dordogne River valley.

A First Stake

The prelate from Bordeaux was accompanied by the bishops of Cahors, Limoges, Agen and Bazas, by the Viscount of Turenne, the Count of Clermont, and the lords of Gourdon and Castelnau. This army captured Bigaroque on the Dordogne and destroyed Gontaud, east of Marmande, two fiefs held by Martin Algai. This Navarrese, a former *routier* who had become John Lackland's seneschal in Gascony and Perigord, had married the daughter of Henri of Gontaud, Lord of Biron. The crusaders reached the Garonne River valley, where they sacked Tonneins before they followed the valley of the Lot and besieged Casseneuil. There they were joined by other crusaders who, having left the Vivarais under the leadership of the Bishop of Le Puy, had just exacted ransoms from Saint Antonin de Noble Val and Caussade. In Cassenueil, a first stake was raised for the perfects who had refused to abjure their faith. The troops then moved on to Villemur. Forewarned, the inhabitants set fire to their houses before escaping. Among the inhabitants were about one hundred Cathar perfects, including the deacon Raymond Méric and the sisters Arnaude and Péronne of Lamothe. When Arnaude was interrogated in 1243 by the inquisitor Bernard of Caux, she related how she and her sister had fled to the Lauragais, to Roquemaure and then to Lavaur. After these events, the crusaders dispersed, probably after being informed that Raymond VI had taken the cross, an action that placed his lands under the protection of the Church.

1209

• June: the host leaves from Lyon
• June: crusade in Quercy and death at the stake in Casseneuil
• July 22: Béziers is sacked
• August 1: the host arrives under Carcassonne's walls
• August 15: Carcassonne surrenders, the inhabitants are evacuated from the city, Raymond-Roger Trencavel is imprisoned, Montfort named new Viscount of Béziers, Albi and Carcassonne.

The House of Amours in Saint Antonin de Noble Val, detail.

Indulgence

Whoever took the cross received remission of the sins for which "he had offered to the true God the contrition of his heart and confession from his mouth."

Apostolic Protection

From his departure for the crusades until his return, the crusader and all his possessions were placed under the protection of the Apostolic See. His property thus remained "free, in the state in which they were found, with no trouble."

Debt Moratorium

A crusader's creditor, at the request of the crusader, can be forced by the Church to free him from his promise to pay interest on the sums lent him and to defer the settlement date at which the debts are to be paid.

WITH A BUTTONED FOIL

I n Servian in July 1206, during the contradictory debate opposing them, Thierry, a former canon of Nevers won over by heretical ideas, addressed Diego and said to him: "I know who you are; in truth, you have come in the spirit of Elijah." And the Bishop of Osma retorted, "And you, you have come in the spirit of the Antichrist."

The Sack of Béziers

From Saint Gilles, Raymond VI, Milon and Tedisio travelled up the Rhone valley as far as Valence, where they joined up with the crusaders. The Count of Toulouse received a warm welcome from his cousins, the Count of Auxerre, Pierre of Courtenay, and his brother Robert. Their father, the son of King Louis VI, was Raymond VI's mother's brother. Raymond-Roger Trencavel came to meet the crusader army and offered his submission to Arnaud-Amaury, who refused it; if Trencavel in turn took the cross, there was no more reason for a crusade. The young viscount quickly returned to Carcassonne. He passed through Béziers and asked the city's inhabitants to put the city in a state of defence. After crossing the Rhone at Beaucaire, the crusaders arrived in Montpellier, which Innocent III had asked them to spare in a letter sent on March 1st. The city, which had always shown itself to be completely orthodox, belonged to the wife of Pedro II of Aragon, the pope's vassal. On July 20, the crusaders left Montpellier and after occupying Servian, abandoned by its inhabitants, arrived before Béziers on July 21, setting up their camp on the banks of the Orb River.

At the time, Béziers had a population of about twenty thousand. Catharism was certainly strongly established if we recall that in 1206 Diego, Dominic, Pierre of Castelnau and Raoul spent two whole weeks debating there. The bishop of Béziers, Renaud of Montpeyroux, came out to meet the crusaders and introduced himself to Arnaud-Amaury. He had a list of two hundred and ten names of Cathars, either perfects or known believers, who were living in the town. The leader of the crusade, through the intermediary of the prelate, addressed an ultimatum to the city's consuls: either they delivered the heretics or they would share their fate. The townspeople refused. This response was partly linked to the confidence the inhabitants had in the strength of their citadel. "The crusaders will break their fangs on our fine walls," said the *Canso.* They were also sure that they could withstand a long siege, especially

Saint James Church in Béziers

Bridge over the Orb and Saint Nazaire Cathedral in Béziers

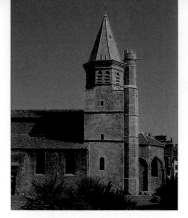

Magdalen Church in Béziers

....

I n the *Historia Albigensis*, Pierre
of Les Vaux de Cernay
remarked that it was also on a
July 22nd, Saint Magdalen's Day,
and in the church dedicated to
her, that Raymond Trencavel
had been assassinated in 1167,
forty-two years earlier, by the
dissatisfied burghers of Béziers.

since they considered that the crusade was going to suffer from supply problems, given their great numbers. Furthermore, they knew
that some of the lords would leave once their forty-day obligatory
service was over. And finally, they counted on the return of their viscount. But there was also a moral reason for their refusal –religious
tolerance was one of their values, and a political one– they owed
fidelity to their viscount and did not want to jeopardize their institutions such as the consulate, which had been obtained only after
much struggle, as was the case in most other towns of Languedoc.

On July 22, the leadership of the crusaders gathered in a tent
around Arnaud-Amaury to discuss the strategy they should adopt. A
few citizens of Béziers came out of the town and right up to their
camp to provoke the crusaders. They were pursued by a group of
camp followers. The besieged did not have time to close the city
gates and Béziers was quickly invested, first of all by the hangers-on,
then by the knights. As the author of the *Canso* put it, "It was a
healthy terror". Some of the inhabitants took refuge in the
churches. Seven thousand of them, men, women and children,
according to Pierre of Les Vaux de Cernay, were massacred in Saint
Magdalen's Church. The town was sacked and set on fire. The flames
destroyed everything, including the booty, to the great displeasure of
the crusaders. A few hours later, nothing remained but smoking
ruins. In the report they addressed to Innocent III, the legates spoke
of twenty thousand dead, probably an exaggerated number but one
which gives a good idea of the scale of the massacre.

"KILL THEM ALL, GOD WILL RECOGNIZE HIS OWN"

In the *Dialogue of Miracles*, a collection of *exempla* written between
1219 and 1233 by the monk
Cesarius, the novice master at the
Cistercian abbey of Heisterbach, near
Bonn, there is a chapter entitled *The
Heresy of the Albigensians*. After mentioning the extension of Catharism in
Languedoc and giving a brief description of Cathar beliefs, Cesarius talks
about the crusade of 1209. In particular, he provided an original version of
the massacre of July 22nd. "[The cru-
saders] arrived at a great city, which
was called Béziers […] and besieged
it […] A few foot soldiers, burning
with the zeal of faith […] placed ladders and climbed […] the ramparts.
[…] They opened the gates […]
and took the city. Learning […] that
the Catholics were mixed with the

heretics, they told the abbot
[Arnaud-Amaury]: 'What should
we do, Lord? We cannot tell the
good from the wicked.' It is said
that the abbot, fearing […] that
those who remained would pretend
to be Catholic […] and would
return to their perfidy after their
departure, answered 'Massacre
them, because the Lord knows his
own'". What should one think of
the authenticity of this terrible reply
that the Cistercian of Heisterbach
was alone among his contemporaries
to attribute to the pontifical legate
Arnaud-Amaury, himself the Abbot
of Citeaux? Many historians have
considered this thorny question,
among them A.Borst, M. Roquebert
or J. Berlioz. Their analyses lead to
the conclusion that although the

reply's authenticity cannot be proved,
it is nonetheless quite plausible. And
although the legate can surely not be
accused of being the author of the
order that led to the savage killing in
Béziers, he was still guilty of knowing
about it and letting it happen. As for
knowing whether God recognized
his own, the English cleric Gervase
of Tilbury held no doubts. Presenting
in his *Otia Imperialia* of 1215 a ghost
questioned in Beaucaire about the
massacre of the Albigensians, he
has him say, "God in His judgement
wanted the good to be distinguished
from the wicked. The good, who
did not sully their faith with heresy,
sinned by tolerance. But those who
were burnt here on earth in their
bodies are burnt even more in spirit
after death."

The Siege of Carcassonne

On July 25th, the crusading army set off towards Narbonne. A delegation led by Archbishop Berenger and Viscount Aimery came to meet it to present the town's submission. On the road to Carcassonne, the host found abandoned villages so they helped themselves to abundant supplies. A week later, on August 1st, the crusaders could see the ramparts of Carcassonne. On his arrival in Carcassonne, Trencavel had mobilized his vassals, built up reserves and organized the city's defences. At the time, the city had only one set of walls on which stood about thirty towers and that, in the west, supported the count's castle. Outside the wall, it was flanked by two neighbourhoods, the Bourg in the north and the Castellar in the south. Saint Nazaire Cathedral stood within its perimeter. The viscount had had local mills destroyed so that the crusaders could not use them for supplies. As soon as the crusading troops passed under his ramparts, Trencavel wanted to make a sortie, but Pierre-Roger of Cabaret dissuaded him. Nothing happened on August 2nd but in the morning of the next day, August 3rd, the crusaders captured the Bourg and occupied the eastern bank of the Aude River, cutting the defenders off from their water supplies. Two or three days later, the arrival of their overlord, Pedro II of Aragon, and a hundred of his knights under the walls of the city revived hope among the defenders. The Aragonese were received at the crusader camp. The king paid a visit to his brother-in-law Raymond VI, who had settled away from the others, on the slope of Mary's Hill, south of Castellar. The pope had written to Raymond VI on July 27th, congratulating him for having reconciled with the Church. Inside his tent, Pedro II had something to eat and then, accompanied by three knights, presented himself at the city gates "without arms and without a shield". Received by Trencavel, his vassal, he offered to mediate and then returned to the crusader camp where the abbot of Citeaux and the French lords agreed to let the viscount and ten of his men come out if he delivered the city. As it was related by the author of the *Canso*, the response was to the point –"I would rather see all mine skinned before me, kiss their corpses and be the last to die." Pedro II went back to Catalonia. On August 7th, the Castellar was attacked. With their war machines, the French bombarded the suburb and, protected by a wooden cover, approached the wall in which they made a breach. The Castellar fell, its defenders retreated into the city where the situation was becoming untenable. The heat was intense in August, the wells were dry, men and animals were dying from disease. The smell was nauseating. A few days later, a French knight asked to parley with Trencavel. The meeting took place outside the walls. The *Canso* relates that the French knight, "one of the greatest among the crusaders' leaders", introduced himself as a "relative" of Raymond-Roger. It may have been the Count of Auxerre, Pierre of Courtenay, first cousin of the viscount's mother. One hundred knights accompanied the viscount; thirty came with the Count of Auxerre. Trencavel had to surrender to save his city and its inhabitants, his vassals and his soldiers. He gave himself up and on

Bishop's Tower in Carcassonne

THE HOLE OF THE CITY

A legend, repeated in an anonymous prose chronicle of the crusade, related that after Trencavel's surrender, the inhabitants of Carcassonne had escaped from the town through an underground passage leading to the castles of Cabaret, four leagues north. And the path taken today by visitors to the castles of Lastours crosses a cave called the Hole of the City, at the foot of Quertinheux.

Cabaret, the Hole of the City

SIMON DE MONTFORT

"Let us mention first his illustrious origin, his unshakeable courage… he was a tall man, his hair was remarkable, his face elegant, his shoulders prominent, his arms muscular, his trunk graceful… his speech was eloquent, his courtesy accessible to all, his camaraderie pleasant, his chastity absolute, his humility exceptional…"
Pierre of Les Vaux de Cernay,
Historia Albigensis

The Montfort's fief was located north of Yveline Forest, over which they had jurisdiction. These lords therefore had rights over hunting in this forest, a possession of their vassals. Simon III de Montfort had three sons from a first marriage: Amaury, Simon, born about 1165, and Guy. His second marriage was to Amicie of Leicester. At the death of his father, Simon IV inherited the family fief and the rights of succession to Robert of Leicester, Amicie's brother, who had died childless. In 1188, Simon was in Gisors where he attended the meeting between Philip Augustus and Henry II of England. The two monarchs decided to leave for the Holy Land. But in 1190 Simon was not at the side of the King of France and of Richard the Lionheart –Henry II having died in 1189– when they left from Vézelay. He married Alix of Montmorency who was not only a faithful and attentive wife but, in Languedoc, his strongest supporter. In 1194, he was at the side of the king, back in France, at the siege of Aumale and proved his bravery by routing the troops of Richard the Lionheart who had come to help the

town. On November 28, 1199, Simon and his brother Guy participated in the great tournament held in Escry sur Aisne, organized by Thibaud of Champagne who, for the occasion, had invited the kingdom's greatest barons. The knights had broken many lances when Foulque of Neuilly, named by Pope Innocent III to preach the fourth crusade, invited them to take up the cross in a vibrant, fiery sermon. This time Simon and Guy de Montfort answered the call. The crusaders were supposed to leave from Venice on June 24, 1202, on ships placed at their disposal by the Venetians for the considerable amount of ninety-five thousand marks. Fifty thousand marks were lacking. Dandolo, the Doge, proposed to the crusaders' leader, Boniface of Montferrat, to make a payment in kind. For the benefit of Venice, the French knights and their men were supposed to capture Zara, today's Zadar, a city on the Dalmatian coast, occupied by the King of Hungary. On November 11, 1202, the fleet arrived before Zara

Simon de Montfort

and, despite Innocent III's interdiction and the opposition of Guy, Abbot of Les Vaux de Cernay, a Cistercian abbey close to the Montfort's lands, as well as of Simon, his brother and their companions, the town was sacked. The crusaders were then called on by Alexis, the son of the Byzantine emperor, to capture Constantinople where power had just been usurped by his uncle. On April 7, 1203, the crusaders set sail for Constantinople where they carved out the short-lived Latin empire of the East. Montfort, his brother Guy, his companions, Simon of Neauphle, Robert Mauvoisin, Dreux of Cressonssacq, and Guy of Les Vaux de Cernay, had not followed them. They were sailing to the Holy Land. When they arrived in Jaffa, a truce had just been signed. Montfort stayed for a short time with the King of Jerusalem, Amaury of Lusignan. Then in the autumn of 1204, he returned to France. His brother Guy, who had just married Heloise of Ibelin, descendant of a great local family, remained. On his return to France, since his uncle Robert had died, Simon inherited the county of Leicester, which was immediately confiscated from him by John Lackland. After the murder of Pierre of Castelnau, Innocent III called for another crusade on March 10, 1208. Arnaud-Amaury and Guy of Les Vaux de Cernay were charged with convincing the French knights to take part in it. The Duke of Burgundy was one of the first to take the cross. Through the intermediary of Guy of Les Vaux de Cernay, he convinced Simon de Montfort to join the host which was about to gather in Lyon. The latter, a sincere and convinced Catholic, an intrepid captain, loyal to the pope and a friend to the Cistercians, turned out to be a precious auxiliary in settling the affair of Peace and Faith.

August 15th, the besieged left Carcassonne in "shirts and trousers", noted Guillaume of Puylaurens, "carrying only their sins", said Pierre of Les Vaux de Cernay. The viscount was thrown into a dungeon of the crusader-occupied city, where he died three months later on November 10th, from dysentery for some, poisoned, according to others. What is certain is that he was betrayed, because the act of surrender, as related by Guillaume of Puylaurens, provided that "he would remain hostage until the execution of the treaty".

On August 15th, Arnaud-Amaury called the principal barons of the crusade together in the courtyard of the count's castle. The defeated Trencavel was declared forfeit of his titles, his properties were confiscated. Everything was to be given to another viscount. Sounded out, the Count of Nevers, the Duke of Burgundy, the Count of Saint Pol, refused them. They had accomplished their duties in the host and planned to return home. They also did not consider the legal situation as very clear. On one hand, loyal to Philip Augustus and authorized by him to participate in the crusade, they were well aware of the king's reticence about the operation. On the other hand, they knew that Trencavel's direct suzerain was Pedro II of Aragon who, absent, had not been consulted. But for Arnaud-Amaury, as chief of the crusade, it was important to display Trencavel's dispossession and to name a new viscount. Indeed, the latter had to receive homage from his vassals, placing them *ipso facto* in the camp of orthodoxy. Those who refused would be fought against both for not respecting feudal laws and also as abettors of heresy. An electoral college was formed and included the abbot of Citeaux, two bishops and four knights. It named a lord from Ile de France to become Viscount of Béziers, Albi and Carcassonne. After a first refusal, he accepted. His name was Simon de Montfort.

As he had in Béziers, Raymond VI remained passive and impassive in the face of events. After Trencavel's surrender, he brought his son Raymond, aged twelve, from Toulouse to Carcassonne, to introduce him to the crusading knights who welcomed him cordially.

Stone showing the siege, St Nazaire Basilica, Carcassonne

Military Loyalists

In August 1209, when their host service had ended, unlike most of the great barons, some of the crusaders remained at the side of the new viscount, Simon de Montfort. The group would be strengthened in December 1211 by the arrival of Guy de Montfort, Simon's brother, on his return from the Holy Land. Some of the most faithful among the loyalists would even settle in Languedoc. Their geographical origins were very different.

From Montfort's area

• Bouchard of Marly, cousin of Alix of Montmorency, the wife of Simon de Montfort
• Pierre of Richebourg, Montfort's vassal
• Amaury, Guillaume and Robert of Poissy, and their cousin Simon
• Guy of Lévis, called the Marshal

From the Orléanais

Guy of Lucy

From Normandy

• Perrin of Cissey
• Roger of Andelys
• Roger of L'Essart

From Picardy

• Gaubert d'Essigny
• Robert of Forceville
• Robert de Picquigny

From Burgundy

• Lambert of Thury
• Guillaume of Contres

From Champagne

Robert Mauvoisin

From England

Hugo of Lacy

From various or unidentified origins

• Rainier of Chauderon
• Raoul of Agis
• Pons and Jean of Beaumont
• Rouaud of Donges

THE CITÉ OF CARCASSONNE

At the foot of the Montagne Noire, where the Aude R. coming from Razès changes direction and flows towards the Mediterranean, Carcassonne has always occupied a strategic position and commercial crossroads. During the 3rd century B.C., the Gallic tribe of Volcae Tectosages occupied the *oppidum* of *Carcaso*, the hill on which the *Cité* stands today. In 118 B.C., Narbonensis was founded, the *Pax Romana* rapidly reigned over the *Provincia* and Carcassonne prospered. The Barbarian threat became pressing during the 3rd century and the town surrounded itself with walls from which about thirty towers jutted upwards. In the 5th century, the Visigoths, who had made Toulouse the capital of their kingdom, settled there. Pepin the Short expelled the Saracens who had entrenched themselves there at the beginning of the 8th century. This was the episode at the origin of the legend of Dame Carcass. According to this story, the Moors were besieged in Carcassonne; their King had been killed and supplies were running short. The deceased's wife, Dame Carcass, had a sow stuffed with wheat thrown to the foot of the ramparts. The Franks, believing that the besieged still had large reserves of food, struck camp. In the 11th century, Bernard-Aton Trencavel became Viscount of Carcassonne. Perhaps it is him shown fighting the Moors on a fresco in the count's castle. During the 12th century, his descendants had a first castle built at the western edge of the Lower Empire wall, which still today makes up the town's principal fortifications. After the events of the crusade, the viscounty of Carcassonne became a royal possession. After Trencavel's failure in 1240 to recapture the lands of his fathers, the boroughs of Saint Michel and Saint Vincent were razed. King

Louis IX had the city's fortifications strengthened and authorized the foundation of a new town (*bastide*) on the left bank of the Aude. Philippe le Hardi and Philippe le Bel had the exterior ramparts built, making Carcassonne an impregnable site that the Black Prince refrained from attacking in 1355. He simply set fire to the bastide. After the Treaty of the Pyrenees was signed in 1659, the fortress lost much of its importance and suffered from damage over time. In the 19th century, Prosper Mérimée, Cros-Mayrevielle and Viollet-le-Duc promoted its restoration. Carcassonne's ramparts consist of two concentric walls with lists between them. The inner wall stands on what used to be the Gallo-Roman enclosure. The covered way runs around the top of the ramparts, protected by merlons and crenellations. The outer wall measures one thousand, five hundred metres, and encloses nearly twenty hectares. The two sets of walls are flanked by numerous towers: thirteen towers set in the outer wall, and twenty-six on the inner one. Integrated into the inner rampart, the Treasury Tower in the north-east is a building with vaulted rooms with Gothic-style windows. The Tower of Justice is a round tower, reinforced during the reign of Louis IX. The Inquisition Tower was the seat of the Inquisition tribunal. The square Bishop's Tower was built astride the lists. The postern gate of Saint Nazaire Tower was only accessible by a ladder which could be pulled up in case of danger; this tower was intended for the defence of Saint Nazaire Cathedral, located just behind it to the north. Outside the exterior wall, the Vade Tower is a five-storey cylinder, in which were installed latrines, wells and a fireplace. Some of the towers opened with grooves and

form a protruding half-cylinder on the outside of the ramparts so they could not be used as a place attackers could lean on if they tried to invest them. The ramparts still show the different stages of their construction. In the north, on the first wall, near the tower of the Avar mill, the enormous stones of the Roman wall are still visible at the base of the walls. Above, the layers of bricks and ragstones were brought in the 4th and 5th centuries. During the 10th century, the curtains were raised with smooth, regular cut ashlar and topped with merlons and crenellations. The Narbonnaise Gate is the Cité's main entrance. It is surrounded by two towers with spurs; a *châtelet* (small fortress) and a barbican complete the defensive system. The Aude Gate is also strongly fortified with a barbican, a châtelet and an enormous machicolation overlook the access ramp that runs along the western curtains of the second enclosure. The count's castle is a citadel within a citadel. The Trencavels built it during the 12th century. At the time it did not have the fortified wall topped with wooden corbels that surrounds it on three sides within the Cité. This enclosure, built after Carcassonne was annexed to the royal domain, probably in 1226 and 1245, is surrounded by a wide ditch. It was intended to protect the seneschal and the French garrison from a largely hostile population. A short time later, a covered way of which vestiges remain, was built to link the castle to the barbican outside the ramparts on the western side. The count's castle was built to withstand a siege. It had a large cistern and bakeries whose bread ovens are still visible in the wall leaning against the Gallo-Roman enclosure. Today, the count's castle contains a museum about stones. Its collections cover a long period from Antiquity to the Middle Ages: military milestones, Gallo-Roman vestiges, Merovingian and Carolingian sarcophagi, sculpted modillions and corbels mainly coming from shrines in the city, funerary stele, a sandstone recumbent figure of a 13th century knight. There is also a very fine lavatorium from the second half of the 12th century, which may have come from Fontfroide Abbey or Lagrasse Abbey. In 1096, Pope Urban II blessed the first stone laid for Saint Nazaire Cathedral, to the two buildings that no longer stand today. It was during the bishopric of Radulphe, in 1260, that enlarging the cathedral was considered so that it would be seen as tangible proof of the victory of orthodoxy over heresy, even though in reality, that victory was not yet complete, far from it. Work on this enlargement began during the bishopric of Radulphe's successor, Bernard of Capendu, and was finished at the beginning of the 14th century. The architectural choice was to extend the building northern and southern ends of the transept. Some of these stained glass windows are Gothic: those in the apse presenting the lives of Christ, of saints Peter, Paul, Nazaire and Celsus; the stained glass window in the first chapel in the transept's northern arm presents the theme of the tree of Jesse; those in the first chapel of the southern arm illustrate the parable of Saint Bonaventure, a Franciscan, and the tree of life. The northern rose window is dedicated to the Virgin and the southern one to Christ. The sculpture programme is equally remarkable, in particular on Radulphe's tomb. This son of a family of serfs from Trèbes was most certainly gifted with exceptional qualities. To be accepted as a student at the cathedral's chapter, he had to pay for his freedom with cash. One by one, he climbed all the steps of the diocesan hierarchy before becoming Bishop of Carcassonne in 1255, and he remained in the post until 1266. Below a bas-relief of an image of the bishop, an embedded sarcophagus is carved with various scenes, including one of the deceased's funeral. The tomb of another bishop of Carcassonne, Pierre of Rochefort, who died in 1321, stands in a chapel he had built in the northeast corner of the Romanesque nave. Twenty-two sculpted statues on the pillars of the choir are topped with small baldaquins in lacy stonework. Among the personalities presented, there is a beautiful Virgin with Child and the patron saints of the cathedral, Nazaire and Celsus. In the southern arm of the transept, a funerary slab is set into the wall. It was discovered in the 19th century and for a long time considered to be that of Simon de Montfort. Carved with a chisel, it represents a knight in armour, dressed in a surcoat covered with lions and the cross of Toulouse.

a - Narbonnaise Gate	h - Justice Tower
b - Aude Gate	i - Saint Nazaire Tower
c - Count's Castle	j - Treasury Tower
d - Theatre	k - Vade Tower
e - Avar Tower	l - Upper lists
f - Bishop's Tower	m - Lower lists
g - Inquisition Tower	n - Saint Nazaire Basilica

Map of the Cité of Carcassonne

whose construction had just begun on the site of a Carolingian shrine. Work was completed in 1130. As related by Pierre of Les Vaux de Cernay, in 1209, in order to strengthen the walls of the besieged city, although "the inhabitants, perverted people without faith, had demolished the canons' refectory and cellar… and even, even more atrocious, the choir stalls in the church", the church itself was not damaged. Guy of Les Vaux de Cernay, Bishop of Carcassonne and the chronicler's uncle, took charge of repairing damage caused eastwards by rebuilding the choir and by placing a transept between the nave and this choir. The 13th century nave of Saint Nazaire Basilica is Romanesque, while its choir and transept, dating from the 13th and 14th centuries, are Gothic. The apse enclosing the choir is lit by six stained glass windows. Along the eastern side of the transept, a narrow side aisle serves six chapels with flat chevets, each of them opening with a large stained glass window that bathes the transept with coloured light, as do the two rose windows placed at the

Western ramparts and Justice Tower in the Cité of Carcassonne

SIMON THE CONQUEROR

In thanksgiving, the new viscount Simon de Montfort ceded three houses to the Order of Cîteaux: one in Carcassonne, one in Sallèles and one in Béziers. He wrote to Innocent III to ask him to confirm his election. He entrusted Robert Mauvoisin with taking the letter to Rome. In this letter, he also requested the pope's support. "Without your help and that of the faithful, I will not be able to govern this land for long." He had analyzed the situation well. Trencavel's vassals had taken refuge in their castles, most of which had been built with serious attention to defence. The highest-raking barons, like the Count of Nevers, left the crusade one by one; the Duke of Burgundy departed in mid-September, and only about twenty lords remained at Montfort's side. For nearly ten years, they would make up the hard core of a host periodically strengthened by lords coming from France, or even the Empire, to accomplish their forty-day service.

An Army of Occupation

The crusaders with Montfort at their head took the direction of Fanjeaux. On their way, they found Alzonne abandoned, just as Montréal had been deserted by its lord Aimery and the heretics, about a dozen perfects, the deacon Pierre Durand as well as fifty credenses, who had been living there. The picture was the same in Fanjeaux from which Guilhabert of Castres and several perfects had gone to join Montségur, where they found the bishop Gaucelin, Raymond of Péreille and his mother, Fournière, a perfect. Montfort set up his headquarters in Fanjeaux. Besides the town's strategic position, it was also a symbol, because this *castrum* was one of the nerve centres of Catharism in Languedoc. In order to reach Limoux, Montfort and his men followed the valley of the Aude River, south of Carcassonne. They besieged Preixan, a possession of Raymond-Roger, Count of Foix, which had shown resistance. The Count of Foix arrived and, after some discussion, agreed to allow the French to enter. Montfort then returned to Fanjeaux, but after passing through Carcassonne and Alzonne, where a delegation from Castres recognized him as their lord. He crossed the Montagne Noire to reach Castres, where he received the submission of the knights of Lombers and took to the stake two perfects he had flushed out. Since Cabaret was practically on his way back and he could still count on the presence of the Duke of Burgundy, he launched an assault which was easily repelled by Pierre-Roger of Cabaret and his brother Jourdain. The Duke of Burgundy then returned to France. In Fanjeaux, Montfort found a message from Abbot Vital of Saint Antonin of Frédelas, who complained of exactions committed against the monastery by the Count of Foix and invited Montfort to replace Raymond-Roger as co-lord of Pamiers. Before going to Pamiers, Simon made a detour through Mirepoix. As he approached, Cathars and their sympathizers, including the *castrum*'s co-lords, fled. Among these co-lords there was Pierre-Roger of

November 10: Death of Raymond-Roger Trencavel	1209
• July 22: end of the siege of Minerve. One hundred and forty perfects die at the stake. • August: Council of Saint Gilles. Confirmation of Raymond VI's excommunication. • November 23: The crusaders capture Termes, and take Puivert a few days later.	1210
• January: Conferences of Narbonne and Montpellier. Pedro II of Aragon accepts Montfort's homage for the viscounty of Carcassonne. • Springtime: surrender without a fight by Cabaret. The crusaders capture Lavaur. Three to four hundred perfects led to the stake. • End of June: First siege of Toulouse. • July: The lords of Quercy swear homage to Montfort in Cahors. Montfort makes a pilgrimage to Rocamadour. • End of September: Battle of Castelnaudary.	1211
• July 16: Battle of Las Navas de Tolosa. • September 8: Surrender of Moissac. • December 1st: Promulgation of the statutes of Pamiers.	1212

143

Roquefort Castle

Fanjeaux seen from St Dominic's Path

GUILLAUME OF ROQUEFORT

In November 1209, the abbot of Eaunes, accompanied by two monks and a lay brother, were going from Carcassonne back to their abbey, located less than two leagues south of Muret. He was returning from Saint Gilles, where the Count of Foix had sent him to defend his position with the pontifical legates. The four Cistercians were set on by Guillaume of Roquefort. The abbot and the lay brother were killed. One monk was left for dead. The other was able to go and alert Carcassonne. The presumed assassin, even though there was no doubt at all for Pierre of Les Vaux de Cernay, was a lord from the Montagne Noire, whose castle was set on the right bank of the Sor River. His brother was the Catholic Bishop of Carcassonne and his mother was a Cathar perfect. He took part in the defence of Termes in 1210 and was killed during the first siege of Toulouse in 1211. A knight from Montgey, Pierre de Corneille, questioned by the Inquisition in 1243, revealed that in the autumn of 1209 Guillaume of Roquefort had strengthened the defences of his castle to receive three hundred Cathar perfects looking for a safe place in which to take refuge.

View of the Lauragais from the Seignadou in Fanjeaux

Mirepoix the Younger, cousin of Raymond of Péreille. Chased out of their *castra* or their castles, these lords, both great and small, became *faydits* (lords without fiefs). Dispossessed and uprooted, many took part in operations against the French, taking shelter between two sieges or raids in friendly places that had not yet fallen. Some, heretic believers and relations of the Lord of Péreille, went to Montségur. Montfort entrusted Mirepoix to Guy of Lévis and then went to Pamiers where a new act of pareage was established in the presence of Foulque, the Bishop of Toulouse. Montfort returned to Fanjeaux through Saverdun, which surrendered; in Lombers, he received the oath from the knights; then, in Albi, homage from the bishop. But after these events in Mirepoix, Pamiers and Saverdun, the Count of Foix began to react. He recaptured Preixan, but his attack on Fanjeaux on September 29th was beaten back.

On November 10th, Raymond-Roger Trencavel died in his Carcassonne jail. He was twenty-four years old. Montfort had his dead body exposed and paid him a funerary homage before leaving for Montpellier where, in the presence of Milon, Viscount Aimery of Narbonne, and the bishops of Agde and Béziers, Trencavel's widow ceded Montfort all her rights and those of her son, in return for an annual payment of three thousand *sous* and the reimbursement of her dowry, worth twenty-five thousand sous. The young Raymond was given into the guardianship of the Count of Foix. Still in Montpellier, Simon de Montfort met Pedro II, his legitimate overlord, to whom he wished to pay homage, but the King of Aragon refused. During this time, the smouldering revolt of the Southerners burst into flame. First of all, Guiraud of Pépieux, a lord from the Minervois who had joined Montfort after the sack of Béziers, captured the castle of Puisserguier and its French garrison, which he had locked up in the keep after first isolating two knights whose eyes he put out, cut off their noses, ears and upper lips, and sent naked to Carcassonne. He thus took revenge for the death of his uncle who had been killed by a French knight, even though Montfort had had the knight buried alive for his crime. Montfort

SAISSAC CASTLE

Bernard of Saissac, former tutor of Raymond-Roger Trencavel and his vassal, did not accept Montfort as his overlord. He abandoned his castle and became a *faydit*. The castle was entrusted to Bouchard of Marly. It stood on a peak carved out of the rock by the Aiguebelle and Vernassonne Rivers, on the southern slope of the Montagne Noire. In 1240, Raymond-Roger's son recaptured Saissac for a while. It passed into the hands of Lambert of Thury before becoming a possession of the Lévis family.

Saissac Castle

arrived too late, freed the rest of the garrison and razed the castle. He then learned that Amaury and Guillaume of Poissy were being besieged in Miramont Castle, on the northern flank of Alaric's mountain, to the east of Carcassonne. Montfort flew to their rescue but the French had all been massacred. Near Saissac, Gaubert of Essigny and Bouchard of Marly, accompanied by fifty men, were ambushed by men from Cabaret. The former was killed, Bouchard was held prisoner by Pierre-Roger of Cabaret. Castres, followed by Lombers and Montréal, rose up. At the end of this difficult year for Montfort, the return from Rome of Robert Mauvoisin with Pope Innocent III's response confirming the August election provided some consolation. At the same time as he wrote to Montfort, the pope addressed nearly all of Christendom, prelates and sovereigns, except Philip Augustus, to ask for financial and military help.

After the fall of Carcassonne, Raymond VI returned to Toulouse where Simon de Montfort and Arnaud-Amaury had sent a delegation charged with getting the heretics, a census of whom had been carried out by Foulque, turned over by the count and the consuls. Both the count and the consuls refused. The count claimed that, being pardoned in Saint Gilles, he did not have to take any orders; the consuls claimed that all the Cathars had been burnt at the stake and, if any had escaped, they should be judged according to canon law. Arnaud-Amaury excommunicated the consuls and placed the city under interdiction. At the beginning of September, a council was held in Avignon in the presence of Milon and Hugo of Riez. Informed about Raymond VI's attitude by Arnaud-Amaury, the legates excommunicated the Count of Toulouse. The Count set off on a journey on September 20th. He first went to his suzerains King Philip Augustus and Emperor Otto in order to, according to Guillaume of Puylaurens, "take counsel about the threats hanging over him", then to Rome to have a meeting with the pope, who had also received an embassy from Toulouse. At the end of January 1210, the pope wrote several letters. In the one addressed to the archbishops of Arles and Narbonne, to the Bishop of Agen and the legates Tedisio and Hugo of Riez –Milon had died in December, 1209– he asked that legal procedures be respected in the matter of Raymond VI, and that after a complaint had been made, a council should meet within three months to take a decision after hearing both the accusation and the defence. If the count was able to justify his behaviour, he should be acquitted; in the opposite case, the file should be transmitted to the pope who would take the final decision after examining the evidence and holding new auditions if necessary. He also addressed Arnaud-Amaury, requesting that he cancel the interdiction placed on Toulouse and the excommunication of its inhabitants and of Raymond VI, so that he could fulfil his engagements. The pope's attitude must be seen as the expression of his desire that these matters, delicate from a legal point of view, as he was reminded by Philip Augustus in 1207, be carried out according to the rules. But the purpose remained clear. Did he not write to Arnaud-Amaury, "Tedisio will be the instrument that you will use, he will be like the fish-hook that you will use to take out of the water the fish from whom it is necessary to hide the metal that it detests".

Vestiges of Miramont Castle

The castles of Lastours, with Cabaret Castle in the back

Tower of Bishop's Palace, Castres

Saissac

147

EVEN THE CYPRESSES HEAR THE GOOD...

"Cabaret resisted Christianity and our count more than the others: it was a centre of heresy. Its lord, Pierre-Roger, an old man of evil nature was a heretic and a declared enemy of the Church."
Historia Albigensis,
Pierre of Les Vaux de Cernay.

The chronicler of the *Historia Albigensis* was well-informed when he spoke of Cabaret in the autumn of 1209. This *castrum* contained a large Cathar community which profited from the protection and sympathy of its lords, Pierre-Roger and Jourdain of Cabaret. The presence of a perfect, Pons Bernardi, was already attested in 1194, in what was probably the seat of a Cathar deaconate of which Arnaud Hot was in charge at the beginning of the 13th century. The troubadour Raymond of Miraval was well-known in the place. Of course, he used to come to entertain the seigniorial clan, but also to visit his cousin Gaucelm of Miraval, a Bon Homme. There were houses of perfects, according to declarations made to the Inquisition in the middle of the 13th century by Maurine Bousquet of Villesicle and two sisters, Florence and Raymonde, from Mas Saintes Puelles. In 1210, Pierre-Roger of Cabaret negotiated his surrender but was careful to evacuate the heretics pursued by the crusaders beforehand. Under the cover of the Occitan reconquest, in 1222 Pierre-Roger and Jourdain regained possession of their fief, like Pierre of Laure, one of their most constant and loyal allies, who recovered his *castrum* in the Minervois. This became the home of Bartholomew of Na Maureta, a

famous Cathar personality and perhaps the author of the anonymous *Cathar Treatise*. And naturally, heretics, openly or not, returned to Cabaret which had become the seat of the bishopric of their Carcassès Church and where they could attend sermons by their bishops, Pierre Isarn and later Guiraud Abit. Isarn Bozom, a knight of Hautpoul, attended the sermon preached at Christmas 1227. After the royal crusade of 1226, Cabaret, like Limoux, was a centre of resistance to French occupation. The *faydits* who had taken refuge in Cabaret harassed the troops of Imbert of Beaujeu. They included Pierre-Roger of Cabaret, Bernard-Othon of Niort, Pierre-Roger's brother-in-law, and Olivier of Termes. As for Jourdain, Pierre-Roger's brother, he had submitted to Louis VIII but, captured by the *faydits*, ended his days in a prison of the Count of Toulouse. In 1229, after the Treaty of Paris, the village's defenders decided to "return Cabaret to the King and the Church." As in 1210, they did all that was needed so that the Cathars could reach a safe hiding-place. The French troops invested the town and immediately razed all the village houses after

At the foot of Surdespine

evicting their last occupants *manu militari*. The French crown then had four castles built on the summit of the crest, placed in echelon from north to south: Cabaret, Tour Régine, Surdespine and Quertinheux, reaching for the sky like the tall cypresses that bristle on the hill. This group of castles that can be seen from the belvedere arranged near the road leading from Lastours to Salsigne has perhaps nothing to do with the castle controlled by Pierre-Roger of Cabaret. In fact, the castle of Tour Régine was built during the second half of the 13th century. As for the three others, although there is evidence of their presence in the 11th century, they were perhaps simply watchtowers that stood half-way up the western slope of the ridge. In any case, scrupulous excavations carried out in Cabaret over eighteen years by Marie Élise Gardel have provided a large quantity of precious information. The Cathar Cabaret stood to the north of the present village of Cabaret, there where the Grésilhou and the Orbiel come within a hundred metres of each other, before they flow apart before their confluence at the village of Lastours. The well-defended castral centre was surrounded by a village whose houses sheltered a large community of believers and clerics for a period of thirty-five years, except from 1209-1222. They lived their faith in peace, working as smiths, weavers, and stone-cutters. But it does appear that the rock of Cabaret, this high point of solitude, was destined to be the *inspired hill* of Catharism. According to the Inquisition register of Jean Galand, the royal castellans of Cabaret, Surdespine and Quertinheux, as well as the members of their families, died consoled between 1273 and 1284.

Attacking the Fortresses

Early in the month of March 1210, Montfort went to Pézenas to join his wife, Alix of Montmorency, who had returned from France bringing reinforcements. She was accompanied by their two children, Amaury and Amicie. On the way to Fanjeaux, Montfort dealt ruthlessly with Montlaur, which had revolted, and hanged some of the insurgents, reoccupied Alzonne and invested Bram. There he hanged a cleric who had delivered Montréal in the previous September, then took one hundred men, cut off their noses, ears and upper lips, and sent them off to Cabaret, led by a man whose one eye he had spared. Montfort had not forgotten the mutilations that Guiraud of Pépieux had inflicted on two of his knights. In mid-April, he besieged the castle of Miramont, which fell two weeks later. He then continued on to Pamiers where Pedro II of Aragon, wishing to improve the situation, had invited him along with Raymond VI and Raymond-Roger of Foix to participate at a meeting, but nothing came of it. They then fought skirmishes on lands belonging to the Count of Foix, even going as far as provoking him at the foot of his castle. Raymond VI returned to Toulouse from Pamiers. Arnaud-Amaury was already there, having come to absolve the population of Toulouse on the instructions of Innocent III. The absolution ceremony took place on March 25, 1210. Pedro II remained active. From Pamiers, he went to Muret then to Portet, where in mid-May he met Arnaud-Amaury, but once again fruitlessly. Having received messages from Pierre-Roger of Cabaret,

Toulouse

INCASTELLAMENTO

F ollowing Bram's example, in the 11th century many inhabited zones organized themselves by grouping their houses around the castral core. The population simultaneously put itself under the authority of the lord.

Bram

Minerve

Dove by Jean-Luc Séverac in Minerve

SYMBOL OF PEACE

The Cathars, for whom the material world was the world of Evil, left few material vestiges –no shrines, no statues, no symbols. However, in the 19th century, Napoléon Peyrat and his followers began to search for false "Cathar doves" in Montségur and Ussat, false since the dove symbolized the Holy Spirit in Christianity. The dove visible in Minerve is a modern work by the sculptor Jean-Luc Séverac.

Raymond of Termes, and Aimery of Montréal, he went to Montréal. These former vassals of Trencavel, who had also been a vassal of the Aragonese king, offered to recognize him as their overlord in return for his support. In exchange, the King of Aragon asked them to hand over their castles immediately, which they refused. Pedro II asked Montfort, who was besieging Bellegarde, not far from Montréal, for a truce, which was accepted to the advantage of the Count of Foix until Easter 1211. Then Pedro II crossed back over the Pyrenees, reaching Teruel on June 13th.

At the end of June, the military leader of the crusade undertook the siege of Minerve, where he was joined by Viscount Aimery of Narbonne, the operation's instigator, and his men. He wanted to take advantage of the arrival of other important reinforcements to capture a number of castles, which were used as pockets of resistance and shelters for heretics. The location of Minerve, a rocky spur surrounded by two ravines dug out of the causse by the Cesse and the Brian, winding rivers that were often dry and whose confluence was at its foot, provided his best defensive argument. The siege was organized and the crusaders installed mangonels and a stone-throwing machine. The village was pounded with stones. During a sally, the besieged failed in their attempt to set fire to the stone-thrower. Installed on the edge of the causse, to the east, it was causing enormous damage. Access to Minerve's only water supply was through a covered and fortified passage leading to a well close to the riverbed of the Cesse. The crusaders destroyed it. Without water, in the summer heat, with the wounded and ill, the besieged could not hold out for long. After five weeks of siege, Guillaume of Minerve agreed to talks with Montfort. At this moment, Arnaud-Amaury and Tedisio arrived, on their way from Toulouse to Saint Gilles, where the council judging the case of Raymond VI was to be held. Montfort let the crusade's spiritual leader set the terms of the surrender. Minerve would become Montfort's possession and its inhabitants' lives would be spared; Guillaume of Minerve would receive lands in the region of Béziers. On July 22nd, the crusaders entered Minerve singing the *Te Deum*. Guy, the abbot of Les Vaux de Cernay tried, in vain, to convince the Cathar perfects to renounce their errors. The prediction made by Arnaud-Amaury and reported in the *Historia Albigensis* was confirmed. When Robert Mauvoisin had questioned his clemency, Arnaud-Amaury allegedly replied, "Do not worry about anything, I believe very few will convert." One hundred and forty perfects were led to the stake set up on the banks of the Cesse. Only three women, whom the mother of Bouchard of Marly had managed to convince, escaped the ordeal. The example of Minerve was to leave its mark. Roger of Ventajou handed over his castle, which Montfort had razed; Aimery of Montréal exchanged his *castrum* for a property in the plains, and the Lord of Laurac also submitted to the crusaders. Montfort called his war council at Pennautier, near Carcassonne. His wife, Alix of Montmorency, joined him there. Montfort's most important companions were Robert Mauvoisin, Guy of Lévis and Guillaume of Contres. A decision was made to besiege the castle of Termes. The operation was likely to be a lengthy one. Guillaume of Contres was to remain in Carcassonne to hold it. He was also charged with organiz-

The well in Minerve

ing the transportation of the war machines, in pieces, that were still standing near Carcassonne, since they would be indispensable for the capture of Termes. They were collected on the shores of the Aude River, below the walls of the city. One night, three hundred men, including several *faydits,* coming from Cabaret led by Pierre-Roger attempted to destroy and burn them. A rapid reaction by Guillaume of Contres and his knights prevented what would have been a great loss for the crusaders. The next day, a convoy of chariots set off with the machines for Termes, where Montfort and his men were waiting.

The siege of this impregnable castle, which overlooked the gorges of the Termenet, began in August 1210 and lasted three months. Behind solid ramparts, fifty knights surrounded Raymond of Termes, "an old man with an evil nature and a confessed heretic" who "feared neither God, nor men", according to Pierre of Les Vaux de Cernay, and his family –his wife Ermessinde of Corsavy, his two daughters and two sons, including Olivier. One of the knights came from the Montagne Noire. His name was Guillaume of Roquefort; his mother, a Cathar perfect called Marquesia, was at his side. As for his brother, Bernard-Raymond, the Catholic Bishop of Carcassonne, he was at the foot of the ramparts, a few hundred metres below, in the camp of the crusaders. There were more crusaders than at any time since August 1209, because they had received reinforcements from many different regions and were led by the bishops of Chartres, Beauvais and Bordeaux, the archdeacon of Paris, and the counts of Dreux and Ponthieu. The crusaders were more numerous but the castle and its well-defended outskirts contained large reserves. Furthermore, the convoys supplying the crusaders were regularly attacked by Pierre-Roger of Cabaret on their way from Carcassonne, and the men escorting them came to an unhappy end. Montfort's men captured the first outskirts, but the defenders immediately took it back. They occupied Termenet Tower which, by placing the attackers in the crossfire of the besieged, was a key element in the castle's defence through its nearby location. As in Carcassonne and Minerve, the heat and lack of water soon began to pose serious problems for the besieged.

Montréal

Window in Termes Castle

Termes Castle

Durfort Castle

TERMES CASTLE

According to Pierre of Les Vaux de Cernay, Termes Castle "… was marvellously, indeed unbelievably, strong and in human estimation appeared to be quite impregnable." This *castrum* which appeared frightful to the chronicler of *Historia Albigensis* was, in 1210, the fief of the lords of Termes who were mentioned for the first time in 1061. These loyal vassals of the Trencavels also owned neighbouring Durfort Castle, at the exit of the Termenet Gorges, and Aguilar Castle in the Corbières. Becoming *faydits*, with Olivier of Termes they became loyal supporters of the Occitan cause. After the crusaders' capture of Termes Castle, Simon de Montfort entrusted its keeping to Alain of Roucy. In January 1224, Amaury de Montfort ceded it to Arnaud-Amaury, the spiritual leader of the crusade, who had become Archbishop of Narbonne. But it is likely that the Lords of Termes took advantage of the French rout and occupied it from 1221, the year Alain of Roucy died defending Montréal, until 1226. After the signature of the Treaty of Corbeil in 1258, the French crown built a citadel on the site of the *castrum* of Termes. This would become part of the line of defence in the south of the kingdom, consisting of the five sons of Carcassonne. After the Treaty of the Pyrenees in 1659, having lost all its strategic importance, the royal fortress of Termes was destroyed. The cost of the demolition work was fourteen thousand, nine hundred and twenty-two *livres* and ten *sols*. Of the outside wall, only some sections of the curtains remain, pierced here and there with arrow slits, as well as the north-west postern gate. Very little remains of the inner wall but the imagination can locate the keep and the still-standing wall of one room, with its cross-shaped window that appears drawn on the blue background of the sky.

A CATHAR FAMILY

When Montfort besieged Puivert, its lord was Bernard del Congost. His wife Arpaïx, the sister of Raymond of Péreille, Lord of Montségur, had received the *consolament* of the dying in 1208. Bernard took refuge in Montségur with his son Gaillard and his nephew Bertrand. About 1215, Gaillard, then seven years old, attended a sermon by Gaucelm, Bishop of the Cathar Church of Toulouse. Bernard died consoled in Montségur in 1232. Through their family ties, the two cousins Gaillard and Bernard, and their close kin, were part of the seigniorial clan of Montségur. The two men took part in the expedition to Avignonet in 1242, and defended the *pog* (hill) until the surrender in March 1244. After the crusaders captured Puivert, the castle was entrusted to Montfort's companions, Lambert of Thury and then Thomas Pons of Bruyères, one of whose descendants, Thomas II, transformed the castle of Congost after marrying Isabeau of Melun in 1310. Through matrimonial alliances, the fief passed into the hands of the Voisins and then the Joyeuses. The door opening in the east tower of Puivert provides access to the lower courtyard, surrounded by curtains and overlooked by the keep's mass with its thirty-two metre height. Entrance to the keep was on the second floor, through a door topped with two shields carved with the arms of the Bruyères and the Meluns. The Musicians Hall occupies the top level of the keep. The ribs of the vault rest on eight sculpted brackets showing musicians playing instruments of the period: bagpipes, vielle, tambourine, a portable organ, rebec, psaltery and guiterne. These instruments, as well as the mouldings on the brackets, are exhibited in the Instrumentarium Room of the Quercorb Museum in Puivert village.

Puivert Castle

Guiterne player, bracket in Musicians Room in Puivert

Raymond of Termes negotiated his surrender with Guy of Lévis. He agreed to hand over his fortress if it was going to be returned to him at Easter, 1211, and if he could keep the rest of his properties. Montfort, who could see the number of his soldiers decreasing daily as the forty-day obligations ended, accepted. Raymond of Termes promised to hand his castle over the next day. But during that night, a storm and torrential rains filled all the castle's cisterns. In the morning, Guy of Lévis arrived at the castle gate but the lord of Termes broke his promise. The Bishop of Chartres, one of the rare prelates who had stayed with Montfort, advised him to appoint the Bishop of Carcassonne as an assistant to his marshal. The two men were received by Raymond of Termes who maintained his position, and refused to let the bishop talk to his brother, Guillaume of Roquefort, and his mother. The siege continued. But the net was loosening, despite the arrival of crusaders from Lorraine. Autumn arrived and the November weather was terrible. During the night of the 22nd to the 23rd of November, the crusaders' sentries detected movement around the castle. Its occupants were beginning to abandon it because the polluted water in the cisterns had made the entire garrison ill. Worn out by dysentery, the defenders had placed the women and children in safety in the keep, and saw flight as the only possibility of safety. Some managed to get away, like Guillaume of Roquefort; others, including Raymond of Termes, were captured when, according to the *Canso*, he returned to get something he had forgotten. The lord of Termes ended his days in a jail in Carcassonne, where he died in 1213. Montfort left Termes and moved westwards. He found the castle of Coustaussa abandoned. Next, Bernard Sermon, a known Cathar believer, surrendered his castle of Albedun. Montfort crossed the Aude River, entered the Quercorb, and captured Puivert after a siege lasting three days. He entrusted that seigniory to Lambert of Thury. He then moved northwards, retaking Castres and Lombers. By the end of the year 1210, one single important site of the former viscounty of Trencavel had not fallen –Cabaret. But the crusaders settled in for the winter…

Vault in Puivert Castle

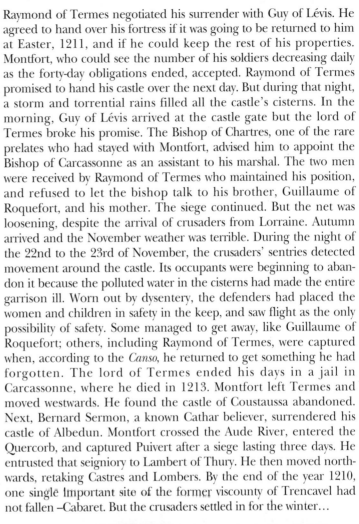

Coustaussa Castle

Albedun

Vestiges of Minerve's ramparts

ABOUT RAYMOND VI

....

T he portrait of Raymond VI
  drawn by Pierre of Les Vaux
de Cernay was not flattering.
The author repeated the grievances
about Peace and Faith that had led
to sanctions against the count but
he also described the count as "a
receptacle of iniquities", a depraved
man who probably abused his own
sister, and who, as an adolescent,
had taken advantage of the charms
of his father's mistresses. Of course,
this chess-player liked women and
there is no doubt that this tolerant
man mixed with heretics, as did his
people. An investigation made in
1247 at the request of Raymond VII
would shine a much more favourable
light on the personality of his late
father, the Count of Toulouse. One
hundred and ten witnesses, mostly
clerics, were heard by commissioners
named by Pope Innocent IV. They
said that Raymond VI had been the
benefactor of many abbeys and
churches, that he was devout, he
fasted and practiced charity, that
he advanced the construction of
the new Saint Stephen's Cathedral
in Toulouse. A chronicler was to
write about him: "There was
nothing mediocre about Raymond,
[...] his soul was noble, his ability
great; he possessed the art of
keeping his neighbours attached to
his interests; adversity never
overcame him; it appeared that
fortune made him greater as it
persecuted him more..."

A Humiliated Prince

After the surrender of Minerve, Arnaud and Thierry gave themselves up to Saint Gilles, as planned. Pope Innocent III's instructions were clear. Although the council before which Raymond VI appeared in August 1210 might acquit the Count of Toulouse, the pontiff reserved the right to condemn him. But, using a rather free interpretation of the Holy See's instructions, the council confirmed the excommunication that had been pronounced against Raymond of Saint Gilles in Avignon in 1209. In the *Canso*, William of Tudela remarked that the count "weighed down like a serf under a bundle of thorns and riding hunched over, returned home." The legates explained to the pope that the council's decision had been motivated by the fact that no trust could be given to the oath of a man who had fulfilled none of the engagements promised at Saint Gilles in June 1209. On November 17, 1210, Innocent wrote to Raymond VI. He reproached him with not having fulfilled his promises in the struggle against heresy and reminded him of the threat of having his properties offered "as spoils". He did not however confirm the measures taken by the Saint Gilles council. On the same date, he wrote once again to Raymond VI but also to the Counts of Foix and Comminges as well as to the Viscount of Béarn, to invite them to provide help to Simon de Montfort; otherwise, they would be considered as abettors of heresy. A few weeks later, as Christmas was nearing,

The seal of Raymond VI

Raymond VI met Simon de Montfort in Ambialet on the banks of the Tarn River, upstream from Albi. Some of the knights in the count's entourage behaved suspiciously and the crusade's leader had some misgivings. Had they planned to kidnap him? But the matter was dropped.

The two men met again in Narbonne at the end of January 1211. They had been summoned, along with Pedro II and Raymond-Roger of Foix, by Arnaud-Amaury who was accompanied by Tedisio and a new legate, Raymond, Bishop of Uzès. After a new refusal, the King of Aragon finally accepted Montfort's homage for the vis-county of Carcassonne. Arnaud-Amaury made new proposals to Raymond VI, described by Pierre of Les Vaux de Cernay as "a great favour and mercy". If he expelled the heretics from his lands, the count would retain all his properties. Over the heretical localities of his fief, he would maintain the rights of lodging, of armed service from his vassals, and of direct taxation, and for those not in his fief, a third or a quarter of them would be attached to his domains. The conference then moved to Montpellier on January 27th. The establishment of good relations between Pedro II and Montfort in Narbonne was sealed by the promise of marriage between James, Pedro's two and a half year-old son, and Montfort's barely older daughter, Amicie. The king entrusted the crusader chief with the upbringing of the son who was to become James the Conqueror. However, the king set conditions on his new vassal. Montfort was to limit his conquests to the Trencavels' former domains, leave the Count of Foix in peace and return what had been taken from him, except for Pamiers. Two months later, in Montpellier, in agreement with the Millau accords of 1205, Sancia, the King of Aragon's sister, married Raymond the Young, son of the Count of Toulouse. Committments between Raymond VI and Pedro II had been honoured and strengthened their family ties. During the Montpellier conference, in a charter he handed to him, Arnaud-Amaury reminded the Count of Toulouse of the promises he had made in Saint Gilles in June, 1209. He furthermore compelled him to go to the Holy Land, to serve in the Templar or the Hospitaller Order and to stay as long as the ecclesiastical authorities decided; his vassals were to deliver or demolish their castles before settling in the countryside "like villeins". This was too much, and, after reading the charter to Pedro II, a flustered Raymond VI left Montpellier immediately. His response was obvious. As was the sanction pronounced on February 6, 1211: he was once again excommunicated by the legates, who sent the abbot of Saint Ruf to Innocent III to have the pope confirm their decision. The pope did so on April 15, 1211. From then on, the Count of Toulouse was no longer a crusader and his lands could be seized as spoils. He returned to Toulouse and went on to Montauban, Moissac and Agen. He informed all who listened –clerics, consuls, knights, burghers– of the charter's contents. His indignation was shared by all and a profound feeling of revolt was born. Raymond called on his vassals and on neighbouring lords: the Counts of Foix and Comminges, the Viscount of Béarn, and Savary of Mauléon, Seneschal of the King of England. It was war.

Rights and Taxes

Albergue

Right of lodging due to the lord.

Ban

Right of commanding and punishing. The term also refers to all a lord's vassals, who were capable of bearing arms. Hence the terms *"lever le ban* and *l'arrière-ban"* was the mustering of all these vassals, and the vavasour, the vassals of the vassals.

Banalities

The obligation of using a means of production belonging to the lord, such as an oven, mill or press, in return for a fee.

Chevauchée (or Cavalcade)

Armed service due by the vassal to his lord, beyond the seigniory of the lord.

Host (or Ost)

Armed service for forty days due the lord by his vassal. The term also designates the army made up of all the vassals carrying out this service.

Peage (or Pedage)

Right levied by lords for the use of roads or rivers or bridges, the payment was intended for maintenance and to guarantee the user's safety.

Queste

A direct tax levied by the lord on the villeins of his fief.

Tallage

A direct tax levied by the lord while exercising his right of ban.

Tithe

Levying of one-tenth of a harvest or the value of the harvest for the benefit of the Church. Applied to all laymen, it could be paid in kind or in money.

East ramparts in Carcassonne

THE BLACKS AND WHITES

······································

The White Confraternity that came to help the crusaders in Lavaur in the spring of 1211 had been formed in Toulouse by Foulque to aid in the struggle against heresy and also to curb abuses by usurers. Recruitment for this militia, which was favourable to the crusade, was mainly carried out among the inhabitants of the city. Those of the suburb soon reacted by forming a Black Confraternity, hostile to the crusade and favourable to Raymond VI. "Between the two groups there were frequent battles, with weapons, standards and equipped horses," wrote Guillaume of Puylaurens.

At the Gates of Toulouse

At the beginning of the year 1211, Foulque went to France to preach the crusade. This was not much appreciated by Philip Augustus, who wrote to the pope. By mid-March, Foulque's appeal had been heard and many crusaders, including Robert of Courtenay and the Count of Nevers, already present in 1209, gathered in Carcassonne. The decision to besiege Cabaret was taken. It was then that Bouchard of Marly arrived, after having been kept prisoner for a year and a half by Pierre-Roger of Cabaret and freed in order to negotiate the latter's surrender. The author of the *Canso* related that the lord had treated his prisoner particularly well since he "dressed him nobly, offered him the finest palfrey on his lands and put three dashing pages at his service." Hence Montfort became the master of the principal seigniory of the Montagne Noire without a fight and, in compensation, he ceded Pierre-Roger lands in the Béziers area. The crusaders changed their target and moved towards Lavaur, on the banks of the Agout River, and besieged it. Lavaur, a fief of Dame Guiraude, a well-known heretic and the sister of Aimery of Montréal, contained a large number of perfects, some of whom had come from Cabaret after Pierre-Roger's surrender. Lavaur was also the refuge of many *faydits*. There were thus eighty knights at the side of Aimery. In order to lend the crusaders a helping hand, Foulque's White Confraternity had mobilized five thousand volunteers. As they approached Lavaur, the besieged at first were overjoyed, taking them for the Count of Toulouse's men. A short time later, Raymond VI arrived with several knights to help Lavaur's defenders. These knights, led by the seneschal Raymond of Ricaud, were able to enter the town while the count went to negotiate with Simon de Montfort. The crusader chief received new crusader reinforcements led by the bishops of Bayeux and Lisieux, the counts of Châlons and Auxerre. Others were supposed to join them. Indeed, announcements were made of five thousand German and Frisian crusaders. On their way from Carcassonne, they were

St Alain's Cathedral, Lavaur

Montgey

attacked at the foot of Montgey Castle by Raymond-Roger of Foix, his son Roger-Bernard, and Guiraud of Pépieux, at the head of their troops and a corps of *routiers*. They were all massacred. The siege of Lavaur, during which Roger of Comminges came to pay homage to Simon de Montfort, continued. It had been going on for over a month. The crusaders managed to advance a "cat" as far as the foot of the ramparts. The sappers dug a breach in the wall. Lavaur fell on May 3rd. Dame Guiraude was thrown alive into a well and then stoned to death. Aimery and the *faydits* were supposed to be hanged but the first to be punished was the Lord of Montréal. The weight of this colossus made the gallows collapse. Since there was not enough time to build another one, the others had their throats cut. The perfects, between three and four hundred of them according to the sources, were led to the stake. As for Raymond of Ricaud's Toulousains, they were simply taken prisoner. The *castrum* was looted. The large amount of booty was entrusted to Raymond of Salvanhac, a *Cahorsin* who was managing the crusade's finances.

The crusade set off once again. The abandoned castle of Montgey was razed. Puylaurens, which surrendered, was entrusted to Guy of Lucy. The *castrum* of Les Cassès belonging to the lords of Roqueville, whose mother was a perfect, did not resist for long. Its defenders' lives were saved but the sixty perfects, who had sought refuge in a tower, perished at the stake. Raymond VI began to react. Les Cassès lay on his lands. He knew that Castelnaudary was a strategic location, but its site was difficult to defend. He therefore had it evacuated before setting it on fire. He then drew back to the castle of Montferrand, which controlled the watershed of Naurouze, and entrusted it to his brother, Baudouin. Montfort besieged Montferrand. Surrounded by fourteen knights and several men at arms and despite the castle's mediocre defences, Baudouin fought gallantly but finally surrendered and went over to the crusade. Raymond VI would never forgive him for this treachery. After placing a garrison in Castelnaudary and raising its walls, Montfort and his men went on campaign in the Albigeois at the

The Auvezines stele

THE SINEWS OF WAR

In the Middle Ages, the term *Cahorsin*, sometimes with a pejorative meaning, referred to bankers, or even usurers, since a number of businessmen from Cahors took part in these lucrative activities. Starting in 1210, a *Cahorsin* named Raymond of Salvanhac was the crusade's financier. After the capture of Minerve, Simon de Montfort ceded to him the seigniories of Pézenas and Tourves as payment for his services.

Puylaurens Castle

Fortified gate in Montferrand

beginning of June. Rabastens, Montégut and Gaillac in the Tarn River valley submitted without a fight, and were followed by Cahuzac, Saint Marcel and Laguépie at the confluence of the Viaur and the Aveyron. The host followed the Aveyron River to Saint Antonin Noble Val, which also surrendered. The Count of Toulouse was at Bruniquel. Baudouin intervened. He suggested to the knights in Bruniquel to transfer the homage they owed to his brother to him and that he would take them under his protection. Curiously, Raymond VI agreed to free the knights from their oath and immediately left for Toulouse, certainly the next target for the crusade. Baudouin settled in Bruniquel and welcomed William of Tudela, the author of the first part of the *Canso*. The crusaders followed the Vère valley and occupied Puycelci. They next moved south to Montgiscard, on the banks of the Hers, where on June 15 they received reinforcements led by Thibaud, Count of Bar. Toulouse was threatened. The city's consuls sent a delegation to the crusaders' camp where Arnaud-Amaury and Foulque set their conditions. If the inhabitants of Toulouse repudiated their count and swore homage to Montfort, the city would be spared. The consuls refused, not wanting to weaken a county power that guaranteed their municipal liberties which had been so difficult to obtain. They were also confident that the city would be able to defend itself. Foulque then laid an interdiction on Toulouse and asked all the clergy to leave, taking the holy sacraments with them. Raymond VI attempted a sortie to destroy the bridge of Montaudran but was opposed by strong resistance from the crusaders. His illegitimate son, Bertrand, was taken prisoner during this skirmish and was freed for a ransom payment. On the morning of June 17th, the crusaders were at Toulouse. The ring of ramparts, with its fifty towers, was over five kilometres long. Behind the ramparts, many knights, including the Count of Foix, and the entire population stood together to defend the city. It was not going to be easy for the crusaders whose numbers were not very high. During the siege Montfort, with the legates Arnaud-Amaury, Tedisio and Raymond of Uzès at his side, received homage from the bishop and lord of Cahors, Guillaume of Cardaillac, who thus removed himself from the sovereignty of Raymond VI. The next to visit the crusade's military chief were the abbot of Saint Antonin of Fredelas, a monk from Grandselve and another from Obazine, Dominic of Caleruega. But there was conflict among the crusaders: the Count of Bar in favour of opening discussions with Raymond VI was opposed by Arnaud-Amaury. Furthermore, supplies were irregular because the convoys were attacked regularly. And finally, on June 27, Hugues of Alfaro, Raymond VI's son-in-law, destroyed the crusaders' camp. The next day the siege was lifted. In the month of July, the consuls wrote to the King of Aragon to comment on what had happened and request his help. This letter is the only source about the discussions that preceded the siege between consuls and crusaders, an episode that is not mentioned by the chroniclers. We learn that, after the fall of Montferrand and Bruniquel, the count had twice, but in vain, proposed surrendering to Montfort in return for a guarantee that he and his heirs would not lose their fiefs.

Window in Bruniquel Castle

AN ILL-LOVED BROTHER

Baudouin was the last child of Raymond V of Toulouse and Constance, sister of Louis VIII, King of France. He was thus the younger brother of Raymond VI. His parents had separated in 1165, shortly before his birth, so he was born at the French court. At the death of Raymond V, he returned to the County of Toulouse and had a hard time having his rights recognized. He even had to return to France to obtain evidence that proved to Raymond VI that he was his brother. But Baudouin received neither *apanage* nor seigniory, despite his great victory over the Lord of Baux in the conflict opposing the latter and the House of Toulouse over the possession of Marseille. In the will written by Raymond VI in September 1209, before going to visit the King of France and the emperor, he had planned to entrust the guardianship of his eldest son to Baudouin, to leave him some property and to pay him an annuity of one thousand Melgorian sous. But the wound could not be healed so easily.

Bruniquel Castle

On All Fronts

From Toulouse, Montfort rode towards the lands of the Count of Foix. He left a garrison in Auterive, but a band of *routiers* invited by the inhabitants attacked it. Montfort passed through Pamiers, of which he was co-lord and then, a short distance before Foix, he left his men in Varilhes which he had found abandoned and burnt. He destroyed vineyards and orchards near the Count of Foix's castle, of which he burnt one of the outskirts, and although he avoided that castle, he ruined others. He returned to Pamiers where the Bishop of Cahors, now his vassal, asked him to come to Quercy to have his rights confirmed. Montfort therefore went northwards, in the direction of Cahors, attacking Caylus in passing and setting a few houses on fire. In Cahors, he received homage from the most important lords of Quercy: Bertrand of Cardaillac, Bertrand of Gourdon and Ratier of Castelnau. The last two had taken part in the Quercy crusade in June 1209. Leaving Arnaud-Amaury in Cahors, Montfort, with several German crusaders who were going home, made a pilgrimage to Our Lady of Rocamadour, where he left Robert Mauvoisin, and went to recruit new crusaders in France. On his way back south, Simon went through Cahors and, accompanied by Arnaud-Amaury and Baudouin, went back towards Carcassonne via Saint Antonin and Gaillac, where he learned that Lambert of Thury and Gautier Langton, whom he had left in Pamiers, were held prisoner by the Count of Foix. He immediately

The Valentré Bridge in Cahors

THE VALENTRÉ BRIDGE

Construction of this bridge, a fine example of medieval military architecture, that spans the Lot River in Cahors was undertaken only in 1308, or nearly a century after Montfort had received homage from Quercy's lords in the city. According to legend, the architect called on the Devil to help finish the bridge but avoided going to hell by sending his assistant to bring water in a sieve, which of course the poor devil could not fill.

Rocamadour

St Peter's Abbey Church in Gaillac

ROCAMADOUR

In the heart of Gramat causse, the village, shrines and castle of Rocamadour cling to the sides of the steep, rocky cliff on the edge of the narrow valley of the Alzou. During Christianity's early years, a hermit retired to this solitude. This lover of the rock, an *amadour* of the rock, gave this name to a primitive shrine dedicated to Our Lady, the site of a pilgrimage that developed under the impetus of Eble, abbot of the Cistercian monastery in Tulle, supported by his brother, the Viscount of Turenne. In 1166, a dying believer expressed a wish to be buried near Our Lady's Chapel. When the tomb was being dug, an intact corpse was discovered and recognized as being that of Amadour. He was rapidly assimilated into Zacheus, the Virgin's servant and the husband of Veronica, with whom he allegedly landed on the coast of Médoc, before retiring to the Quercy causse. The ever more numerous pilgrims, some of whom were bound for Santiago de Compostela, used to come to honour the relics of the saintly founder of the shrine and to pray to the Virgin, whose miracles were collected in 1172 as one hundred and twenty-six tales in *The Book of Miracles of Our Lady of Rocamadour*. Bernard of Clairvaux came to Rocamadour in 1147, Henry II Plantagenet and Thomas à Becket in 1159. During the summer of 1211, Simon de Montfort, passing through Cahors, naturally came to Rocamadour, fifteen leagues north of the city on the banks of the Lot. According to the chronicle of Trois Fontaines Abbey, it was the standard bearing the effigy of Our Lady of Rocamadour that, in the following year, 1212, led the Christian troops to victory over Miramamolin's Almohads at Las Navas de Tolosa in Spain. Louis IX and his mother, Blanche of Castile, made the pilgrimage to Rocamadour in 1244.

A knight

went to their rescue, on his way capturing a castle and slaughtering the garrison except for three knights retained as bargaining chips to free his two companions. He arrived in Pamiers and learned that the inhabitants of Puylaurens, a place he had entrusted to Guy of Lucy, had revolted after the latter's departure to join the Catholic armies in Spain, and had recalled Sicard, their former lord. Back in Carcassonne at the end of September 1211, Montfort was informed that his enemies had made up a powerful army and were preparing to march on Castelnaudary. On the advice of Hugues of Lacy, Montfort immediately went there. The Occitan coalition consisted of Raymond VI of Toulouse, Raymond-Roger of Foix, Bernard IV of Comminges, Gaston VI of Béarn and Savary of Mauléon. Towns like Montauban, Moissac and Castelsarrasin had sent men to join the troops of the four great southern lords. The Occitans, "covering the ground like locusts", we are told by Pierre of Les Vaux de Cernay, set up camp on the Pech, a hill facing Castelnaudary, whose garrison had received reinforcements from Montferrand.

Castelnaudary

A PERFECT KNIGHT'S EQUIPMENT

Wearing a helmet on his head, the top of his body covered by a hauberk or a coat of mail, his hands and feet protected by iron gauntlets and chausses, the knight warded off blows with his shield. His most distinctive weapon was the lance but he also carried one or two swords, the longest of which was attached to his saddle. All this equipment was bulky and heavy, so when he went to war the knight had three mounts: the destrier, a heavy war-horse; a palfrey for transportation; and a pack-horse. In the camp and on the battlefield, he was helped by his squire and two or three valets, the team being known as an *écu*. The knight proudly wore his colours on his surcoat, a cloth tunic covering his coat of mail, on his shield and on the banner attached to his lance. He was thus identified and could identify his adversaries. During battle, the knight looked for one-on-one combat, and as in tournaments, he liked to break lances. He therefore did not much appreciate crossbows whose use spread in the early 13th century. This defensive weapon, heavy and difficult to set, killed anonymously from a distance.

They bombarded Castelnaudary, but it was not besieged since the defenders were able to go out and harvest the grapes. Montfort called back all crusading knights scattered throughout the area. Bouchard of Marly and one hundred horsemen, accompanied by Martin Algai, Lord of Biron, arrived from Lavaur. But the Lauragais was in turmoil: Avignonet, Montferrand, Les Cassès, Saint Felix and other localities had freed themselves from the crusaders' yoke. In order to reach Castelnaudary, Bouchard's troops had to pass through Castres and cross the Montagne Noire and get back to the lowlands through Saissac. The Count of Foix and a contingent of his men went to Saint Martin Lalande, a few kilometres east of Castelnaudary, to attack Bouchard of Marly's group. But Montfort foresaw the manoeuvre and sent about forty horsemen as reinforcements. Bouchard's crusaders, outnumbered thirty to one according to Pierre of Les Vaux de Cernay, had a hard time resisting the Count of Foix's attack. Some like Martin of Algai even ran

The Orant Stele in Cassès

LIKE A PRAYER

Stele have been found in Carcassès and the Lauragais. The village of Cassès maintains a collection of stele that are mainly disc-shaped, engraved with the Cross of Toulouse, pictures of weapons or other symbols. One of them is sculpted in high-relief with a strange person who seems to be praying, l'*orant*. A stele stands near Fanjeaux. Another, from Baraigne, presented in the Petiet Museum in Limoux, shows a weaver's loom. One at Labarthe Castle shows Christ as a living cross. Some people mistakenly wished to see Cathar or even Bogomil symbols when, in fact, they present very common Christian themes.

The Fanjeaux Cross

Labarthe Stele

away. Montfort then came from Castelnaudary with sixty knights, took the Occitans from the rear and routed them. The other southern lords had not moved. They struck camp and burnt their war machines. However, the Occitans claimed victory and made it known. On hearing the news, over fifty castles, *castra* or villages rallied to Raymond VI, including Gaillac, Cahuzac, Saint Marcel, Laguépie and Saint Antonin, despite Baudouin's intervention, especially at Lagrave, to try and prevent these defections.

In France, since the summer Foulque and Guy of Les Vaux de Cernay had been preaching to encourage other lords to take up the cross and it finally bore fruit. At the beginning of December, Robert Mauvoisin was able to return to Languedoc with about one hundred horsemen. By this end of the year, Montfort had to face several minor problems. He freed Quié, besieged by the Count of Foix, took back La Pomarède and went to make sure of the doubtful loyalty of Bernard Sermon, Lord of Albedun in the Haut Razès.

La Pomarède Tower

GUY OF LES VAUX DE CERNAY

G uy of Les Vaux de Cernay
was mentioned for the first
time in 1181 as being the head
of the Cistercian abbey in Yvelines
Forest, near the lands of the
Montforts. At the request of
Innocent III, he took part in
preparing the fourth crusade and
in 1202, before Zara, he tried to
prevent the crusaders from
capturing the city for the
Venetians. After their return from
the Holy Land in 1204, Guy
maintained close relations with his
abbey's neighbouring lords, the
future crusaders of 1209: Simon
de Montfort, Simon of Neauphle
and Robert Mauvoisin. After a
first journey to Languedoc in
1207, when he accompanied
Arnaud-Amaury and other
Cistercians to participate in holy
preaching, he returned there in
November 1209, at Innocent III's
request, to support Montfort.
From 1210 to 1215, he dedicated
himself to preaching the
Albigensian crusade. Named
Bishop of Carcassonne in 1212, he
died in his bishopric in 1224. He
did however often return to his
favoured abbey. In 1226, Thibaud,
the son of Bouchard of Marly, one
of Montfort's loyal companions,
entered Les Vaux de Cernay and
became its abbot in 1235. Thibaud
was canonized.

In Castres, where he celebrated Christmas, he was joined by his
brother Guy returning from the Holy Land, accompanied by his
wife, Heloise of Ibelin. At the end of the winter, Montfort started
his endless cavalcade throughout his viscounty to impose his domination over these lands. He first moved in the Albigeois, where he
played hide-and-seek with the counts of Toulouse, Foix and
Comminges. He successively captured les Touelles, today's
Briatexte, putting its inhabitants to the sword, then Cahuzac,
Gaillac, Montégut and Rabastens. In Saint Marcel the siege lasted a
month. The place was defended by Guiraud of Pépieux supported
by three southern counts accompanied by five hundred knights.
Montfort finally gave up. On March 23, 1212, he was in Albi where
he met with Arnaud-Amaury, who had been named Archbishop of
Narbonne in the place of Berenger, and Guy of Les Vaux de
Cernay, the appointed successor of Bernard-Raymond of Roquefort
at the head of the bishopric of Carcassonne. Guy was accompanied
by his nephew, Pierre, a monk in the same Cistercian abbey, who
became the crusade's invaluable chronicler. Montfort returned to
Castres and then undertook the siege of Hautpoul, deserted four
days later by its defenders who disappeared in thick fog. On May 2
in Narbonne, ceremonies consecrating the new Archbishop of
Narbonne and the new Bishop of Carcassonne took place. Arnaud-
Amaury awarded himself the Duchy of Narbonne at the same time
and hence received the homage of Viscount Aimery, ignoring the
rights of Raymond VI and Montfort's opinion. Three weeks later,

Les Vaux de Cernay Abbey

THE CHRONICLERS OF THE ALBIGENSIAN CRUSADE

Three great medieval texts relate episodes from the Albigensian Crusade: The *Song of the Albigensian Crusade* or *Canso de la Crosada*, *Albigensian History* by Pierre of Les Vaux de Cernay, and finally, the *Chronicle* of Guillaume of Puylaurens. Each of these three works shines a distinct light on the facts. The *Canso de la Crosada* is a chanson de geste of 9,578 lines. Only a single manuscript of this poem written in *langue d'oc* has been preserved. The *Canso* narrates the events of the crusade from the invasion of the Midi by the crusaders and follows them until the day after the death of Simon de Montfort (1218), with the arrival of Philip Augustus' son, the future King of France Louis VIII, before the walls of Toulouse. Under the single title, the *Canso* in fact consists of the work of two different authors. The first, William of Tudela, composed the first 130 couplets. He stopped at the moment that Pedro II of Aragon was preparing to enter the war against Simon de Montfort (early 1213). The second poet wrote the following 83 couplets. A cleric originally from Tudela in Navarre, William crossed the Pyrenees in about 1199. A troubadour, he settled in Montauban where, in 1210, he began to write his work and completed it as events took place. Towards 1212, the situation in Montauban became threatening. William decided to go to Bruniquel, a seigniory belonging to Baudouin, the brother of the Count of Toulouse but who had crossed over to the crusaders' side. And when, in May 1212, Simon de Montfort entrusted Saint Antonin to Baudouin, William was named the locality's canon. Although he did not possess the literary talent of his successor, William was a well-informed and trustworthy chronicler. Though

favourable to the crusaders and happy about their victories, he nonetheless expressed his compassion for the victims of Béziers or Lavaur, and his sadness about the war's destructive fury. William stopped writing in early 1214. Did he follow Baudouin to Lolmie and was he kidnapped and hanged like his master? Was his manuscript taken by the Toulouse fighters as war booty? In any case, his quill passed into the hands of a new poet, strongly anti-clerical even though he was a Catholic, and a sworn adversary of the French. Remaining anonymous, he related the great episodes of the period 1213-1218: the battle of Muret, the Lateran Council, the siege and capture of Beaucaire by the young count, Toulouse's revolt against Simon de Montfort, and the battle of Baziège. His vibrant, passionate work, with its style on occasion eloquent or else cutting, displayed great purity of language and unquestionable poetic qualities. Beside the Occitan *Canso*, appeared two Latin chronicles, the *Historia Albigensis* by Pierre of Les Vaux de Cernay and the *Chronicle* of Guillaume of Puylaurens. A monk in the Cistercian abbey of Les Vaux de Cernay, near Paris, Pierre was the nephew of the abbot Guy, who had been in charge of Les Vaux since 1181. He took part in the fourth crusade (1202-1204) and then joined his uncle, who had become Bishop of Carcassonne in 1212, in Languedoc. He followed the military operations of 1212, attended the Parliament in Pamiers and the Lavaur Council in January 1213. Returning north with his uncle a short while later, Pierre did not witness the battle of Muret. In April 1214, he rejoined Simon de Montfort at Saint Thibéry and followed the army to the Agenais and Rouergue. He was

at the side of Prince Louis in 1215. In 1216, he attended the siege of Beaucaire and the revolt in Toulouse. His trace is lost after 1218, when he returned to the north. Very well-informed, he had access to archives (pontifical and council notes…). He was perhaps the official historiographer of the crusade. The first version of his *Historia*, finished at the beginning of 1213, contained a preface dedicated to Pope Innocent III. It was completed by two continuations written as the events happened. The overall plan was in three parts: the Cathar heresy, the Roman Catholic Church's preaching, and the crusade. Pierre heaped praise on the crusaders, come to rid Christendom of Satan's henchmen represented by the heretics and their protectors. Despite his excesses, he remained accurate and lucid about the weaknesses of his own side (rivalry between the Duke of Burgundy and the Count of Nevers, the duplicity and indiscipline of the army…). As for Guillaume of Puylaurens, probably starting in 1249, he wrote a short chronicle devoted to the crusade and the annexation of the County of Toulouse to the French crown. Born just after 1200, Guillaume studied in Toulouse. About 1228-1230, he entered into the service of Bishop Foulque, then of his successor Raymond of Le Fauga, whom he accompanied as a notary to Provence in 1241. In 1237-1240, Guillaume received the cure of Puylaurens (Tarn, diocese of Toulouse). Writing in a more moderate tone than Pierre of Les Vaux de Cernay, Guillaume might have consulted the latter's work. He also used obituaries (books of the dead), official texts and also his own youthful memories. His namesake was the chaplain of Count Raymond VII.

Façade detail on the Wolves' House in Caylus

Biron Castle

on May 22, Arnaud-Amaury accompanied by three hundred horsemen left for Toledo, Spain, where the Catholic armies were regrouping before their confrontation with the Almohads at Las Navas de Tolosa on July 16. In the meantime, Montfort recaptured a great number of the localities in the Lauragais that he had lost during the autumn of 1211: Cuq, Montmaur, Saint Felix, Les Cassès, Montferrand, Avignonet. In Puylaurens, the Count of Toulouse had settled in with a corps of *routiers*, but at the approach of the crusaders he and the inhabitants fled to Toulouse. So many volunteer crusaders were arriving that Montfort charged his brother Guy, and Guy of Lévis, to make them into a second army corps. The leader of the crusade finished recapturing the Albigeois and started on Quercy. The towns fell one after the other: Rabastens, Montégut, Gaillac, Lagarde, Puycelci; Saint Marcel abandoned by Guiraud of Pépieux was burnt down, as was Laguépie. On May 20, Saint Antonin Noble Val was besieged; it resisted but then surrendered. Its lords Adhemar and Pons Jourdain were imprisoned in Carcassonne. The town was ceded to Baudouin. During the siege Montfort had received a letter from the Bishop of Agen asking him to come. On his way, he retook Caylus and found Montcuq abandoned. Its bailiff had entrenched himself with Hugues of Alfaro and four hundred men in Penne d'Agenais. On June 3, Simon left his army in front of Penne's walls to go on to Agen, where he became co-lord of the city and received the oath of its inhabitants. He returned to Penne where he was joined by the second crusader corps led by his brother Guy, which had captured Lavelanet in the meantime. On July 17, Robert Mauvoisin left Penne to take Marmande. A week later, Hugues of Alfaro negotiated his surrender in exchange for freedom for himself and his men. Having received new reinforcements led by the Archbishop of Reims the following day, Montfort put a garrison in Penne. With some troops, he went to besiege the castle of Biron, the fief of Martin Algai, a former ally of the crusaders who had crossed over to the Occitan side. Montfort wanted to make him pay for this treachery. Martin Algai was delivered to the French by his own men. He was dragged through the crusaders' camp attached to a horse's tail before being hanged. After Montfort's return to Penne, Alix of Montmorency, Baudouin of Toulouse and Guy of Les Vaux de Cernay arrived with a new contingent of knights. The crusader army left Penne at the beginning of August. It moved in the direction of Moissac where it arrived on August 14. The previous day another three hundred men, essentially *routiers*, had arrived as reinforcements. The war machines were put in place. The siege lasted three weeks. While it was going on, Castelsarrasin, Verdun sur Garonne and Montech came to submit to Montfort. The captured nephew of the Archbishop of Reims was cut into pieces and the parts of his body were catapulted into the crusader camp by the defenders. The city finally surrendered. Montfort demanded that the *routiers* paid by Toulouse be handed over and had them all killed. He entered Moissac on September 8 and on the 14 signed an agreement with the abbot of Saint Peter's Abbey, later looted by the crusader army, by which he took the place of

Calatrava Castle

LAS NAVAS DE TOLOSA

I n early 1212, the Caliph al Nasir, alias Miramamolin, brought together 300,000 men in Sevilla. At the request of Alfonso VIII, King of Castile, Innocent III called for a crusade against the Almohads and granted those who agreed to take the cross their share of indulgences. At the end of May, the crusaders met in Toledo. There were 60,000 Castilians led by Alfonso VIII, 50,000 Aragonese behind Pedro II and 40,000 *Francos* accompanied by the bishops of Narbonne, Bordeaux and Nantes. The Archbishop of Narbonne, Arnaud-Amaury, had come from Languedoc with about a hundred knights. After the capture of Calatrava, the host received reinforcements from Sancho VII the Strong, King of Navarre, but many crusaders from the other side of the Pyrenees left, disappointed by Alfonso VIII's half-hearted attitude towards the Muslims and the distribution of booty. Arnaud-Amaury and his followers took part in the battle of Las Navas de Tolosa on July 16, 1212. While the battle was raging, Miramamolin was reading the Koran in his tent, surrounded by thousands of slaves chained together and armed with lances. Informed of his troops' defeat, he fled to Sevilla. Pedro II's contribution to this Christian victory, the beginning of the end of the Almohad kingdom, provided his name of Pedro the Catholic.

A MASTERPIECE SPARED

After the surrender of Moissac on September 8, 1212, the town and St Peter's Abbey were looted by the crusaders. A fire destroyed the upper sections of the cloister and the abbey church as well as convent buildings. Fortunately, the sculpture programme on the doorway of the abbey church and cloister were spared. The abbey's foundation, attributed to Clovis, was more likely the work of Didier, Bishop of Cahors from 630 to 655. It was destroyed by Moorish raids in 721 and 732, rebuilt, then once again ruined by Norman razzias in 850 and 864, and Hungarian ones in the 10th century. Odilon, the fourth abbot of Cluny, accepted the Benedictine establishment's affiliation with the Cluniac Order in 1047. Durand of Bredons, the first Cluniac abbot, undertook reconstruction of the abbey church, consecrated in 1063. His successor, Hunand of Gavarret, carried out important work in the cloister, whose sculptures were carved during the abbacy of Ansquitil (1085-1115). The sculptures on the doorway were begun during the same abbacy but finished under Roger, Ansquitil's successor, as was the steeple-porch. On the doorway's tympanum, the artists expressed their vision of St John's Apocalypse, watched by the procession of twenty-four old men. The piedroits hold up images of Saint Peter on the left, and Isaiah on the right, while, leaning on the central pier, Saint Paul and the extraordinary Jeremiah, with his simultaneously kind and serious face, turn their backs to each other. In the cloister, the sculptures are placed in bas-relief on the eight pillars supporting the galleries and on the column capitals. Intended for the monks, they express a cycle taken from the Old and the New Testaments, the Acts of the Apostles, John's Apocalypse but also from the lives of Saints Benedict, Martin, Sernin, Laurence, Augurus…

Jeremiah, detail on pier in St Peter's Abbey Church, Moissac

The cloister in Moissac Abbey Church

Raymond VI as the city's protector. After Moissac, Montfort decided not to take on Montauban, defended by Roger-Bernard, the son of the Count of Foix. Instead, he considered taking action in the Ariège River valley, a zone of contact and hence trade and communication between the counties of Toulouse and Foix. He therefore moved towards Pamiers and recaptured Saverdun, which the Counts of Foix and Toulouse had just left, and Auterive. From there he headed for Muret where the bishops of Comminges and the Couserans joined him and suggested that he go to Saint Gaudens to receive an oath from the local lords. From Saint Gaudens Montfort returned to Muret, but only after carrying out several destructive raids in the Couserans. On October 9, he received homage from Bernard-Jourdain, the lord of L'Isle Jourdain, before returning to Pamiers where he set up his winter quarters. The crusade's leader had reason to be satisfied at the end of 1212: he had conquered the entire county of Toulouse, where only the cities of Toulouse and Montauban still held out. However, in reality, the situation was not that simple and Montfort wanted to provide a new legal framework for his possessions. In Pamiers, he called a parliament composed of his principal companions-at-arms and vassals, the Archbishop of Bordeaux and seven bishops. The parliament named a twelve-member committee charged with writing new statutes for the conquered territories. It consisted of the bishops of Toulouse and the Couserans, a Templar and a Hospitaller, four French knights, two lords and two local burghers. The statutes, issued on December 1, 1212, consisted of forty-six articles concerning religious, political, military, social and fiscal matters. Although they were clearly aimed at eradicating heresy, they were also intended to reinforce the power of the French in Languedoc. The articles opened with a preamble in which the formula *Ad abolendam haereticorum pravitatem* from the Verona decretal was repeated. A convention was added specifying that "successions will be made according to custom and usage in France around Paris."

Steeples of Notre Dame du Camp, the Cathedral and the Cordeliers, Pamiers

The Statutes of Pamiers

Regarding Religion

- Restoration of first-fruits and tithes.
- Respect of immunity of clerics and churches.
- Destruction of fortified churches.
- Obligation of creating places of worship where there had been heretics' houses.
- Any person declared a heretic to be expelled. Whoever does not do so loses his land and his person is placed at the disposal of Simon de Montfort. A heretic, even if reconciled with the Church, cannot hold a position in the magistracy.
- Obligation of attending mass on Sundays, a day when fairs and markets will be forbidden.

Regarding Politics and the Military

- It is forbidden to supply Toulouse.
- Creation of a permanent army corps under the orders of Simon de Montfort and, for a period of twenty years, composed exclusively of non-local knights. Mobilization should be completed within two weeks.
- It is forbidden to restore works destroyed by Simon de Montfort without his authorization.

Regarding Social Matters

- It is forbidden for young women and widows to marry locals without previous authorization by Simon de Montfort.
- Prohibition of private prosecution.
- It is forbidden to create leagues and associations without Simon de Montfort's authorization.
- Expulsion of prostitutes from towns to the countryside.

Regarding fiscal matters

- A tax of three Melgorian *deniers* per household in aid of the Church.
- It is forbidden for Simon de Montfort's vassals to increase tallage without his authorization.
- Suppression of tolls put in place over the past thirty-four years.
- Regulation of transmission and collection of quit-rents.

THE COUNTY OF COMMINGES

In the 10th century, Count Arnaud of Carcassonne possessed the counties of Carcassonne, Razès, Comminges and the Couserans. At his death, one third of the county of Comminges, mentioned for the first time in 980, and the Couserans went to his son Roger, Count of Carcassonne, and the other two-thirds to Raymond of Rouergue, a cousin of the Count of Toulouse. At the beginning of the 12th century, through alliances and conventions, the two parts of the county were reunited. In 1130, the County of Couserans, until then attached to the County of Foix, became part of Comminges, which then consisted of the Garonne valley from Muret to the Val d'Aran, as well as the Couserans. The Count of Comminges recognized no lord as being superior. Hence, during the war opposing Aragon and the House of Toulouse from 1179 to 1185, he did not enter the coalition against the latter that included the Lord of Montpellier, Trencavel, the Viscount of Narbonne, the Count of Foix, the Viscounts of Béarn and Bigorre. The county of Comminges had privileged relations with Toulouse, strengthened by the marriage of Alphonse-Jourdain's daughter and the future Bernard III of Comminges. In 1244, Bernard VI, while paying homage to Raymond VII, recognized holding his domains from the Count of Toulouse and solemnly declared that the lands of the Comminges and Couserans dioceses had never been held as fiefs by his family and that they had always been allodial. In about 1120, Bertrand of L'Isle Jourdain, Bishop of Comminges, had built Saint Mary's Cathedral on the acropolis of the ancient Gallo-Roman city of *Lugdunum convenarum*. At the end of the 13th century, Bertrand de Got, future Pope Clement V, had this cathedral of Saint Bertrand of Comminges enlarged.

St Just of Valcabrère and St Bertrand of Comminges

Adam and Eve, capital in Collegiate Church, Saint Gaudens

THE NORTH AGAINST THE MIDI

In September 1212, Raymond VI travelled south of the Pyrenees to request help from Pedro II of Aragon, still basking in the glory of his victory over the Almohads at Las Navas de Tolosa, a feat of arms that earned him the name Pedro the Catholic. This meeting between the two brothers-in-law took place either in Barcelona, the county's capital, or Zaragoza, capital of the kingdom of Aragon, the sources are not specific. The two men, conscious of the worsening situation in Languedoc, had devised a plan to put an end to the crusade and thus safeguard the rights of the great feudal lords of the Midi and intended to submit it to Pope Innocent III.

A Pope Under the Influence

The plan elaborated by the King of Aragon and the Count of Toulouse was presented to Innocent III by an Aragonese embassy led by the Bishop of Segorba and Master Columbus. Montfort's actions were strongly criticized. Of course, fighting against heresy was a duty but, by paying homage to Pedro II for Trencavel's former viscounty in Montpellier in January 1211, the crusade's military leader had promised to limit his conquest to that viscounty and to leave the Count of Foix in peace. He had however attacked the possessions of the Counts of Foix and Comminges and of the Viscount of Béarn, he had intervened militarily on lands spared by the heresy, he had attacked the County of Toulouse, mixing up good Catholics and heretics, he had received homage from inhabitants and lords and hence ridiculed the rights of the superior suzerain. This was particularly notable in the case of Agen, since the town and the Agenais had been part of the dowry brought to Raymond VI by Jeanne, the sister of Richard the Lionheart. Therefore, Montfort had to return the possessions he had conquered or granted himself beyond Trencavel's former viscounty. Pedro II, his suzerain, had the right to demand he do so. It was true that there were wrongs that Raymond VI had to admit, but he was ready to submit to all the Holy See's demands and accomplish all the penances the pope required. As proof of his good faith, he was ready to immediately abdicate in favour of his fifteen-year-old son, whose upbringing was entrusted to the King of Aragon. Until the younger Raymond was old enough to reign, Pedro II would be his guardian and would impound all of Saint Gilles County. In case Raymond VI breached any of his promises, his county would be confiscated by the King of Aragon. Innocent III accepted the project. Why would he not approve the outline of a vast trans-Pyrenean kingdom over which his vassal Pedro II would reign? The Pope himself had crowned Pedro II in Rome in October 1204, and the King had just won glory against the soldiers of Islam. Innocent also thought the crusade had dealt a severe blow to heresy and Christendom was in greater danger on the banks of the Jordan than on those of the Garonne. In January 1213, the pope ordered the end of the crusade. On January 15, he wrote to Montfort to

173

remind him of his vassalage duties with respect to Pedro II, and to Arnaud-Amaury not to waste any more indulgences on the Albigensian crusade, since Islam posed a greater threat to Rome. On January 17, Innocent III wrote another letter to Montfort telling him to return the wrongfully captured lands. The pontiff reminded Montfort that the purpose of the crusade was to chase the heretics off their lands and not to capture those lands while the heretics remained on them. The pope wrote, "By maintaining them on their domains, you have implicitly recognized that they are Catholics, given that you do not intend to appear to be an abettor of heretics…" And he concluded by telling the crusader chief, "You have used the crusader army to spill the blood of the just, you have wronged the innocent." On January 18, Arnaud-Amaury, Tedisio and Hugo of Riez were in turn honoured by papal correspondence. The pope explained Pedro II's plan to them, and lectured them sharply. "You have put your greedy hands on lands that no suspicion of heresy had ever touched…" It was obvious that the Holy Father had been informed of Arnaud-Amaury's temporal takeovers in Narbonne. He requested that they convoke a council of prelates and great barons to study the Aragonese plan, and to tell him of their conclusions to enable him to make a final decision. But at the moment that Innocent III began to write these letters, a council was held in Lavaur to, once again, examine the case of Raymond VI.

At Epiphany, 1213, Pedro II was in Toulouse. He had come accompanied by the bishops of Tarragona, Barcelona and Vich, two royal notaries, two scribes from his chancellery, and thirty knights. He was received by Raymond VI at the Narbonnais Castle. On January 14, a meeting was organized between Toulouse and Lavaur, at the initiative of Pedro II. Arnaud-Amaury attended with twenty prelates, Simon and Guy de Montfort. The King defended the Counts of Toulouse, Foix and Comminges and the Viscount of Béarn, pleading for their reconciliation and requesting the restitution of their properties. He was asked to write a report on the subject and to transmit it to the Council of Lavaur, where it was read out on January 16. On January 18, Pedro II was notified that his requests were rejected. On January 21, the council wrote a letter addressed to Innocent III in which, first of all, the legitimacy and necessity of the crusade were reaffirmed and, secondly, the excommunication of Raymond VI, who had no more fulfilled his promises than he had in 1210, was maintained. At the end of the council, while the bishops of Toulouse and Carcassonne were on their way to France to preach the crusade, Tedisio and four prelates left for Rome carrying the council's letter. Pedro II, confident in the pope's promises, did not worry about the council's positions and began to put his plan into action. In the presence of the Count of Foix, the Count of Comminges and his son, and the Viscount of Béarn, on January 27, he received oaths of loyalty from Raymond VI and his son, ratified by the consuls of Toulouse, and in the succeeding days, the oaths of several of the Toulouse count's vassals, including Olivier, Lord of Penne d'Albigeois. In the course of the month of February, Pedro II left Toulouse. A judge remained in

Capital, Lavaur Cathedral

TOLOSA DOLOSA

From Lavaur, Tedisio went *ad limina* to deliver the letter from the council fathers to the pope. He went through Orange, where the Metropolitan of Arles had gathered his suffragans and the abbot of Saint Gilles. This provincial council, which had also written a letter intended for Innocent III, gave it to him on February 20. The terms in the missive were immoderate. Obviously in high sprits, the prelates were playing word games in Latin with *Tolosa dolosa* – Toulouse, the crafty – which were later taken up by Pierre of Les Vaux de Cernay.

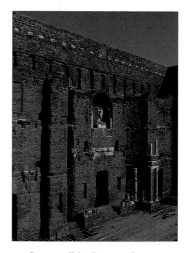

Stage wall in Orange theatre

Penne d'Albigeois

the Saint Gilles' capital to represent him and the seneschal of Catalonia, Guillaume-Raymond of Montcade, set up his quarters there with several knights and a corps of Aragonese *routiers*. Pedro II sent messengers to Montfort to warn him that he would defend his vassals if he, Montfort, threatened their interests. Simon sent his companion Lambert of Thury to the king and, while affirming that he had never failed in his duties as a vassal, he asked the king to take the quarrel that opposed them, in other words, the confiscation of lands belonging to heretics or those protecting them, to Rome. Since Pedro II answered that the Church had no say on a matter strictly belonging to feudal law, Lambert of Thury handed him a letter from the leader of the crusade breaking the link between vassal and suzerain. Pedro II also sent an embassy to Philip Augustus with copies of Innocent III's bulls from the month of January. The embassy was supposed to transmit a request to the King of France for the marriage of his daughter, Marie of France, to Pedro II. But the embassy did not accomplish this because the validity of the marriage of Pedro II and Marie of Montpellier had just been confirmed by the pope, hence prohibiting the union.

Puycelci

It was true that the King of France had other worries. He had not appreciated the decision in January 1213 of his son Louis to go to Languedoc. And when he considered organizing a landing in England, he wanted to be able to count on the future Louis VIII and all his knights. Prince Louis's crusade in Occitan lands would have to wait. At the beginning of 1213, several prelates were preaching the crusade in France. Of course there were the bishops of Toulouse and Carcassonne for the Albigensian crusade, despite Innocent III's instructions to Arnaud-Amaury, but also Robert of Courçon, the pope's legate for a crusade in the Holy Land. This competition reduced recruitment for the southern bishops who, nonetheless, managed to convince the bishops of Orléans and Auxerre who were to arrive in Languedoc in May with several knights. The crusaders' side had received papal bulls which Tedisio learned about when he arrived in Rome in mid-March to hand over the account of the Lavaur Council. The pope had meanwhile been informed by Pedro II about the oaths sworn by Raymond VI and his son. Although Innocent III received Tedisio rather coldly in March, two months later, on May 21, 1213, he had completely changed his position. In a letter addressed to the King of Aragon, the pope questioned his plans, declared the oaths pronounced on January 27 null and void, asked the king not to interfere in the crusade's affairs and to sign a truce with Montfort. He nevertheless told Montfort to respect the vassal's homage he owed to the King of Aragon, revoked the order to restore the lands to the Counts of Foix and Comminges and the Viscount of Béarn, who were invited to return to the community of the faithful, announced the sending of a bull to Foulque telling him to reconcile those Toulousains wishing to return to the Church. Even though the Supreme Pontiff did not accept all the requests of the Lavaur Council, although he announced the sending of an observer –a new legate, Peter of Benevento, and well knowing that the information he received from the crusaders was not objective, the pope had chosen his side.

In the field, Innocent III's January bulls had no influence on the crusaders' behaviour. In Fanjeaux, Montfort received the reinforcements led by the bishops of Orléans and Auxerre. Together they went to Muret near Toulouse and began to devastate the city's outskirts because they were unable to besiege it given their reduced strength. Montfort returned to Carcassonne and then went on to Castelnaudary, where his thirteen year-old son, Amaury, was dubbed on June 24. The young lord received the apanage of Comminges. Meanwhile, Guy de Montfort and Baudouin tried, with great difficulty, to recapture Puycelci, a place conquered by the crusade in the spring of 1212 but then lost. In fact, Guy and Baudouin agreed to lift the siege after receiving a promise from its defenders to no longer fight the crusaders and to surrender without resisting if the castle nearby of Penne d'Albigeois, an invincible adversary of the crusade, capitulated or was captured. On July 4, Bernard IV of Comminges met the King of Aragon at the monastery of Sigena. At the very moment when Montfort broke his oath of vassalage, Pedro II began to mobilize his troops. Together they began their preparations for a confrontation that had become inevitable. In Toulouse, the Occitan side knew that they could count on Aragon. Raymond VI had his son at his side, as well as the Counts of Comminges and Foix, and the seneschal of Catalonia. The crusaders had invested Le Pujol, a position five leagues from Toulouse, south-west of Lanta. It was held by three Norman barons: Perrin of Cissey, Roger of L'Essart, and Simon the Saxon.

Sigena Monastery

Feudal Terms

Apanage

Part of a fief ceded by a lord to his younger sons or to his brothers to guarantee that they have resources. The beneficiary had only limited rights.

Dubbing

Rite through which a man became a knight. During the ceremony, the candidate received his weapons and his armour.

Feudatory

Holder of a fief.

Fief

A domain, seigniory, rights and properties, inalienable in principle, granted to a vassal by a lord to whom he paid homage. In return, the vassal promised not to harm his lord and to provide him with *auxilium et concilium*, aid and counsel.

Homage

Procedure by which a vassal placed himself under a lord's protection. During the ritual, the vassal kneeled and placed his joined hands in his lord's before swearing an oath of loyalty on a holy book or relics and, if necessary, sealing the feudal contract by the *osculum*, a kiss on the mouth.

Knight

In the 10th century, an individual possessing his own horse, arms and armour. After the 12th century, knighthood formed a caste that could be entered through dubbing.

Suzerain

Lord to whom a vassal has paid homage. The King is the superior suzerain.

Tenure

Situation of dependence of a vassal's fief with respect to that of his lord.

The Toulousains wanted to capture the place. It had to be done quickly because crusader reinforcements were coming from Carcassonne and Montfort was riding back fast from Comminges, where he had accompanied Amaury to receive homage from the local lords. This was not accomplished easily because, in order to have his rights recognized, Amaury had to besiege the castle of Roquefort on the Garonne. During the attack on Pujol, Roger of L'Essart was killed, Perrin of Cissey and Simon the Saxon were imprisoned in Toulouse. On July 20, they were murdered in their jail by the people. Attached to a horse's tail, their bodies "were dragged like carrion out of the city", reported Guillaume of Puylaurens. The capture of Pujol and the announcement of Pedro II's arrival stimulated the Occitan side and worried the crusaders, who saw the departure back to France of the crusaders who had come with the bishops of Orléans and Auxerre, once their forty days of service were fulfilled and their indulgences granted. Montfort asked his son to return from Comminges and, with the agreement of Arnaud-Amaury and Foulque, sent the abbots of Caunes and Lagrasse to ask the King of Aragon to obey the pope's instructions of May 21. The king's response to the messengers on August 16 was both laconic and ambiguous. "I will always obey the orders of the Supreme Pontiff." At the head of his army, the King of Aragon moved towards Toulouse. He arrived in Huesca on August 22, crossed the Pyrenees on the 28, and set up camp in Muret on September 8, ready to meet his fate.

Lagrasse Abbey

CAUNES ABBEY

In 791, Anian, a disciple of Benedict of Aniane, founded the abbey of Caunes and opted for the Benedictine Rule. The abbey church has retained its 11th century Romanesque chevet. The 12th century transept is closed by two bell-towers in the north and the south. Its two apsidal chapels are set on either side of the choir. Several capitals from the Carolingian monastery have been reused in the northern bell-tower.

Lagrasse

LAGRASSE ABBEY

···

T he charter founding the abbey of Lagrasse dates from before the year 800. According to legend, the future Charlemagne was allegedly at its origin. In 1070, the abbey came under the influence of the Count of Barcelona, Ramón Berenguer I, and was attached to Saint Victor's Monastery in Marseille. Several abbeys or priories were affiliated with Lagrasse. In the area, Saint Polycarpe, east of Limoux, and Saint Martin des Puits, between the abbey and Termes; in Catalonia, Saint Andre of Sorède, Saint Martin of Canigou, Sant Pere of Galligants, San Felíu of Guíxols. The abbey is located on the left bank of the Orbieu. The keep/bell-tower built at the beginning of the 16th century overlooks the abbey buildings from its forty-two metre height at the end of the southern arm of the transept, which, with its three apsidal chapels, dates from the 11th century. The abbey church was built at the end of the 13th century. Work in 1989 uncovered a Romanesque capital with sculptures attributed to the chisel of the Master of Cabestany, who also made the abbey church's doorway, of which, unfortunately, only a few scattered vestiges of voussoirs remain.

Abbey of Sts Peter and Paul, Caunes-Minervois

Fresco in Saint Martin des Puits

St Nicholas Tower, La Rochelle

TWO COUNTS' OATHS

I t was in the Archbishop's Palace of Narbonne that the Counts of Foix and Comminges reconciled with the Church on April 18, 1214. Before Peter of Benevento, they promised under oath to reject all heresy, to be neither a believer, nor defender, protector nor abettor of heretics, to obey the legates on questions of peace, orthodoxy, employing *routiers* and penance. And finally, each one pledged a castle as security. The Count of Foix pledged Foix Castle; the Count of Comminges, one in Salies du Salat, and also had to give one of his sons as a hostage, the one "who is not a knight".

Keep in Salies du Salat

The Occitan Princes Reconcile with the Church

Tireless, Montfort went away again to fight in the county of Foix after having sent his brother, Guy, to occupy Rabastens, abandoned by its inhabitants after they heard about the terrible defeat. He learned that in the Rhone valley crusaders and their supply convoys were frequently being attacked by two of Raymond VI's vassals, Pons of Montlaur and Adhemar of Poitiers, the Count of Valentinois, even though the latter had taken the cross in 1209. Montfort decided to remedy the situation, but, on the way, he realized that the situation was far from favourable. Narbonne, Montpellier and Nîmes, where he spent the beginning of October, refused to open their gates or made difficulties. In Largentière, Pons of Montlaur was quickly brought back into the fold, unlike Adhemar of Poitiers, who eventually did submit when he saw the arrival of new crusader reinforcements led by the Duke of Burgundy and the archbishops of Lyon and Vienne. On December 4, Montfort and the Count of Viennois agreed on the marriage of their children, Amaury and Beatrice. By mid-February 1214, Montfort was in Béziers. Reprisal raids were being carried out in the Lower Languedoc by Catalan-Aragonese troops because Montfort had refused to give back Pedro II's son, James. At the same time, the situation was worsening in the Agenais and the Quercy. First of all, on February 16, John Lackland landed in La Rochelle and received homage from his Aquitaine vassals, including those in Mas Agenais, who had been forced to submit to Montfort during the summer of 1212. Next, the Count of Toulouse, with the support of the Count of Foix, tried to rally the Quercy's lords to his side. On February 17, Baudouin, who had taken part in the Battle of Muret on the crusaders' side, was in Lolmie, near Montcuq. He was accompanied by Guillaume of Contres. *Routiers*, paid by his own vassals and led by Ratier of Castelnau and the lord of Lolmie, kidnapped him while he was sleeping and took him to Montcuq, before imprisoning him at Montauban Castle. Raymond VI arrived and, in the presence of the Count of Foix and his son, had his brother hanged on the banks of the Tarn River. Then he left to besiege the French garrison in the castle of Moissac after its population had given its city over to him. In Narbonne, a great gathering of prelates and Catalan-Aragonese lords was organized to obtain the liberation of Pedro II's son. After riding around and waging war near Toulouse, Montfort returned to Carcassonne at the end of March. He came to Narbonne, attacked the resisting city and was preparing to besiege it when the legate Peter of Benevento arrived at the beginning of April. He asked Montfort to free James and reconciled the Counts of Foix and Comminges with the Church on April 18, 1214. One week later, on April 25, the legate went to Castelnaudary, where he received oaths of fidelity from the consuls of Toulouse. The pope had received their embassy and, on January 25, 1214, had told his legate that a reconciled Toulouse would be placed under the Holy See's protection "without being bothered, in the future, by the Count of Montfort and the other Catholics". On this same April 25, the future King Louis IX, the son of Louis of France and Blanche of Castile, was born in Poissy. A few days later,

Foix Castle

THE COUNTS OF FOIX-BÉARN

About 945-949, a certain Count Arnaud, theoretically a vassal of the Count of Toulouse, was at the head of the counties of Carcassonne and Razès, the lands of Foix, the county of Comminges and the Couserans. At his death in 957, his eldest son, Roger the Old, received the county of Carcassonne, the lands of Foix and the Couserans, and part of Comminges. In 1002, Roger wrote his will and testament, dividing his properties between his sons, his daughter Ermessinde having married the Count of Barcelona, Ramón Borrell (992-1035). Most of the churches and abbeys on his lands were given to his son Pedro, the future Bishop of Gerona; the eldest, Raymond, received, among others, the county of Carcassonne, part of Razès, half of Volvestre and part of Comminges. Bernard, the youngest, received Sabarthès, the county of Couserans, the other half of Volvestre, the castle and lands of Foix, and half of Boulbonne Forest between the Hers and Ariège Rivers. The will specified that if either of the heirs died childless, the other would receive his lands. Bernard's son, Roger 1, was the first to hold the title of Count of Foix in 1034. His uncles Raymond and Pierre being dead, Roger of Foix inherited important rights over Carcassonne, confirmed in 1063 by his cousin Roger III, Raymond's son. But when the latter died childless in 1066, his niece and heiress, Ermengarde, wife of Viscount Raymond-Bernard Trencavel, was afraid that Roger of Foix would claim his rights over Carcassonne. She decided to place herself under the protection of the powerful Count of Barcelona Ramón Berenguer I (†1076), to whom she sold for a high price not only Carcassès and Razès, but also the lands of Foix, Comminges and Sabarthès. Roger 1st dying in the

meantime, Ermengarde attached little importance to Pierre-Bernard, Roger's brother. However Barcelona's sovereignty was no longer exercised over the lands of Foix after 1076, and Pierre-Bernard's son, Roger II († c. 1124), Count of Foix and Couserans, had his rights restored. On the eve of his departure for the crusades in 1095, Roger II reconciled with Ermengarde and her son, Bernard-Aton Trencavel, to whom he left all his properties should he die heirless. But Count Roger returned from the crusades before 1108. Soon he had to decide what position to take in the conflict opposing Barcelona and Toulouse. Bernard-Aton Trencavel had chosen Toulouse, since its count had helped him subject Carcassonne when it had rebelled against his authority in 1120. Roger II of Foix chose Barcelona, and confirmed it by the marriage, in 1117, of his son Roger III (†1148) and Chimena, daughter of Ramón Berenguer III. But in the second half of the 12th century, Toulouse lost a strong ally, the Viscount of Albi-Carcassone-Béziers, Raymond Trencavel, who joined Ramón Berenguer IV in 1150. The following

year, Cecile, the daughter of Raymond Trencavel, married the Count of Foix Roger-Bernard 1st. The marriage produced Raymond-Roger, Count of Foix from 1188 to 1223, and Esclarmonde who was ordained a perfect in Fanjeaux in 1204. Raymond-Roger married Philippa, herself a future perfect in Dun. Their son, Roger-Bernard II (1223-1241) married a believer, Ermessinde, daughter of the lord Arnaud of Castelbon. Although it did not emerge unscathed, the county of Foix survived the crusade and the conquest of the Midi. In 1252, Roger IV (1241-1265) obtained for his son, Roger-Bernard III (1265-1302), the hand of Marguerite of Moncade, heiress of Viscount Gaston VII of Béarn. The union produced Gaston 1st (1302-1315), who added the title of Viscount of Béarn to that of Count of Foix. His grandson, Gaston III (†1391), the son of Agnes of Navarre, was one of the great princes of the kingdom. This patron of the arts, nicknamed *Phoebus* for his blonde hair and his love of letters, composed in the *langue d'oil* a treatise on his favourite leisure activity, *The Book of the Hunt*, translated into English in 1413.

Roquefixade Castle, a possession of the Counts of Foix

Raymond VI met the legate in Toulouse and made amends. He abdicated in favour of his son and submitted to the Church. In Narbonne, Montfort was informed of the siege of Moissac and galloped to help his troops. By the time he arrived Raymond VI had already struck camp, so Montfort continued on to Penne d'Agenais on April 13, then to Mas d'Agenais to try to retake the place. At the time, John Lackland was in La Réole, where the inhabitants were trying to prevent the crusaders from crossing the Garonne. With few means, Montfort organized the siege of Mas d'Agenais but had to lift it three days later because Peter of Benevento called him to Narbonne in order to free James of Aragon. The two men met in Capestang, beside Béziers. The legate accompanied the future king, just over six years old, to Aragon. James entered the castle of Monzón, where Guillaume of Montredon, Grand Master of the Templars in the kingdom of Aragon, took charge of his upbringing.

Fresco, Templar chapel, Cressac

St Peter's Church, La Réole

TEMPLARS AND HOSPITALLERS

The Order of Hospitallers of Saint John of Jerusalem was founded in 1113. In 1119, Hugues of Payens created the confraternity of the Poor Knights of Christ, which became the Order of the Templars at the Council of Troyes in 1128. At the beginning of the 13th century, Hospitallers and Templars owned many houses and commanderies in Languedoc. They influenced the architecture of some churches, like in Rieux-Minervois, built on the model of the Holy Sepulchre in Jerusalem. The Hospitallers maintained strict ties with the local princes. In his will dated 1218, Raymond VI even presented himself as a Hospitaller Brother in Toulouse, *ad succurendum*, perhaps to ensure he would obtain a Christian burial that he did not in fact receive. In the Peace and Faith affair, although the Hospitallers were monks and soldiers, hence men of the crusade, they were not called on to intervene against the heretics and their protectors in a land they knew well. The Templars on the other hand were present at several military operations at the crusaders' side, such as the siege of Minerve in 1210.

Cavalcades in Quercy, Perigord and Rouergue

New crusaders had just arrived in Montpellier. Preaching in France by Guy of Les Vaux de Cernay and the archdeacon of Paris, but also by the legate Robert of Courçon who was now working for the crusade, had been fruitful. Coming from Capestang, Montfort joined them in Saint Thibéry at the beginning of May 1214. He had come through Agde, where Bernard-Aton, Viscount of Agde and Nîmes, and a vassal of the Count of Toulouse, had transferred his domains to him. He accompanied the new crusaders to Carcassonne and went to Valence to arrange the final details of the marriage of his son Amaury to Beatrice of Viennois. The ceremony took place in early June in Carcassonne, and the wedding blessing was made by Dominic of Caleruega, recently named parish priest of Fanjeaux by Foulque. Before leaving for the Valentinois, Montfort had asked his brother Guy to take command of the crusaders who had just arrived and to intervene in Rouergue. From Carcassonne the troops, now joined by Robert of Courçon, passed through Castres and Albi before occupying Najac. The neighbouring village of Morlhon resisted but eventually surrendered. Seven Waldensians were captured. The crusaders led them to the stake "with extreme joy", reported Pierre of Les Vaux de Cernay. Guy de Montfort and his men rode towards the Lower Quercy, razed Castelnau-Montratier, and Simon joined them in Mondenard around June 10. They had to go to Montpezat, where lords from the Agenais had readied it for defence. When the crusaders arrived, the place had been abandoned; the fortifications were destroyed. The crusaders continued westwards as far as Marmande, conquered by Robert Mauvoisin in 1212, but retaken by the English since the arrival of John Lackland. The city's inhabitants had fled by boat upriver along the Garonne to La Réole, but the city was besieged, captured and looted. The English garrison, entrenched in the keep, surrendered. On June 19, John Lackland had begun a siege of La Roche aux Moines in Anjou, but he lifted it on July 2 at the approach of the French army led by Prince Louis. Less than a month

Eleanor of Aquitaine

NAJAC

The castle of Najac stands on top of a hill overlooking a meander in the Aveyron River. The fortress was built by one of the sons of Raymond IV of Toulouse, Bertrand, at the beginning of the 12th century, and was rebuilt in 1253 by Alphonse of Poitiers. As part of Eleanor of Aquitaine's dowry, it passed under English domination when the Duchess, repudiated by Louis VII, married the King of England, Henry II Plantagenet. In 1183, Eleanor's son, Richard the Lionheart, met Alfonso II of Aragon in Najac to conclude an alliance against Raymond V of Toulouse, who was contesting Alfonso's rights over Provence. In 1214, the castle surrendered without a fight to the crusaders led by Guy de Montfort. The presence of seven Waldensians, captured several days later in Morlhon, proved the existence of heretical households in the region. A few years later, in 1251, Uc Paraire, a consul of Najac convicted of heresy, also died at the stake and, in 1258, the town's inhabitants were sentenced for their heretical sympathies to build Saint John's Church. In the 17th century, the castle fell into the hands of the rebelling *Croquants* and their leader, Bernard Calmels, was sentenced to being broken on the wheel in October 1643.

Old houses on the Agout River, Castres

Najac Castle

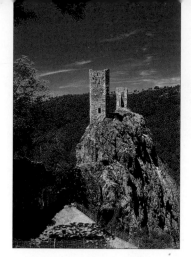

Peyrusse-le-Roc Castle

JANUS

The portrayal of Bernard of Cazenac, Lord of Domme, Montfort and Castelnaud by Pierre of Les Vaux de Cernay is rather unflattering. The author of the *Historia Albigensis* accused him and his wife, Hélis de Montfort, "that new Jezebel", of having horribly mutilated one hundred and fifty men and women that the crusaders found in Sarlat monastery. A few years later, during the spring of 1218, Bernard of Cazenac came with five hundred men to provide reinforcements for the Toulousains besieged by Simon de Montfort. The anonymous author of the *Canso* described his arrival. "I have never seen a more perfect knight, for his uprightness, which was equal to his strength […]; he respects a vassal's Homage and leads Valour; to restore Uprightness and abolish Pain, he came, through love, to aid Toulouse and the count." The House of Toulouse remembered. When Raymond VII recaptured Castelsarrasin in 1228 from Imbert of Beaujeu, he handed it over to Cazenac. From the Inquisition's reports, Bernard of Cazenac, a "miserable blackguard" for one chronicler, "gifted with wisdom, generosity and an imperial heart" for another, frequented the city's Cathar community led by the deacon Bernard of Lamothe.

later, on July 27, 1214, Philip Augustus defeated Emperor Otto at Bouvines. On June 28, Montfort, joined by the Viscount of Turenne, besieged Casseneuil where the local insurgent lords had gathered. Robert of Courçon had to leave, but first of all he confirmed Montfort in his possession of the lands conquered or to be conquered in the dioceses of Cahors, Agen and Albi. One attack failed on August 17. Casseneuil fell the next day, and was pillaged and razed. The crusaders' next target was Perigord. The castles of Domme and Montfort, owned by Bernard of Cazenac, the brother-in-law of the Viscount of Turenne, were destroyed and a garrison settled into Castelnaud, spared. In vain, Montfort asked the Lord of Beynac to return the possessions he had extorted from churches. His castle was dismantled. Montfort went through Penne d'Agenais once again before entering Quercy through the Lot valley. From Cahors he went to Figeac where the monastery's abbot gave him the castle of Peyrusse-le-Roc, then to Capdenac where the lords submitted. In Rodez, the bishop, who had been present at the siege of Casseneuil, had organized Simon's taking possession of Rouergue. Henry, Count of Rouergue, reluctantly paid homage to Simon on November 7. Sévérac Castle, at the edge of the Gévaudan, was held by Déodat III, another of Turenne's brothers-in-law. On November 30, Déodat negotiated his surrender and obtained that his castle be handed over to the Bishop of Rodez by Montfort. On December 6, Simon was in Moissac to settle with Abbot Raymond of Proet the problems caused in 1212 when crusaders had damaged his abbey. In the space of six months, with the support of the Viscount of Turenne, an ally from the very first, Montfort had confirmed his hold over Perigord, Quercy and Rouergue. He had also taken advantage of support by Robert of Courçon who, by confirming Montfort's rights in Casseneuil over lands already conquered or to be conquered by him, had forgotten the heretofore unquestioned concept of "unjustly conquered lands" introduced by the pope in his bulls dated January 1213. On December 7, 1214, from Reims the legate wrote to Arnaud-Amaury to ask him to call a council to settle the question of the crusade.

Sévérac Castle

Bouvines, July 27, 1214, One Sunday…

After his marriage in January 1212 to the heiress of the counties of Flanders and Hainaut, Ferrand of Portugal, Prince Louis's brother-in-law, paid liege homage to Philip Augustus. But a short time later, in February, Louis had captured two of his towns, Aire and Saint Omer. Ferrand did not appreciate this poor behaviour. In 1213, he refused to supply the King of France with the contingent he was requesting for a landing in England, forcing Philip Augustus to abandon his plans. Furthermore, at the beginning of 1214, Ferrand concluded a treaty with John Lackland. Philip Augustus' army went to confront the troops of Ferrand and Renaud of Dammartin, Count of Boulogne, in Flanders. In the spring of 1214, John Lackland arrived in La Rochelle to create a diversion but he was routed at La Roche aux Moines by Prince Louis on July 2. It was then that Otto IV of Brunswick brought reinforcements for Ferrand and Renaud's troops. By the end of July, the French were in Tournai and the coalition was twelve kilometres to the south. Philip Augustus, cut off from his rear base, wanted to retreat towards Lille. He headed for the bridge of Bouvines to cross the Marcq. In fact, he was not really sure where the enemy was located. The Viscount of Melun and Friar Guerin, a Hospitaller later named Bishop of Senlis by Innocent III, went on reconnaissance and realized that the coalition forces were on their heels, in battle order and with standards flying. The King of France was hoping that the Truce of God would be respected on this Sunday, July 27. Besides, most of his troops were already on the other side of the river. While most of the French barons advised the king to continue on his way, Friar Guerin convinced him to stand fast and join battle with the enemy. Philip Augustus gathered his men on the river's right bank. After praying in a little chapel, he put his armour back on and had the bridge destroyed –no-one was to run away. His army spread out in three corps on the plateau extending northward from Cysoing Abbey. Friar Guerin led the right wing against Ferrand. The coalition, surprised by the rapid French reaction, also had the sun in their eyes. They were routed. The emperor and his knights fled. Ferrand was captured along with many other knights. Kept prisoner at the Louvre, he was freed only in 1227. The amount of booty was enormous; the joy of the French people, indescribable; Philip's return to Paris, a triumph. This victory put an end to English and German interventionist inclinations. Otto was definitively replaced by Frederick II as the head of the empire. The Capetian established the authority of his dynasty durably and brilliantly. And yet the French, with one thousand three hundred knights, as many mounted sergeants, and four to six thousand sergeants on foot, were numerically inferior to their adversaries. But the French cavalry did wonders in a battle in which the mystical element was primordial. Philip Augustus had God on his side against the excommunicated Otto, who did not even respect the Lord's day. As for Friar Guerin, Philip Augustus' strategist, he was to be at the side of Prince Louis during his actions in Languedoc in 1216, 1219 and 1226.

The Battle of Bouvines

Beynac

DISAPPOINTMENTS

In 1115, disciples of Geraud of Sales founded a hermitage at Cadouin, on the edge of Bessière Forest, ten leagues west of Domme. In 1117, the hermitage received the Holy Shroud as a gift from crusaders coming from Antioch. The establishment was affiliated with the Cistercian Order in 1119, and the precious relic made the Perigord abbey the site of an important pilgrimage. Richard the Lionheart, Louis IX and Blanche of Castile were among the famous pilgrims. In 1214, after investing Domme, Montfort, Castelnaud and Beynac, Simon de Montfort awarded the Abbey of Cadouin an annual rent of twenty-five *livres* to be taken from the revenues of Castelnaud, but which the monks never received. As for the Holy Shroud, an examination in 1933 showed it to be Fatimid material with a Kufic inscription to the glory of Allah.

Castelnaud Castle

Abbot's chair in Cadouin

A gallery in Cadouin cloister

Tower Gate in Domme

La Babote Tower, Montpellier

Statue of St Trophime, Arles

All Roads Lead to Rome

The Council opened in the church of Notre Dame des Tables in Montpellier, on January 8, 1215. Among the participants were the archbishops of Narbonne, Aix, Arles, Embrun and Auch, twenty-eight bishops and many abbots, French barons and Occitan lords who had come over to the crusaders' side. In the unavoidable absence of Robert of Courçon, the council was presided over by Peter of Benevento, back from Aragon where he had accompanied the child James back home. Montfort could not attend the council since the city's inhabitants had forbidden him to enter, and he had to wait in a nearby castle. The council was unanimous in wanting to give Montfort, with the title of "*Dominus et Monarcha*" or "lord and ruler", rights over the conquered lands and the county of Toulouse. Pierre of Benevento could not condone a decision that would depose Raymond VI because his mandate did not cover it. Indeed, his mission was to make the counts of the Midi and the inhabitants of Toulouse respect the previous year's sworn engagements. Anything else had to be decided by the pope. The council immediately sent the Archbishop of Embrun to Rome. While waiting for the

Embrun

pope's reply, Montfort did not sit still but trampled on the Count of Toulouse's rights, with the complicity of the local prelates. Where iron, fire and blood had not been used to despoil the count, trickery, money and legal rules written off as a loss did the trick. Hence, on January 30, the Archbishop of Arles enfeoffed his castles of Beaucaire and Argence and their dependencies onto his ecclesiastical province. Hence, on March 6 in Carcassonne, Montfort granted to the Bishop of Uzès all of Raymond VI's properties and privileges in his diocese, in other words, twenty castles and localities, retaining the right of justice for himself. At the Council of Montpellier, Peter of Benevento asked Foulque to go back to the bishopric of Toulouse, which he had abandoned in May 1211, and as provided for by a clause of Raymond's oath of 1214, to occupy Narbonnaise

Les Baux de Provence

Castle on behalf of the Church. Foulque, helped by the clerics returning with him, took Toulouse in hand and was joined by Dominic. On April 25, Pierre Sellan, who had just inherited from his father, granted three houses to the Castilian who settled in with half a dozen disciples, including Pierre Sellan. Foulque authorized Dominic to preach, paid him part of the diocese's tithes, and granted him a hospice that took in repentant prostitutes.

Raymond VI returned from Rome to Toulouse and, since his palace was forbidden to him, settled with his family in the house of a local burgher, David of Rouaix. The meeting with the pope had gone well. On February 4, the Holy Father, who had not yet received the Archbishop of Embrun, wrote to Peter of Benevento to tell him of Raymond VI's good behaviour, that the count had pledged him his possessions and rights in a notarized act, and of his absolution. Raymond VI's case would be studied and the final settlement of the Albigensian crusade would be treated at the Lateran Council that the pope had called for the following November. The pope even asked his legate to pay the expenses of Raymond's voyage out of his legation's budget, the count being ruined by the crusade. In the same letter, the pope ordered that the Marquisate of Provence be entrusted to the Lord of Les Baux while waiting for the council. Unfortunately for Raymond VI, after his departure the delegation sent by the Montpellier Council arrived in Rome. It was a repetition of the scene from early 1213. The prelate denounced Raymond VI's hypocrisy, and presented Montfort as the sole rampart against a heresy that was far from eradicated. The pope let himself be convinced and, while waiting for the great Lateran meeting, agreed to place Raymond VI's domains in commendam to Montfort. The pope remained neutral. He told Peter of Benevento and the crusade's leader of his decision in letters dated April 2, 1215. In early May, Montfort was in Saint Gilles, where he accompanied Prince Louis who had taken the cross according to his wish of 1213. There he met the Archbishop of Embrun carrying the pope's letters.

AU HASARD BALTHAZAR

I t was in the 10th century that the lords of Les Baux had built their castle on this rocky spur in the heart of the Provencal Alpilles. They traced their origins to one of the Magi, and their coat of arms proudly bore the star of the nativity as well as the fine motto "Au Hasard Balthazar". Through his marriage in 1120 with Étiennette of Gévaudan, daughter of Gilbert, last Count of Provence in the Boson dynasty, Raymond of Les Baux believed he had rights over the county of Provence. But his dynasty was unable to turn them to good account against the Catalonian counts, despite support from Alphonse-Jourdain, Count of Toulouse, and despite his participation in the Baussenque wars from 1142 to 1162. The dynasty's consolation was obtaining the principality of Orange in 1162. In the first canto of his *Calendal*, Mistral praised this "race of eaglets, never vassals".

Castelnaud Castle

FOIX CASTLE

....

The rocky spur topped by Foix Castle had been occupied by a Celtiberian *oppidum* and then by a Roman fort. In 867, the abbey of Saint Volusien, on the left bank of the Ariège, had been protected with ramparts, but a primitive castle was built in the 10th century, probably on the slopes of the spur, by Roger 1st of Carcassonne. Construction of the castle, still in admirable condition, took place subsequently in several stages. Seals affixed in 1229 and 1240 are illustrated with a castle with only two square towers linked by a crenelated main building. They provide an idea of the castle that was besieged, in vain, by Simon de Montfort, who claimed, as related by William of Tudela, to "make the rock of Foix melt like fat and grill the master on it". Philip the Bold tried too in 1272. The round third tower in the south is thus from a later date, probably the mid-15th century and not from the period of Gaston Phoebus, to whom its construction was attributed for a long time. A spiral staircase leads to four hexagonal rooms with ribbed vaulting that take up the different levels of this last tower. They contain part of the collections of the Ariège Museum.

Prince Louis' Pilgrimage

The prince left from Lyon on April 19, 1215 and Montfort went to welcome him in Vienne. After Bouvines, there was no longer anything to prevent Louis from leaving for Languedoc. Some of the crusade's leaders questioned the young Capetian's intentions. But this pilgrimage took place absolutely normally, even though it allowed the King of France to find out more about the situation in the Midi and reminded everyone that he was the "superior suzerain" of the Count of Toulouse. From Saint Gilles, Prince Louis, accompanied by Guy of Les Vaux de Cernay, the legate, and by Simon de Montfort, arrived in Béziers where, at the legate's request, he ordered the destruction of the ramparts of Narbonne. After the events of 1214, Montfort had given the same order, but had been opposed by Arnaud-Amaury. The same decision was applied to Toulouse's fortifications. Louis and his suite went from Carcassonne to Fanjeaux and Pamiers, where the legate gave Montfort Foix Castle in commendam. Montfort sent his brother Guy to Toulouse to begin dismantling the ramparts, filling in the ditches, and destroying fortified houses. The Toulousains were obviously in no hurry to obey orders and the demolition took over a year. At the beginning of June, Louis and Montfort entered Toulouse. The Saint Gilles, both father and son, were absent. At the end of his forty-day service, Louis returned to France. On June 8, Montfort went to Montauban to receive homage from Gerard, Count of Armagnac and Fezensac. He then returned to Carcassonne, from where he accompanied Peter of Benevento, on his way to Rome, as far as Saint Antonin Monastery near Vienne. In July and August, other homages were paid to Montfort and, on August 24, he settled his quarrel with Lagrasse Abbey over the possession of ten castles and localities. He returned to Perigord to take back Castelnaud from Bernard of Cazenac, who had expelled the garrison put in place in 1214. All the defenders were hanged except for Bernard of Cazenac who managed to escape. Montfort went back to Carcassonne. The Lateran Council had begun.

Foix Castle

The Roman Curia

The council opened on November 11, 1215 in Holy Saviour Basilica. Eighty ecclesiastic provinces were represented in this huge gathering of Christendom, with the attendance of nineteen cardinals, four hundred and twelve archbishops and bishops, the five patriarchs of the Greek churches, eight hundred abbots and priors, and over one thousand clerics or laymen. The agenda concerned several subjects, including the condemnation of the doctrine of Joachim of Flora, transubstantiation, and, of course, the Peace and Faith Affair that was of prime importance to Guy of Les Vaux de Cernay, Peter of Benevento and Robert of Courçon, Tedisio, Arnaud-Amaury, and Foulque, who were all present. Montfort had stayed in Carcassonne, but sent his brother Guy. For the Midi, there were Raymond VI, his son, the Count of Foix, Arnaud of Villemur, Pierre-Raymond of Rabastens, Raymond of Roquefeuil, Arnaud of Comminges, Guillaume Porcelet. Debates on the Languedoc affair began on November 14. Innocent III described the situation: Raymond VI's absolution, the pledging of his possessions given temporarily in commendam to Simon de Montfort. The Count of Foix mentioned that he had pledged his castle in Foix to Peter of Benevento in May, 1214. Foulque began to speak and launched into a violent diatribe against Raymond-Roger. The Bishop of Toulouse added that the count's sister was a perfect and that he was harbouring an evil monster in the *castrum* of Montségur on his lands and that he had carried out the massacre of German crusaders in Montgey in 1211. The *Canso*'s anonymous author related the reaction of Arnaud of Villemur: "My lords, if one called to this place the victims who suffered from combats, killings and mass graves, I call before you my tortured people." The Count of Foix replied point by point. He was not his sister. He possessed no seigniorial rights over Montségur. And the German crusaders were criminals who had come to devastate his lands. As for Foulque, he just about called the bishop a travelling acrobat when he recalled his past as a troubadour. On the subject of the Count of Foix, Innocent III ordered a further enquiry. Raymond of Roquefeuil, in the name of the young Trencavel, came to ask to have his lands returned. The case of Toulouse was dealt with at the next meeting. On their side, the prelates claimed that returning the conquered lands would call into question all the accomplishments of the crusade. The pope's opinion was that confiscating the lands of the Count of Toulouse would be a denial of justice. The pope made a first concession – Montfort would keep all the properties of proven heretics but not those of repentant or absolved accomplices of heresy, nor those of heretics' widows or orphans. This excluded the Count of Toulouse and the former Viscount Trencavel. Foulque counter-attacked with the support of many prelates, with the notable exception of Arnaud-Amaury who realized that if Montfort had his way, he himself would lose the Duchy of Narbonne. Alone against the others, Innocent III defended his point of view, reproaching Montfort, along with his companions-at-arms to whom he had entrusted lands, with having harmed good Catholics. He defended the Saint Gilles, saying that even supposing that

One of the great concerns of Innocent III's pontificate was "to avenge the wrong done to the crucified", to defend the Holy Sepulchre in the Holy Land. In 1198, when the young Lotario Conti was elected to Saint Peter's throne, Jerusalem had been in Muslim hands for eleven years. Muslims had also severely defeated the troops of Alfonso VIII, King of Castile, at Alarcos in 1195. Therefore, shortly after his election, in April 1198 the Pope organized a new crusade – the fourth, but its purpose was diverted and it ended in 1204 with the sack of the Byzantine capital and the foundation of the Latin Empire of Constantinople. In 1208, the year the pope called for the Albigensian Crusade, the Affair of Peace and Faith, he sent a legate, Cardinal Saint Mary in Porticu, to France to deal with the question of the Cross. The spirit of the crusade was still alive but not always well controlled, and the Children's Crusade in 1212 came to a tragic ending. In April 1213, Innocent III invited Christendom to participate in a fifth crusade. The Lateran Council of 1215, in its third and final session on November 30, prepared the text of the constitution *Ab liberandam Terram sanctam*, promulgated on December 15. This text specified and completed the clauses of apostolic protection that had been set by the pope in 1208 and 1209. It allocated one twentieth of ecclesiastic revenues to the Holy Land for three years. Innocent III died in July 1216. After his death, Duke Leopold VI of Austria, King Andrew II of Hungary and King Hugo I of Cyprus gathered in Acre. The crusaders led by Jean of Brienne, King of Jerusalem, went to Egypt where they captured Damietta in 1219 but failed to take Mansurah in 1221.

Raymond VI was guilty, why dispossess his son? The Archbishop of York, supported by the Abbot of Bewley, reminded the council in John Lackland's name that the dowry of Jeanne of England, mother of Raymond the Younger, consisting of the Agenais and Quercy, was inalienable. The sentence was handed down on November 30. Innocent III was beaten. Raymond VI, dispossessed of his titles and properties, was condemned to exile; he would receive an annual payment of four hundred marks. His county was granted to Montfort "reserving the rights of the superior suzerain". In a slight consolation for the pope, one clause excluded the heretofore unconquered lands from this enormous plundering and temporarily entrusted the Marquisate of Provence to the Lord of Les Baux. The church was to sequester it and return it to the young Raymond. A few weeks later, the last of the Saint Gilles was received in a private audience by the pope, to whom he intimated that nothing was finished and that all was beginning. According to the *Canso*'s poet, Innocent III told him, "Even the most awful night ends in daybreak." The pope died seven months later, on July 16, 1216, in Perugia and was succeeded by Honorius III. After the council, Raymond VI went to Viterbo, where he spent Christmas with Raymond-Roger of Foix, who had recovered his castle through the bull of December 8. Berenger, Abbot of Saint Thibéry gave it back to him after holding it since April 18, 1214. In January 1216, Raymond VI made a pilgrimage to Saint Mark's relics in Venice, from where he continued on to Genoa to see his son. They set sail for Marseille.

Palace of the Popes in Viterbo

Innocent III

Perugia

VICARIUS CHRISTI

Innocent III made the Holy See the *Imperium Mundi* that he wanted to command from the Vatican Palace he had built. He wrote, "Just as the Moon receives its light from the Sun, so is royal dignity only a reflection of pontifical dignity." He therefore intervened constantly to impose his will on the powerful leaders of Christendom. He took the side of Otto of Brunswick, crowning him Emperor in 1209 and excommunicating him a year later, opposing him with Frederick II Hohenstaufen and supporting the King of France, Philip Augustus, who defeated Otto at Bouvines. In England, he named Stephen Langton Archbishop of Canterbury against the advice of John Lackland, who immediately confiscated the cathedral's properties. In 1212, Innocent III excommunicated the King of England, placed an interdict on his lands and freed his subjects from their feudal contract, forcing John to submit in 1213 and accept the pope's suzerainty. However, in France, he did not manage to break the will of Philip Augustus when, despite the interdict placed on his kingdom in 1200, the King refused to take back Isambour, his repudiated wife, nor would he participated in the Albigensian crusade. And at the Lateran Council, Innocent had to give way before the will of the clerics and princes who had grabbed Languedoc. He died a few months later in Perugia. The day after his death, July 17, 1216, Jacques of Vitry arrived in the Umbrian city, residence of the curia, to be consecrated Bishop of Acre. The night before, the pope's body had been presented in the cathedral. During the night, the body was stripped of its precious clothes and ornaments that were supposed to be buried with him. The naked and decomposing corpse lay there abandoned. And Jacques of Vitry could only note "how brief and vain is the deceptive splendour of this world."

Archbishop's Palace in Narbonne

Narbonne

YESTERDAY'S FRIENDS

As soon as he was informed in the month of January about the Lateran decisions, Montfort wanted to be recognized as the Duke of Narbonne, even though the council had not discussed this question. Arnaud-Amaury, the city's archbishop, had the same claims and, on his return from Rome, ordered Viscount Aimery to pay him homage and cancel whatever he owed Montfort. From Lézignan, two hours away on horseback, Montfort appealed to the pope about the situation and informed the crusade's former spiritual leader, then in Fontfroide. The situation envenomed. Arnaud-Amaury threatened to excommunicate Montfort if he tried to enter Narbonne. Despite mediation by the Archbishop of Embrun, the Bishop of Béziers and the Archdeacon of Narbonne, despite the holding of a crisis council, Montfort paid no attention and forced the barrage placed at the city's entrance by the prelate and settled into the Viscount's palace. Arnaud-Amaury anathematized Montfort. He asked Innocent III to confirm the excommunication but the pope had just died. In March, 1217, the new pope, Honorius III, took the side of his prelate "of whom Simon de Montfort is the vassal". The affair was not seriously settled, but the cause was understood for Montfort. In April 1217, Philip Augustus received his liege homage "for the Duchy of Narbonne, the County of Toulouse, the Viscounties of Béziers and Carcassonne."

Romanesque recess, Narbonne

HONOUR AND HIGH BIRTH

Raymond VI and his son Raymond the Young landed in Marseille. There they met up with their wives, Eleonore and Sancha, both sisters of Pedro II of Aragon, at the Tolonée Palace. A few days later, the consuls of Avignon came to pay them homage and assured them of their loyalty and the support of their Provencal subjects and vassals. The Saint Gilles understood that all hope was not lost and, the following day, they went to Avignon. During this time, after passing through Lézignan, Montfort had to go to Narbonne to settle, once and for all, the quarrel opposing him and Arnaud-Amaury. On March 7, he was in Toulouse at Narbonnais Castle, to receive homage from the city's consuls and to grant himself the titles of Count of Toulouse and Leicester, Viscount of Béziers and Carcassonne, Duke of Narbonne. On March 8, he promised the Toulousains to be a good lord, which did not prevent him from telling them to continue dismantling the fortifications. However, he prepared Narbonnais Castle for defence and had direct access to the castle built from outside the city. In April, at Pont de L'Arche, he paid homage to Philip Augustus and received the lands he had conquered as a fief from his suzerain. The Capetian king thereby clearly reasserted his suzerainty over the county of Toulouse, whose vassalic links had been greatly loosened, and over the former Trencavel viscounty which had not been part of his tenure for many years. On April 30, Montfort returned to the south through the Rhone valley. On his way, he learned that his brother Guy had suddenly left Toulouse for Nîmes. Provence had risen up.

The Siege of Beaucaire

It was a jubilant population of Avignon that welcomed Raymond VI and his son. The Count of Toulouse left for Salon, where Guy of Cavaillon was waiting for him at the head of an armed troop. They all returned to Avignon together. Many lords rallied to the Toulousain banner: Adhemar of Poitiers, Dragonet of Mondragon, Guiraud-Adhemar of Montélimar, Pons of Saint-Just, Lord of Pierrelatte. The lord of Les Baux promised to remain perfectly neutral. There were also numerous *faydits* in Provence. Among them was Guillaume of Minerve who was certainly fretting in his Hospitaller commandery. Raymond VI named Guy of Cavaillon Seneschal of the Venaissin before leaving to obtain more support in Catalonia and Aragon. The town's inhabitants delivered Beaucaire to Raymond the Young and the French garrison, led by Lambert of Thury, took refuge in the castle. When Montfort arrived in Nîmes, Guy had already left for Beaucaire to bring help to the French knights. Montfort joined him there on June 6. The Provencal cavalry came out and placed itself in front of the town's walls. The French charged. The confrontation was violent and everyone returned to his position. Montfort was forced to besiege the town. But the situation was not favourable. Via the Rhone

Reference Dates

• January: Saint Gilles father and son land in Marseille • March 7: Montfort receives homage from the consuls of Toulouse • April: Montfort pays homage to Philip Augustus for his new fiefs • June: Beginning of the siege of Beaucaire, lifted on August 24 • September: Montfort's soldiers loot Toulouse • November 6: Marriage of Guy de Montfort and Petronilla of Bigorre, in Tarbes	1216
• May 22: Guillaume of Peyrepertuse submits to Montfort • Early September: Conference in Saint Lizier • September 13: Raymond VI returns to Toulouse. Start of the siege of the city.	1217
• June 7: Raymond the Young arrives in Toulouse • June 25: Death of Simon de Montfort • July 25: The siege of Toulouse is lifted	1218
• Springtime: Battle of Baziège • June 2: Arrival of Prince Louis in Marmande and sacking of the city • June 6: Beginning of the siege of Toulouse by Prince Louis; siege lifted on August 1.	1219
• June: Beginning of the siege of Castelnaudary by the French • July 20: Death of Guy de Montfort, Simon's son, below the walls of Castelnaudary	1220
February: The siege of Castelnaudary is lifted	1221
• August: Death of Raymond VI • September 21: Raymond VII takes the title of Count of Toulouse	1222
July 14: Death of Philip Augustus	1223
January 14: Surrender of Amaury de Montfort at Carcassonne. The French leave Languedoc.	1224

War Machines

Assault Tower, Castle, Belfry

A tower with wheels allowing it to be brought close to the ramparts. It contained several platforms, the top one being level with the top of the rampart which the attackers could mount over a small drawbridge. The wooden planks it was made from were protected by skins of freshly-killed cattle, to prevent the defenders from setting fire to it.

Cat

A hut built at the foot of ramparts. It contained men who filled the ditch so that the assault tower could be brought forward, or who sapped the base of the walls. The cat was not used with undermining, when the base of the ramparts was reached from underground.

Catapult, Ballista

Machine to throw projectiles, the force coming from a spring.

Trebuchet, Mangonel

A machine to throw projectiles, based on the principle of a pendulum, also called a stone-thrower. The trebuchet was the most powerful of these machines. Its support, a frame made of large beams, held a pivot with a rotating arm. A counterweight was placed at one end of this arm. A leather pouch to hold the projectile, usually a rock, was attached to the other end by straps, making a kind of sling that increased the strength of the shot. Cables and winches let its operators hoist the counterweight which hurled the projectile when loosed. The arsenal of projectiles mainly consisted of rocks, but also of firebombs made of sulphur or pitch, decaying animals – an early biological weapon to provoke epidemics, or pieces of an enemy's body, an equally formidable psychological weapon.

River, the besieged Southerners received weapons, food and reinforcements, while the French had difficulties ensuring their supplies in hostile territory, and the situation became ever more precarious for Lambert of Thury and his companions. Although Montfort ordered construction of a catapult, a cat and an assault tower, his attempts to attack, even the fiercest on August 15, all failed. He sent a messenger to Dragonet of Mondragon, asking him to mediate between him and Raymond the Young. An agreement was made. On August 24, the siege was lifted. Lambert of Thury and the French knights had their lives spared. As for the new Count of Toulouse, he rode flat out for the capital of his county; he had just learned that Raymond VI was heading for Toulouse coming from south of the Pyrenees. At the announcement of Montfort's arrival, Raymond VI preferred to avoid a confrontation. After Beaucaire, Raymond the Young was warmly welcomed by the inhabitants of Saint Gilles, to the great despair of the monks, who left their abbey taking away the holy sacrament and "fulminating interdiction and anathema", related Pierre of Les Vaux de Cernay.

Beaucaire Castle

Tolosa Dolorosa

At the beginning of September 1216, Montfort was in Montgiscard where he was joined by his knights from Carcassès, Razès, the Lauragais and the Toulousain. A delegation from Toulouse that came to meet him was surprised by his belligerent attitude. A furious Montfort wanted to make Toulouse pay for the affront of Beaucaire and the cost of the siege. The city's representatives were imprisoned in Narbonnais Castle. Meanwhile, Foulque, accompanied by the abbot of Saint Sernin, tried to mollify the inhabitants who, on learning that their representatives had been taken hostage, were afraid that the French soldiers led by Guy de Montfort would invade and plunder the city. A riot broke out. The Toulousains used any weapon they found: axes, scythes, knives and sticks. Barricades were piled up. Various projectiles were thrown from rooftops. The Saint Rémésy and Jewish quarters were set on fire. Montfort wanted to invest Saint Stephen's Cathedral Square and then enter into the street "straight ahead coming directly from the cross of Master Baragnon". He was pushed back. Neither could he enter through the Cerdane Gate. The French retreated to Narbonnais Castle where Montfort threatened the hostages. Foulque offered to mediate and convened the notables of the Villeneuve quarter. He promised Toulouse and the Toulousains the Church's protection if they surrendered. Whether it was Foulque's trick or innocence abused by Montfort, the latter had the notables arrested and ordered a round-up. All of Toulouse's burgers and knights were placed under guard at the Borde, a farm outside the city. The next morning, the inhabitants were called to Saint Pierre des Cuisines Church. They were ordered to choose between surrender or exile. The city, humiliated and deprived of its consuls, had to pay a fine of thirty thousand gold marks. The hostages were sent to various castles controlled by Montfort. And the people were condemned to finish demolishing the ramparts of their city. "The beauty of Toulouse is in the hands of barbarians", wrote the poet of the *Canso*.

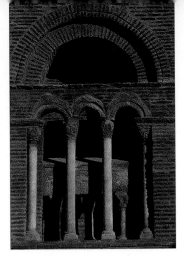

Niche at Saint Pierre des Cuisines

Saint Pierre des Cuisines Church in Toulouse

A SPECIAL REGIME

As soon as he received the county of Toulouse in commendam in April 1215, Simon de Montfort set up his own court of justice, taking their judicial power away from the local consuls. Becoming the Count of Toulouse according to a decision made by the Lateran Council, he came to take possession of his domain on March 7, 1216. That day, he received homage from the city's consuls. Their mandate continued until April 9, 1216. It is likely that there were no new elections and that, in fact, the consulate was abolished. The anonymous author of the *Canso*, who dedicated at least seven hundred lines to the repression against Toulouse after the Beaucaire episode, did not make any reference to the city's consuls. In September 1217, with time lacking to organize new elections, Raymond VI himself named the twenty-four new consuls.

THE BEST OF CITIES

S et on the right bank of the Garonne, at the place where, coming from the Pyrenees, the river is swollen by the Ariège and curves towards the north-west on its way to the ocean, the capital of the Volcae Tectosages, an *oppidum* and important port by the 3rd century B.C., enjoys a privileged location. It is connected to the Atlantic but also, in the east, through the long depression of the Hers that runs through the Lauragais, with the Mediterranean. A Roman city in 118 B.C., *Tolosa* prospered during the first century, trading with Bordeaux and, via Narbonne, with Italy and north-eastern Spain. The seat of a bishopric by the second half of the 3rd century, in 418 the city became the capital of the vast Visigothic kingdom that, during the reign of Euric (466-484), extended from south of the Loire to the Strait of Gibraltar. Passing into Frankish hands after Clovis's victory in Vouillé in 507, Toulouse stopped being a capital and, in the 8th century, became a military base for expeditions against Muslim Septimania and Spain. The city regained its high rank in 781, with Charlemagne's creation of the new kingdom of Aquitaine. It became the seat of a county whose Count Guillaume, famous for his exploits in battles in the future *Marca hispanica*, founded the Abbey of Gellone and was the hero of a series of *chansons de geste* in the 12th century. After 814, the county freed itself and continued to grow under the Saint Gilles dynasty. The northern section of the city of Toulouse, limited by the Roman ramparts, was the seat of episcopal and county power. Starting in the 12th century, came the incorporation of the town of merchants and craftsmen founded around Saint Sernin's Basilica, a famous stage of the *via Tolosana* leading to Santiago de Compostela. Toulouse endowed itself with an urban consulate in 1152, a period of demographic and economic growth.

Saint Sernin's Basilica in Toulouse

Saint James's Hospital in Toulouse

From the Adour to the Rhone

Montfort had designs on Bigorre. Since a good marriage was better than a bad war, he broke up the marriage of Nuno Sanche, Pedro II's nephew, and Countess Petronilla and married her off to his younger son, Guy, fifteen years younger than his wife. The ceremony took place in La Sède Cathedral in Tarbes on November 6, 1216. Nuno Sanche and the Viscount of Béarn occupied the castle of Lourdes that Montfort vainly besieged. Simon returned to Toulouse, where he completed the demolition of the ramparts, after making a detour through Saint Lizier. Here he arbitrated, in favour of the Bishop of Couserans, the disagreement opposing the Bishop and the Count of Comminges with the Lord of Montégut for the temporal control of the city. Montfort next passed through Aspet. Foix Castle had just been returned to Raymond-Roger, to Montfort's great displeasure. On February 6, 1217, he undertook the siege of Montgrenier, a castle that the Count of Foix had built beside Montgaillard. The place was defended by the count's son, the Viscount of Couserans, Roger of Comminges, and several *faydits*, including Pierre-Roger of Mirepoix. Its position on a steep hill and a severe winter made the besiegers' task more difficult. As for the besieged, a lack of water made their conditions nearly as hard. After several weeks, negotiations led to signing of a truce for one year. On March 25, 1217, the defenders could leave freely with their weapons and baggage and a French garrison occupied the castle.

La Sède Cathedral, Tarbes

PETRONILLA

Petronilla of Bigorre, the daughter of Bernard IV of Comminges and Stephanie of Bigorre, was born in Muret in 1184. In 1196, she married Gaston VI of Moncade, Viscount of Béarn, who died in 1214. Petronilla's next husband was the son of the Count of Roussillon and nephew of the late Pedro II, Nuno Sanche. At the siege of Toulouse in 1217, Guy de Montfort, whom Petronilla had married in 1216, was wounded by his father-in-law, the Count of Comminges, who called to him, "I believe I might have stung you! However, since you are my son-in-law, I will give you the county," Guy, the father of her two daughters, Alix and Petronilla, died at the siege of Castelnaudary on July 13, 1220. In 1222, she married Aymeric of Rancon. He accompanied Louis VIII on his royal crusade and died at the siege of Avignon in 1226. The wedding of Petronilla and Boson of Matha, Lord of Cognac, her last husband, was celebrated in 1227. In 1228, she gave birth to a third daughter named Mathe. Petronilla always maintained good relations with the Montforts. Becoming a widow in 1247, in return for an annual payment she granted the county of Bigorre to Guy de Montfort's brother, Simon V, before retiring to the Cistercian abbey of L'Escale-Dieu, where she died in November 1251.

Lourdes Castle

In April 1217, Simon de Montfort spent a few days with his family in Narbonnais Castle. He was surrounded by his wife, Alix, and his youngest children: Simon the Young, Robert, Amicie, Laura and Petronilla. His sons Amaury and Guy and their wives, Beatrice of Viennois and Petronilla of Bigorre, were also present. Montfort knew that Raymond VI had returned to Provence and that, with the help of Raymond the Young, he was rallying to his cause more and more towns and lords. He entrusted the guard of Narbonnais Castle and the fate of his wife, his daughters-in-law, his sister-in-law and all the children to Gervais of Chamigny and left for the Rhone valley. Passing through Carcassonne on May 7, he learned about the unrest in the Corbières area, where the *faydits* in Termenès had recaptured some castles, including Montgaillard, north of Padern Castle, and others between Aguilar and Peyrepertuse. Montfort took back Montgaillard. Calm was re-established and the message was understood; on May 22, despite the defensive qualities of his formidable castle, Guillaume of Peyrepertuse made an act of submission. To maintain order, Montfort left a large armed troop in Carcassonne, under the command of the seneschal Philippe Goloin, with the two Guy de Montfort, his brother and his son, and several loyal companions from the early days: Guy of Lévis, Alain of Roucy, Foucaud of Berzy and Hugues of Lacy. He set off again for Provence, which Raymond VI had left for Catalonia and Aragon. Since the gates of the Saint Gilles were closed to him, Montfort captured Posquières and Bernis, which he destroyed after having the defenders hanged. This regime of terror had the desired effect since many of the area's castles, except for Beaucaire and Saint Gilles, were abandoned by the fighters of Provence. On July 14, at Pont Saint Esprit, Montfort received homage from Raymond Pelet, Lord of Alès, before going to try to convince Adhemar of Poitiers. He was at that time joined by the new pontifical legate, Cardinal Bertrand, who was staying in Orange. East of Viviers, he was able to cross the Rhone on boats put at his disposal by the Bishop of Viviers, despite opposition by the Provencaux who were waiting for them on the river's left bank. Montfort captured Montélimar. He was joined by Guillaume of Les Baux, who had forgotten his promise to stay neutral towards Raymond VI, by the bishops of Valence and Die and by one hundred French knights who had arrived as reinforcements. He devastated Adhemar's lands and besieged him in Crest. During the siege, he received a message from Alix of Montmorency saying that Raymond VI had returned to Toulouse and that the population had risen up against the French. Montfort kept the terrible news to himself so that his opponents would not gain any advantage, and the Counts of Valentinois and Diois finally surrendered. As proof of his neutrality, Adhemar pledged three of his castles to Montfort. To seal the reconciliation, there was even talk of marrying Guillaume, the count's son, to Amicie, Simon's daughter, who had earlier been promised to James, son of Pedro II. Dragonet of Mondragon, the mediator of Beaucaire, surrendered in turn. And, accompanied by the pontifical legate, Montfort rapidly rode back to Toulouse.

Montgaillard Hill

Peyrepertuse Castle

Padern Castle

La Garde Adhémar

PEYREPERTUSE CASTLE

Peyrepertuse Castle stands on an impressive site, built on a narrow rocky crest of the Corbières, stretching east and west, north of the Verdouble River valley. With the sky as a background, the crest's outline looks like a ship's hull, holding proud, dead ruins: the lower castle, taking up the quarter-deck, and standing on the forecastle, San Jordi Castle. A terrace links the two, making a fortress three hundred metres long and fifty wide, its surface the size of the Cité of Carcassonne. The place was probably occupied at the beginning of our era, but the first written mention of the rural district of *Petre Pertuse* dates from 842 in a charter of Charles the Bald. At her marriage in 1018 with the Viscount of Narbonne, Garsinde, the daughter of Bernard, Count of Besalú, brought Peyrepertuse as part of her dowry. Its existence had been mentioned three years earlier in her father's will. The castle remained within the sphere of influence of the Counts of Besalú, since in 1083 Berenger of Narbonne paid them homage for the castles of Quéribus and Peyrepertuse. In 1107, they granted the latter to Ramón Berenguer, Count of Barcelona. This annexation to the Catalonian County house was confirmed in 1140 by the oath sworn by Berenger of Peyrepertuse, a member of the younger branch of the viscounty lineage of Fenouillet, to Count Ramón. Hence, by 1209, Peyrepertuse was the fief of the Viscount of Fenouillet, a vassal of the Viscount of Narbonne, who in turn paid homage to the Counts of Barcelona, also Kings of Aragon since 1162. Until the Battle of Muret in 1213, this vassalic link spared Peyrepertuse from the crusade. Montfort captured the castle

without a fight in 1217 and its lord Guillaume recognized him as his suzerain, in the presence of the Count of Narbonne. In 1226, Louis VIII entrusted the castle to Nuno Sanche, Count of Roussillon, as the price of rallying to him. But in 1229, Sanche ceded it back to the French crown for twenty thousand Melgorian sols. Until 1240, date at which the place was taken by Jean of Beaumont, control of Peyrepertuse, first by the Montforts, then the Capetians and Nuno Sanche, had been largely theoretical because it was a place of refuge

the signature of the Treaty of the Pyrenees, its strategic interest disappeared but a garrison remained there until the Revolution. Access to the lower castle is through the north gate onto which a narrow, steep path opens after running along the curtains flanked by two semi-cylindrical towers. Once the zigzag is passed, an oblong courtyard extends to the eastern spur, at the south of which stands the main building. At the south-west corner, a door leads to the old keep which is built around a courtyard called "of the shirt" (de la *chemise*), between

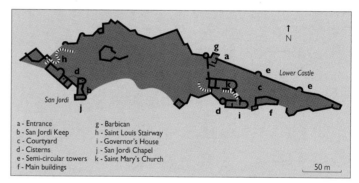

a - Entrance
b - San Jordi Keep
c - Courtyard
d - Cisterns
e - Semi-circular towers
f - Main buildings
g - Barbican
h - Saint Louis Stairway
i - Governor's House
j - San Jordi Chapel
k - Saint Mary's Church

50 m

Layout of Peyrepertuse Castle

for many *faydits*. After its surrender in 1240, in compensation Guillaume of Peyrepertuse received the castle and lands of Cucugnan, while Peyrepertuse became a royal fortress. At the time the castle consisted only of the lower castle. Work got underway in 1242, and during the period 1250-1251 San Jordi was built. The original castle received its flanking towers. During construction, the *petra pertusa*, the pierced stone that gave the site its name, was destroyed. Peyrepertuse was a key element in the defensive system of the French kingdom against Aragon. In 1367, Henry of Trastamare took shelter there and, in 1580, it was captured by Huguenots. In 1659, at

St Mary's Church and the governor's house. Between the lower castle and San Jordi, the terrace is protected by fortifications running along the edge of the cliff. Between the void and the curtains, the sixty steps of the Saint Louis staircase climb, and that is the right word for it, towards San Jordi. The width of the smooth and irregular steps, and the presence of a railing, help to overcome the drop. Through the door, San Jordi rock rises on the west side. The keep in the east provides a reward for the effort made getting there: a fine viewpoint of the lower castle at the visitor's feet, and in the distance, melting into the mountains – Queribus.

The Great Siege of Toulouse

At the beginning of the month of September 1217, Raymond VI had crossed the Pyrenees and gathered a certain number of his loyalists in Saint Lizier, in order to organize his return to Toulouse. Roger-Bernard, son of the Count of Foix, the Count of Comminges, the Viscount of Couserans and his vassals, *faydits* and emissaries from Toulouse were present. The army led by Raymond VI crossed the Garonne near Cazères. At La Salvetat, it was engaged by a troop led by Joris, one of Montfort's lieutenants, but quickly freed itself. On the evening of the 12, after having followed the Garonne's left bank, it arrived at the ramparts of the suburb of Saint Cyprien, where Raymond VI was welcomed by the leaders of the group resisting French occupation, organized in Toulouse after the city had been plundered a year earlier. On the morning of the 13, taking advantage of a thick fog, Raymond VI crossed the

Cathedral fresco, Saint Lizier

SAINT LIZIER

The town in which Raymond VI prepared his return in September 1217 had been the seat of a bishopric in the 5th century. The former capital of the *Consoranni* used to be called *Austria. Glycerius,* or *Licerius,* was its bishop from 498 to 542. In 503, the town on top of the hill overlooking the course of the Salat, was besieged by Ricosinde, Alaric's lieutenant. Licerius-Lizier, a miracle-worker often invoked to cure rabies and whitlow, managed to have the Visigoths lift their siege through prayer. At the death of its holy bishop, the town took his name. Other misfortunes struck Saint Lizier. In 736 and 793, the Saracens devastated it. In the 10th century, a plague epidemic was stopped by the intercession of the Virgin of Marsan, whose nearby chapel became a pilgrimage site. In 1117, the Romanesque cathedral containing Saint Lizier's relics was consecrated by Saint Raymond. It was rapidly flanked by a cloister. Starting in 1120 and for nearly a century, the bishop's authority over the town was bitterly contested by the Counts of Comminges and the Lords of Montégut who, in 1216, saw their claims condemned by Montfort. In 1208, Navarre, Bishop of Couserans, was named pontifical legate. At his death in 1213, Brother Dominic, approached about succeeding him, refused.

Chevet of Saint Lizier Cathedral

The Bazacle ford in Toulouse

PRETZ E PARATGE

··

The anonymous poet of the *Canso* wrote lyrically about the return of Raymond VI to Toulouse in September, 1217. "Now, we have with us Jesus Christ and the morning star, the star that has recovered its brightness for us, because here is our lord who was lost for a long time. Hence Merit and High Birth, which were in a tomb, have come back to life and vigour and health and healing." Thus, for the Toulousains, their count returned, Merit, personal merit, and High Birth, nobility of soul, *Pretz e Paratge* in Occitan, vanquished treachery, *Engans*, and bad faith, *Falhimens*, perfectly embodied by Montfort and his henchmen.

Garonne at the Bazacle ford and entered his city through the borough of Saint Sernin. He was welcomed by jubilant Toulousains, who grabbed weapons and pursued the French and those who had collaborated or colluded with them. Those who were able to reach Narbonnais Castle survived. Others found safety only behind the walls of Saint Stephen's Cathedral or within Saint Sernin's Abbey. Raymond VI immediately began working to restore the city's defences. Ramparts and towers were raised, ditches were dug, Narbonnais Castle was isolated, and the bell-towers of Saint Stephen's and Saint Sernin's were placed in a state of defence. The city was a huge construction site in which all the inhabitants took part – men and women of all social classes. Speed was absolutely necessary because Montfort was coming. The atmosphere was festive. Work continued during the night by torchlight. Before the end of September, Raymond VI re-established the consulate and, after the purge of September 13, he acted as a unifier. Since time was too short to organize elections, he named the twenty-four consuls. Among them were Hugues Déjean, Raymond Beranger and Guillaume of Rouaix, the son of David. On September 22, Guy de Montfort, Simon's son, attacked Saint Stephen's quarter but was repulsed by Roger-Bernard of Foix. Meanwhile, his uncle Guy vainly tried to free Narbonnais Castle. The French settled outside the city. Southern reinforcements, Raymond VI's vassals and *faydits*, flocked to the ramparts of the city, which soon became a huge, entrenched camp. Montfort arrived in Baziège, five leagues south-east of Toulouse, at the beginning of October. He had already sent messages to Pope Honorius III and the Archbishop of Auch asking for their help. His brother Guy came to meet him and the next day they went together towards Toulouse. The French camp was set up near the suburb of Saint Michel, east of the city, facing Narbonnais Castle not far from the Garonne. Gascon reinforcements led by the Archbishop of Auch soon arrived while, on the Occitan side, the Count of Foix entered the city despite the opposition of Amaury de Montfort. On December 29, the pope addressed Raymond-Roger of Foix, telling him to leave Toulouse. On the same day, he wrote to the Aragonese, asking them to stay away from these events this time. The next day and on January 3, 1218, he made an urgent appeal to the archbishops of France and to Philip Augustus in favour of the crusade. Montfort wanted to block the Saint Cyprien suburb on the left bank of the Garonne, which commanded the two bridges, the Old Bridge and the New Bridge, built in 1192, but his attack failed. He was forced to establish a siege. The length of the perimeter formed by the ramparts prevented a blockade. The end of the autumn and the winter passed calmly, with both camps observing each other. But hostilities began again at Easter, 1218. The besieged attempted many sorties. Some, like that on Montolieu Field, were very bloody. At the beginning of May, Alix de Montfort, who had gone to France with Foulque to find reinforcements, arrived with thirty barons and their knights. Montfort abso-

Window of Narbonnais Castle

NARBONNAIS CASTLE

Near the Garonne, flanking the eastern rampart of the city, the castle of the counts of Toulouse was built on the site of a 3rd century fortification. At the beginning of the 13th century, the structure of large bonded stones possessed two towers framing the main building.

The inhabitants fortifying Toulouse, by Jean-Paul Laurens

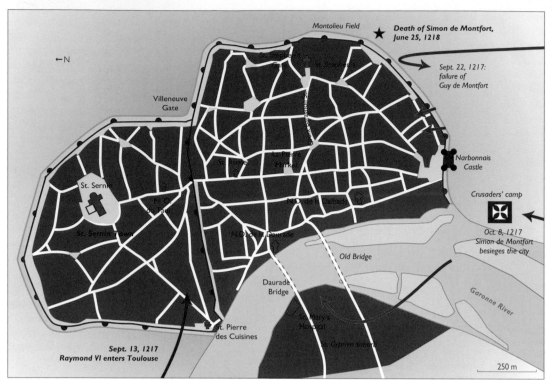

The siege of Toulouse

St James Hospital, Toulouse

lutely wanted to invest Saint Cyprien. He went to cross the Garonne at Muret, followed its course along the left bank and launched an attack on the suburb that was repulsed by the men of Roger-Bernard of Foix. Shortly afterwards, three days of torrential rain caused the river to flood and overflow its bed. The suburb was flooded. Montfort could thus occupy it since its inhabitants and defenders had abandoned it. He fortified Saint James's Hospital, but Saint Cyprien had lost much of its strategic value since both bridges had been washed away by the waters. On May 30, in the presence of Bernard, Count of Comminges, Raymond VI made his will in which he bequeathed the income from his farms to the Hospitallers and Templars of Toulouse. On June 2, an offensive by the French cavalry was broken on the defenders' first line of defence, organized at the foot of the ramparts, behind the ditches and palisades. On the French side, construction of an enormous cat was started. On June 7, the bells of Toulouse rang for the arrival of Raymond the Young at the head of a troop from Provence. Montfort called together his military leaders. He wanted to put an end to the dissensions that were threatening his troops. He gave himself one month to capture Toulouse. On Sunday, June 24, he began a general attack but the attackers could not get close to the ramparts, the defenders' first line of defence doing its job perfectly. Rocks flew through the air and the cat was made unusable. On Monday the 25, combat started again. The besieged made a sally on the side of the French camp. Montfort flung himself into the battle. On Montolieu Field, his brother Guy was shot in the side by a bolt from a crossbow. Montfort was running to him when a stone, hurled by a stone-thrower brought from Saint Sernin and used by women and young girls, smashed his head open. And the poet of the *Canso* wrote, "And the stone arrived right where it was supposed to..." Behind the ramparts there was much rejoicing. On June 26, the cardinal legate Bernard invested Amaury de Montfort with his father's titles and domains in the name of the Holy See. There was a period of calm in the hostilities and Raymond the Young was able to get away from Toulouse to go to L'Isle Jourdain, to place the city in defence, since it was the fief of Bernard-Jourdain. He was back by July 1. While a group of crusaders was preparing to leave since their forty-day service was over, Amaury ordered a new attack. Fighting was bloody but it failed. It was to be the last attack. On July 8, Amaury, the legate and the barons went to Pamiers. In the church of Saint Antonin of Fredelas Monastery, Amaury took possession of the city and its castle as its co-lord. They returned to the walls of Toulouse. His uncle Guy and Alain of Roucy dissuaded Amaury from continuing the siege. The cardinal legate decided to give up, still claiming that the crusade was not over. And indeed, in his bulls of August 11, 12 and 13 and September 5, Honorius III addressed the archbishops of France and Provence, the King of France and his son Louis asking them to give their support to the crusade. The bishops of Toulouse, Tarbes and Comminges, as well as Alix of Montmorency left for Île de France to find reinforcements and subsidies. On July 25, the French set fire to their camp and their war machines as well as to Narbonnais Castle, whose fire was rapidly put out by the Toulousains. Amaury de Montfort left for Carcassonne, taking away his father's corpse in a leather bag. He intended to bury it in Saint Nazaire Cathedral. He was twenty years old. Behind the ramparts of Toulouse, another young man enjoyed his victory when he saw the vanquished attackers, Raymond the Young was twenty-one.

Flagstone with a knight

MORE GALLICO

The lifeless body of Simon de Montfort was treated according to French custom. The corpse was boiled to separate the skeleton from the flesh and the entrails, which were buried nearby. The bones were placed in the final burial place. Those of Montfort were buried in an apsidal chapel of Saint Nazaire in Carcassonne. They were exhumed and taken away by Amaury in 1224. The remains of the crusading lion were definitively buried in the church of the Hautes Bruyères Priory, near Chevreuse, founded in 1112 by the lord of Montfort and Louis VI.

St Nazaire Cathedral, Carcassonne

Nave in Condom cathedral

A Difficult Legacy

After the death of the crusade's leader, the southern liberation movement, started when the Raymonds landed in Marseille in January 1216, developed even though Amaury de Montfort could still count on a few, rare southern allies like the Lord of Les Baux. The latter was taken prisoner when he attacked Avignon; he was skinned alive and dismembered. The heir of the Montforts, dealing with what was most urgent, had to intervene in the Albigeois, Quercy and the Agenais. In September, he ceded the lease of the old castle to the Bishop of Albi to ensure his loyalty. Then, in Moissac, he renewed the agreements that his father had made with Saint Peter's Abbey. In October, he recaptured Gontaud. He next went to Comminges where he took Cazères and massacred the inhabitants. His next trip was to Lagrasse where he had been told that the abbot had contact with *faydits*. At the end of December, his mother Alix, still busy helping, arrived with French reinforcements. Amaury had sufficient troops with which to besiege Marmande. On their side, the counts of Comminges, Toulouse and Foix were also actively reconquering their domains. As soon as the siege of Toulouse was lifted, Bernard of Comminges returned to his castle in Salies. He began to pursue Jordi, who had captured Saint Gaudens, and caught up with him in Meilhan, where the former ally of the crusaders was now fighting for himself and was besieging Meilhan in Astarac. "A blow through his body knocked him into the dust", commented the *Canso*'s anonymous author, and Jordi was taken prisoner. As usual, Raymond VI preferred to negotiate. In Perpignan on October 9, he gave some of his possessions as fiefs to his grandson, Pierre-Bermond of Anduze, who promised to serve him faithfully. In November, his daughter-in-law, Sancia of Aragon, confirmed the privileges of Nîmes, a city that had rallied to the House of Toulouse. Meanwhile, Raymond the Young had reconquered the Agenais: he invested Condom, Marmande, Clairac and Aiguillon. On January 6, 1219, he was in Najac where, in the presence of Centule of Astarac, he gave as fiefs the castles of Loupian and Balaruc, and the church of Palais, to two lords of Languedoc. As for the Count of Foix, in early 1219, after travelling through the Lauragais, he settled in Baziège, five leagues south-west of Toulouse, with his two sons, Roger-Bernard and Loup, his knights and several *faydits*: Chabert of Barbaira, Jourdain of Cabaret, Guillaume of Niort. They were joined by Raymond the Young and several knights, including Arnaud of Villemur, Hugues of Alfaro, Bernard-Jourdain of L'Isle, followed by a corps of militia from Toulouse. Since Amaury and his army had just begun to besiege Marmande, it was the French stationed in Carcassonne who were to try and dislodge them. The French approached Baziège. They were led by Foucaud and Jean of Berzy, and Alain of Roucy. The Southerners came out of the town, using the classic opposition of three corps. The first was that of the Count of Foix, the second consisted of fighters from Comminges, the third, the reserve, was placed under the command of Raymond the Young. The French heavy cavalry was first of all damaged by the much more mobile light cavalry of their adversaries. The fast destriers carrying

In All the Campaigns

In the spring of 1219, when Amaury de Montfort had already started besieging Marmande, Prince Louis set off for Aquitaine. The heir to the French throne had come at the head of a large army to bring him support. The anonymous author of the *Canso* spoke of 25,000 *écus*. Since an *écu* consisted of one knight and three to five men at arms accompanying him, the total number in this army would have been about 100,000 men. This is probably exaggerated but other chroniclers also mentioned that it was very large. At the side of Prince Louis, there were about twenty prelates and thirty-three counts, including the Count of Saint Pol, Gaucher of Châtillon. He had been fighting for over thirty years. He had gone to the Holy Land on the third crusade with Philip Augustus and had fought at his side during the siege of Acre, in July 1191. He had been part of the host that had invaded Languedoc in 1209. In 1214, he had won renown at the Battle of Bouvines, and in 1215 accompanied Prince Louis on his pilgrimage to Languedoc. He died a few months after the sacking of Marmande, in October 1219.

riders armed with bows, crossbows and slings circled around the crusaders loaded down with armour. The Occitan heavy cavalry then intervened and, with the help of foot-soldiers from the Toulouse militia, finished them off. The French were massacred. The Berzy brothers were taken prisoner. Pierre-Guillaume of Séguret, a treacherous Southerner, was hanged. In Marmande, the city's defenders continued to resist. On June 2, Prince Louis arrived under the city's walls with a strong armed contingent. The Capetians had indeed received the repeated messages from Honorius III. Centule of Astarac, Marmande's defender, parleyed: their lives saved in return for the town's surrender. He was imprisoned in Puylaurens and exchanged for Foucaud of Berzy. But the town, handed over to the soldiers, was pillaged, and the population – men, women and children – slaughtered. There were five thousand dead. These gratuitous murders, carried out under the eyes of and perhaps on the orders of the future King of France, had only one purpose: to terrorize in order to maintain Amaury's ever more contested legacy from his father. On June 17, the crusaders, with Louis, Amaury and the legate, moved towards Toulouse.

At the approach of the crusading troops, Raymond the Young had called his council together. Pelfort of Rabastens suggested being recognized as one of Louis's vassals, since Amaury, who held his titles and domains from the Church, had not yet been invested by the King of France. Raymond VI's son excluded this solution. He placed Toulouse in a state of defence. The eighteen fortified places of the city were given into the command of knights like Hugues of Alfaro or Bertrand of Toulouse, his half-brother; allies like Roger-Bernard, son of the Count of Foix, or Arnaud of Comminges; *faydit* heretical believers or sympathizers, like Guillaume of Minerve, Jourdain of Cabaret, Arnaud of Villemur, Guillaume Hunaud of Lanta, Pelfort of Rabastens, Guiraud of Gourdon and Sicard of Puylaurens. The crusaders arrived before Toulouse on June 6. The siege was lifted on August 1. It had failed. Prince Louis returned to France, leaving Amaury a contingent of two hundred men for one year.

St Sernin's Basilica, side aisle

A HOLY PROTECTOR

After Raymond VII had held his council, as Prince Louis's army approached Toulouse in June 1219, in the abbey church of Saint Sernin the inhabitants exhibited "the body of Saint Exupère, surrounded by lights and candelabra", at least according to the anonymous author of the *Canso*. According to tradition, this Bishop of Toulouse from the beginning of the 5th century had prevented the Vandals from destroying the city. In 1226, Prince Louis, who had become Louis VIII in 1223, led a new crusade to the Midi. When they learned of this plan, the consuls voted an annual subsidy of ten Toulousain *sous* in favour of the confraternity in charge of maintaining the oil lamps that, day and night, illuminated with their flickering flames Saint Exupère's altar in Saint Sernin's, so that "God and the Lord Jesus Christ, through the intercession of the Blessed Virgin Mary, the Blessed Bishop Exupère, and the other saints, protect the city and the town from all evil, all danger, and all enemy attack." In the autumn of 1226, Louis VIII did not come close to Toulouse.

Crypt in Saint Sernin's Basilica, Toulouse

The Occitan Triumph

After the siege of Toulouse was lifted at the beginning of August 1219, Amaury took up quarters in Castelnaudary. Until the end of the year, the two adversaries tried to reinforce their respective positions. The Raymonds received homage from several vassals, and Amaury, on September 3, came to some agreements with Tedisio, the former legate who had become Bishop of Agde, over disputes about several domains in the diocese of Agde. There were skirmishes between the partisans of the two sides. In one, the two Berzy brothers, Jean and Foucaud, after being freed in exchange for Centule of Astarac, were taken prisoner in the Languedoc after they began a reign of terror there. They were beheaded and their impaled heads were carried around the streets of Toulouse. The Pope named a new legate, Conrad, Bishop of Porto and former abbot of Citeaux. At the beginning of the year 1220, when his wife had just given birth to a girl, Jeanne, Raymond the Young set off on campaign once again. With the help of Sicard of Lautrec, who had abandoned the crusaders' side, he captured Lavaur and the garrison was massacred. Puylaurens, still held by the widow of Foucaud of Berzy, surrendered; the lady's and the defenders' lives were spared. Of course, the Occitanians went to Castelnaudary. Amaury had evacuated the *castrum*. But they had barely invested it when Montfort's son came back to besiege it. The siege of Castelnaudary lasted for eight months. During an attack on July 20, Guy de Montfort, Amaury's younger brother, was killed. During the siege, Pope Honorius III depended on his legate to try to recover control. He addressed the local clergy but also the Southerners, lords, consuls and the population, to regain the crusading impetus, while at the same time he was insistently demanding that the Counts of Toulouse, Foix and Comminges lay down their arms or else suffer serious consequences. The siege of Castelnaudary was finally lifted in February, 1221. Amaury withdrew to Carcassonne. Raymond the Young and his troops followed, capturing Montréal on their way through. The population had opened the gates for them but the French garrison, entrenched in the castle, defended itself. Alan of Roucy, one of the most loyal followers of Simon de Montfort, was mortally wounded. His son surrendered the place. In May, Raymond the Young was in Avignon to confirm the inhabitants with a certain number of rights and privileges in return for services rendered. In July, he did the same thing with the inhabitants of Gaillac. This was when Amaury de Montfort saw the arrival of reinforcements in Carcassonne with, at their head, the Archbishop of Bourges and the bishops of Limoges and Clermont. He left with them for Agen to guarantee the loyalty of its inhabitants. But one month later, Agen returned to the Raymondin fold. In October, realizing that Raymond the Young had not paid any attention to his warnings, Honorius III delivered a judgement through which he disinherited him. In March 1222, after arranging the election system of the consuls of Toulouse, Raymond the Young went to the Gevaudan and, on his return on March 27, 1222, received an oath of fidelity from the population of Moissac. Amaury's domain was

Old man, Moissac Abbey Church

Fortified gate, Penne d'Agenais

Cité of Carcassonne

inexorably shrinking. Little remained in the Agenais and Quercy, where only two places –Penne d'Agenais and Verdun sur Garonne– remained loyal to him. The inhabitants of Béziers and the Minervois areas had revolted in 1221 just as Conrad arrived in Béziers. On April 28, 1222, the legate excommunicated thirty localities in the area, including Narbonne. By now, Amaury had almost nothing besides the Carcassès. In May 1222, he sent an embassy consisting of the bishops of Nîmes and Béziers to Philip Augustus. Honorius III supported the move. Amaury suggested the King of France cede him all the lands he had conquered. On June 16, Raymond the Young undertook a similar step. In the letter he addressed to the King of France, taking up Pelfort of Rabastens' idea during the siege of Toulouse in 1219, he denounced his "shameful disinheritance" and asked the king to recognize him as a vassal. The king answered neither one nor the other. Two months later, in August 1222, Raymond VI died in Toulouse at the house of Hugo Déjean. He was sixty-six. His body was handed over to the

RETURNING HOME

Taking advantage of the Occitan reconquest, *faydits* and perfects returned to their *castra*, the fortified villages and castles evacuated by the French. Hence, when Amaury de Montfort was besieging Castelnaudary in 1220, inside the town were Gaucelm, the Bishop of the Cathar Church of Toulouse; his *filius major*, Guilhabert of Castres, who succeeded him; Raymond Agulher, the deacon of Sabarthès and future Bishop of the Razès Cathar Church. To put them in a safe place, during the siege three *faydits* believers – Bernard-Othon of Niort, Guillaume of Lahille, and Bernard of Saint Martin – organized the escape of Guilhabert of Castres and Raymond Agulher whom they led to Foix to the home of Raymond Sans de Rabat, after making an incognito stopover at Boulbonne Abbey. In 1222, Guilhabert of Castres, following a short stay at Mas Saintes Puelles, returned to settle in Fanjeaux which he made into the temporary seat of his bishopric.

Nave in St Sernin's, Toulouse

Death of An Occitan Prince
....

Raymond VI of Toulouse died in August 1222. That morning, he had gone to pray in the Daurade Church and it was on his return to Hugo Déjean's house in the borough of Saint Sernin, where he was living, that he was suddenly struck down by illness. He asked to be attended by Saint Sernin's abbot, who was slow in coming. When the latter arrived at his bedside, the count was already speechless. Through gestures, placing his hands within those of the abbot, he managed to make the abbot understand that he wanted to be absolved and reconciled with the Church. Hospitallers of Saint John, in whose properties the count wanted to be buried, were present. One of them put on his coat emblazoned with a cross. Raymond of Saint Gilles kissed the material and passed away. At the request of Raymond VII, in 1247 Innocent IV charged commissioners with an enquiry. They heard more than one hundred and ten witnesses and made a report very favourable to Raymond VI. But the count's remains stayed in a coffin placed in a shed at the Hospitallers'. With time, the bones were scattered but the authors of *A General History of Languedoc* relate that, at the beginning of the 18th century, "the skull [of Raymond VI] was still being shown in Saint John's House in Toulouse."

members of the Order of Saint John of Jerusalem according to his wishes in his will and testament of 1218. But the count could not be buried because his excommunication had not been lifted. His widow, Eleonore of Aragon, retired to the charterhouse of La Valbonne, three leagues west of Pont Saint Esprit. On September 21, 1222, Raymond the Young took the title of Raymond VII during a ceremony at Saint Pierre des Cuisines Church in Toulouse. The reconquest continued. In December, Raymond VII tried to take back Penne d'Agenais and Verdun sur Garonne. On March 27, 1223 in Pamiers, Raymond-Roger of Foix received homage from the twelve co-lords of Mirepoix, including Pierre-Roger of Mirepoix, Isarn of Fanjeaux and his cousin Arnaud-Roger, the brother of Raymond of Péreille. Shortly afterwards, during the springtime, just before Raymond-Roger died he recaptured the town from Guy of Lévis. Many perfects then returned to settle on the banks of the Hers. Amaury, who had received reinforcements in April, left for Penne d'Agenais to free the garrison besieged by Raymond VII. He ended up proposing a truce to be discussed at Saint Flour. Marriage between Raymond VII and one of Amaury's sisters was even considered. The two young men met again in Carcassonne but, even though they stayed in the same lodgings, their talks led nowhere. At the beginning of May, Conrad learned that the King of France planned to convoke an assembly in Melun to discuss the Occitan question. He wrote to the king asking him to intervene. Amaury even went to the sovereign to renew the request. But Philip Augustus was very ill. The Melun meeting would probably not be held at all. Conrad called for a council to be held in Sens on July 9. Philip Augustus, who was at Pacy sur Eure, wished to attend and asked that the meeting be held in Paris. But he died on his way there, on July 14. According to his own words, his kingdom fell "into the hands of a woman and children". His son, Louis, was crowned King in Reims on August 6. Conrad was present and took care to alert Louis VIII about the situation in Languedoc, before leaving for Rome from where the pope addressed a letter to the new king. One was sent on December 13, another on the 14, congratulating him, to be sure, but also urging him to intervene in Languedoc. Amaury returned to Carcassonne, which had been besieged in vain during his absence by the Counts of Toulouse and Foix. The circle of his loyalists was constantly shrinking, leaving at most twenty knights including his uncle Guy, the Marshal of Lévis and Lambert of Thury. The situation was difficult; despite support from Arnaud-Amaury, still Archbishop of Narbonne, he had been forced to return to his domains in Île de France to raise new troops, while the Viscount of Narbonne had just joined the Occitan side. The game was over for Amaury who, on January 14, 1224, signed his capitulation before his adversaries in a tent set up on the banks of the Aude, at the foot of the ramparts of Carcassonne. The next day, he presented pastures in the Minervois mountains to Fontfroide Abbey, and the castle of Termes to Arnaud-Amaury, thus thanking them for their support to the very end. Then he set off on the road to France, taking the remains of his father wrapped in an oxskin.

Consuls' House in Mirepoix

Joists in Consuls' House, Mirepoix

MIREPOIX

Although Guy of Lévis lost Mirepoix in 1223, he would regain this *castrum*, located on the "Marshal's lands" in 1229 by clauses in the Treaty of Paris. In 1279, waters of the Hers carried away the part of town set on the river's right bank. According to legend, an Aragonese princess staying in Puivert wished to have lowered the waters of a lake at the foot of the castle, which retained the waters of the Blau, a tributary of the Hers. The excavation work undertaken to satisfy the princess's whims were allegedly at the origin of this catastrophe – the waters carrying away the princess and engulfing Chalabre and Puivert downstream. Jean of Lévis, husband of Constance of Foix, had the town rebuilt on the other bank. This was a bastide built in a systematic, orthogonal lay out. Nowadays, the bastide of Mirepoix retains fine vestiges of its medieval past with a central square edged with wooden covered walks, opening onto fine coloured half-timbered facades, like the Consuls' House from the 15th century. The ends of its joists are decorated with sculptures of heads of men and horrible monsters and fantastic animals. Mirepoix was raised to a bishopric by Pope John XXII in 1317, and the bastide's church, consecrated in 1298 to Saint Maurice, was raised to cathedral rank for a while. In 1327, when Jacques Fournier left the bishop's seat of Pamiers for that of Mirepoix, work began to enlarge the cathedral. The Lévis family put down roots in the region and, at the beginning of the 14th century, Guy III of Lévis enlarged and restored Lagarde Castle, a former possession of the Counts of Foix, two leagues upstream from Mirepoix, on the Hers.

Chevet of Saint Stephen's Cathedral in Bourges

THE ROYAL CRUSADE

After Amaury de Montfort's departure, the Counts of Toulouse and Foix gave Carcassonne back to the young Trencavel. He was only sixteen years old. He entered into the possession of the lands of his fathers and became, "through the grace of God, Viscount of Béziers, Lord of Carcassonne, the Razès and Albi". On January 23, 1224, Arnaud-Amaury and the bishops of Nîmes, Uzès, Agde and Béziers sent a letter from Montpellier to Honorius III telling him of the defeat and departure of Amaury de Montfort. For them, it was a return to the *statu quo ante*. Everything had to begin again...

Into the Lion's Mouth

The Languedoc prelates were correct. The Occitan princes had recovered their domains and heresy was stronger than ever. At the end of January, Louis VIII answered the pope's December letters. He agreed to intervene in Languedoc, accepted the donation of Amaury de Montfort, to be acknowledged in February, but set conditions. He wanted the Holy See to confer on him the authority to name the archbishops of Bourges, Sens and Reims as the crusade's spiritual leaders and to recognize the conquered lands as his property. He also demanded that the prelate of Bourges be named a legate. In January, Honorius III received four embassies from Raymond VII, coming to present him with the Count's submission. Faced with such demands, he answered the King of France at the beginning of April. Since he was negotiating peace with Raymond VII, intervention in Languedoc was no longer urgent, but he would appreciate Louis VIII maintaining the threat of it to make the Count of Toulouse more receptive to admitting his errors. The King of France would not play the pope's game. He announced his refusal to the legate Conrad and demanded that his rights as suzerain be respected. On June 3 in Montpellier, Arnaud-Amaury called together Raymond VII, Roger-Bernard of Foix and Raymond Trencavel. They submitted to the Church but asked that the accords with the Montforts, the investitures conceded to him by the Holy See, and the enfeoffing of their lands by Montfort to the advantage of Philip Augustus be cancelled. The Pope agreed on July 11. A council was held in Montpellier on August 22. Despite protests by Amaury de Montfort, the council ratified the peace with the Occitan princes who swore to expel the *routiers* from their lands, fight heresy and promote the Catholic faith. The Archbishop of Arles travelled to Rome to transmit these oaths to the pope. Everything seemed so simple. But, not everyone had had their last word. Louis VIII sent Guy de Montfort to Rome where the reconciliation proceedings were dragging on. On February 13, 1225, the Pope sent him Cardinal of Saint Ange, the new legate named in December. Meetings were held in Paris between the legate and the king in May, then in Tours and Chinon in June. A new council was organized in Bourges in the month of November.

Reference Dates

1225
- August: A council is held in Montpellier
- November 29: Opening of the Council of Bourges

1226
- Cathar "council" in Pieusse
- January 28: Louis VIII takes the cross
- June 6: Beginning of the siege of Avignon
- September: Avignon surrenders on the 12. Louis VIII names a seneschal in Beaucaire and in Nîmes. Submission of Carcassonne; the King installs another seneschal there.
- November: Death of Louis VIII in Montpensier.
- Death at the stake of Pierre Isarn, Bishop of the Cathar Church of Carcassonne

1227
- Wars of Limoux and Cabaret
- Labécède is besieged by Imbert of Beaujeu. The population is massacred. Death at the stake of the Cathar perfects who lived there.

1228
- Death of Guy de Montfort, Simon's brother.
- Destruction by Imbert of Beaujeu of crops and vineyards around Toulouse.

1229
- April 12: Signature of the Treaty of Paris by Raymond VII and the Crown of France
- June 16: Surrender of the Count of Foix at Saint Jean de Verges.

THE "COUNCIL" OF PIEUSSE

....

According to witness' accounts during interrogations by the Inquisition, it was in early 1226, while the royal crusade was being organized, that about a hundred perfects met in Pieusse. The Cathars of Razès wished to have their own Church, since they no longer knew whether they depended on Carcassonne or Toulouse.
For Pierre Isarn, bishop of the latter, referring to the limits set at Saint Felix in 1167, the Razès depended on his Church. But the moral authority of Guilhabert of Castres was compelling and a new bishopric was created. The bishop named at its head was Benedict of Termes, probably the brother of Raymond of Termes, and Oliver's uncle. His *filius major* was Raymond Agulher and *filius minor*, Pons Bernardi. The first bishop of the Razès Cathar Church died at Quéribus in 1241.

14 archbishops, 123 bishops and 520 abbots attended the council, whose sessions opened on November 29, 1225. Two prelates from Languedoc, known from the crusade, did not attend: Guy of Les Vaux de Cernay, Bishop of Carcassonne, had died on March 21, 1224, and Arnaud-Amaury, Archbishop of Narbonne, had died in Fontfroide on September 29, 1225. Speaking before the assembly, Raymond VII renewed his Montpellier promises, begged the Cardinal of Saint Ange to make sure he respected them, asked for absolution and declared himself ready to carry out any penance asked of him. The council noted the count's declarations but set forth one condition: in his own name and that of his heirs, he had to renounce his domains forever. Masks had been dropped and the trap snapped shut. Raymond VII refused. He was therefore not reconciled with the Church. A new crusade could be organized in Languedoc. The council asked Louis VIII to lead it. In Paris, on January 28, 1226, the king called the vassals who pledged to support him in a parliament, and on the 30, he took the cross from the hands of the legate who excommunicated Raymond VII and declared him a "condemned heretic". Every crusader would be given indulgences; his lands and person would be under Church protection. On March 29, another parliament set the date for the expedition. Before his departure, Louis VIII pronounced a royal edict against heretics and their abettors. And on May 17, Easter Sunday, the host gathered in Bourges. Amaury de Montfort and his uncle Guy, but also Bouchard of Marly, were at the side of Louis VIII.

Quéribus Castle

St Nazaire Gate in Carcassonne

A Crusader Named Louis

The decisions taken at the Council of Bourges rapidly became known in Languedoc, where lords, consuls and people were dismayed. How could they imagine that these lands still scarred by fifteen years of war would once again suffer from another crusade? Submissions therefore multiplied even before the crusader host had gathered. After the Lord of Laurac, Bernard of Aillou presented his submission before the abbot of Ardorel at Usson Castle on March 16. On the same day, Raymond of Roquefeuil did the same to Pierre Amiel, the new Archbishop of Narbonne. Before leaving Bourges, Louis VIII and the legate had taken care to make sure of the neutrality of James I of Aragon and of Nuno Sanche, Count of Roussillon. The pope too had written to the King of England so that he would not attack the King of France during his crusade and not provide support for Raymond VII. The inhabitants of Avignon, informed that the crusaders would pass through their city, made it known that they would not oppose them. Bertrand of Gourdon and Bernard-Othon of Niort, who wrote directly to the King of France, also submitted, as did, in April, the lords of the Béziers area and the consuls of Béziers. As planned, the crusaders arrived in Lyon on May 28. On June 7, they arrived in Avignon and discovered that the city's gates were closed to them. Raymond VII had managed to change the minds of the city's authorities. The crusaders besieged it, but also warned its suzerain, Emperor Frederick, of their intentions. The

SENESCHALS OF THE LORD KING

After the surrender of Avignon on September 12, 1226, Louis VIII named a seneschal "of the lord King of France in Beaucaire and in Nîmes". This was a French knight, Peregrine Latinier. Several weeks later, he installed another French knight, Adam of Milly, at the head of the new royal seneschalsy of Carcassonne.

The ramparts of Avignon

Statues in Clermont Cathedral

The Young Girl of Montpensier

The illness that killed Louis VIII in Montpensier was considered curable through the act of the flesh. Judging the king's condition desperate, a member of his entourage, Archambaud of Bourbon, went in search of a beautiful, well-born damsel, to whom he explained what was expected of her. Finding her in his room when he awoke, Louis VIII was surprised at her presence. She explained the situation. The king refused to commit what would have been a mortal sin and ordered that she be married honourably. The episode was related by Guillaume of Puylaurens who heard it from Archambaud of Bourbon himself.

siege lasted over three months. Exhausted, Avignon gave in on September 12. The Cardinal of Saint Ange would make the city pay dearly for its about-face. But for the besiegers, the surrender was welcome because the fighting had been fierce and their ranks had been decimated by dysentery. Among the victims were the Archbishop of Reims and Bouchard of Marly. Furthermore, many barons and lords departed once their forty days of service were over and their indulgences were earned. Submissions had continued during the siege. At the beginning of June, the consuls of Nîmes presented theirs to their bishop. The abbot of Castres received that of Sicard of Puylaurens; the Bishop of Albi that of Guillaume-Bernard of Najac; the consuls of Carcassonne delivered theirs to the abbot of Lagrasse. Castres, Albi, Narbonne, Limoux and Beaucaire made acts of allegiance. Some arrived in person before the king, like Bernard VI of Comminges in August. According to Guillaume of Puylaurens, the Count of Foix also came to Avignon. Only one did not bend: Raymond VII of Toulouse. From Avignon, the king reached Beaucaire, Béziers, and then Carcassonne, where Jourdain of Cabaret, the provost named by Trencavel, who had abandoned the place, submitted in his turn. In October, the crusaders went to Pamiers, where Louis VIII received his rights as the city's co-lord from Amaury de Montfort. But the king was ill. It was autumn and Toulouse, still loyal to its count along with a few rare places like Gaillac and Rabastens, was an important obstacle, especially since the Counts of Toulouse and Foix had signed a new alliance in Toulouse at the end of September. Louis VIII departed for Île de France. On his way, he passed through the Lauragais. In Belpech, he enfeoffed Nuno Sanche, the Viscount of Fenouillèdes and the Perapertusès. His itinerary took him through Castelnaudary, Lavaur and Albi. In Albi, he increased the annuity of Agnes of Montpellier, the wife of Raymond-Roger Trencavel, who had died in Carcassonne's prison in 1209, and entrusted the army he left in Languedoc to Imbert of Beaujeu. His route passed through Rodez, Espalion, Saint Flour, Clermont, and stopped in Montpensier where the king died on November 8.

Rodez Cathedral

The Old Bridge in Espalion

Scorched Earth

Cabaret and Régine Tower

Certainly, Imbert of Beaujeu could count on the support of experienced men like Guy de Montfort, Guy of Lévis or Pierre of Voisins, even Amaury de Montfort. Certainly, he could count on the seneschals the king had named in Beaucaire and Carcassonne. But Louis VIII was dead and his widow, Blanche of Castile, had to accept the regency since Louis IX was only twelve years old. She first had to control several unruly French barons before dealing with Languedoc. Imbert of Beaujeu was quite forlorn. The submissions of 1226 had lost some of their strength as the person who had benefited most from them, *intuitu personae*, the King of France, was no longer of this world. Pockets of resistance were forming. For two years, 1226 and 1227, Limoux was controlled by Trencavel and the Count of Foix, surrounded by about forty *faydits* including Pierre-Roger of Mirepoix and Arnaud of Villemur. And as soon as Amaury left in January 1224, the Bishop Pierre Isarn had made Cabaret into the seat of the Cathar bishopric of Carcassès. Since then, many perfects had arrived there, as well as several *faydits* such as Bernard-Othon of Niort, one of the co-lords of Cabaret since he was married to Nova, the sister of Pierre-Roger and Jourdain, and Olivier of Termes. In 1226, Imbert of Beaujeu captured Pierre Isarn on the road to Toulouse. He delivered him to the Archbishop of Narbonne and the bishop of the Cathar Church of Carcassès perished at the stake in Caunes. In 1229, Cabaret was supposed to be handed over

LIMOUX AND CABARET

Resistance to Imbert of Beaujeu was particularly strong in Limoux and Cabaret. In their testimonies, people interrogated by the Inquisition often mentioned the "wars of Limoux and Cabaret".

East ramparts of the Cité of Carcassonne

Capital, Notre Dame of Rabastens

THE PRICE OF LOYALTY

....

Noting that Avignon did not allow free passage to the royal crusade, at the beginning of the month of June 1226, the legate immediately excommunicated Raymond VII and proclaimed an interdict on his lands. Four months after the siege, in January 1227, he granted the city absolution and in return the city was penalized with strict sanctions: besides a very heavy fine, Avignon's artillery was to be seized, its ramparts, towers and three hundred houses destroyed. It would furthermore have to send thirty knights to the Holy Land within three months and cover their costs.

Chevet in St Jean de Verges

to the French King; the perfects living there were taken to a safe place by the *faydits*. One who had never submitted was Raymond VII of Toulouse. In the course of the winter of 1226-1227, he captured Auterive from its French garrison and then strengthened the defences of Labécède, whose guard he entrusted to Pons of Villeneuve, the bailiff of Castelnaudary, his future seneschal. During Lent in 1227, the Archbishop Pierre Amiel called a council in Narbonne. The Counts of Toulouse and Foix were anathematized and excommunicated, and anti-heretical edicts decided during Louis VIII's stay in Pamiers in 1226 were confirmed. Meanwhile, Imbert of Beaujeu's troop numbers were dwindling as the forty-day services came to an end. The legate forced the unwilling prelates to support the crusade financially. But Imbert of Beaujeu, a man of action, had no qualms. He besieged Labécède during the summer of 1227. The defenders fled. The population was massacred, even the women and children that Foulque had tried to protect. There had been perfects living in Labécède, including Geraud of Lamothe, the Quercy deacon and brother of Guilhabert of Castres' *filius major*. They were condemned to the stake. One of them did manage to escape from the *castrum* – its lord, Pagan of Labécède. Imbert of Beaujeu pursued his actions, gathering a contingent in Albi, besieging Lagrave and devastating the region of Cordes. During the winter of 1227-1228, Sicard of Puylaurens rallied to Raymond VII, who placed troops in Puylaurens and Saint Paul Cap de Joux. The latter locality contained many perfects. After a short stay in Besplas Castle, Guilhabert of Castres went to Mirepoix and then to Toulouse before coming to Saint Paul Cap de Joux. He was accompanied by his *filius major*, Bernard of Lamothe, the deacons of Saint Paul, Lanta, Caraman and Verfeil, other perfects like Guillaume-Bernard of Airoux, a doctor. Many believers or sympathizers came to visit Guilhabert in his Lauragais retreat, which had become the seat of the Cathar Church of Toulouse. Untamed Toulouse was thus encircled by a chain of places and castles it could count on: Auterive, Puylaurens, Saint Paul Cap de Joux, Rabastens and Gaillac. Imbert of Beaujeu had managed to place a garrison in Castelsarrasin, but Raymond VII recaptured it despite the presence of Bishop Foulque of Toulouse, and Clarin, Simon de Montfort's former chaplain who had become Bishop of Carcassonne in 1226, and despite intervention by the French who had received reinforcements led by the Archbishop of Bourges. Although the French had lost Guy de Montfort, killed by an arrow near Varilhes before the siege of Castelsarrasin, they captured Montech. At the beginning of the summer of 1228, Imbert of Beaujeu received reinforcements of Gascon troops led by the archbishops of Auch and Bordeaux. He set up a first camp at Guilhemery, then moved it to Montaudran, just outside Toulouse. He devastated the area, especially the vineyards, meticulously destroying everything. At the end of September, there was no harvest in the Toulousain. The region's entire economy was seriously and durably affected. Imbert of Beaujeu struck camp and sent the Gascons home. He moved towards Pamiers and continued as far as Saint Jean de Verges, on the banks of the Ariège, one league downstream from Foix.

A Peace of Clerics and the French

In early 1228, the Cardinal of Saint Ange returned to Rome. On March 21, Pope Gregory IX, who had succeeded Honorius III in 1227, agreed to the request of Blanche of Castile who wished that the prelate continue his mission as legate. At the beginning of the summer, the Pope wrote to his legate to encourage him to work for peace between the Capetians and the Saint Gilles. To seal the peace, he considered a marriage between Jeanne, daughter of Raymond VII, and a brother of Louis IX. For this purpose, he granted the necessary dispensation since the mothers of the Count of Toulouse and Blanche of Castile were second cousins. This plan of peace was dramatically different from anything that had been undertaken in Languedoc over the previous twenty years, including the actions of Imbert of Beaujeu who, at the moment that the pope was addressing his legate, was preparing to devastate the Toulousain. This turnaround was probably due to Blanche of Castile. The regent of the kingdom of France knew the price of a war whose outcome was uncertain. Furthermore, she was related to Raymond VII. The legate charged Elie Garin, the abbot of the Cistercian abbey of Grandselve, to begin negotiations with the Count of Toulouse. A first meeting took place in Baziège and several agreements were sketched out. As far as religion was concerned, Raymond VII had to reconcile with the Church and promise to fight heresy to have his excommunication lifted. Politically, he had to recognize the King of France as his suzerain. In return, he would retain his titles and possessions. Raymond VII could only accept these conditions, which were the same as those he had suggested to Philip Augustus in 1222, that he had accepted at the Council of Montpellier in 1224, and that he was waiting to have ratified at the Council of Bourges in 1225. Besides, Languedoc was militarily, economically and morally weakened by twenty years of war. Some Occitan lords had given up, like Olivier and Bernard of Termes who, in Narbonne on November 21, 1228, ceded their castle in Termes to the King of France, whom they recognized as their suzerain for all of their possessions, and to whom they swore loyalty in the presence of the Archbishop of Narbonne, the Bishop of Carcassonne and Guy of Lévis. After the devastation and economic sanctions, the population of Toulouse was suffering from famine. On December 1228, Raymond VII granted full authority to the abbot of Grandselve to reach an agreement with the mediator named by Blanche of Castile, Thibaud, Count of Champagne. A meeting was held in Meaux on the latter's lands. In attendance were Raymond VII and the Toulousains, the Archbishop of Narbonne and his suffragans, Cardinal of Saint Ange and the two mediators. A preliminary document, agreed to by Raymond VII, was drawn up. This was to be the basis for the Treaty of Paris. It was signed on April 12, 1229. Conditions for the negotiation of peace, formulated in Bourges, had become the total capitulation of Raymond VII. The treaty contained thirty-two articles, thirty-one of which were commitments by the Count of Toulouse. In order to reconcile with the Church, he had to promise to fight heresy and to

St Louis, capital in Laramière

LOUIS IX

A t the death of Louis VIII, his son Louis was twelve years old. Blanche of Castile was regent in her son's name until 1242. King Louis IX put important reforms in place within his kingdom. In the judiciary, he abolished duels and set up appeals courts. In the financial sector, he created a commission that, under a successor, Philippe le Bel, would become the revenue court (*Cour des Comptes*). But this profoundly religious king's greatest project was the crusades. In 1248, he left to confront the soldiers of Islam in Egypt. After investing Damietta, he was taken prisoner at Mansurah on February 8, 1250. Freed in exchange for a ransom, he stayed in Syria where he had many Christian soldiers freed, and strengthened the Frankish fortresses. But he had to return home in 1252, at the death of Blanche of Castile who had been in charge of the kingdom during his absence. In 1270, he departed once again for Tunis, landed in Carthage and died from the plague a month later. He was canonized in 1297 by Pope Boniface VIII.

make the peace respected, to expel the *routiers* from his lands, not to entrust public positions to heretics or Jews, to restore to the Church all properties or rights belonging to it. Articles 5 and 6 clearly associated temporal and religious powers in the repression of heresy. As penitence, Raymond VII was supposed to take the cross and leave for the Holy Land before the month of August, 1230, where he was to stay for five years. He was furthermore compelled to pay ten thousand marks to the Church for any damage caused, and four thousand marks to the abbeys of Citeaux, Clairvaux, Grandselve, Belleperche, and Candeil, "as much for damages caused to their personal estates, as for the salvation of [his] soul." The Order of Citeaux was rewarded for its zeal and its action in the service of *negotium pacis et fidei*. Raymond had to pay six thousand marks for "the fortification, reinforcement and guard" of Narbonnais Castle and eight other castles that the king would occupy for ten years, then for five years one thousand five hundred Tournoi *livres* annually to pay for guard costs. According to the terms of Article 13, he had to pay for the salaries of professors at the University of Toulouse, which was to be inaugurated on May 24, 1229, but whose existence was mentioned for the first time in this article. As far as lands were concerned, Raymond VII retained Toulouse and its diocese except for the "lands of the Marshal", the possessions of Guy of Lévis that consisted of Mirepoix and the Pays d'Olmes. He also kept the dioceses of Agen and Rodez, as well as the part of the diocese of Albi located on the left bank of the Tarn, the diocese of Cahors except for the city of Cahors and the fiefs in the diocese held by Philip Augustus at the time of his death. On the other hand, he had to renounce all his lands west of the Rhone in favour of the French crown. This was to be the future seneschalsy of Beaucaire. The Holy See, already owner of Melgueil County, inherited the Marquisate of Provence, for which it became the emperor's vassal. Extremely precise inheritance clauses were attached to the Saint Gilles' new domaine. The daughter of Raymond VII and Sancia of Aragon, Jeanne, was to marry a brother of the King of France. She was to be the sole heiress of the county, even if Raymond VII was to have a son. In fact, it was all planned so that, whatever the case, the County of Toulouse eventually belonged to a man of the Capetian dynasty. Furthermore, thirty of the county's cities and castles, including Toulouse, were to have their defences destroyed. And finally, Raymond VII promised to have the citizens of Toulouse and the lands he retained swear to respect the same commitments he himself had made. On the very day of the treaty's signature, the reconciliation with the Church took place at a public ceremony on the square in front of Notre Dame in Paris. Raymond VII "in a shirt and breeches, barefoot" provided the "pitiful spectacle" of his humiliation, in the presence of the entire French court, the pontifical legate, the archbishops of Sens and Narbonne and the bishops of Toulouse, Nîmes, Maguelone, Paris and Autun. After hearing the treaty read out and swearing to respect his commitments, he entered Notre Dame, led by the legate who lifted his excommunication at the foot of the high altar. A few days later, in line with Articles 5 and 6 of the treaty, the king pronounced an

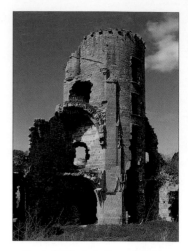

Lagarde Castle in Pays d'Olmes

OF THE RACE OF EAGLES

Article 31 of the Treaty of Paris, dedicated to the sole castle of Penne d'Albigeois, was the longest of all the articles. The chronicles barely mentioned this castle, the seat of a deaconate of the Albi Cathar Church, but enough to let it be understood that this eagle's nest, isolated in the gorges of the Aveyron by a fold in the land, was that of proud lords. In 1213, before the Council of Lavaur, Olivier, Lord of Penne d'Albigeois, came to pay homage to Raymond VII. A few months later, Guy de Montfort lifted the siege of Puycelci in return for its lords' promise to submit if neighbouring Penne Castle surrendered or was captured. Montfort's brother took care not to provoke this. And in 1243, in Lorris, Penne d'Albigeois was still being mentioned and still uncontrolled since on April 22, Raymond VII wrote to Louis IX to tell him he could not hand Penne over to him because its knights would not obey him. In 1248, the Count of Toulouse's promise to become a crusader earned him the restitution of Penne d'Albigeois, Puycelci, Najac and Laurac. At that time therefore, the eagles of Penne had folded their wings.

Notre Dame of Paris

The Count's castle in Carcassonne

Bonnefont Abbey

BOULBONNE ABBEY

In about 1129, a Benedictine monastery had been set up at the edge of Boulbonne Forest, south-east of the present town of Mazères. In 1147, the community decided to adopt the Cistercian rule and the abbey became the daughter of Bonnefont Abbey in Comminges and, thus, granddaughter of Morimond. This first Cistercian abbey in the County of Foix developed rapidly thanks to numerous privileges and exemptions granted it by the Houses of Foix, Aragon and Toulouse. It owned many granges that practiced breeding and transhumance. Starting in 1188, the abbey became the burial site of the Counts of Foix. In 1216, coming from Fanjeaux, Simon de Montfort stopped there on his way to Muret. At the end of the 13th century, Armand Nouvel was a monk in Boulbonne, as was his nephew Jacques Fournier at the beginning of the 14th century. The monastery was ruined by Hugenots in 1567 and rebuilt in the 17th century in Tramesaygues, at the confluence of the Hers and Ariège Rivers.

anti-heretical edict that, among other conditions, offered a reward for any heretic denounced. At the same time, an appendix to the Treaty of Paris was signed, providing for twenty Toulouse hostages "until five hundred toises of the walls of Toulouse have been demolished and as many toises of ditches have been filled." In the end, there were only ten hostages, but Raymond VII was one of them. Among the nine others were Hugues of Rouaix, Raymond of Alfaro, the son of Hugues Déjean, a Maurand. From his captivity at the Louvre, Raymond VII wrote to Roger-Bernard, Count of Foix, on April 25, asking him to join the peace accord. Indeed, at the end of September 1226, in Toulouse, each of the two counts had agreed not to conclude any peace with the King of France without the other's consent. On June 16, the Count of Foix met the vice-legate, Pierre of Colmieu, the pope's former chaplain, and Mathieu of Marly, the king's lieutenant, at Saint Jean de Verges. The two men, named to register the Occitan agreement to the Treaty of Paris and to apply the anti-heretical edict pronounced by the King, had, on May 17, just received oaths from the Narbonnais. Following the advice of the Count of Toulouse, Roger-Bernard submitted to Louis IX in the presence of the Archbishop of Narbonne, the bishops of Carcassonne, Couserans and Toulouse, the abbots of Lagrasse and Boulbonne, Guy of Lévis and Pierre of Voisins. On June 3, Raymond VII was freed from the Louvre, having kept his three promises preliminary to his freedom. His daughter Jeanne had been handed over to the king's emissaries in Carcassonne; he had delivered five of his castles; demolition of Toulouse's ramparts had begun. He was made a knight by Louis IX and accompanied him to Moret sur Loing to attend the engagement of Alphonse of Poitiers, the king's brother, and his daughter. The two children were just nine years old. Raymond returned to Toulouse only in September. In July, during his absence, the city had been reconciled with the Church by Pierre of Colmieu. He was soon followed by Cardinal of Saint Ange who was to prepare the Council of Toulouse. By the autumn of 1229, the French crown had in fact annexed all of Languedoc. Through the Treaty of Paris and the Act of Saint Jean de Verges, it now controlled the Counties of Toulouse and Foix. Through the donation Amaury de Montfort had made in February, 1226, it also possessed the former Trencavel viscounty. As a precautionary measure, several days after the Treaty of Paris was signed, Louis IX had Amaury confirm this donation since it also concerned the County of Toulouse. To establish his power over the Midi, he could count on the seneschalsies of Carcassonne and Beaucaire, and he had named a constable, Mathieu of Montmorency, the brother-in-law of the late Simon de Montfort and cousin of Mathieu of Marly. At his death in November 1230, the brother of Alix of Montmorency was replaced by his nephew, Amaury de Montfort. Obviously, the crown of France showed its gratitude to the Montfort clan since, after the Treaty of Paris, Philip, Guy's son, was granted the fief consisting of the area of Albigeois on the left bank of the Tarn, except for Albi. The nephew of the crusade's leader made Castres the capital of his seigniory.

2

THE TIME OF THE INQUISITORS

Although the political situation in Languedoc seemed settled by 1229, heresy was far from being eradicated. In 1233, Pope Gregory IX entrusted the Inquisition to the Preaching Friars. One year earlier, the Cathar Bishop of the Toulousain had made Montségur "the head and seat" of a hounded Church. In vain, Trencavel and the *faydits* tried to reconquer their lands. In vain, Raymond VII and the kings of Aragon, Castile and England united against a triumphant crown of France, while the *Good Christians* of the *pog* were delivered to the fire in 1244. Some survivors went into exile in Lombardy and, after 1296, the Authié preached and consoled again in Occitania. But the Inquisition had the last word. Belibaste, the last known perfect, died at the stake in Villerouge-Termenès in 1321.

House the Rue Saint Rome, Toulouse

WANTED NOTICE

The one-sided contents of the Treaty of Paris inspired only indignation in the Midi. The fact is well described in *A General History of Languedoc*, though it was written by Benedictine monks. "It can be seen in this treaty that the main instigators of the war against Raymond were less concerned with ensuring his Catholicity than with depriving him of his domains and getting rich from the spoils." Even Guillaume of Puylaurens noted, "Of the many conditions obtained and contained in this peace, a single one would have sufficed as a ransom, if the king had found the count against him in a fight in open country." Harsher were the troubadours, who wrote numerous sirventès on the subject, like the Toulousain Guilhem Figueira who launched a violent diatribe against the Church. "Rome, your felony is so great/About God and his saints no-one cares/Your reign is damned, Rome is false and perjured/It's through you melts/sickens and merges/All joy down here. With what outrageousness/Do you overwhelm Raymond!" The Church and French crown implemented the conditions of the treaty very quickly. Hence, on May 24, 1229, at Saint James Church, in the Saint Gilles' capital next to the cathedral, Hélinand of Froidmont gave the opening sermon inaugurating the University of Toulouse, established at the beginning in the convent of the Preaching Friars, rue Saint Rome.

Canons' Law

The Council of Toulouse was held in November 1229. Debates were conducted by the Cardinal of Sant'Angelo. The Archbishop of Narbonne and most of his suffragans including the Bishop of Toulouse, the archbishops of Auch and Bordeaux, Raymond VII and the other princes concerned, except for the Count of Foix, two Toulouse consuls – one for the city, one for the borough, and the seneschal of Carcassonne, André Chaulet, were in attendance. The measures taken by the council were contained in forty-five canons. They contained the seeds of the future Inquisition as an institution. Did not Canon 18 stipulate that, "Will be considered as accused of heresy those concerned by public rumour or those who, upon denunciation by honourable and serious people, will have been considered as such, legally, by the bishop"? The purpose was clearly to put an end once and for all and by any means to the Affair of Peace and Faith. The Cardinal of Sant'Angelo did not hesitate to make the council into a framework for practical work. In fact, he had entrusted Foulque with carrying out an investigation aimed at having a certain number of people suspected of heresy appear before an assembly that turned into a tribunal. There were spontaneous abjurations, such as that of Guillaume del Soler. This former perfect, *socius* of the deacon Bernard of Lamothe, had lived in the entourage of Guilhabert of Castres, who had been in Toulouse during the royal crusade in 1226. In return for his abjuration, the former heretic received a canon's prebend.

THE FOUNDATION OF THE UNIVERSITY OF TOULOUSE

"But the degenerates are the doctors and the fire and sword that exterminate them, and Foulque the holy prelate who cuts them down in the city." John of Garland, *De triumphis Ecclesie*

In Article 13 of the Treaty of Paris Raymond VII promised to assign four thousand marks to have fourteen masters teach in Toulouse. This was the announcement of the creation of Toulouse University. Under the leadership of the legate Romano of Sant'Angelo, the Cistercians and Dominicans took part in the foundation of the new institution. The Cistercians were the organizers; Elie Garin, the abbot of Grandselve, "chose as masters learned Parisians", according to John of Garland, and Foulque, the Bishop of Toulouse, once again in Garland's words, "brought care and consolation to the new university". As for the Preaching Friars, they were particularly involved in teaching theology. No time was lost and barely two months after the signature of the Treaty of Paris, on Ascension Thursday, 1229, another Cistercian, Helinand of Froidmont, pronounced the speech inaugurating the University of Toulouse in Saint James's Church. The same white monk was charged with the opening and closing sermons of the Council of Toulouse, whose first session was held in November 1229. Apparently, the university that Helinand hoped for was going to be characterized by blind obscurantism. He took care to attack the universities of Paris, Orléans, Bologna, Salerno and Toledo as dens of iniquity, and to challenge philosophers in a long diatribe. "Yes, they knew nothing about this art [of salvation], those philosophers who, in their long research, only concluded by betraying their powerlessness to discover anything…; they only tried to make a name for themselves on this earth and to perpetuate it in their disciples named Pythagoreans, Platonists, Aristotelians, Epicureans…". And he continued, "Real science is the science of the saints… There is even the stupidity of thinking oneself rich because one possesses earthly treasures and to believe oneself wise because one knows liberal arts or letters. One does not become wise until one renounces this stupidity." But for the Dominicans who had come to Toulouse, as recalled by Guillaume Pelhisson who was later to become an inquisitor in the Albigeois, this university had been founded above all "to introduce in Toulouse the teaching of the faith and to eradicate heresy." At first, the institution's foundation seemed to begin favourably. The material conditions of its masters were ensured, they lived on prebends or on gifts from their students. Recruitment too was favourized, both for students and teachers, by the strike that affected the University of Paris in 1229, a sign of protest after students had been killed by royal sergeants on February 26 and 27. The strike lasted until 1231. Furthermore, the masters who came to Toulouse in a crusading spirit received plenary indulgences. But the euphoria was not to last. By 1230, John of Garland, an English master who came to Toulouse, addressed "the masters and students from the entire earth" to attract them to the banks of the Garonne. He praised the charms of the city, "another Promised Land where honey and milk flow…where Bacchus reigns over the grapevines and Ceres over the harvests." He also spoke of the program that included Roman law, medicine and even Aristotle. Old Helinand must have been upset. But Garland's appeal received little response. It must be said that the Toulousains did not accept the university and did not much appreciate the methods of one of the masters of theology, Roland of Cremona. Roland had entered the Dominican Order in 1218, and studied at the University of Bologna before teaching in Paris. He never hesitated before launching into vehement preaching in public places, using threats and intimidation and, especially, having the bodies of suspected heretics exhumed and burnt, as he did with Jean-Pierre Donat, a Cathar, and Galvan, a Waldensian. In 1231, the city's consuls complained to the prior of the Preaching Friars, and the inhabitants went as far as interrupting the masters during their lectures. John of Garland and Roland of Cremona soon left Toulouse. The failure was obvious. Although, in a bull dated April 30, 1233, the pope reminded the Count of Toulouse of his obligation of paying the masters' remuneration and of granting important privileges to the university, such as *jus ubique docendi*, the university had a hard time recovering from this failure. Even theology was removed from the program. The Dominicans taught it entrenched within the walls of the Jacobins Church. On April 22, 1233, eight days before the pope issued the bull reminding Raymond VII of his obligations to the masters of the university, the Dominicans were entrusted with the charge of running the tribunals of the Inquisition by Pope Gregory IX.

Within the framework of his investigation, Foulque had produced witnesses whose declarations were carefully written down. Among those suspected of heresy, some defended themselves by asking the names of those who had testified against them simply with the intention of harming them. The legate refused but, nonetheless, supplied them with the list of all the witnesses before leaving for another council that was being held in Orange at the end of December. He took with him all the investigation's documents so that they would not fall into the hands of anyone eager for revenge on the informers. On December 29 in Mornas Castle, he handed over to Foulque the letters of penitence for those who had been convicted of heresy in Toulouse. Their contents would be made known to those concerned in Saint James's Church. The situation remained tense in the county of Toulouse. Foulque demanded the restitution of Verfeil, which had been ceded to him by the Treaty of Paris. The local lords did not agree and, with the help of Bernard-Othon of Niort, confronted the armed troop that the prelate had had to hire to have his rights respected. The lord of Niort, seriously wounded by an arrow in his forehead, was taken to Laurac where Guilhabert of Castres came to console him. One of the ceremony's witnesses, André Chaulet, provided the information after he was captured by the seneschal of Carcassonne. The seneschal organized an expedition into the lands of Sault, Bernard-Othon's fief but, after leaving Quillan, he was ambushed near Coudons and killed. Meanwhile in Toulouse, where informers and investigators were being murdered, Raymond VII did not manage to convince the local clergy of his good intentions. The Bishop of Carcassonne was even sent in an embassy to Rome to tell the pope that the Count of Toulouse was not paying the masters of the university. As for the count, he addressed the Holy Father to tell him that the payments he had to make to the Church prevented him from paying for his journey to the Holy Land. On July 9, 1230, the pope granted him extra time before his departure so he could honour his financial promises and, on September 18, he wrote to his legate, to the Bishop of Toulouse and the Abbot of Grandselve, asking them, on behalf of Raymond VII, to conduct the trial of a post mortem reconciliation of Raymond VI and the Church so that his body could finally be buried. In October, with several knights including the Count of Rodez, the Viscount of Lautrec, Olivier of Termes, Sicard of Montaut, Bernard Hunaud and Jourdain of Lanta, and Bernard-Othon of Niort, Raymond VII rushed to help Marseille, besieged by the Catalonian Count Ramón Berenguer V, who backed off. On November 7, the city of Marseille recognized him as its overlord. On January 2, 1231, the pope demanded that he pay the amounts the Treaty of Paris had prescribed for the Cistercian abbeys and, in November, Raymond VII used part of his income from the tolls of Marmande to make a first payment to Citeaux Abbey. On his return from Provence, Raymond VII had to go to Castelnaudary, where the new legate named by Honorius III, Gautier of Marnis, Bishop of Tournai, had convoked him to request that he honour his promises. On August 6, 1231, James I of Aragon was in Montpellier and granted its

Council of Toulouse

In the struggle against heresy

Heretics will be hunted down and denounced, their shelters destroyed and their property confiscated. Those suspected of heresy will be judged by the local bishop or any other ecclesiastic authorized to do so. Those indicated by public rumour shall be indicated as accused of heresy. Repentant heretics will have to leave their place of residence and wear two crosses on their clothes; they will be excluded from public positions and struck by legal incapacity. Anyone suspected of heresy will not be allowed to practice medicine.

On orthodox practices

Any man over fourteen years of age and any woman over twelve years of age must abjure all heresy and promise to serve the Catholic faith. The oath must be renewed every two years. Laymen will not be allowed to own the Old and New Testaments. Every parishioner must go to church on Sundays and holidays. Four times a year, priests will remind their parishioners of the measures of the Council of Toulouse.

On fiscal measures

Laymen will have to pay tithes, with no deductions, to clerics who are furthermore exempted from tallage and tolls.

On peace

All men over fourteen years of age will have to promise to respect peace. All relations with *faydits* are forbidden. Whoever lodges them will violate the peace. It is forbidden "for barons, lords, knights, inhabitants of towns and cities and even for peasants" to constitute associations, leagues or confraternities. Any construction of a new castle and any reconstruction of a demolished castle will be forbidden. Any woman or widow possessing a castle or fortress, or who inherits one, may not marry an enemy of the peace or the faith under penalty of confiscation of this castle or this fortress.

In the heart of Montagne Noire

inhabitants various privileges for the help they had provided in the conquest of Majorca. Foulque, the old Bishop of Toulouse, died at Christmas. He was buried in Grandselve Abbey. His successor, Raymond of Le Fauga, a provincial prior of the Preaching Friars, was elected on February 11, 1232. One week later, the pope addressed his new legate, Gautier, Bishop of Tournai, asking that he adopt a more flexible position with respect to Raymond VII and to "nourish him with the milk of the Church". It was probably to make this return to grace more obvious that an unenthusiastic Raymond VII accompanied Raymond of Le Fauga to the Montagne Noire to capture nineteen perfects, including Pagan of Labécède who, once again, managed to escape from the stake. The consuls of Toulouse too were supposed to become involved in the anti-heretic struggle but they were more concerned with protecting their citizens from the excesses of the Preaching Friars, by forbidding them to claim that there were heretics in their city. One of these Dominicans, Roland of Cremona, a master at the university, learning that a donor to Saint Sernin had been buried in the cloister after receiving the *consolament*, had his corpse exhumed and burnt. The same fate awaited the body of a Waldensian, which was carried around the streets of Toulouse. The masters of the university were held in contempt. It was better for them to leave the city. In 1232, John of Garland left Toulouse, soon followed by Helinand of Froidmont. Roland of Cremona did the same in 1233.

A PLEDGE OF GOOD FAITH

B efore Montségur had become the seat of the Cathar Church, Massip of Gaillac, the lord of Fanjeaux and bailiff of Raymond VII, went to the *pog* (hill) on several occasions to worship the perfects. He returned to Montségur at the head of an armed troop, without meeting any opposition, to arrest Jean Cambiaire, the *filius minor* of Guilhabert of Castres and three other perfects he handed over to the Count of Toulouse. This was declared before the Inquisitor Ferrer by Berenger of Lavelanet on April 21, 1244. The defender of Montségur specified that the actions took place "more than twelve years earlier", setting them in about 1232 and that the three Bons Hommes had been led to the stake. But the existence of Jean Cambiaire was attested in 1237. Had he escaped? Were his companions burnt at the stake? But where? Was the operation only a pretence by the Count of Toulouse to give the Church and the king a pledge of his good faith at a moment when his sincerity had been seriously questioned?

The seal of Raymond VII

The Jacobins cloister in Toulouse

Capital, St Stephen's Cathedral

WARMING UP

F errer had not waited to be
named Inquisitor to start
attacking heretics. In 1234, this
Catalonian, a master of theology at
the University of Paris, was a prior at
the Preachers' convent in Narbonne.
Having learned that there were
several followers of heresy in the
town, he had a certain Raymond
of Argens, an artisan by trade,
arrested. But the town's artisans
stood together. In 1219, they had
even formed the confraternity of
Amistats. They had their colleague
freed. When the police came to re-
arrest him, a riot started and soon
degenerated into a confrontation
between the borough, a fief of the
viscount, and the city, the domain of
the archbishop. On March 24, 1234,
Archbishop Pierre Amiel, declared
an interdict on the borough and
excommunicated the rebels. The
consuls asked for mediation by the
consuls of Toulouse, who sent
Olivier of Termes and Geraud of
Niort. Had Raymond VII wanted
to fan the flames, he would not
have acted otherwise. And the
situation did not improve. At the
end of the year, the Preachers'
convent was sacked. A truce was
arranged between the two sides
in 1236, mediated by the abbot
of Fontfroide. As for Ferrer, his
interrogations of the survivors of
Montségur at least had the merit
of supplying precious information
about the lives of the *pog*'s
occupants until March 16, 1244.

D'inquisitio, Enquiry

Noting once again Raymond VII's lukewarm application of certain
articles of the Treaty of Paris, the papal legate complained to the
King of France who, in the autumn of 1232, called the Count of
Toulouse to Melun. There Raymond VII found the Archbishop of
Narbonne, the legate and several bishops from the south. Under
the supervision of the Bishop of Toulouse and the knight Gilles of
Flageac, he was invited to proceed with the reforms consistent with
his promises of 1229. On April 29, 1233, the list of these reforms
was made publicly to the count, in the presence of the new pontifical legate, Jean of Bernin, Archbishop of Vienne, in the cloister of
Saint Stephen's Cathedral of Toulouse. The count promulgated
them as decrees essentially repeating the measures decided by the
Council of Toulouse. On April 20, 1233, just over a week before
Raymond VII placed his seal on the document, committing the
county power to the struggle against heresy, Pope Gregory IX had
addressed a letter to the priors of the Preaching Friars in the arch-
bishoprics of Bordeaux, Bourges, Auch and Narbonne, informing
them that he had entrusted eradicating heresy to their Order. In
1231, the Pope had promulgated the constitution *Excommunicamus
et anathemisamus*, confirming sentencing to death at the stake for
heretics and excommunication of persons guilty of having relations
with enemies of the faith. Through the letter dated April 20, the
Dominicans became "judges delegated by the authority of the Holy
See to the Inquisition of heretical perversity". On April 22, the
pope asked Romeu of Llivia, the provincial prior of Provence, to
name the first inquisitors from among his friars. The list the prior
submitted to the legate, the Archbishop of Vienne, consisted of
three names: Pons of Saint Gilles, Guillaume Arnaut and Pierre
Sellan. At the beginning of 1234, they were confirmed in their
posts for the dioceses of Cahors and Toulouse. Arnaud Cathala
and Guillaume Pelhisson were named for the diocese of Albi;
Ferrer and Pierre of Alès, for that of Carcassonne.

Domini canes, fresco in Santa Maria Novella Chapel, Florence

Baptism of Saint Dominic in Caleruega church

THE INQUISITION HOUSE

On April 25, 1215, Friar Dominic received a group of three houses close to Toulouse's Narbonnais Castle from Pierre Sellan, the son of Bernard Sellan, provost to the Count of Toulouse. Dominic settled his disciples here. But Toulouse was living through troubled times and two months later, Simon de Montfort moved into Narbonnais Castle and strengthened its defences, destroying one of the houses in doing so. As the situation became more difficult and even dangerous, Dominic's friends moved to Saint Romain's priory before finally settling at the Jacobins in 1230. But in 1233, the tribunal of the Inquisition took up residence in Pierre Sellan's house. In 1648, the trial room of this tribunal was destroyed and replaced by a rectangular chapel whose ceiling was decorated, between 1648 and 1650, by Baltasar-Thomas Moncornet. This Dominican also painted six paintings intended for an oratory in the Sellan house. The fifteen panels of this ceiling and the six paintings present episodes from the life of Saint Dominic, from his baptism to his death in Bologna, with his miracles, his receiving the rosary from the Virgin, and the confirmation of the Dominican Order's preaching mission by Pope Honorius III on January 21, 1217.

Near Montréal, Dominic protects a companion from a great storm

Last sacraments of Dominic

AN INVESTIGATION INTO HERETICAL DEPRAVITY

"It is a great and fine privilege of the Inquisition tribunal that the judges are not obliged to follow judicial order, and omitting several formalities of the law does not taint the proceedings."
Nicolas Eymerich,
Inquisitors' Manual (1376)

In the face of the danger that the Cathar heresy represented for the established Church, the peaceful struggle using words and examples preached and tried by Friar Dominic in the Languedoc at the beginning of the 13th century did not provide the immediate results expected by the papacy. Therefore the pontifical Curia decided to use other means to eradicate heresy, which, in 1199 through the bull *Vergentis in Senium*, was assimilated into divine lese-majesty. Repression was progressively codified by the popes starting in 1184 and, in 1215, the Fourth Lateran Council confirmed all the anti-heretical measures established so far. Presided over by Innocent III, the council prescribed a new method of criminal proceedings: the automatic or inquisitorial procedure, introduced in 1213 with the decretal *Licet Heli*, in trials of heretics. Contrary to accusatory procedures, where the lawsuit was brought by a victim making a complaint, the inquisitorial procedure – from the Latin *inquiro* "try to discover, make an enquiry" – was engaged by a judge on his own initiative, allowed to pursue anyone vaguely suspected of heresy or defamed by public rumour. The trial then took place *simpliciter* and de *plano* "without useless formalities and straight to the point". It was a sum-

mary procedure, "without lawyers' clamour or figures of verdict", wrote Bernard Gui. In 1215, the role of inquisitors was still held by bishops. In 1229, during the pontificate of the new Pope Gregory IX, the Council of Toulouse set up a permanent, exceptional episcopal tribunal, charged with hunting down heretics according to the new procedures. However, despite the energy of secular judges, despite the institution, right after Gregory's accession in 1227, of synodal witnesses charged with denouncing heretics to the episcopal tribunals, and finally, despite sending legates to stimulate the bishops' inquisitorial fervour, the latter, especially in Languedoc, appeared rather lacking in zeal for their new duties. Furthermore, seigniorial or diocesan borders hobbled the coordination of proceedings. Hence, through a series of edicts ratified in 1231, Pope Gregory IX set up permanent and itinerant judges, delegated by him directly. Their jurisdiction extended over a huge area, with no consideration for episcopal or seigniorial boundaries. Bishops were ordered not to interfere in the work of these independent judges, who enjoyed widespread power allowing them to ignore all appeals. The pontifical Inquisition was born. Through his bull *Excommunicamus* of 1231, Gregory IX specified the penalties incurred by heretics and their protectors – life imprisonment or death at the stake for heretics; excommunication, banishment and other punishment for their protectors. At this time, the Supreme Pontiff delegated his first inquisitor to Germany, Conrad of Marburg. In early 1233, Brother Robert, called the Bugger, was in turn delegated to Burgundy, Champagne and Flanders. Then, in April of the

same year, a series of bulls consecrated the official instauration of the pontifical Inquisition over the entire Capetian kingdom, with its itinerant tribunal of exception, particularly charged with pursuing heretics. The Preaching Friars, trained in theology and rhetoric on the benches of the university, and whose Order was not placed under the jurisdiction of bishops but under the direct supervision of the papacy, were chosen by Gregory IX in 1233 to carry out the work of inquisitors. The pope did not hesitate to confer on these judges extraordinary powers, such as condemning the least suspect to life imprisonment, or of having the corpses of supposed former heretics exhumed to be burnt. In 1234, inquisitorial tribunals were set up in Toulouse, Montpellier and Avignon. The inquisitors presiding over them were provided with complete administrative teams: clerks and notaries took part in investigations and interrogations; the inquisitors could name vicars to whom they delegated their powers, and *prosecutors* charged with interrogating suspects. In 1235-1237, the Inquisition was established in northern Italy. Soon recruitment of inquisitorial personnel spread to the Friars Minor. In1238, Gregory IX named the provincial Dominicans but also Franciscans of Aragon and Navarre as inquisitors in these two kingdoms. In 1254, Franciscans were charged with repressing heresy in central Italy. Of course, the new institution clashed with the local population and clergy. In Germany, Conrad of Marburg was murdered in 1233; in Avignonet, in the Lauragais, the inquisitors Guillaume Arnaut and Étienne of Saint Thibéry were assassinated in 1242. Faced with such popular hostility, the Inquisition was even temporarly suspended by the papacy in 1238. But these attacks did not prevent the inquisitors from avidly continuing their task, nor from setting up, during the second half of the 13th century, an efficient administration and radical procedures against heresy. Bernard of Caux, an inquisitor at the tribunal of Toulouse in 1243, wrote a manual in 1249 destined for his colleagues, the *Processus Inquisitionis*, in which he defined a set of rules and customs to be observed. Similarly, the Toulouse inquisitor Bernard Gui, named in 1307, described in his *Treatise on the Practice of the Inquisition* between 1321 and 1324 the methods for an efficient struggle non only against Cathars, but also Waldensians, pseudo-apostles, Beguins, without forgetting sorcerers and Jews. Inquisitorial proceedings were broken up into several specific steps by the end of the 13th century. It began with the *general sermon*, pronounced by the inquisitor in front of the church in the chosen locality. It recalled orthodox dogma, denounced heresy, and proclaimed the sentences that would be carried out in public. The assembled crowd would be allowed some time to consider, or *period of grace*, during which the inquisitor called for repentance but especially for denunciation. With the information obtained from informers, lists of suspects were drawn up, and they were soon called for interrogation. During the interrogation, the suspect was alone, without a lawyer, before the inquisitor or his replacement, in the presence of a notary charged with writing down the statement and two clerks. He would not know nor be informed of the exact charges against him, and would not learn the identity of the informers. He was left with the anxiety and vul-

nerability of secrecy, one of the great principles of inquisitorial proceedings. The inquisitor began by asking the suspect to swear "to tell the whole truth, about himself and others living and dead, about the incrimination of heresy". Then he ordered him to make a religious confession, in which he was supposed to confess the sins and actions of his existence, without forgetting to mention his genealogy (parents, brothers, sisters, spouse, children…). The suspect was not to omit anything that he may confess later or he would be condemned for perjury. Once this *confessio* heard, the inquisitor generally asked for details – if the deponent confessed to having seen Cathar perfects, he had to specify where they had come from, with whom they had left and for where. Mentioning the place was important because, if a house contained heretics, it was destroyed in application of the measures adopted at the Toulouse Council of 1229. The deponent also had to tell whether he had taken part in any preaching, given anything to Cathar dignitaries, or received books or objects from them. The Inquisition considered receiving the *consolament*, called "heretication", as the principal crime of heresy. But whoever had practiced the *melhorier*, called "adoration", was equally guilty because he was considered as approving all the errors of Catharism. If the court judged the confession as insufficient, the suspect was put in prison to await the next interrogation. There were several degrees of incarceration, called *Murus*, the wall. Strict immuration implied fasting, sleep deprivation, chains on the hands and feet. Broad immuration meant a common prison. Torture – punishment on the rack, or hot coals – permitted by the papacy

in 1252, was used to obtain confessions. During interrogations, the suspect was subjected to physical pressure, but also to increasing psychological pressure. Because the inquisitor was allowed to use any weapons he wished, "tricks and shrewdness" as well as "dissembling and lying", wrote Eymerich. Once the crime of heresy had been proved through confession, the guilty had no other alternative than to persevere in his error – and being judged *pertinax* – or to abjure under oath. The sentence was soon pronounced: life imprisonment sanctioned convicted heretics who abjured. The *pertinaces* and *relapsi*, those who fell back into error after abjuring a first time, were handed over to the secular arm who inflicted the *animadversio debita*, a euphemism for death at the stake. Some, abjuring at the last moment through fear of death, were sent back before the inquisitor to be interrogated once again, then thrown into prison or given to the secular arm for *animadversio debita*. But it often happened that the inquisitor pronounced absolution, with or without penitence. Penitence consisted of wearing signs of their infamy – a yellow cross, the obligation of going on a pilgrimage, fines, and confiscation of property. The Inquisition declined after 1350, partly a victim of its own success since heresies had practically disappeared. In the 15th century, the tribunals that pursued sorcerers and witches were ineffective against the Hussites of Bohemia. But it was reborn in Spain at the request of the Catholic Kings. Pope Sixtus IV in 1478, allowed the Spanish Inquisition, with the Grand Inquisitor Torquemada at its head, to expel between 150,000 and 200,000 Jews in 1492. Pursuing Marranos, Moriscos and Protestants, it was officially abolished only in 1838.

Jacobins nave in Toulouse

GUILLAUME PELHISSON

....

Guillaume Pelhisson entered the Preaching Friars in Toulouse in 1229. Named an inquisitor at the beginning of 1234, he seconded Arnaud Cathala in Albi. He then accompanied, as an inquisitor, Pierre Sellan to Quercy, and as a witness he went to the Lauragais with Bernard of Caux and Jean of Saint Pierre in 1245 and 1246. Starting in 1248, he was in charge of construction of the Jacobins Church in Toulouse. Before his death in 1268, he wrote a chronicle intended for young friars relating events he had been involved in or witnessed during the period 1229-1244. Despite several chronological approximations, the document supplies precious information on the fifteen years following the signature of the Treaty of Paris, especially the establishment of the Inquisition in Toulouse. He tells the episode of the old lady of L'Orme Sec, specifying that it took place the day the friars were celebrating the canonization of their Order's founder. Guillaume Pelhisson was also in Albi on June 15, 1234, when Arnaud Cathala participated in excavation work, using a pickaxe to exhume the body of a heretic called Boissène. He was attacked by a hostile crowd who beat him up. Handling anathema better than a pickaxe, "Brother Arnaud, once he arrived at the cathedral church, immediately excommunicated the city, in the presence of the bishop and clergy."

Days of Grace

The first inquisitors were already in place by the beginning of 1234. They took their new responsibilities very much to heart. Nobody suspected of heresy could receive a Christian burial and, since a heretic had to be burnt, they even took it out on the dead, like in Cahors and Albi, where exhumed remains were thrown into the flames. But of course, the living did not escape the repression. Some managed to escape, like Jean of Lagarde from Moissac, who took shelter in Montségur where he was ordained as a priest but died at the stake in 1244. Others however, like Pierre Pechperdut and Pierre Bonmassip in Albi, two perfects handed over to the secular arm by Arnaud Cathala and Guillaume Pelhisson, were immediately burnt. Some Cathars preferred to abjure, like Raymond Déjean, a perfect from Albi, who admitted his errors. The local population had difficulty with this permanent atmosphere of informing and repression. In carrying out their holy task, the inquisitors soon ran into serious difficulties, especially in Toulouse, where they met with opposition from the consuls and the inhabitants. One Toulouse artisan, called a heretic by his neighbour, lodged a complaint for slander with the consulate. The neighbour, condemned to pay a fine, appealed to the episcopal tribunal where he was acquitted thanks to the support of Pierre Sellan and Guillaume Arnaut. The condemned artisan had to flee to Lombardy. Another inhabitant of Toulouse, Jean Tisseyre, appeared in court. He denied being a heretic but the inquisitors, believing him to be a perfect, handed him over to Raymond VII's provost. Faced with the crowd's hostility, he could not be led to the stake and was placed in a dungeon that he shared with perfects arrested in Lavaur. He asked them to ordain him and submitted to the ordeal of fire with them. On August 5, 1234, a crippled old woman from the Rue de L'Orme Sec received the *consolament* of the dying. The inquisitor Pons of Saint Gilles was informed. The Bishop of Toulouse, Raymond of Le Fauga, went to her bedside and, pretending to be Guilhabert of Castres, took down the ill woman's confession. She was thrown onto the stake in her bed. At the beginning of 1235, the inquisitors organized a large general preaching. Wanting to take advantage of the time of grace they had been granted, the Toulousains who wanted to confess at the Preachers' Convent on Friday, April 6 were so numerous that the Dominicans had to call for reinforcements from the Franciscans and the city's priests. Arnaud Domergue did not go to confess and was arrested. Threatened with the supreme punishment, he denounced seven perfects who were captured at Cassès. He was murdered at his home in the middle of the night. An old man, Guillaume Delort, a former consul, was also arrested. Freed by friends who hid him, he was nonetheless condemned in his absence. Meanwhile, more corpses were exhumed, carried around the city in processions and then burnt. The population of Toulouse muttered angrily and to calm it down, Raymond VII had to dismiss Durand of Saint Bars, who was too passive in the face of the inquisitors' excesses, and named Pierre of Toulza in his place.

St Francis by Cimabue, San Francesco Basilica in Assisi

St Francis feeding the birds, San Francesco Basilica in Assisi

FOR THE LOVE OF LADY POVERTY

The son of a wealthy cloth merchant in Assisi, Francis, born about 1181-1182, spent a festive youth, full of the chivalrous ideals of courtly literature. In 1205, Pope Innocent III organized an expedition to Apulia. Francis joined in but fell ill in Spoleto. A vision convinced him to return to Assisi where, in 1206, despite paternal opposition he put on a penitent's habit to dedicate himself to serving the poor and lepers. In 1208, the words of Jesus Christ sending his disciples to preach in complete deprivation (Matt. 10, 7-16) revealed his path to Francis. With several friars, he formed an itinerant community, based at Porziuncola Church in Assisi. In 1209, the *Minors* –or very small– received the authorization to preach from Innocent III. Living in absolute poverty, dividing their existence between prayer, work, preaching and being present among the poorest in towns, they spread throughout central Italy, encouraging vocations such as Clare in 1212, who founded the Poor Clares Order. In 1217, the Porziuncola General Chapter decided to send the brothers beyond the Alps. In 1219, Francis, wishing to go to the Holy Land, arrived in Egypt. There, while the crusaders wanted to attack Damietta, he established a dialogue with the sultan. But he had to return to Italy in 1220 because of troubles within his community, which consisted of three thousand brothers. It had to be organized and created into an Order, whose rule was approved by the papacy in 1223. But Francis missed the evangelical poverty of his beginnings. Ill, he received the stigmata in 1224 and, blind, composed the *Canticle of the Sun*, before dying in 1226, leaving behind a *Testament*. He was lucky not to see his brothers implicated in the Inquisition. The Spirituals (Zelanti) and Fraticelli attempted to return to his ideals in the 14th century.

Guillaume Arnaut had momentarily left Toulouse for Carcassonne for the investigation the pope had ordered about the Niort family on April 8, 1233, entrusting it to the Bishop of Toulouse. On his return, he summoned twelve notables, known as heretical believers to appear before the tribunal of the Inquisition. Not only did they not appear, but they told him to leave the city or to stop the inquisitorial procedure. The inquisitor refused and was expelled from the city. In October 1235, he wrote from Carcassonne to Pons of Saint Gilles and the Toulouse clergy asking them to carry on with the procedure. The consuls had them expelled from the city in their turn, threatening death to those who attempted to replace them and blockading the Preachers' convent. The forty Preaching Friars of Toulouse were even expelled from a city whose bishop had already left a month earlier after being subjected to various humiliations. The operation, carried out *manu militari*, took place on November 5 and, on November 10 Guillaume Arnaut excommunicated eleven consuls and Raymond VII as abettors of heresy. Raymond of Le Fauga and Pons of Saint Gilles went to see Pope Gregory IX in Perugia to tell him of the situation. The pope reacted vigorously. On April 28, 1236, he wrote a reproachful letter to Raymond VII, reminding him of the many promises made in 1229 which had not been fulfilled, concerning payments to be made to the Church, and the departure for the Holy Land that the Holy Father set for Easter, 1237. He also addressed King Louis IX, telling him to be more demanding with the Count of Toulouse. Raymond VII, on his return from Orange where he had gone to receive homage from his vassals, passed through Carcassonne, where, with Guillaume Arnaut, he organized the return of the inquisitors and the Preachers to Toulouse for September 4, 1236. The most Raymond VII could obtain was the replacement of the over-zealous Pierre Sellan at the side of Guillaume Arnaut by a more moderate Franciscan, Étienne of Saint Thibéry.

In Toulouse, the inquisitors occupied Pierre's Sellan's house, close to Narbonnais Castle. But in the autumn of 1236, perhaps afraid that Toulouse would once again become restless, Guillaume Arnaut and Étienne of Saint Thibéry left for the Lauragais. They visited Puylaurens, Avignonet, Laurac, Fanjeaux and Castelnaudary. In February 1237, the Dominican left his companion for a month to go and finish the Niort affair in Carcassonne. The two men met at the end of March in Castelsarrasin. On the 29, they handed a letter of penitence to Pons Grimoard, Raymond VII's seneschal in Quercy who, during the period of grace, had come to confess his heretical sympathies. In order to atone for his offence, he was supposed to feed a pauper until the end of his life and before Easter, 1239, go on a pilgrimage to Rocamadour, to Saint Gilles, to Le Puy and to Santiago de Compostela. On April 2 in Toulouse, the two inquisitors took down the conversion of the perfect Raymond Gros, which produced enough confessions that the Dominicans considered that a miracle had occurred. On May 26, they were in the cloister of the Preaching Friars' convent in Toulouse, which had been transferred from the Rue Saint Rome to its present location at the Jacobins. They read the condemnation of Alleman of Rouaix to life imprisonment

THE NIORT AFFAIR

Esclarmonde, the daughter of Blanche of Laurac, had married Guillaume of Niort, Viscount of Sault. She raised their five sons in the understanding of Good. Although one became Abbot of Olet, the other four, including Bernard-Othon, were heretical believers. After the Treaty of Paris, the Niort chose their side. In 1230, they prepared an ambush for the royal seneschal of Carcassonne and, in 1232, robbed Pierre Amiel, the Archbishop of Narbonne, causing their excommunication. In March 1233, Pope Gregory IX ordered an enquiry into them. Interrogated by Pierre Amiel, Esclarmonde answered, "My belief is better than yours and that of all the prelates of this world." Male and female perfects and believers found a welcome and a refuge in their isolated castles of Niort, Roquefeuil and Dourne. Guilhabert of Castres and Raymond Agulher, before going to Montségur in 1232, stayed in Dourne for six months. To re-establish order, royal troops fought the "Roquefeuil war" in the land of Sault. Pierre-Roger of Mirepoix arrived with other *faydits* to give a hand to the Niort, who did not concede an inch of land. In February 1237, the Niort were summonsed to appear in Carcassonne to be judged. One hundred and fourteen witnesses were heard. Only Bernard-Othon and Guillaume attended the trial. They were sentenced by Guillaume Arnaut to life imprisonment. Their brothers Geraud and Guillaume-Bernard and their mother were sentenced *in absentia*. In 1240, Geraud of Niort was at the side of Trencavel. He surrendered to the French at Peyrepertuse and, on December 13, submitted to Louis IX at Issoire, negotiating the liberation of his brothers and his mother. But the Niort had to cede their fief and their impregnable castles to the French crown.

Cloister detail, Jacobins in Toulouse

Roquefeuil

THE JACOBINS

"This church of Toulouse
surpasses in beauty all the other
churches of the Preaching Friars.
I therefore choose it for
Saint Thomas…"
(Urban V's bull of June 15, 1368)

In 1229, Saint Romain's Priory had
become too cramped and the
Dominicans of Toulouse decided
to install their convent to the north
of the Daurade parish, on lands
belonging to the Garrigues gardens
and to Pierre de l'Orme. The buildings of the Jacobins convent, named
for its Parisian counterpart in the
Rue Saint Jacques, were built in several stages. From 1230 to 1235, a
first church flanked by a cloister
was built. The building measured
forty-six metres by twenty-two and
was topped with a wooden roof.
During the years 1245-1252, the
church was extended eastwards.
A new period of construction was
undertaken in 1275 and was completed in 1292. The chevet whose
entire vaulting is supported on one
pillar dates from this period. This
vault is divided into eleven sections
supported by twenty-two ribbed
arches, their lierne ribs resting on
eleven keystones. This ribbed
springing topping the pillar provided
its name of "Jacobins' Pillar".
In 1298 the steeple was built to
contain the university's bell. It was
to lose its spire during the
Revolution. Between 1306 and 1310,
a new cloister replaced the original
one and was placed on the western
façade of the church in order to
receive laymen coming to study
theology. The second cloister disappeared completely during the 18th

and 19th centuries. From 1325 to
1335, the nave was enlarged and
vaulted. Seven twenty-two metre
high columns provide this nave
with its extraordinary height. The
cloister's galleries led the Preaching
Friars to the chapter house and
Saint Antonin's Chapel, but also to
the infirmary and the refectory, the
kitchen, dormitory and cells. The
chapter house was built from 1299
to 1301. Extended by an apse that
was used as a chapel, it stands out
for the narrow diameter of its two
interior hexagonal pillars supporting
the vault. Work on the refectory,
one of the largest medieval monastic
refectories, was completed for
Christmas of 1303. Construction and
decoration of Saint Antonin's Chapel

were paid for by Dominic Grima,
the fourth bishop of Pamiers. Work
started in 1335 and was finished in
1341. The chapel was supposed to
be used as a funerary chapel for the
Dominicans and the canons of
Pamiers, whose patron saint was
St Antonin. The paintings on the
vaults present the sacrificed lamb
praised by the twenty-four old men
of the Apocalypse. Through a bull
dated June 15, 1368, Pope Urban V
presented the relics of Saint Thomas
Aquinas to the Preaching Friars convent of Toulouse. The relics were
ceremoniously handed over to the
convent on January 28, 1369. During
the Revolution, they were placed in
Saint Sernin's but were returned to
the Jacobins convent in 1974.

The Jacobins palm tree

in absentia, since the man in question had not appeared. He continued to lead his life in Toulouse, flouting clerics and inquisitors. He would finally surrender to the Inquisition eleven years later and undergo his punishment. In September, while many bodies of supposed heretics were being exhumed, exhibited and burnt, the perfect Arnaud Rougier, who was to be the successor of Bernard Mary as the Bishop of the Cathar Church of Toulouse after the fall of Montségur, was condemned *in absentia.* At Bousquet near Lanta, the abbot of Saint Sernin's had the former lord of the *castrum,* Guillaume-Bernard Hunaud, captured. The latter had become a perfect and had carelessly left his retreat in Albedun to visit his family. He was burnt alive in Albi, as was his *socius,* Arnaud Giffre. And on February 19, 1238, thirty-five Toulousains, repentant but suspected of having returned to their past errors, were condemned to life imprisonment.

Although he had been forced to accept the inquisitors' return to Toulouse in September 1236, Raymond VII did not stop opposing their mission and attempting to obtain for himself the easing of the constraints of the Treaty of Paris. He knew that the conflict between the pope and the emperor allowed him to move his pawns on the diplomatic chessboard. And, as a son worthy of his father, he was good at it. At the end of 1236, he had addressed the King of France to delay his departure for the Holy Land and to ask him to make Guillaume Arnaut and Étienne of Saint Thibéry leave. His answer, dated February 9, 1237, came from the pope. His departure for the Holy Land could wait until June 24 and the legate was invited to study the grievances expressed by the Count of Toulouse with respect to the inquisitors who had to follow the rules, insisted the Holy Father. But conflict soon reappeared between Raymond of Saint Gilles and the pope, the former having intervened in Marseille against Count Berenguer, a loyal papal supporter in the affair opposing the pope and the emperor. On May 20, the pope changed his attitude and addressed to Louis IX a violent indictment of the Count of Toulouse who had not fulfilled any of his promises of 1229.

Fossanova Abbey Church nave

SAINT THOMAS AQUINAS

The son of the Lord of Aquino, Thomas was born in 1225 in Roccasecca Castle in the Kingdom of Naples. At the age of five, he entered the Benedictine abbey of Monte Cassino as an oblate. When he was sixteen, he entered the Dominican Order. He continued studying theology in Paris, where he became the disciple and friend of Albertus Magnus, whom he followed to Cologne when Albertus became the director of the *studium generale* established in that city. On his return to Italy in 1259, Thomas wrote his *Summa contra Gentiles.* He taught at Anagni, Rome, Orvieto and Viterbo in Latium. In 1266, he undertook the writing of his major work, the *Summa Theologica,* a synthesis of traditional thinking by the Fathers of the Church, particularly Saint Augustine, and the demands of rationality in his own time, marked by the rediscovery of Aristotle. He continued working on it in Paris from 1269 to 1272. He returned to Naples in 1272 to direct the theology teaching at the city's university. In 1274, he was convoked as a consultant to the Council of Lyon, called by Pope Gregory X to try to unite the Greek and Latin Churches. But on his way, he fell ill and died at Fossanova. His writings decisively influenced the doctrinal tendencies of the medieval Church.

Belvoir Castle in the Holy Land

Raymond VII, who had perfectly analyzed the strength of his position, remained unruffled and sent an embassy to Rome, charging it with reaffirming his loyalty to the pope and submitting several complaints to him. He obtained satisfaction for some of them: no final date was set for his departure for the Holy Land and the length of his exile was shortened to three years; the excommunication pronounced against him and the consuls of Toulouse in 1235 was lifted. On the other hand, the pope did not authorize the burial of Raymond VI. And it was probably too much to ask that the Inquisition be taken away from the Preaching Friars. However, the punishments decided by the inquisitors were commuted into less serious penalties. On May 13, 1238, the Bishop of Palestrina, James of Pecoraria was named legate replacing John of Bernin, and the Inquisition was suspended for three months, and then for six. The new legate, who could not leave Italy which was controlled by the emperor, received twelve letters from the pope between the date he was nominated and the end of June. All of them told him to be benevolent towards the Count of Toulouse and to moderate the inquisitors' fervour. Since the new legate had still not been able to leave Italy by early August, the pope named Guy, Bishop of Sora, in his place. Guy got Raymond VII to pay for the salaries of the masters at the University of Toulouse, and obtained the freedom of several people who had been sentenced to life imprisonment by the Inquisition. By the end of the year 1238, Raymond VII had managed to slow the inquisitorial machine for a while.

Ramparts in Jerusalem

THE ARAGONESE INQUISITION

In 1237, the Council of Lerida organized a search for heretics in the Kingdom of Aragon. The task was entrusted to the mendicant orders. In the Viscounties of Cerdagne and Castelbon, fiefs of the Count of Foix, eighteen corpses of suspected heretics were exhumed and burnt. Others, who were still alive, perished at the stake.

The men of the Holy Office, by Jean-Paul Laurens

Lerida

Peyrepertuse Castle

The bottom of Peyrepertuse Castle seen from the eastern spur

Trencavel's Return

In 1239, the Count of Toulouse continued the undermining work he had begun to recover his titles and domains, to ensure the perpetuity of his dynasty and to provide his father with a burial place. In October, James of Pecoraria, disguised as a pilgrim, was able to leave Italy and reach Provence. He met Ramón Berenguer V who gave him a charter confirming his support of the Holy See. But the Catalonian did so as the Count and Marquis of Provence, attracting the anger of Emperor Frederick II who, from his residence in Cremona, banished him from the Empire and took away his possession of the County of Forcalquier, which he gave to his other vassal, Raymond VII, whom he asked to intervene. The Count of Toulouse besieged Ramón Berenguer in Arles. He had come accompanied by the Counts of Comminges, Rodez and Auvergne, as well as Olivier of Termes. The pope's reaction was rapid; the count and his allies were excommunicated at the Council of Viviers on July 15. Intercession by the Kings of France and England put an end to the crisis and Raymond VII returned to Toulouse. On his way home, he stopped at Pennautier. It was the end of the month of August. Guillaume of Ormes, Seneschal of Carcassonne, asked Raymond for help against Trencavel. Indeed, the son of the hero of 1209 had returned. Many of his father's former vassals or their sons as well as many *faydits* had rallied to his cause: Olivier of Termes, Bernard-Hugues of Serralongue, Guillaume of Peyrepertuse, Pierre of Fenouillet, Geraud of Niort, Chabert of Barbaira, Pierre of Mazerolles, Guillaume of Minerve, Jourdain of Saissac, Jourdain of Lanta. Pierre-Roger of Mirepoix, Raymond of Marceille and Guillaume of Lahille had come from Montségur. Strongholds fell one after the other –Montréal, Saissac, Montolieu. In Carcassonne, with the complicity of several inhabitants, he was able to capture Bourg Saint Vincent, but was not able to invest the Cité. On October 11, after thirty-four days, he had to lift his siege because of the arrival of a relief army sent by the King of France, led by Jean of Beaumont. Trencavel took refuge with his family in Montréal, which was besieged in turn by the French. The noble ladies took part in the defence of Montréal, where the Bishop of the Cathar Church of Carcassès, Pierre Paulhan, and several perfects were staying. Their escape was organized by Jourdain of Lanta, Pierre of Mazerolles and Guiraud Hunaud. The Bons Hommes found refuge in Besplas. Diplomatic intervention by the Counts of Toulouse and Foix put an end to the siege of Montréal. Although the Occitan army was allowed to leave safe and sound, the *castrum* was razed, as were the other localities that had provided support for Trencavel. Those suspected of heresy had a cross marked on their foreheads with a hot iron. Jean of Beaumont began to pursue the Occitan army, captured its rearguard and hanged several *faydits*. He besieged La Roque de Fa, defended by Olivier of Termes. Though forced to surrender, Olivier was not disturbed and six months later he presented his submission to the King of France. On November 16, after a siege lasting three days, Guillaume of Peyrepertuse delivered his fortress in the Corbières. The surrender of Geraud of Niort in Duilhac followed. As for Trencavel, he returned to his Catalonian exile.

The Narbonnaise Gate, Carcassonne

LIKE MOLES

At the announcement of Trencavel's arrival, the seneschal of Carcassonne sent a messenger to King Louis IX, who was then in Bourges. When the messenger returned from his mission, he told him that a relief army led by Jean of Beaumont was coming. From then on, Guillaume of Ormes knew he had to resist behind the walls of the Cité, where he was joined by the Archbishop of Narbonne, the Bishop of Toulouse and several barons and clerics. After investing the town, Trencavel's men mined the ramparts in seven places, "like moles", wrote Guillaume of Puylaurens. The operation consisting in digging tunnels from neighbouring houses to make sections of the ramparts collapse. The besieged retaliated by digging other tunnels to drive out the invaders, "with blows, smoke and quicklime", and by erecting palisades in the threatened areas as a palliative in case of their destruction. Ever since its beginning, this siege had been the object of a report by Guillaume of Ormes to Blanche of Castile. He told her that at the announcement of Jean of Beaumont's arrival, the besiegers "had set fire to the town's houses and completely destroyed the lodgings of the Friars Minor and those of Saint Mary's Convent."

Chevet of Angoulême Cathedral

FLUCTUAT ET MERGITUR

O verland travel in Italy was not very safe so the pope entrusted his treasurer Gregory of Romany with arming a fleet to take the prelates of France, Normandy, Aquitaine, Provence and Languedoc from Genoa to Rome, so that they could attend the council in Rome. The pontifical legates, James of Palestrina and Otto of Saint Nicholas, the archbishops of Auch, Bordeaux, Besançon and Rouen, the bishops of Nîmes, Carcassonne, Agde, Le Puy, Asti and Pavia, the abbots of Cluny, Citeaux and Fécamp reached Genoa by sea from Nice. On March 15, 1241, the pope wrote to his treasurer to warn him of danger –Frederick II had armed twenty-five galleys. He asked him to add sixteen galleys to the prelates' fleet. On May 3, off Monte Cristo Island, this fleet was attacked by pirates in the pay of the emperor. The Archbishop of Arles and the Bishop of Le Puy died in the confrontation. Most of the prelates were taken prisoner. They were released some time later, although the Bishop of Nîmes died in captivity.

A Count Facing His Destiny

Raymond VII was in a difficult position. He had not provided military support to his overlord the King of France, who had requested it. He therefore had various issues requiring forgiveness. Furthermore, he needed the pope, the only one who could annul his marriage to Sancie of Aragon, thus allowing him to remarry and try to have a male heir, the only possibility of preventing the dispossession of his dynasty. In February 1241, Raymond met the Bishop of Palestrina in Clermont and swore to support the pope against the emperor. On March 1, he asked his vassals and the Count of Foix to make the same promise before the Bishop of Agen. On March 14, he was in Montargis where he renewed his vassalic homage to Louis IX and repeated his willingness to respect the clauses of the Treaty of Paris, at least those that remained topical. He even promised to destroy Montségur as soon as he could. Within the year, he indeed sent an army troop there which carried out a sham siege that had no results. From Montargis, he went with the Bishop of Toulouse to Marseille, where he was supposed to embark for Rome, where Pope Gregory IX had convoked a council. Beforehand, on April 18 at Lunel, in the presence of Guy Foulcoy, the future Pope Clement IV, he concluded an alliance with James I of Aragon, and met Ramón Berenguer V to discuss his projected marriage with Sancie, the daughter of the Catalonian count. He then joined the Bishop of Toulouse in Marseille but, learning of the attack on the prelates' ships by a fleet paid by Frederick II, he decided not to travel to Italy. In September, he returned to Toulouse and discovered that the inquisitors were back at work. Indeed, in May 1241, Guillaume Arnaut and Étienne of Saint Thibéry had delivered new letters of penitence to inhabitants of Toulouse and, in the month of August, Pierre Sellan distributed over seven hundred of them in Quercy. On the 21 of the same month, Gregory IX died and was succeeded by Celestine IV in an extremely brief pontificate lasting only two weeks. It was only eighteen months later that Sinibaldo Fieschi became Pope under the name of Innocent IV. During this vacancy of the apostolic seat, the Inquisition was left to its own devices. In October 1241, Guillaume Arnaut and Étienne of Saint Thibéry left again for the Lauragais. They went to Saint Paul Cap de Joux where, on the 17, they condemned in their absence Guillaume of Balaguier, Guillaume of Lahille and Bernard of Saint Martin. They were in Lavaur in November. In 1242, their travels took them to Auriac, Saint Félix, Labécède, Castelnaudary, Laurac, Fanjeaux and Sorèze. By May they were in Avignonet.

Raymond VII went to Angoulême in mid-October 1241. A pact was sealed with Hugues of Lusignan, Count of Angoulême and the March. The King of Aragon was also involved. They fomented a coalition against Louis IX. On June 24, 1241 in Saumur, the latter had granted Poitou and Auvergne in apanage to the Count of Toulouse's son-in-law, Alphonse of Poitiers. In application of the measures of the Treaty of Paris, Alphonse had married Jeanne of Toulouse in 1237. Hence, Poitou and Auvergne were taken from Richard of Cornwall, the brother of the King of England, Henry III.

Cloister of Saint Papoul Abbey

SAINT PAPOUL

In 1241, the Inquisition got hold of the deacon Guillaume Vital, who was taken under escort to Saint Papoul Abbey. The abbot demanded a ransom of one thousand sous to free him and forty *credentes*, too naïve in this case, arrived with the money at the abbey only to be taken by guards. One believer was killed. Guillaume Vital was not released and probably died at the stake. The abbey of Saint Papoul had been founded during the Carolingian period. It had originally been consecrated to Saint Peter before being dedicated to Saint Papoul, Saint Sernin's disciple and the evangelizer of the Lauragais. During the 11th century, the community had opted for the Rule of Saint Benedict and after 1119 the abbey was attached to Alet Abbey. In 1308, Saint Papoul Abbey was associated with Fontfroide within the framework of the investigation of the trial of Bernard of Castanet, Bishop of Albi. At that time, Saint Papoul became the seat of a bishopric. Its first bishop, Robert of Mostuéjouls, with Jacques Fournier led the court that judged Bernard Délicieux in 1319. The 12th century abbey church has a single nave. Its chevet is buttressed by five columns topped with capitals, two of which are historiated, sculpted by the Master of Cabestany, showing Daniel in the lion's den and lions eating men.

A capital by the Master of Cabestany, St Papoul Abbey

Detail of St Papoul Cloister

Compostela cathedral

MARRIAGE PLANS

I n June 1241, Raymond VII had reason to be satisfied for several reasons. In Lunel on the 16, he received homage from Roger IV, the new Count of Foix. A few days earlier, his marriage to Sancie of Aragon had been annulled. Immediately, James I of Aragon, Ramón Berenguer, Count of Provence, and Raymond VII organized the latter's marriage with Sancie, Ramón's daughter. Subject to papal dispensation, the ceremony took place in Aix on August 11 but by proxy, with Raymond VII represented by the King of Aragon. The alliance was doomed because of the death of Pope Gregory IX on August 21. In 1243, the Count of Toulouse married Marguerite of the March, but the marriage was invalidated in 1245 since there was still no papal dispensation. That was not a problem, Ramón Berenguer had another daughter, Beatrice, but she married Charles of Anjou in January, 1246. Raymond VII then went on a pilgrimage to Santiago de Compostela. Guillaume of Puylaurens reported rumours that he had taken a wife there. As for Ramón Berenguer's other daughters, all of them found good matches: Marguerite married Louis IX, King of France; Eleonore married Henry III, King of England. And Sancie was quickly consoled by Richard, Henry III's brother, and became the Queen of Cornwall.

These were the sons of Isabelle of Angoulême, the widow of John Lackland, who had remarried Hugues of Lusignan who, along with other lords of Poitou, did not recognize the King of France as their lord. On this occasion, Raymond VII, forgetting Sancie, agreed to a marriage with Marguerite, the daughter of the Count of the March. On October 17, he was in Barcelona where James I of Aragon received homage from Raymond Trencavel for the viscounties that had been despoiled from his father Raymond-Roger in 1209. On December 4, Trencavel himself would receive homage from Bernard VII of Comminges, whose father, Bernard VI, had died on November 30. According to the plan elaborated by Raymond VII and his allies, Henry III would land in Royan, the Poitevins would rise up and Raymond VII would arrive with the reinforcements of his vassals, whose support he made sure of during the coming autumn and winter. Roger of Foix joined him on April 5. By the end of the month of April, 1242, the Count of Toulouse was in Penne d'Agenais. Still trying to reduce the inquisitorial role of the Preaching Friars, he met the Bishop of Agen and asked him to take charge of the anti-heretical struggle in his diocese. He did the same thing in letters to the bishops of Albi, Cahors and Rodez. He did not, however, repeat his action with Raymond of Le Fauga, a Dominican who had become Bishop of Toulouse. Was this when he planned the assassination of Guillaume Arnaut and Étienne of Saint Thibéry? It is not impossible. The two inquisitors were hated by the Occitan population and getting rid of them could only favour the coalition's success. All the operations simply had to be properly coordinated. The King of England landed in Royan on May 20. On the 26, in Montségur, Pierre-Roger of Mirepoix received a visit from Guillaume of Plaigne, carrying a letter addressed to him by Raymond of Alfaro, loyal to Raymond VII and bailiff of Avignonet where the two inquisitors and their followers were to be found that day. Pierre-Roger called on fifty loyalists and set off for Avignonet. On the way, the troop was joined by Pierre of Mazerolles and twenty-five men, then in Antioche near Mas Saintes Puelles by Jourdain of the Mas. On May 28, the day before Ascension, three knights –Guillaume of Balaguier, Guillaume of Lahille and Bernard of Saint Martin, perhaps not accidentally– and twelve sergeants moved towards Avignonet, leaving the rest of their companions in Antioche. They counted on collusion inside the *castrum*. At nightfall, after the inquisitors had gone to bed, they entered the castle and climbed up into the keep where the inquisitors' dormitory was, broke the door down with axes and then used the axes to murder the eleven people inside: Guillaume Arnaut, Étienne of Saint Thibéry, two Dominicans, a Franciscan, the archdeacon of Lézat and his clerk, two bailiffs, the prior of Avignonet, and the court clerk. Allegedly the victims died singing the *Te Deum*. The killers took everything they found, destroyed the inquisitors' registers and then disappeared into the night. It is said that Pierre-Roger of Mirepoix reproached the murderers for not bringing him the head of Guillaume Arnaut so that he could make a goblet out of it. Consternation reigned on the Catholic side which grieved for its new martyrs. The country was full of joy. On June 6, the inquisitors from Carcassonne, Ferrer and Guillaume Raymond,

The Murder of the Inquisitors, painting in Avignonet church

Tower of Taillebourg Castle

THE BATTLE OF TAILLEBOURG

O n May 13, 1242, Henry III of England landed in Royan with his brother Richard of Cornwall and his brother-in-law Simon V de Montfort. It was ironic to see the son of the lion of the Albigensian crusade on the side of the Count of Toulouse against the King of France! Richard and Simon were returning from the Holy Land where they had ransomed Amaury de Montfort, captured in Gaza in 1239, but who died on his way home in Otranto, Italy, on April 23, 1241. The King of England called all of his Aquitaine vassals, among them Boson of Matha, Lord of Cognac and husband of Petronilla of Bigorre. In July, Henry III's troops occupied Saint James's field on the left bank of the Charente, facing Taillebourg Castle, whose lord, Geoffroy V of Rancon, owed homage to the King of France. On the other bank, the French troops of Louis IX were preparing their offensive. Their crossbowmen crossed the Charente in boats and their bolts rained down on their enemies, who retreated towards Saintes. The main body of the French troops was then able to cross the river over the bridge Henry III had fortified. On July 22, the battle raged below the walls of Saintes. Completely overrun, Henry III withdrew into Saintes before fleeing to Bordeaux.

excommunicated Raymond VII who, on June 11, requested that the consuls of Agen place their city in a state of defence. The military plan got under way. Raymond VII, the Viscount of Narbonne and Trencavel rode victoriously through the Razès, Termenès and Minervois. The seneschal of Carcassonne took refuge in Béziers, where he was joined by Pierre Amiel, the Archbishop of Narbonne, a city that had just been invested without opposition by the Count of Toulouse. On August 8, the count took back the title of Duke of Narbonne. Raymond VII learned that Louis IX had beaten Henry III and the coalition at Taillebourg on July 22, and that Hugues of Lusignan had already capitulated. He went to Bordeaux to where Henry III had retreated and, on August 28, the king and the count strengthened their alliance and agreed not to sign a separate peace. Then, boldly, Raymond VII went to besiege the French army stationed in Penne d'Agenais. During the siege, he received a letter from the Count of Foix, Roger, who had succeeded his father, Roger-Bernard, at his death on May 20, 1241. The letter was dated October 5, 1242. It informed the Count of Toulouse that not only was his lifelong ally the Count of Foix abandoning the coalition, but that furthermore, he was declaring war on him. In his answer dated the 10, Raymond VII wrote, "Remember that you told me several times that if I were to lose my domains, you would not want to keep your own." He understood that negotiations were needed. From Penne d'Agenais on October 20, he wrote to the King of France to make amends and to swear loyalty. To make his submission formal, he met the Bishop of Toulouse and then the three commissioners that the King had named, Imbert of Beaujeu and the Bishop of Clermont, first in Alzonne and next in Saint Rome in the Lauragais. On December 28, he rejoined the King of France in Lorris, in the Gâtinais, where in January, 1243 he signed a peace accord and renewed the promises he had made in the Treaty of Paris. Before returning to Toulouse, he stopped in Angoulême where he married Marguerite of the March, on condition of obtaining a papal dispensation, necessary because of their kinship, but which was never in fact delivered. Back in Toulouse, he ordered a search for the authors of the Avignonet massacre. Four of them were found. Three, including Guillaume of Balaguier, were hanged. On April 18, Raymond attended the Council of Béziers to blame the inquisitors of Carcassonne for excommunicating him without evidence, while he could not appeal the sentence because of the vacancy in the Holy See. Three days later, he wrote to the bishops of Agen, Cahors, Rodez, Albi and Toulouse (he had nothing more to lose), asking them to take over the struggle against heresy. On June 25, Innocent IV was elected. Raymond VII went to Italy in September. In Apulia, he negotiated with the emperor about recovering the Comtat Venaissin and Provence for himself. At the beginning of November, he was in Rome. He obtained absolution from the new pope and, in vain, requested that the pope remove the Inquisition from the hands of the Preaching Friars. Beforehand, the Holy Father had received a delegation from the Dominicans which had come to ask him the same thing, although obviously for different reasons. He had refused. He was even to strengthen their position.

Gemelled windows of a house in Penne d'Agenais

Castel del Monte, one of Frederick II's castles

The *pog* of Montségur

Montségur

In 1206, at the time of the "council" of Mirepoix, the Cathars had asked Raymond of Péreille to rebuild the *castrum* of Montségur. In 1209, fleeing before the advance of Montfort's army, the Cathars of Fanjeaux, including Guilhabert of Castres, withdrew temporarily to Montségur. But the seat of the Cathar Church of the Toulousain remained in Saint Paul Cap de Joux, even though its bishop, Gaucelm, occasionally went to Montségur. Faced with the threat that the Treaty of Paris signed in 1229 posed for the Cathars, the Cathar hierarchy reacted quickly. With the support of a network of sympathizers, bishops of the Cathar churches, deacons and perfects found refuge in places that offered the most security. Benedict of Termes, Bishop of the Church of Razès, went to the eagle's nest of Queribus, and Guilhabert of Castres, Bishop of the Toulouse Church, left Saint Paul Cap de Joux as soon as the treaty was signed and joined Albedun in the Haut Razès. For three years, Guilhabert led a nomadic and clandestine life which took him, successively, to Montréal, Dourne, the Sault lands, Estavar, Cerdagne, to Laurac where he consoled the wounded Bernard-Othon of Niort, to Verfeil, Besplas, Fanjeaux, to Miramont in Sabarthès, to Labécède, and finally, to the Gaja Forest.

The Seat and the Head of the Cathar Church

During the autumn of 1232, Raymond of Péreille, who had just settled in Montségur with his family, received a message from Guilhabert of Castres asking him to come and join him in Villeneuve d'Olmes. The old lord and several of his men found Guilhabert surrounded by about twenty perfects. They had come from Gaja Forest, escorted by three knights – Raymond Sans of Rabat, another co-lord of Mirepoix, Isarn of Fanjeaux, Raymond of Péreille's cousin, and Pierre of Mazerolle, co-lord of Gaja. Raymond of Péreille led all these Bons Hommes to Montségur, where Guilhabert requested that "he receive them under the castle so that the Church could have its seat and its head there". "So Raymond of Péreille, after many words and prayers, agreed to the request of these perfects," declared Berenger of Lavelanet before Ferrer the inquisitor on April 21, 1244. Accompanying the Cathar Bishop of Toulouse were his *filius major*, Bernard of Lamothe and his *filius minor*, Jean Cambiaire; the Bishop of Agenais and his *filius major*, Vigouroux of La Bacone; the deacons Pons Guilhabert, Bernard Bonnafous and Raymond of Montouty. For nearly twelve years, the male and female perfects, essentially from the Cathar Church of Toulouse, were able to carry out their ministry under the protection of the family clan of the lords of Péreille and Mirepoix. It is true that in 1232 Massip of Gaillac, Raymond VII's bailiff, had come to Montségur with an armed troop to arrest Jean Cambiaire, the *filius minor* of Guilhabert of Castres, and three other perfects. It is true that in 1241, Montségur was besieged by troops of the Count of Toulouse, but with little enthusiasm and for

Reference Dates	
"Council" of Mirepox. The Cathars invite Raymond of Péreille to rebuild the *castrum* of Montségur.	1206
At the Lateran Council, Foulque, Bishop of Toulouse reproaches the Count of Foix for sheltering heretics in his *castrum* of Montségur.	1215
• Guilhabert of Castres makes Montségur the "seat and head" of the Cathar Church of Toulouse, of which he is bishop. • John Cambiaire, *filius minor* of Guilhabert of Castres, and three perfects are arrested in Montségur by Raymond VII's bailiff.	1232
Siege of Montségur by troops of the Count of Toulouse.	1241
• May 26: Pierre-Roger of Mirepoix receives a visit from Raymond of Alfaro. He leaves Montségur with about fifty men in the direction of Avignonet. • May 28: murder of the inquisitors in Avignonet.	1242
• The siege of Montségur begins at the end of springtime. • December: the besiegers capture the position of Roc de la Tour. • A few days before Christmas: the treasure of the Cathar Church is evacuated.	1243
• Early January: Arrival of Bertrand of La Vacalerie, an engineer in war machines, in the camp of the besieged. • March 2: Pierre-Roger of Mirepoix starts discussions with the seneschal Hugo of Arcis. A fifteen-day truce is negotiated. • March 16: More than two hundred and twenty perfects and consoled die at the stake. • From March 10 to May 27: The inquisitor Ferrer gathers statements from the occupants of Montségur.	1244

Raymond of Péreille's Relations

- Raymond of Péreille, his wife Corba, and his perfect mother-in-law, Marquésia Hunaud of Lanta.
- Jourdain, his son
- Arpaix, his daughter and her husband Guiraud of Rabat
- Philippa, his other daughter
- Pierre-Roger of Mirepoix, cousin of Raymond of Péreille whose daughter Philippa he had married; their son Esquieu
- Arnaud-Roger of Mirepoix, brother of Raymond of Péreille, his wife Cecile of Montserver, and his perfect mother-in-law, Braida of Montserver
- Gaillard del Congost, nephew of Raymond of Péreille, his wife Blanche, his sister Saissa, a perfect, his cousin Bertrand
- Alazais of Massabrac, sister of Raymond of Péreille, her two sons, Alzieu and Othon, her daughter Fays and the latter's husband, Guillaume of Plaigne

Raymond of Péreille's entourage

- The bailiffs of Raymond of Péreille and Pierre-Roger of Mirepoix
- Four attendants and the nurse of Esquieu, wife of Pierre-Roger's bailiff
- A doctor, Arnaud Rouquier, his wife and his daughter

Defenders

- 12 knights, including Berenger of Lavelanet, with his wife, his son and their two daughters
- 10 equerries
- 55 sergeants, including Imbert of Salles with his wife Lombarde of Lavelanet
- An engineer for catapults, Bertrand of Vacalerie
- Ten liaison men
- Regular visitors and entourage

Religious Community

- Over 200 male and female perfects, 49 of whom known (34 men and 15 women, 3 from the Péreille clan)
- Bertrand Marty, Bishop of the Toulouse Cathar Church, and Pierre Sirven, his *filius minor*
- Raymond Agulher, Bishop of the Razès Cathar Church
- The deacons Guillaume Déjean, Pierre Bonnet and Raymond of Saint Martin

good reason – they were led by Jourdain of Lanta, the son of a perfect who had died at the stake, and Pons of Villeneuve, a benefactor of Montségur. Before this non-threatening danger, India of Lahille and seven other perfects were taken to Queille to the house of Arnaud of Lescure. But from 1232 to 1244, Montségur enjoyed the same impunity as it had done since the beginning of the crusade in 1209. The best explanation is probably linked to a complex feudal situation. Nobody really knew whether Montségur fell under the influence of the Counts of Foix or the Counts of Toulouse, or even the Viscounts of Carcassonne or Béziers.

Just before the siege, the castle and village built at its foot contained between four and five hundred people. The lord Raymond of Péreille lived with his family, including Pierre-Roger of Mirepoix, his son-in-law and military chief. The seigniorial clan was surrounded by a civil community of equerries, men-at-arms, *faydits*, and their families, and by a religious community of over two hundred people. This entire community was perfectly organized. There was a porter, Sergeant Guillaume of Gironda; a miller, the perfect Pons Aïs, a public baker, Guillelme Marty. Both Bons Hommes and Bonnes Femmes worked; the former in a tailor's workshop, making doublets for the soldiers; the latter as seamstresses managed by Marquésia Hunaud of Lanta, making clothes for women and chausses for men. Each of these workshops employed about a hundred people. One perfect was a barber, another a shoemaker. There was even a doctor, Arnaud Rouquier. The community did not live cut off from the world. There was continuous movement of perfects coming and going out on missions, but also believers coming on pilgrimages. They could listen to sermons by Bernard Marty, who succeeded Guilhabert of Castres as head of the Toulouse Cathar Church in about 1240, or by Raymond Agulher, the Bishop of the Razès Cathar Church. The ill came to be consoled. Peasants from neighbouring localities also came to the summit of the *pog* (hill) to supply Montségur with food and basic supplies.

The courtyard and keep of Montségur Castle

Waiting for Raymond

It was probably at the Council of Béziers in April 1243 that the decision to besiege Montségur was taken. According to the expression of Blanche of Castile, it was necessary "to cut off the dragon's head". More than ten years earlier, Montségur, the "synagogue of Satan" in Guillaume of Puylaurens' words, had become the seat and the head of the Cathar Church. Furthermore, the expedition to Avignonet had left from Montségur. By the end of the spring of 1243, the French army led by the seneschal Hugues of Arcis was moving towards the fearsome rocky spur whose invulnerability had earned it the name *secure mount*. As the number of troops was not very high, conscription had to be organized among the population and was sometimes rather forced, given that it was not enthusiastically welcomed. Fortunately, the seneschal was able to count on the Church's collaboration. On his side, the Bishop of Albi was able to raise one hundred and fifty men. The Archbishop of Narbonne, Pierre Amiel, joined the besiegers, but had to return to Albi at the end of 1243 to take charge of a council to specify and supervise inquisitorial procedures. The siege was established at the end of May. The net was however sufficiently loose that the besieged were able to continue having contact with the outside world even though supplies of food and merchandise had rapidly become practically impossible. But this inevitable encircling had been foreseen and Montségur had been provided with large reserves of food. Sporadic fighting broke out between the besiegers and the besieged, who began to have their first casualties. During the early days of the siege, Raymond of Ventenac, the equerry of Arnaud-Roger of Mirepoix was mortally wounded and received the *consolament* from the perfects Raymond of Saint-Martin and Guillaume Razoul. The same fate befell Sicard of Puivert in June and Guillaume of Gironda in August. For Raymond of Péreille and Pierre-Roger of Mirepoix, the most important thing was to play for time. They knew the area and that winter would be their precious ally. Furthermore, they were well-informed. They knew that the Count of Toulouse was in Italy straightening out his problems with the emperor and the pope, and that he was the sole possibility of outside intervention on their behalf. They could no longer count on their direct overlord, the Count of Foix, who had joined the French. But although they had paid homage to the lords of Foix for the lands of Olmes and Montségur, it had been "on condition of fidelity to the Count of Toulouse". Not having been consulted, and for good reason, they did not care about the measures of the 1229 Treaty of Paris, which directly annexed the "Land of the Marshal", given by Montfort to his faithful lieutenant Guy of Lévis, to the French crown. Therefore, on two occasions, Raymond of Péreille and Pierre-Roger of Mirepoix sent messengers to obtain information about Raymond VII. The first messenger was Escot of Belcaire, who communicated his answer by lighting a fire at the summit of the Vidorle, near Belvis in the land of Sault. The second message was carried by two sergeants who went to obtain information about the Count of Toulouse from the brother of Pierre-Roger

Miglos Castle

ARNAUD OF MIGLOS

On June 24, 1244, Arnaud of Miglos, who ten years earlier had come to the *pog* to hear sermons by Guilhabert of Castres, told Ferrer the inquisitor that "one year ago" Guillaume Dejean of Lordat had come to see him on behalf of Pierre-Roger of Mirepoix. The latter was requesting "ten or twelve ropes for a *gousse* –a throwing machine– and a catapult". The messenger returned to Montségur with the ropes, the catapult and also with a crossbow. Before the inquisitor Bernard of Caux in 1246, Arnaud specified that this had taken place "when the castle of Montségur was besieged by the Count of Toulouse". Hence in 1241.

Stele with crossbow, Carcassonne

of Mirepoix, Isarn of Fanjeaux, in Queille. In both cases, the information that they managed to obtain provided them with a little bit of hope – Raymond of Toulouse was supposed to return to his lands before the end of the year. The morale of the besieged remained high even though, in September, Alzieu of Massabrac was wounded and though, in October, the sergeant Guillaume Claret was killed. Before the end of October, a letter addressed by the heretics of Cremona, Italy, to Bertrand Marty crossed the enemy lines, through which Escot of Belcaire also managed to slip to bring other good news about the Count of Toulouse, transmitted by Raymond of Niort and his wife, Marquésia, a daughter from the first marriage of Pierre-Roger of Mirepoix. Among the besiegers, Hugues of Arcis was well aware that he had to try something before the arrival of the first snows. In December, a group of his soldiers, lightly armed and led by men who knew the area, arrived along dangerous paths above the gorges of the Lasset, at Roc de la Tour. They caught out the sentries who occupied the small fort at the eastern end of the upper ridge of the *pog*, killed them and invested the position. Of course, this place was nearly seven hundred and fifty metres from the castle and three hundred and fifty metres below it, but for the besiegers it was to provide a very important stepping-stone from which they could launch attacks on their principal target, the castle, and its outpost, the barbican. The bolts, arrows and the many cannonballs found on this crest testify to the intensity of the fighting.

A Montségur cannonball

USSON CASTLE

At the upriver entrance to the gorges of the Aude River, at the place where the river receives water from its tributary the Bruyante, Usson Castle is hidden in the heart of the hilly terrain. Like Pierre-Roger of Mirepoix and Raymond of Péreille, its lords, the brothers Bernard of Aillon and Arnaud of Usson, were *credentes* or believers of the heretics and used to come to listen to the perfects' sermons at Montségur. From 1232 to 1244, protected by its very isolation, the castle was practically an annex to Montségur, as attested by testimony gathered by the inquisitor Ferrer during the spring of 1244. Hence, in about 1236, Arnaud of Vivier, son of the perfect Raymonde of Vivier, led Guilhabert of Castres from Usson to Montségur. Perfects moved permanently between the two strongholds. At the beginning of the siege of Montségur, Imbert of Salles, coming from Usson, arrived on the *pog* in the company of a crossbowman. And early in the year 1244, Bernard of Aillon and Arnaud of Usson sent twenty-five sergeants as reinforcements to the besieged. After the great stake of March 1244, four perfects went to Usson before going to recover the treasure of the Cathar Church in the high county of Foix.

The Roc de la Tour, Montségur

Usson Castle

Arrow slit in Montségur keep

The Fall of Montségur

It was a hard blow for the besieged. Prudently, Bertrand Marty had the treasure of the Cathar community evacuated. A few days before Christmas, the deacon Pierre Bonnet and the perfect Mathieu descended the sides of the *pog*, stumbled onto the guard posts held by men of Camon, neighbours, who let them pass and even showed them the way. The two men reached a *spoulga*, a fortified cave, in the high county of Foix where they hid their precious load. At the beginning of the month of January 1244, an engineer for war machines entered the castle by night. A native of Capdenac, his name was Bertrand of la Vacalerie. Early in the March truce, to restore their confidence, he called together knights and sergeants, assuring them that he had been sent on behalf of Raymond VII by his lieutenant Sicard Alaman and his bailiff Bertrand of Laroque, and that the Count of Toulouse's intervention would not be long in coming. At the beginning of 1244, an inhabitant of Saint Paul Cap de Joux, Jean Rey, brought a second letter from the bishop of the Cathar Church of Cremona for Bertrand Marty. It informed him that his Church lived in peace and asked him to send him two perfects. During the first half of February, the attackers were on the point of investing the castle with ladders but their attack only just failed. It was probably during this operation that Jourdain of the Mas, son of one of the co-lords of Mas Saintes Puelles, grandson of the perfect Garsende who died at the Inquisition's stake, was mortally wounded defending the barbican. Although he could not speak, he was consoled by Bertrand Marty's *filius minor*, Pierre Sirven, and the deacon Raymond of Saint-Martin. A short time before he had done his *convenenza*. The besieged suffered from other losses during the month of February and there were many who asked to do their *convenenza* in order to be able to be consoled even if they were unconscious. In the third week of February, the perfect Mathieu returned to Montségur accompanied by two sergeants and two crossbowmen, and supplied with weapons and money in order to recruit new defenders. One of the two sergeants brought a message from Isarn of Fanjeaux: the besieged had to hold out until Easter "because the Count of Toulouse was arriving in the country with great reinforcements from the emperor." But the situation was desperate. On March 2, Pierre-Roger of Mirepoix, after consulting Bertrand Marty, began negotiations with the seneschal. A two-week truce was granted. At the end of it, Montségur would be delivered to the Church and the King. An amnesty would be granted to the members of the Avignonet commando. Male and female perfects would be handed over to ecclesiastical authorities and would have to abjure. Those who refused would be taken to the stake. The other inhabitants or defenders of Montségur would be interrogated by the inquisitor Ferrer. The statements of eighteen interrogations made by this inquisitor from March 10 to May 27, 1244, have been preserved. During the truce, the perfects distributed the provisions and the meagre possessions that they still had. They gave Pierre-Roger of Mirepoix a blanket filled with silver from donations made by believers. On Sunday,

THE TREASURE OF MONTSÉGUR

Montségur did not live within a closed economy. Commercial exchanges took place with the outside and the *pog*'s occupants possessed monetary means and certainly had savings. Furthermore, the Cathar Church needed resources to finance its activities. Hence, Montségur possessed capital in the form of money, but perhaps also precious metals transformed into objects, jewels or ingots. After the besiegers captured the Roc de la Tour, it was normal for Bertrand Marty to have a large part of the treasure of his church evacuated and placed in security in a fortified cave (*spoulga*) in the high county of Foix, held by a trustworthy man, Pons-Arnaud of Châteauverdun, the brother-in-law of Pierre-Roger of Mirepoix but also a known Cathar believer. As the tragic ending approached, the perfects or consoled who had chosen to die donated to the others what they had in cash but also their meagre belongings. They did not forget to pay those who had defended them for nine months; each sergeant received five *toulzas* sous and Pierre-Roger of Mirepoix was given four hundred *toulzas sous* by the deacon Raymond of Saint-Martin "to distribute as a salary or as a gift".

The fortified spoulga of Bouan

Prat del Cramats stele, Montségur

LORDAT

I n his interrogations from March to May, 1244, the inquisitor Ferrer tried to obtain from his witnesses the names of people who had stayed in Montségur or who had come there to listen to or "adore" the perfects. We know that the *castrum* of Lordat, in Sabarthès, to the south of Montségur on the southern slope of Tabe Mountain, had supplied a large number of heretical believers. Indeed, at least ten of them came from this castle, including Raymond Salles, the lord, and his son Guillaume.

March 13, twenty-one *credentes* asked to be consoled, *ipso facto* implying that they accepted to share the fate of the perfects who refused to abjure their faith. Among them were Corba, the wife of Raymond of Péreille, and her daughter, Esclarmonde, four *faydits* including Guillaume of Lahille and Raymond of Marceille, the latter's equerry, a merchant from Mirepoix, two liaison men including Jean Rey, two women, one of whom was Guillelme Aicart who left behind her husband and two children. Bertrand Marty consoled the believers of his diocese and Raymond Agulher, those of his own. At dawn on March 16, Hugues Arcis took possession of the castle in the name of the king. Pierre Amiel, the Archbishop of Narbonne, gathered together the perfects, all of whom refused to abjure. Over two hundred and twenty people, perfects and consoled, men and women, perished at the stake raised at the foot of the *pog*. Guillaume of Puylaurens wrote, "Refusing the conversion to which they were invited, they were burnt in an enclosure made of pales and stakes which was set on fire and they passed into the flames of Tartarus." It should be noted that the Inquisition had not intervened in setting up this tragedy but it was certainly present at its conclusion. The night preceding the holocaust, four perfects, Amiel Aicart, Hugon, Peytavi and Pierre Sabatier, were evacuated from the *castrum* over the precipice by means of ropes. Their mission was to recover the treasure evacuated in December from the spoulga in the lands of Foix. They passed through Caussou and Prades to reach Usson. On the way, they met Mathieu. They put the treasure in a safe place. Peytavi and Pierre Sabatier carried the tragic news to the Bishop of Cremona. Trace was lost of all those who managed to escape from Montségur except Pierre-Roger of Mirepoix who, fifteen years later, was still a *faydit*, and Bernard of Scopont, who was interrogated by the inquisitor Bernard of Caux in May 1245. This defender of Montségur reached Italy and became a perfect. Montségur was given to Guy of Lévis, the son of Simon de Montfort's lieutenant. The houses that had sheltered heretics were all destroyed according to the measures of the Treaty of Paris.

Lordat Castle

Montségur Castle

MONTSÉGUR, FROM CATHAR CASTRUM TO LÉVIS'S FORTRESS

In the heart of the Ariège department's Pyrenees, the *pog* or hill of Montségur, the limestone peak crowned by the ruins of the castle, at an altitude of 1,208 metres, appears as an outpost of the Tabe range from which the peaks of Soularac and Saint Barthélemy emerge to the south-west. The source of the Lasset is at their foot. Before it reaches the Hers at Fougax-et-Berrineuf, the river cuts deep gorges, called Carroulet, out of the eastern face of the *pog*, separating it from the Frau mountain. Nothing remains of the original Péreille castle, nor of the one Raymond of Péreille had rebuilt towards 1210 at the request of the Cathar hierarchy. When Guilhabert of Castres settled there in 1232, Montségur's defences were organized around the original keep. By making the best use of the terrain, the defences stood on the edges of the cliffs. They were reinforced even further on the south-western side which was, relatively, the most easily accessible. This is the side that today contains the path used by visitors. To the east, about one hundred and fifty metres from the *caput castri*, there was an outpost called a barbican. At the eastern tip of the summit's plateau, the watch post of the Roc de la Tour topped the eighty metres of the steep cliff that dropped into the Carroulet gorges. Vestiges of walls and passages, found in the rectangular, inclined space separating the Roc de la Tour and the eastern defences of the castle, allow us to imagine that this place was developed and defended. The village in which the Cathar community lived was located "below

the castle", on the narrow ledge separating the northern walls of the keep from a precipice that was so sheer that any access by this northern face was completely impossible. The houses were squeezed and entangled together, rising on rocky ground and using the shapes of the relief and the smallest ledges of the terrain as support for their wooden structures and walls, mostly drystone. This village was razed in 1244. Excavations carried out on site have brought to light a large quantity of objects, some of which are presented at the Museum of Montségur. An analysis of this material, completed by records of interrogations by the inquisitor Ferrer, has provided much information about life on the *pog* before the fall of Montségur. Water was supplied by the Lasset and brought to the mountain's summit on muleback, but was also collected in cisterns fed by rainfall. Mills worked by hand provided flour and, starting in 1243, there was a woman baker, Guillelme Marty, who baked bread. Wine from neighbouring villages was drunk by the *pog*'s occupants, who ate vegetables and meat produced on the spot but also, and more surprisingly, fish from the sea, probably dried, such as skate, bass, mullet, and sea bream. Several instruments —scissors, thimbles— are evidence of sewing and clothes-making activity. Exchanges with the outside were therefore numerous and the various monies found on the spot confirm this. The castle whose vestiges are visible nowadays was rebuilt after 1244 by the Lévis, lords of Mirepoix, and direct vassals of the King of France. This fortress was one of the defensive links of the

kingdom of France against Aragon. A garrison was still in place there in the middle of the 15th century. The castle is seventy metres long and its maximum width is twenty metres. The north-western tip is occupied by a rectangular keep measuring fifteen metres by eight. Towards the south-east it is prolonged by a seven hundred square metre enclosure, whose blind curtain walls open only through doors at the north and the south, at one time defended by hoarding. At the centre of the encroachment of this enclosure, the one hundred square metre courtyard was roughly of the same shape and used to be surrounded by the main building that was three storeys high but is now completely destroyed. Three staircases led to the wall walk. The second floor of the main building communicated with the main room of the keep, the lord's dwelling place. This room opened through four great openings with stone benches and possessed a fireplace and a cistern. A spiral staircase led from this room down into the lower room with its five loopholes that lay next to the cistern. The same staircase led up to the terrace on top of the keep. None at all of this architecture, dating from after 1244, is linked to any cult of the sun. It is simply the product of the rigour of its builders who adapted their construction to the military requirements of their time, to the layout of the terrain and also the climatic demands of this windswept place, extremely cold in winter and sometimes scorching hot in summer. But the castle of Montségur, turned into a symbol, continues to fascinate and strike the imagination.

WITH A FINE-TOOTHED COMB

A fter the murder of the inquisitors Guillaume Arnaut and Étienne of Saint Thibéry in Avignonet in 1242, the work of the Toulouse court was carried out for three years by the tribunal of Carcassonne, at the time under the leadership of Ferrer. In 1245, after short missions in Agenais and Quercy, the inquisitors Bernard of Caux and Jean of Saint-Pierre took charge of the Toulouse court. Their great investigation in the Lauragais took place from May 1, 1245 until August 1, 1246. The inhabitants of about a hundred localities of the Lauragais and the Montagne Noire were subjected to their interrogations, including Mas Saintes Puelles, Saint Julia, Hautpoul, Montmaur, Montgey, as well as Toulouse. The number of these interrogations is estimated at five thousand. They took place at the cloister of Saint Sernin's Abbey where the suspects were convoked, most of them having attempted to take advantage of the period of grace. The inquisitors had a house near the abbey that was used as a temporary prison. Sentences were delivered from March to July 1246 and from November 1247 to June 1248, during practically weekly general sermons. There are indeed fifty-two of them. Condemnations particularly concerned believers, with the two inquisitors preferring an undermining process rather than pursuing disguised heretics, who were less numerous and more careful since Montségur. Generally, the penalties were confiscation of property and life imprisonment. In 1248, Bernard of Caux and Jean of Saint-Pierre were charged with the Carcassonne court for a year, replacing Pierre Durand and Guillaume Raymond, disavowed by Pope Innocent IV. In 1249, Bernard of Caux worked in Agen to create a Preachers' convent, which opened in 1252, shortly after his death.

Vestiges of Hautpoul Castle

Montmaur Castle

LANGUEDOC, LAND OF FRANCE

Within thirty years of the tragedy of Montségur, Languedoc and a part of Provence would be annexed to the kingdom of France. Even though the scenario for the Raymondine possessions unfurled as planned by the Treaty of Paris of 1229, the situation was less obvious for the former Trencavel viscounties.

The Last Years of Raymond VII

The besieged in Montségur had waited in vain for the arrival of the Count of Toulouse. Raymond VII had remained in Italy to have his excommunication lifted and to recover his title of Marquis of Provence. In order to obtain the latter goal, he had to play a fine diplomatic hand between the pope and the emperor and was therefore retained in Rome until the month of April 1244. As for the lifting of his excommunication, it had been decided by the pope in December 1243 and was to be promulgated by the Archbishop of Narbonne on March 14, 1244, two days before the mass deaths at the stake at Montségur. On his return journey, Raymond VII stopped in Narbonne, where the archbishop was reconciled with Viscount Aimery. Raymond VII had reason to be satisfied. He had recovered nearly all his lands and titles and had been welcomed back into the Church. In his capital, he received homage from many vassals, such as the Counts of Astarac and Comminges in November. Hence, for the Christmas celebrations of 1244, he held a great court in Narbonnais Castle, described by Guillaume of Puylaurens as "sumptuous and magnificent". But in his mind, there remained one essential task to be accomplished. He wanted the Inquisition taken away from the Preaching Friars and entrusted to prelates. He wished to provide his father, whose corpse had been rotting in a shed at the Hospitallers Convent in Toulouse for over twenty years, with a proper Christian burial. And finally, he wanted to have a male heir, the only way of preventing the measures of the Treaty of Paris coming into force after his and his daughter's deaths, and leading to the end of his dynasty.

In the spring of 1245, when the inquisitor Bernard of Caux was starting his great investigation in the Lauragais, Raymond VII went to Paris to see King Louis IX. On the way he stopped in Lyon, where a council was being prepared, and met Pope Innocent IV with whom he evoked the question of the dispensation he needed to validate his marriage with Marguerite of the March. Returning from Paris, he went through Lyon where the council was under way. There he met the Count of Provence, Ramón Berenguer, whose daughter, Sancie, he had planned to marry in 1241. But the Catalonian had another daughter, Beatrice, who, in the eyes of the Count of Toulouse, was a much better match than the daughter of the Count of the March. An enquiry into the validity of the marriage between Raymond VII and Marguerite had begun on June 13. Its results were known on August 3. Since the two spouses were related to the third and fourth degree, the pope annulled the marriage. Raymond VII

The ramparts of Aigues Mortes

Laurac

OPEN THE DOOR

O ne of the twenty-two miracles attributed to James the Greater and related in the *Codex Calixtinus*, a work preserved in the archives at Compostela Cathedral, presents one of the ancestors of Raymond VII, Count Pons of Saint Gilles (1037-1060) who, arriving in front of the closed doors of the cathedral in Compostela, saw them being opened by Apostle James in person.

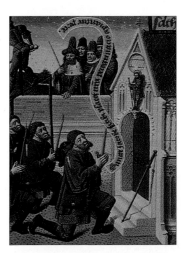

Pons of Saint Gilles in Compostela

could now dream of joining to his own Marquisate of Provence the County of Forcalquier, of which Beatrice was the sole heiress. But Beatrice had other suitors who rapidly appeared a few weeks later, after the death of Ramón Berenguer. At the time, Raymond VII was in Toulouse and he rushed to Provence. James I of Aragon, who wished to have his son marry his cousin, beat him to it. But Blanche of Castile too had a son to marry off, Charles of Anjou. She met the pope at Cluny in November to ask for the necessary dispensation and, in January 1246, Charles married Beatrice. In the course of the year, the Count of Toulouse went on a pilgrimage to Santiago de Compostela. In early 1247, Louis IX called him to his court and suggested that Raymond VII participate in a new crusade to the Holy Land. The King of France was developing Aigues Mortes, from where he was to embark. In this royal invitation, there was of course on the monarch's part strong faith and religious conviction, but it also involved political calculation. With Raymond VII at his side, the future Saint Louis could hope that Occitania would remain calm. His position on the subject was close to that of Pope Innocent IV who, at the end of 1247, asked the Archbishop of Auch and the Bishop of Albi to commute the penalties of imprisonment imposed on the heretics into an obligation to leave for the Holy Land, either as pilgrims or as crusaders. In response to Louis IX's request, Raymond VII declared that he no longer had the means to organize such an expedition. This was not a problem since Blanche of Castile gave him twenty-five thousand *livres* and, as a bonus, Raymond VII recovered his title of Duke of Narbonne, which he had lost in 1229. The pope was pleased with the Count of Toulouse's new plans and his decision to leave for the banks of the Jordan River. He wrote to the patriarch of Jerusalem recommending the count to him and asking Hugues of Turenne, a Franciscan who preached the crusade in Languedoc, to deduct one-twentieth of the ecclesiastical revenues of the County of Toulouse to pay for the count's crusade. The count, confident in his excellent relationship with the papacy, asked Innocent IV in July, 1247 to authorize his father's burial. An investigative committee put in place by the pope did not respond favourably to the request. In February 1248, Raymond VII's promise to take the cross earned him the French crown's restoration of the castles of Penne d'Albigeois, Puycelci, Najac and Laurac. On February 2, Raymond VII was in Saint Sulpice, on the banks of the Tarn River, in the house of Sicard Alaman. In the presence of the master of the house, of Raymond Alfaro and Guillaume of Puylaurens, his chaplain and namesake of the chronicler, he ceded the property of Pierre of Rouaix, condemned in his absence as a relapsed heretic by the Inquisition on March 18, 1246, and whose goods had been confiscated, to a certain Odon Escot of Linars. Whatever the profound motivations of the Count of Toulouse may have been, this fact reveals the radical change in his attitude towards heresy. The pope could only be very pleased about it, as evidenced by the letters the supreme pontiff addressed to the Bishop of Agen on April 29 and 30, 1248. In the second letter, Innocent IV strengthened the inquisitorial powers of the Bishop of Agen, which could only satisfy Raymond VII.

On June 12, Louis IX left Paris for Aigues Mortes. On August 25, accompanied by his brothers Robert of Artois and Charles of Anjou, Philippe de Montfort, Lord of Castres, his brother Philippe, Lord of Lombers, but also Trencavel and Olivier of Termes, he set sail for the Holy Land. Raymond VII was not a part of this expedition because the ship he had fitted out to cross the Mediterranean was coming from Brittany. He went to wait for it in Marseille, but finally postponed his departure until the following year. The year 1249 arrived, but Raymond VII still did not leave. He took care of his business, received homage from his vassals, and went to Logroño, in Rioja, to meet the Infante of Castile, the future King Alfonso X. On his return to Toulouse, he fell ill. Hardly had he recovered his health, he went off to the Agenais to mediate a conflict between two of his vassals, the Viscount of Lomagne and the Count of Armagnac. Showing excessive zeal, in a pointless and unwarranted action perhaps intended to prove that the anti-heretical struggle did not need the inquisitors, Raymond VII had eighty heretical believers burnt at Béoulaygues. In August, he returned to Aigues Mortes where, on the 26, his daughter Jeanne and his son-in-law Alphonse of Poitiers, accompanied by numerous crusaders, set sail in their turn for the Holy Land. Raymond VII went to Rouergue. He was struck by a high fever in Millau. He turned back to Toulouse, but was forced to stop at Capdenac to take to his bed. The bishops of Toulouse, Agen, Cahors, Rodez, the consuls of Toulouse and many knights hurried to his bedside. It would have been natural to take him to Toulouse but the count wished to return to Millau. In the testament he dictated to the notary Jean Auriol on September 23, he expressed his wish to be buried at Fontevrault next to his grandfather, Henry II, King of England, his uncle, Richard the Lionheart, and his mother, Jeanne. Two days later, in a codicil, he promised that if he recovered, he would leave for the Holy Land; and if he was to die, the money that had been advanced by the French crown and the papacy for the expedition was to be given back. He died on September 27 at the age of fifty-two. On May 1, 1250, his body was buried at Fontevrault.

Millau belfry

Recumbent figure of Richard the Lionheart, Fontevrault Abbey

OLIVIER OF TERMES

At the moment of the capture of Termes in 1210 by Montfort, Olivier of Termes was only three years old. When he was old enough to bear arms, he took part in many battles on the Occitan side. He defended Labécède in 1226. Like many others, in 1228 he submitted for a while to Louis IX, before accompanying James I on his conquest of Majorca the following year. Loyal to Raymond VII, he supported him in his Provencal operations of 1230 and 1236. He was among the numerous *faydits* who gathered under the Trencavel banner in 1240. During the rout, he tried one last-ditch stand by defending La Roque de Fa attacked by the French. Six months later, in Pontoise, he rallied to Louis IX and accompanied him to the Holy Land in 1248. He won renown there, earning the admiration of Joinville and obtaining the restitution of several castles, including Aguilar. He captured Quéribus on behalf of the king in 1255. In 1270, he was in Tunis at Louis IX's bedside when the king died of plague. Olivier died in 1274. His remains were placed in Fontfroide, an abbey of which he was a benefactor.

Aguilar Castle

THE PREACHERS DISAVOWED

On March 12, 1244, Innocent IV and Emperor Frederick II signed the Peace of Saint John Lateran for which Raymond VII had worked so much. But hardly had it been signed that it was denounced by the emperor. The pope had to flee. He went to Genoa before establishing his residence in Lyon. Meanwhile in Italy, Guelfs and Ghibellines confronted each other more that ever. In Lyon, where he was to remain until 1251, the year of the death of the emperor, the pope organized a great council, held in June 1245 and whose principal purpose was the deposition of Frederick II. However, the question of the Holy Land returned to the fore. Indeed, in that same year of 1244, on August 23, Jerusalem fell into the hands of the Khorezmian Turks and, on October 17, the Christian army was annihilated by Egyptian troops at La Forbie near Gaza. In January 1245, the supreme pontiff once more considered the question of the Inquisition in Languedoc, which was causing dissatisfaction not only among the population but among local bishops, who wished to recover their anti-heretical jurisdiction, and asked that the Office suspend its activity until the council was held. His call was not heeded since in May Bernard of Caux and Jean of Saint Pierre were getting ready to go through the Lauragais with a fine-toothed comb. Early in 1246, the pontifical legate Pierre of Colmieu published an ordonnance with eight articles, the first five of which concerned the inquisitors. In particular, they were asked to be lenient towards repentant heretics and to inflict penalties only after consulting with the bishops. In April 1246, the legate organized a council in Béziers. Its thirty-seven canons confirmed the new

trends of the papacy in its struggle against heresy. It was no longer allowed to condemn without proof and, although the stake remained the normal sanction for convicted heretics who refused to abjure, other sanctions were supposed to be imposed with discernment. Among these sanctions, the departure for the Holy Land was a desirable alternative to imprisonment. Although during the first years of the Dominican Inquisition pilgrimages or service in the crusades had been the punishment frequently meted out to repentant heretics, they had been forbidden by Pope Gregory IX who believed that the presence of former enemies of the faith in holy places was incongruous. But circumstances had changed and in June 1245, Innocent IV was forced to call for a seventh crusade. Christendom needed men to go and fight the Egyptians. In November 1247, the pope saw that his message had not been heeded, that terms of imprisonment continued to be imposed and that few of them had

David's Tower in Jerusalem

been commuted into journeys to the Holy Land. He addressed the inquisitors telling them to be more moderate. In the same month, he wrote to prelates that property confiscated from men convicted of heresy should be restored to their Catholic wives. In December, the Archbishop of Auch and the Bishop of Albi were invited to examine the cases of prisoners who would accept to leave for the Holy Land. In 1248, the pope intervened to accelerate the procedure of commuting punishment. Louis IX was on the point of embarking with his army. On April 29, he asked the Bishop of Agen to lead the anti-heretical activity and to be the one who pronounced condemnations after consulting with the appointed inquisitors. These were the measures of the Council of Narbonne of 1243, though the opposite course had been taken. In the same year of 1248, Innocent IV had destituted the two inquisitors of Carcassonne, Pierre Durand and Guillaume Raymond, who had shown themselves too severe in the penalties they had imposed on one hundred and fifty-six inhabitants of Limoux. In March 1249, Algise of Rosciate, the pope's penitentiary, received full powers to reduce, commute or annul penalties or punishments imposed by the inquisitors in the archbishopric of Narbonne. In May, the pope addressed Bernard of Caux and Jean of Saint Pierre to reproach them for their indulgent way of life but also their zeal in the struggle against heresy. The cup was full. After the indignity they had suffered the previous year with the inhabitants of Limoux, the two Preaching Friars soon returned to their convents. For more than six years, the Dominican Order would not be in charge of the Inquisition.

At the time of the death of Raymond VII, Alphonse of Poitiers and Jeanne were sailing towards Egypt to join Louis IX who was at Damietta in the Nile delta. Blanche of Castile was in charge of the kingdom. As soon as she was informed of the count's death, she sent three commissioners to take possession of the late count's lands in her son's name. She had to deal with the extremely intransigent attitude of the lords and consuls of Languedoc who essentially wanted to maintain their prerogatives, especially those of municipal freedoms. On their return from the crusade, Alphonse and Jeanne entered Toulouse on May 22, 1251. Although his first action was to annul Raymond VII's testament, mainly to avoid having to make the various legacies that the document provided for, Alphonse of Poitiers was wise enough not to question the administration that had been set up by his father-in-law and not to Frenchify it too much. Sicard Alaman retained control over the administration of Toulouse, Raymond VII's chancellor continued to be in charge of justice, and Guy Foulcoy, the son of a chancellor of Raymond VII, became the chancellor of the new count. During his reign, marked by rather strict fiscal regulations, he tried to find a solution to the innumerable legal problems born of the half-century of conflict that had affected the county, and founded several bastides, including Montjoie en Couserans, Saint Sulpice sur Lèze, and Villefranche de Rouergue. But also, right after his return from the Holy Land in 1251, Alphonse insistently interceded with Pope Innocent IV to have the Inquisition entrusted to the Preaching Friars. During the summer of 1270, Alphonse set sail once again with Jeanne to go and join Louis IX in Tunisia. When he arrived at the French camp set up before Tunis on August 27, he learned that his brother had died two days earlier. The count and his wife were back at sea in November, and spent the winter in Sicily before reaching Italy in the spring of 1271. Alphonse died in Savona on August 21. Jeanne survived him by only three days. In application of the Treaty of Paris, the county of Toulouse reverted to Philippe III le Hardi, the new King of France.

Covered walk in St Sulpice sur Lèze

TERRITORIAL DEVELOPMENT

During the 13th century, the situation in Plantagenet-controlled Aquitaine and in a Languedoc torn apart by the crusades and their consequences was rather confusing. These regions were also undergoing strong demographic growth as well as being affected by the development of urbanization that concerned all of Europe. This is the background to the multiple foundations of bastides that started in 1230. These bastides were new towns that provided rights and revenue for their developers, whether civil or religious, who thus more easily controlled the populations gathered within them. Installed at the borders of their domains, they provided a certain amount of security. A legal contract called *pareage*, between the owner of the lands –a lord or a cleric– and another royal or feudal authority, as well as a customary charter were the basis for founding a bastide whose inhabitants enjoyed several advantages: the possibility of becoming owners, exemption from tallage and lodging and collection rights, participation in municipal administration through *jurats* or elected consuls. The bastide was usually organized around a central square on which the market hall stood and laid out in a characteristic checkerboard pattern, making square or rectangular plots of land separated by streets and alleys that met at right angles.

Tunis

The Treaty of Corbeil

After his frustrated attempt in 1240, Trencavel lived at the court of James I in Barcelona. He knew that he would not recover the lands of his fathers but also that, legally, the conditions under which his lineage had lost them could be contested. He wanted to negotiate the final renunciation of the former Trencavel viscounties and to obtain forgiveness from those who had supported him in 1240. At the end of 1246, he met the seneschal Jean of Escrennes in Carcassonne and handed over his own son as a hostage. In January 1247, Louis IX suggested that he give up his rights and leave with him for the Holy Land. In return he would receive six hundred *livres* of annual revenue and his supporters could recover their properties if they were to rebuild the churches and monasteries they had destroyed in 1240. The agreement was signed on April 7, 1247 in Béziers. Trencavel's son was then freed. This agreement pre-empted any possibility of future territorial demands by Trencavel, but did not prejudge demands that might be made by James I of Aragon. Indeed, Raymond-Roger of Trencavel was the vassal of Pedro II, King of Aragon and father of James I who, after Simon de Montfort had captured the viscounties, had recognized the latter as his vassal in Narbonne, in January 1211. To the east of the Pyrenees, the kingdoms of Aragon and France were face to face with each other, on either side of the Fenouillèdes whose annexation posed problems. Catalan-Aragonese influence extended over Roussillon, Cerdagne, Vallespir and Conflent, as well the seigniory of Montpellier. The Fenouillèdes, a fief of Pierre of Fenouillet, extended between the final foothills of the Corbières and Agly. In 1242, perfects had stayed in the castle of Puilaurens, according to testimony by Imbert of Salles, one of the defenders of Montségur, to the inquisitor Ferrer on May 19, 1244. Towards 1250, the castle became French in conditions that are still not clear. At the same period, according to the same testimony of Imbert of Salles, other perfects had taken refuge in Quéribus and in the castles of

Keep window in Quéribus

Castel Sabarda and Saint Pierre Castle in Fenouillet

TESTIMONY

On May 19, 1244, Imbert of Salles from Cordes, a defender of Montségur, testified before the inquisitor, Ferrer. "Two years ago this year, in the month of August, [...] I saw in Puilaurens, in the house of Raymond Laurens, these same perfects [...]. And there everybody, me as much as everyone else, adored these perfects. [...] I saw in Puilaurens, Pierre Jacques, Berenger Malcuit, Pierre Brunet, Berenger of Dourgne, Prima and two other perfects whose names I do not know, whom Pierre of Cucugnan supplied with food. [...] Three years ago, I saw, in the castle of Quéribus, Pierre Paraire, deacon of the perfects of the Fenouillèdes, Raymond of Narbonne and Bugarach, the perfects, who kept Chabert there in a cellar." On May 2, 1244, Guillaume of Bouan from Lavelanet had mentioned, before the same inquisitor, the presence in Puilaurens, in 1240, of three perfects, including Raymonde of Vivier who he and his companions "adored".

Puilaurens Castle

PUILAURENS CASTLE

During the second half of the 10th century, the Mont Ardu, the original name of the mountain on which Puilaurens Castle stands, and the Boulzane and Sainte Croix valleys became possessions of Saint Michel de Cuxa Abbey, through a donation in favour of the Benedictine abbey of Conflent from Count Sunifred. The whole formed an enclave inside the Viscounty of Fenouillèdes. In the heart of a cirque of mountains whose flanks were heavily wooded with coniferous trees, at an altitude of 697 metres, the castle tops a rocky spur overlooking the valley of the Boulzane River. It controlled this important passage of communication between

Louis IX ordered its defences strengthened after the capture of Quéribus. It is probable that for a time it was out of the hands of the Cuxa monks and became the refuge of many *faydits* and Cathars, as confirmed by the testimony of Imbert of Salles before the inquisitor Ferrer on May 19, 1244. After the Treaty of Corbeil in 1258, the castle became a royal fortress and underwent important transformations to be able to receive, in 1260, a garrison of twenty-five sergeants under the orders of Odon of Montreuil. In 1262, Saint Michel de Cuxa Abbey, still the legal holder of the fief, was compensated for its loss by an annual revenue. Like

esting path is filled with marvellous scents from the plants alongside it. It arrives at the foot of the castle, on its north-northwestern side. The plant world is replaced by a mineral one. The evergreen is succeeded by the gray of rock and the castle's stones. Over steep steps, the visitor crosses nine walls in chicane to reach the gate in the first rampart, overlooked on

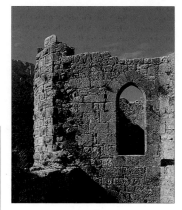

Window in Puilaurens Castle

the left by the wall of the second rampart leaning on the western tower. The courtyard is a vast oblong triangle, measuring seventy metres by twenty-five, running east-west and surrounded by crenellated curtain walls supported by the eastern and southern towers. To the west of the courtyard, the second rampart rises, with the square tower of the keep emerging between the north-west and western towers. The latter is called *Dame Blanche* (White Lady) because Blanche of Bourbon, niece of Philippe le Bel, stayed there. At the entrance to this tower, on the left, a groove in the wall is the beginning of a loud-hailer passage running from the ground floor to a room on the second level, in which a large opening with stone benches opens in the south-east.

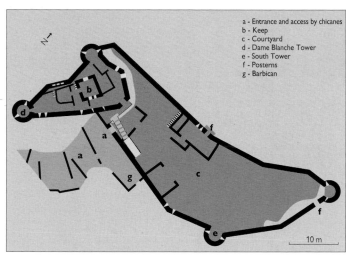

a - Entrance and access by chicanes
b - Keep
c - Courtyard
d - Dame Blanche Tower
e - South Tower
f - Posterns
g - Barbican

10 m

Layout of Puilaurens Castle

the Fenouillèdes and the Catalan *pagus* of Conflent, which came under Aragonese influence in 1162. The castle does not seem to have been directly concerned by the military events of the first half of the 13th century. Pierre Catala in 1217, and Roger Catala in 1247, were mentioned as lords of Puilaurens, which reappeared in the chronicles only in 1255, when

Quéribus, in 1473 the castle was implicated in the conflict opposing the crowns of France and Aragon. And in 1635, it was captured by Spanish troops during the Franco-Spanish War which was ended by the Treaty of the Pyrenees in 1659. Access to Puilaurens Castle is from the west by following a steep path through the undergrowth. This botanically-inter-

Puilaurens Castle

Fenouillet, like Puilaurens possessions of Pierre of Fenouillet, who died consoled in 1243. His son Hugues of Saissac succeeded him. In 1243, Saurine Rigaud, a perfect and sister of a perfect, summonsed to appear by the inquisitor Ferrer, fled and arrived seeking refuge in Fenouillet, where her youngest son died consoled by a deacon. She stayed there for two years, before going to join other perfects at Puilaurens. On July 1, 1229, Pierre of Fenouillet had ceded his lands to the Count of Roussillon, Nuno Sanche "in reparation for damages that he and his knights had caused to him and his vassals". Nuno Sanche having died childless, the lord of Fenouillet paid homage to Aimery of Narbonne on November 8, 1242. At this time he also owned the castle of Quéribus, whose defence he entrusted to Chabert of Barbaira. Chabert had been at the side of Trencavel in 1240 and had taken refuge in Aragonese lands for a time. Quéribus Castle, which overlooks the Grau de Maury and overhangs the Fenouillèdes lands and the Roussillon plain, had in 1229 welcomed the Cathar Bishop of the Razès Church, Benoît of Termes. When, at the beginning of the year 1255, Louis IX gave the order to the seneschal of Carcassonne, Pierre of Auteuil, to capture "this nest of heretics and criminals", it is probable that the castle, defended by Chabert of Barbaira, still contained Cathar perfects. It was not certain and perhaps the King's aim was simply to use Quéribus to strengthen the southern defences of his kingdom while he was about to confront the King of Aragon on the diplomatic chessboard.

PIERRE OF FENOUILLET

In 1262, the inquisitor of Carcassonne, Pons du Pouget, wrote to the archpriest of Fenouillèdes asking him to summons the heirs of Pierre of Fenouillet and his son Hugues of Saissac. On September 5, he ordered that Pierre's corpse be exhumed and burnt. The family appealed, arguing that at the time of the death of their ancestor, in 1243, the Fenouillèdes lands were Aragonese. But the affair dragged on and the sentence was annulled only in 1300. The Count of Fenouillet's remains rested in peace.

St Jean le Vieux in Perpignan

CHABERT OF BARBAIRA

T he Barbaira, vassals of the
Trencavels, owned a *castrum*
to the east of Carcassonne,
between the right bank of the Aude
and Alaric's Mountain. In the
autumn of 1209, Chabert of
Barbaira (1185-1275), who had
become a *faydit*, took part in
recapturing Miramont Castle. In
1219, he defended a besieged
Toulouse and fought at the side of
Raymond the Young in Baziège. In
1223, Nuno Sanche entrusted him
with commanding the garrison of
Perpignan. It was at this time that
he made contact with Pierre of
Fenouillet. In 1229, he was one of
the conquerors of Majorca. In
1240, he was with Trencavel.
Chabert was a Cathar believer. The
request to lift excommunication
addressed by the Count of Foix to
the Bishop of Urgell on March 12,
1244, was very explicit in this
respect: Roger-Bernard justified
his heresy by his friendship with
Chabert, who reconciled with the
Church in 1247. When Olivier of
Termes attacked Quéribus in May,
1255, Chabert had been ambushed
and held prisoner since March in
Carcassonne, hence explaining the
castle's rapid surrender. Chabert
spent the twenty last years of his
life in Catalonia. Shortly before he
died in 1275, on October 4 he
attended the marriage of
Esclarmonde of Foix and James II
of Majorca at Saint John's Church
in Perpignan.

In the autumn of 1254, the King of Aragon had some problems with
his Montpellier seigniory. The city's inhabitants and consuls, supported by the Bishop of Maguelone, were shaking off the Aragonese
yoke. To settle the affair, the King of Aragon asked Louis IX for the
authorization, which was granted, to travel through the Languedoc
coastal area with his army. The King of France simply sent two
observers, Guy II of Lévis and Pierre of Voisins. At the beginning of
the month of May, 1255, the siege of Quéribus by Olivier of Termes
started. It was short and it seems likely that Chabert of Barbaira surrendered quickly, probably without a fight, to a man at whose side he
had fought in 1229 in Majorca and with Trencavel in 1240. He was
imprisoned in Carcassonne where, before the end of the month of
May, he delivered Quéribus to the seneschal and bought his freedom
for a price of a deposit of one thousand silver marks, guaranteed by
Pierre of Voisins and Philippe de Montfort. Still in May, the kings of
France and Aragon decided to entrust the settlement of their territorial conflicts to a committee composed of the Dean of Bayeux and
the Sacristan of Gerona. The conflicts were noteworthy. Indeed,
although James I contested his rights over the Carcassès, the Razès,
the Minervois, the Termenès, the Lauragais, Albigeois, Perapertusès
and even the Gévaudan and the Nîmois with the French crown,
Louis IX could put forward his own rights over the county of
Barcelona, the Besalú, Ampurdan, Roussillon and Conflent, which at
the time of Charlemagne formed the famous March of Spain.
Certainly, over three hundred years had passed since Wilfred the

Pillar room in Quéribus Castle

Quéribus Castle

QUÉRIBUS CASTLE

In the south of the Corbières range, three kilometres from the village of Cucugnan, the keep of Quéribus Castle prolongs the rocky peak on which it was built, at an altitude of 728 metres. It thus controlled the Grau de Maury, the pass separating the Pla de Saint Paul from the rock of Quéribus, ensuring the thoroughfare between the valleys of the Verdouble and the Maury. The view point from the castle's ramparts takes in Peyrepertuse to the north-west, and extends beyond the Roussillon plain as far as the Mediterranean Sea towards the south-east. Looking south, we can see the Pyrenees and the cone of Canigou Peak rising up. It is very likely that even during the distant past the site's defensive qualities were used to good advantage. The existence of Quéribus is mentioned for the first time in 1021, with the name *Cherbucio* that might have meant *an inhabited place on a rock*. Peyrepertuse was also mentioned in the same testament. Until the middle of the 13th century, the fortunes of the two castles ran in parallel. During the 12th century, through the Viscounties of Fenouillèdes and Narbonne, Quéribus came under Catalonian-Aragonese influence, and in 1140, Berenger of Peyrepertuse, from the family of the viscounts of Fenouillet, was lord of both castles. Quéribus, spared by the crusaders, became a refuge for *faydits* and heretics, all the more secure because the lords of Fenouillet, who held it as a fief, were Cathar believers. In 1233, Benoît of Termes, the Bishop of the Cathar Church of Razès, stayed there and died at the castle in 1241. In 1242, the presence of the deacon of the Fenouillèdes, Pierre Paraire, and two perfects, Raymond of Narbonne and Guillaume of Bugarach, was attested by the testi-

mony of Imbert of Salles before the inquisitor Ferrer in 1244. At this time, Pierre of Fenouillet entrusted the defence of Quéribus to Chabert of Barbaira, who also controlled Molhet and Padern. In 1242, Pierre of Fenouillet died consoled and his son Hugues of Saissac succeeded him. In

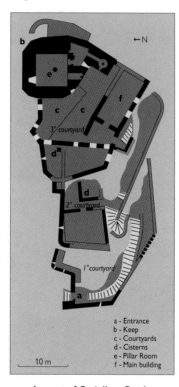

Layout of Quéribus Castle

1255, the seneschal Pierre of Auteuil received orders from Louis IX to capture Quéribus. On May 5, when the siege had already started, he requested support from the Archbishop of Narbonne, Guillaume of la Broue, and his suffrangans, but who provided it only under duress. Olivier of Termes, charged with leading the operation, captured Quéribus. By the month of August, a French garrison of twenty sergeants was placed in the fortress

which, after the signing of the Treaty of Corbeil in 1258, became part of the southern line of defence of the Kingdom of France. In 1473, troops belonging to John II of Aragon came to free Perpignan and the Roussillon, occupied by Louis XI, captured Quéribus but it was retaken by the French two years later. After the signing of the Treaty of the Pyrenees in 1659, Quéribus lost its military importance. The present appearance of the castle is partially a result of restoration work undertaken during the second half of the 13th century and at the end of the 16th century. Three sets of ramparts are adapted to the relief of the rock, with the third enclosing the keep. This wall is the first line of defence on the eastern and northern sides. There are no openings and the walls are four to five metres thick in some places. They resisted attacks by trebuchets set up on platforms one hundred and twenty metres from the castle, at the level of the keep's terrace. The stone balls found on the southern face of the rock show that during the 13th century Quéribus came under fire by these projectiles weighing thirty to forty kilos. Inside the keep, the room with the pillar, dating from the 13th or 14th century, is shaped like a square whose side is seven metres long. It is lit by a cross-shaped mullioned window which, in the south, opens onto the keep's courtyard. The pillar is not centred and spreads into eight ribs, supported by corbels and four crossed arches of varying sizes. This fine Gothic room was to be named Saint Louis's Chapel after the canonization of King Louis IX in 1297. But visitors may nonetheless remember that half a century earlier it was occupied by Cathars, so near to heaven and so far from the madness of man.

Hairy, and the deposition of Raymond-Roger Trencal from his titles and possessions was only half a century old. However the committee was supposed to respond to a problem posed in this way. It did not reach any conclusions by the deadline set for June 24, 1256. In March, 1258, James I sent an embassy to Louis IX. It was led by the Bishop of Barcelona. The two parties finally came to an agreement. The treaty was drawn up and concluded in Corbeil and was ratified by the King of Aragon on July 11. It set the border between the two states. The Catalonian counts remained in Aragon. The Trencavel viscounties, including Perapertusès, were given to the King of France. As for the Fenouillèdes, it was annexed to the former, except for the Boulzane valley, overlooked by the impressive fortress of Puilaurens. This border was not disputed again until the Treaty of the Pyrenees in 1659. The seigniory of Montpellier, whose inhabitants and consuls made amends to James I in December 1258, remained a possession of the Crown of Aragon.

Northwest gate, Termes Castle

Tour de la Dame Blanche seen from the barbican, Puilaurens Castle

THE FIVE SONS OF CARCASSONNE

After the signing of the Treaty of Corbeil in 1258, the Capetians wanted to be able to count on a sure line of defence on the southern border of their kingdom, facing the Catalonian-Aragonese power. They were able to rely on five magnificent castles: Aguilar, Quéribus, Peyrepertuse, Puilaurens and Termes –the "five sons of Carcassonne"– but also on the fortresses of Cabaret in the north, and Roquefixade in the south-west. They began to strengthen the defences to make real "royal citadels". Four centuries after the signing of the Treaty of Corbeil, in 1659, another treaty was signed –the Treaty of the Pyrenees. The official act took place on the Ile des Faisans, in the middle of the Bidassoa River in the Basque country. It was sealed by the marriage of Louis XIV and the Infante Maria-Teresa, daughter of Phillip IV of Spain. The treaty set the border between France and Spain along the Pyrenees watershed and hence removed all the strategic value from these castles which have been more or less abandoned ever since.

St Stephen's Church in Mas Cabardès

Roquefère

Embers under the Ashes

After Montségur, the Cathar Churches of Languedoc were considerably weakened. In Toulouse and the Lauragais, Bons Hommes and Bonnes Femmes and deacons lay low and had great difficulties carrying out their ministries. One such was Arnaud Rougier, Bernard Marty's successor, even though the situation appeared more favourable in the Albigeois, Quercy and Rouergue, as attested by the confession made in 1255 by a converted perfect, Sicard Lunel. On the lands of the seneschalsy of Carcassonne, although Cathar communities were still steadfast, the number of perfects leading them were reduced in number. They were concentrated in the Val de Daigne, between Alaric's Mountain and the Lacamp plateau, west of Lagrasse Abbey; in the Carcassès, between Carcassonne and Saint Hilaire; around Preixan, and between Conques and Alzonne in the piedmont of the Montagne Noire. And on the southern flanks of these hills, in Cabardès, villages that were difficult to reach in the heart of wild country, like Labastide-Esparbairenque, Roquefère, Mas Cabardès, Les Ilhes, La Tourette or Cuxac, became refuges for these communities and their Bons Hommes. However, these active localities of Catharism had not been forgotten by the episcopal Inquisition which, from 1249 to 1255, acted as a replacement in carrying out the repression while the Preaching Friars had temporarily been shunted aside.

La Tourette Cabardès

THE LAST CATHARS

Although they were not able to put an end to their souls and consciences, and kill the deep faith of the numerous remaining believers, the great stake at Montségur and the zeal, or even ruthlessness, of the Dominican inquisitors between 1244 and 1249 did nonetheless manage to disorganize the hierarchy of the Cathar churches in Languedoc, and totally destroyed that of Toulouse. The Cathar Church of Toulouse lost its bishop, most of its deacons, and nearly three hundred perfects died at the stake. To these tragic disappearances must be added those arrested, those who abjured and the exiles. In 1249, the temporary stop of inquisitorial activity by the Preaching Friars was only a short respite.

Perquisites

On his return from a crusade in 1251, after a detour through England and even before going to Toulouse, Alphonse of Poitiers went to visit the pope, who was still in Lyon. Did he encourage him to revive the anti-heretical struggle? In any case, a short time later, on June 17, Innocent IV wrote to the provincial prior of the Preaching Friars asking him to name new inquisitors, but with no result. The hardening of the pope's position, once he returned to Rome, was confirmed by the promulgation on May 15, 1252 of the constitution *Ad extirpendam* authorizing Italian civil powers to have recourse to the question, in other words to use torture, in the struggle against heresy. The same month, he announced to the bishops in Alphonse's county that he had once again entrusted the Inquisition to the Preaching Friars. Still receiving no response, in October 1253 the Supreme Pontiff addressed the prior of the Preachers in Paris, but to no effect. In the springtime of 1254, Alphonse of Poitiers, certainly motivated by the knowledge that intense anti-heretical activity would bring him important financial advantages through the confiscation of properties that it would entail, insisted to the pope that the repression should be more enthusiastic. On July 11, the pope once again wrote to the Parisian Dominicans and ten days later, tried his luck with the Franciscans. Perhaps stung into action, the Dominican prior in Paris reacted and in January, 1255, Renaud of Chartres and Jean of Saint Pierre took charge of the tribunal in Toulouse, whose jurisdiction covered the County of Toulouse. Another tribunal was set up in Carcassonne, with jurisdiction over the royal domain and the County of Foix. The Preaching Friars' taking in hand of the Holy Office was to make life more difficult for the Cathars, concealed or not, and many of them had to go into exile. For the Church of Toulouse, a single perfect, Guillaume Prunel, and his *socius* Bonnet of Saintes, were still preaching in the Lauragais after the return of the Inquisition. Prunel went to Lombardy in 1268. He returned in 1272 with another perfect, Bernard of Tilhols. But the two men were about to be captured when they set off for Italy again in 1274. From then on, among believers more than ever pursued by the Inquisition, sincere or sham abjurations multiplied.

Reference Dates	
The Preaching Friars take over the Inquisition tribunals again.	1255
Cathars captured in Sirmione.	1276
Stake at Verona.	1278
• Sicilian Vespers, the King of Aragon expels Charles of Anjou from Sicily. • Bernard of Castanet becomes Bishop of Albi.	1282
Attempt to steal the Inquisition's archives in Carcassonne.	1284
• Philippe le Hardi's crusade in Catalonia. • Death of Philippe le Hardi.	1285
First inquisition trial in Albi.	1286
Bernard Délicieux refuses to allow the inquisitors to enter the Franciscan convent in Carcassonne.	1295
Pierre Authié leaves for Lombardy.	1296
• Second trial in Albi. • Pierre Authié returns to Languedoc.	1299
December: the Preachers of Albi are surrounded in their convent.	1302
Revolts in Carcassonne, Cordes and Albi.	1303
Journey of Philippe le Bel to Languedoc and plot of Bernard Délicieux.	1304
Bernard Gui is named an inquisitor at the tribunal of Toulouse.	1307
Pierre Authié dies at the stake in Toulouse.	1310
Council of Vienne and promulgation of the constitution *Multorum Querella*.	1312
Beginning of the Templars' trial.	1313
Jacques Fournier carries out the first interrogations of suspected heretics in his diocese of Pamiers.	1318
Trial of Bernard Délicieux.	1319
Guillaume Bélibaste, the last known Cathar perfect, is burnt at Villerouge-Termenès.	1321

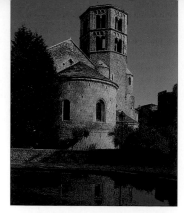

Sant Pere de Galligants, Gerona

SICILIAN VESPERS

O n March 31, 1282, Easter Monday, at the hour of Vespers, the people of Palermo rose up against Charles of Anjou, the foreign king imposed by Pope Clement IV. The revolt soon spread throughout Sicily, where four thousand French were massacred. At the end of April, the island was in insurgent hands. Charles, the brother of Louis IX, reacted and invaded Sicily after attacking Messina. The Sicilians then turned to the King of Aragon, Pedro III the Great, husband of Constance, the niece of Emperor Frederick II. On June 6, Pedro III left the delta of the Ebro at the head of a fleet of one hundred and fifty ships and fifteen thousand men. The expedition's official purpose was to go and receive payment of the tribute the Sultan of Tunis owed to the King of Aragon. After laying off the Tunisian coast for about a month, the armada sailed towards Sicily and defeated the French fleet off Trapani, where Pedro III was welcomed by cheering crowds. The pope excommunicated him and called for a crusade, placing the Aragon's empire as booty. Pedro III hurried back to his lands. Charles of Anjou could not recapture Sicily from him, since it was defended by Admiral Roger of Lauria, a Sicilian emigrant at the Aragonese court, who claimed that "in the western Mediterranean, even the fish are stamped with the Aragonese coat of arms."

Take the Cross and Then Die…

At the death of Alphonse of Poitiers in 1271, the County of Toulouse became part of the Kingdom of France. Philippe le Hardi, who had become King of France in 1270, was in Poitou in 1272 when he learned that the Infant of Aragon, supported by the Counts of Foix and Armagnac and perhaps by the consuls of Toulouse, was scheming to take the county back from him. Gascon castles had been attacked by the two counts and their defenders had been put to the sword. Although the Count of Armagnac submitted to the King of France in Toulouse on May 25, where the king had the opportunity to attend the burning at the stake of a rather unorthodox cleric, Raymond-Bernard III locked himself in his castle, which the French army came to besiege. Finally, the Count of Foix surrendered, following advice from James I of Aragon, whose daughter Isabelle had married the King of France. She was the mother of the future Philippe le Bel, born in 1268. But Toulouse bore the weight of royal administration ever more unwillingly. Philippe understood that he had to make some concessions. In 1279, he granted a "special grace" annulling confiscation of property seized before 1270. Two hundred and seventy-eight Toulousains, including the Rouaix and the Maurands, recovered their family properties.

Philippe le Hardi took the cross in 1285, at the call of Pope Martin IV. The lands up for grabs were those of the King of Aragon, whom the pope had excommunicated after his intervention in Sicily. The King of France received support from James II of Majorca, Pedro III's brother. He besieged Gerona, but his army was decimated by dysentery and his fleet was routed in the Gulf of Rosas by Admiral Roger of Lauria. After re-crossing the Pyrenees through the Panissars Pass, the king died in Perpignan on October 5, 1285. His fate was similar to that of his grandfather, Louis VIII, who died of a sickness probably caught during the siege of Avignon in 1226, on his return from a royal crusade, and that of his father Louis IX, who also died of illness at the siege of Tunis, during the eighth crusade in 1270.

Palace of the Kings of Majorca in Perpignan

In Exile

Ever since Marc, the bishop of the Cathar Church of Lombardy, had come to the Council of Saint Felix in 1167, there had been exchanges between the Cathar Churches of Italy and Languedoc. Thus, in 1220, four Bons Hommes from the French Midi appeared in Milan. One of them was Geraud of Lamothe, the brother of Bernard of Lamothe, the *filius major* of Guilhabert of Castres. In 1227, this deacon from Quercy was back in France and he died at the stake after being captured at Labécède when it was besieged by Imbert of Beaujeu. In 1230, two *credentes* accompanied two female perfects as far as Cremona. On their way, in the Val de Suse they met a barber from Najac who was returning home. The Treaty of Paris, the tribunals of the Inquisition being placed in the charge of the Preaching Friars, the murders in Avignonnet and, of course, the tragedy of Montségur were all events that, to a greater or lesser extent, provoked waves of exiled Cathars, acknowledged or not, from Languedoc to Lombardy. Given the political events taking place on the other side of the Alps, the Cathars were able to live their faith relatively serenely, as the bishop of the Occitan Church wrote from Lombardy in one of the two messages he sent from Cremona to Bertrand Marty during the siege of Montségur. "Here we live in peace and tranquility."

Information about the Church in exile, completely independent from the Italian Cathar Churches but maintaining relations with them, comes from reports of interrogations to which the inquisitors subjected those Cathars who had travelled to Italy. Among them were: Bertrand of Quiders, interrogated by Bernard of Caux in 1246; Guillaume Fournier, interrogated in 1256 by Renaud of Chartres and Jean of Saint Pierre; Raymond Baussan, interrogated in 1274; Bernard Escoulan, interrogated in 1277; Pierre of Beauville, interrogated in 1278, just like Guillaume Raffard. These declarations provide an understanding of the life of Occitan Cathars exiled in Italy, through the traces of their personal itineraries. They tell us that some lived in Cuneo, others in Pavia, in Piacenza or Alessandria, and that the Cathar community in Cremona surrounding Messer Vivent, bishop of the exiled Church of Toulouse, was numerous. That in 1266, after the defeat of Manfred's imperial troops by the Guelphs in Benevento, the communities of Lombardy had to seek refuge, with their bishop, in Guardia-Lombardi, east of Naples, on lands controlled by the emperor. Some of the personalities cited are familiar. Hence, in 1252 in Piacenza, Pierre of Beauville met Messer Vivent who had at his side Athon-Arnaud of Châteauverdun, the nephew of Pierre-Roger of Mirepoix. The same year, Guillaume Fournier went to see Raymond Mercier in Pavia, where he was lodging Peytavi Laurent, one of the four perfects who had escaped from Montségur. Raymond Baussan specified that it was in a house on the via Levata in Piacenza, that the perfects, including Guillaume Déjean and Raymond Bonnet, were living and that he had met Guiraud Hunaud of Lanta, the son of the perfect Guillaume-Bernard, who had died at the stake in Toulouse in 1237. Guillaume Raffard, a native of Roquefort in the Montagne Noire, had been ordained a perfect at

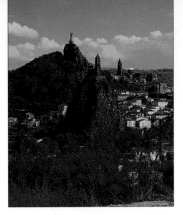

Le Puy en Velay

ITALIAN AFFAIRS

Guy Foulcoy (or Foulques) was the son of a chancellor of Raymond VI. When Alphonse of Poitiers took the title of Count of Toulouse in 1249, this doctor of law, who like another Foulque was a talented troubadour, became one of his closest advisors. Foulcoy entered orders in 1256. After having been Bishop of Le Puy in 1257, then Archbishop of Narbonne in 1259, in 1265 he succeeded Urban IV on the throne of Saint Peter. Very devoted to the Capetians, appreciated by Louis IX, the new Pope Clement IV confirmed the donation of the Kingdom of Sicily to Charles of Anjou right after his accession. The King of France's brother had to deal with the opposition of Emperor Frederick II's heirs, Manfred and Conradin. Having become the champion of the Guelphs, Charles of Anjou won the Battle of Benevento in 1266, beating Manfred who died in combat, and in 1268, beating Conrad at the Battle of Tagliacozzo. On November 29 of the same year, Clement IV died. Fourteen years later, Charles of Anjou lost Sicily to Pedro III of Aragon, after the episode of the Sicilian vespers. Meanwhile, constantly looking for new pipe dreams, he had participated in the eighth crusade in 1270, had been King of Albania in 1272 and King of Jerusalem in 1277.

Detail of Scaligers' tomb

LIKE THE APOSTLES

In 1260, Gherardo Segarelli founded the Apostolic Movement. The man wrapped his evangelical words in a cloak of prophecies very much inspired by Joachim of Flora. He died at the stake on July 18, 1300. His precepts were repeated and turned into a doctrine by Dolcino of Novara, his successor at the head of the movement, who defined the community as "a spiritual congregation living in the manner of the apostles [...] with no outside link of obedience, with only an inner link."

Sirmione at the beginning of the 1270's. At the time, the ramparts of the fortress on the shores of the Lake of Garda contained the Cathar Bishop of Desenzano, the second successor to head the church of Giovanni da Lugio, the author of *The Book of Two Principles*. At his side were members of the Cathar Church of Mantua; Guillaume Peter of Verona, Bishop of the Cathar Church of France, which had been decimated at the stake of Mont Aimé in 1239; Bernard Olieu, a native of Verdun en Lauragais, a perfect who had become a bishop. There were also numerous Bons Hommes, including Guiraud Hunaud of Lanta and Bernard of Scopont, one of those besieged in Montségur, interrogated by Ferrer on March 2, 1246, and who had been ordained. It was an entire network of people who knew each other, who met and moved around. But the victory of the Guelph party in 1266 at Benevento had a certain number of consequences. The Inquisition in Lombardy recovered its vigour. According to the *Annals of Milan*, in 1269 in Piacenza, twenty-eight wagons took Italian believers to the stake. And during the same period, the castle of Mangano, fief of the Count of Cortenuova and a usual residence for known Cathars, was captured by Milanese troops. The fate of Sirmione, where many Lombard, French and Occitan Cathars lived, was soon to be sealed. In December 1273, the Minor friar Timoteo, an inquisitor, managed to get a woman, Constance of Bergamo, into the castle of the Scaligers. She managed to integrate perfectly into the Cathar community, from where she provided information to her mentor. In 1276, Alberto and Martino della Scala, accompanied by Timoteo, now Bishop of Verona, besieged Sirmione, which surrendered on November 12. One hundred and sixty perfects were captured and handed over to the inquisitor of Treviso, Filippo Buonaccorsi. Most of them perished, along with others who had been denounced and caught, in all nearly two hundred people, on February 13, 1278, at the stake raised in the centre of the Roman amphitheatre of Verona. However, not all the Occitan perfects died in Verona since the passage of several of them, like Bernard Olieu in Genoa, was mentioned after the capture of Sirmione.

The Roman amphitheatre in Verona

The Scaligers' Castle in Sirmione

Statues, Saint Nazaire, Carcassonne

Weavers Cross, Mas Cabardès

Cabaret Castle

Dominic, Wake Up

Jean Galand took up his position at the Inquisition tribunal of Carcassonne in 1278, succeeding Etienne of Gâtine. He carried out about fifty interrogations. On January 26, 1282, in Toulouse, he took down the statement of the perfect Guillaume Raffard, who had returned from Sirmione in 1273 and was captured after wandering for five years. In 1284, on March 14 in Carcassonne, he questioned Guillaume Gomesenc for the first time. In the course of the year, he saw this inhabitant of La Tourette in the Cabardès several times, subjecting him to his questions and perhaps, putting him to the question. Because with each interrogation, Gomesenc became more talkative. Galand's method was simple – it was enough to refresh the witness's memory about the *consolaments* he attended, to obtain the names of the perfects who had carried them out and those who had attended, in order to widen the breadth of his investigation. It was enough to summons those implicated and apply the same methods and the number of believers thus discovered would grow exponentially. There were not many perfects remaining. From the testimony he had obtained, it indeed appeared that only two perfects were particularly active, especially in Cabardès and in Carcassès: Guillaume Pagès, back from Lombardy in 1262, and Bernard Coste. For the believers, a majority of whom were nobles, notables or even clerics and royal officers, things were very different. Hence, Gomesenc reported that in the spring of 1281, the parish priest of Roquefère had been consoled, and that in 1282, the lord of Cuxac had also been consoled in the presence of Jean of Pennaveyre, the royal lord of Cabaret. Raymond Marty, named by Gomesenc, was convoked in turn on August 31, 1284. He said that he had attended, in Mas Cabardès in 1283, the *consolament* of Guillaume-Arnaud Morlane, prior of the village and a canon of Carcassonne Cathedral, by the perfect Isarn of Canois. On the 20 and 28 of November, another witness, Arnaud Mazelier, after several interrogations declared that he had attended thirty-three *consolaments* given by Guillaume Pagès and Bernard Coste between 1277 and 1283. Among the consoled appeared the names of Blanche of Villegly, the sister of Olivier of Termes and wife of Guillaume of Minerve, and Pierre of Mirepoix, the royal lord of Surdespine, one of the castles of Lastours. All of these castles had been affected by heresy because Galand discovered that Pierre of Breuil, the lord of Cabaret, had been consoled in 1273, like Gilles of Bures, the lord of Quertinheux in 1284, after his wife Edeline had been consoled in 1283.

In Carcassonne, the means and methods used by Galand continued to pose problems for some notables who were often implicated during interrogations. In the autumn of 1284, some of them even became afraid and planned an operation in which they intended to get hold of the Inquisition's registers. They managed to convince Bernard Lagarrigue, a former perfect who had converted and entered into Galand's service, to steal the documents. The man was accompanied by Bernard Agasse, a public letter-writer, since Garrigue did not know how to read. Although they failed completely because Galand, a careful man, had left taking the cupboard keys with him, they were not caught. But Agasse betrayed the plot when he was interrogated on July 15, 1285. Lagarrigue was immediately arrested and, after several interrogations, finally confessed and informed on the participants and those behind the operation. Among the participants was Arnaud Mathe, a cleric from Carcassonne who, interrogated on October 4, denounced the "heresification" of Castel Fabre, a former tax collector for the seneschalsy. Among the plotters, one of the city's consuls, Guillaume Serre, was arrested and questioned in September, 1285. At the beginning of 1285, after the operation's failure, inhabitants of Carcassonne had denounced Jean Galand's behaviour to the pope, the King of France, and to the Dominican prior of Paris. At the end of July, the inquisitor prudently decided to leave Carcassonne for a while and found refuge in Albi with Bernard of Castanet, the city's lord and bishop since 1282, and who, hardly had

Chevet of Sainte Foy Abbey Church in Conques

Sentences Incurred

Fines

These monetary penalties were inflicted either as the principal or compensatory basis. Any heirs might have to finish paying the fines.

Confiscation of goods

The goods of heretics handed over to the secular arm or condemned to life imprisonment were confiscated.

Destruction of houses

Houses in which perfects were hidden, or where they preached or consoled, were destroyed. Their location had to remain uninhabited and uncultivated but could become a rubbish tip.

Incapacities

These deprived perfects, believers, receivers and defenders of heretics of civil and ecclesiastical rights, even if they had reconciled with the Church.

Imprisonment

The prisoner was placed in a regimen of "bread of pain and water of tribulation". In the "*murus strictus*", his members were shackled.

Pilgrimages

There were two types of pilgrimages: major and minor ones. The first type include: Rome, Santiago de Compostela, Canterbury, Cologne. The second: Le Puy, Rocamadour, Conques, Saint Denis, Saint Guilhem le Désert.

Handed to the secular arm

This sentence, reserved for heretics who refused to abjure and to relapsed heretics, was equivalent to condemnation to the stake.

Signs of Infamy

They consisted of pieces of cloth that those concerned had to sew onto their clothes, on the back or the chest. Repentant heretics wore crosses of yellow felt.

SAINT CECILE OF ALBI

Bernard of Castanet, the new Bishop of Albi, arrived on the banks of the Tarn River on August 15, 1282. The next day, he announced to his canons that he had decided to have a new cathedral built. Work was undertaken immediately but was to last nearly two centuries, since the new cathedral was consecrated on April 23, 1480. The outside of the building looks just like a fortress. Its keep rises to a height of seventy-eight metres. Its walls are reinforced over their entire height by semi-cylindrical buttresses that rise from the embankment encircling the building's base. Between these buttresses, the openings are high and narrow. A staircase of fifty-one steps, defended by a fortified gate and a tower, leads to the only door of the cathedral, which opens under a Gothic baldaquin added during the first quarter of the 16th century. This baldaquin is the sole element of exterior decoration. No statue, no bas-relief exists to attenuate the strictness of the simple and pure lines of this massive, pink brick construction. But in 1282, the Cathar heresy was still present in Albi, where the annexation to the royal domain was still not fully accepted by the population. The new bishop probably did not feel completely safe, just like his predecessor who, several years earlier, had started construction of the Palais de la Berbie, the bishops' residence that resembles a keep. The layout of the cathedral's interior is extremely simple: no side aisles, no transept, no ambulatory around the choir. Albi Cathedral has no relation to the great cathedrals of northern France, nor with the great pilgrimage churches. Its dimensions are impres-sive: thirty metres high and thirty metres wide, with a length of one hundred metres. Although the out-side of the church is very simple, its interior decoration is particularly rich. It was under the bishopric of Louis I of Amboise at the end of the 15th century that the choir and the rood screen were built in Flamboyant Gothic style. In the centre of this gallery, a crucified Jesus Christ is sur-rounded by the Virgin and Saint John, both of them standing on columns. Lower down, Adam stands on the left column and Eve on the right –they who committed the original sin. The western part of the choir is encircled by a double row of stalls, one hundred and twenty of them, topped with sixty statues of angels. On the outside of the eastern section stand statues of the twelve apostles on the inside and statues of the prophets on the outside. Statues of numerous saints decorate the outer sides of the first choir and the rood screen. All of these statues were made in Burgundy. The Last Judgement of Albi takes up the west-ern wall of the nave, at the foot of the steeple. It is a French work from the end of the 15th century. Although the sections showing Christ, the Virgin and Saint John were destroyed during the 18th cen-tury by a bishop, the presentations of Paradise and Hell have been extremely well preserved. The style of these paintings, finished towards 1500, is similar to that of Hieronymus Bosch (1450-1516), whose work was contemporary. The visitor should look at the way the seven deadly sins are represented, each of them sanctioned by some torture. Hence, the lustful has his sexual parts devoured by serpents and toads.

One should also note the absence of Purgatory, which artists had to introduce into their work under pres-sure from the ecclesiastical hierarchy during the Counter Reformation to counter the theses of Luther, who denied the existence of Purgatory. When Louis I of Amboise had been forced to give up his position, his nephew Louis II of Amboise suc-ceeded him in 1502. In 1509, the new bishop brought in Italian painters directed by the master Giovanni Francesco Donella. They undertook the decoration of the vault of the nave. The task was difficult since the vault is divided into twelve bays separated by transverse ribs, and each portion of the vault being fur-ther divided into four sections by two ribs that cross at the keystones. The work was completed in 1512. Renaissance art was then at its high point. Michelangelo had just finished the frescoes in the Sistine Chapel and Raphael had completed those in the Signature Chamber at the Vatican. The parcelling of the ceiling is certainly the reason for the some-what heterogeneous iconography, but some of the scenes are particu-larly well executed, such as the incredulity of Saint Thomas, the para-ble of the Wise and Foolish Virgins, and the Coronation of the Virgin. A constellation of pictures of saints decorates the nearly celestial vault of the cathedral. Some of them can-not be identified. Among the others, there is Saint Anthony curing ergo-tism; Saint Roch with his wound cared for by an angel but without his dog; Saint Catherine of Sienna; Saint Clare of Assisi; Saint Sebastian, the healer of plague; Saint Louis, and, of course, shown twice, Saint Cecile, the patron saint of the cathedral.

Jacques de Molay

he been named to his post, decided to start construction of a new cathedral dedicated to Saint Cecile. Galand returned to Carcassonne in November to conduct the investigations for a trial of the lords of Lastours, before returning to Albi to help Bernard of Castanet who had arrested eleven people suspected of heresy. From January 1286 to April 1287, they were heard in the course of eleven hearings in which the names of four hundred and two believers were cited. Jean Galand soon left the Carcassonne tribunal. Guillaume of Saint Seine, named his assistant in 1284, carried on the inquisitorial mission alone until 1292. He carried out twenty-two interrogations. That of Rica Toupine, questioned in September and October 1290, was particularly productive; she declared having attended forty-two "heresifications". These interrogations implicated several hundred witnesses of *consolaments*. Among the heretics were nobles, like the Viscount Isarn of Lautrec; men of the Church, such as Sans Morlane, the major archdeacon of the Carcassonne bishopric, Arnaud's brother, or the abbot of Montolieu; notaries, consuls, law professors Guillaume Garric and Guillaume Brunet, doctors, tradesmen, and generally people who were rather well-to-do.

At the end of 1290, while Philippe le Bel's investigators were in Carcassonne to carry out administrative controls, they received complaints from the city's inhabitants about the Inquisition's excesses. The king took note and asked his seneschal to put an end to the abuses. He did not want this kind of *State within a State*, which the Office had become, to blame his subjects. Guillaume of Saint Seine was not impressed since in September 1292, before leaving his position, he ordered the priests of the lower town of Carcassonne to excommunicate anyone who impeded the inquisitors' work. Until 1295, while waiting for Nicolas of Abbeville to take on his succession, Bernard of Clermont from the tribunal of Toulouse worked as his replacement. Hardly had Nicolas of Abbeville taken up his post, he convoked seven people including Guillaume Garric and Guillaume Brunet. Some of those among the accused had taken refuge at the Franciscan convent of Carcassonne where Foulque of Saint Georges, the Preachers' prior in Albi, appointed by the inquisitor, went to get them accompanied by an armed troop. The convent's lector, Bernard Délicieux, not only refused to let them enter but alerted the population, who chased away Foulque and his henchmen by throwing stones at them. Philippe le Bel continued to take careful note of the situation. In early January 1296, he forbade his seneschal and other royal officers to arrest anybody on the sole request of the inquisitor. Nicolas was stubborn and on June 28, when he was not able to get hold of the seven suspects, he excommunicated them. Since the pursuit of living heretics was becoming more difficult, he decided to attack dead ones. In 1297, he began a posthumous trial of Castel Fabre, who had died twenty years earlier after having received the *consolament*, according to Arnaud Mathe's testimony. The former notable was buried in the cemetery at the Franciscan convent. The Friars Minor, who still counted Bernard Délicieux in their ranks, refused to give up his corpse, arguing that the man who had been their benefactor had been a good Christian. And his son, Aymeric Castel, appealed to Pope Boniface VIII. But

IT'S A STATUE

Bernard Saisset was to say of him, "It's not a man, nor an animal, it's a statue." He had the beauty of a statue. His acts proved that Philippe le Bel also had the cold and hardness of marble. To finance his campaign against Flanders, he carried out two devaluations, in 1296 and 1297, and taxed the clergy. Pope Boniface VIII condemned him in February 1296 in the bull *Clericis laicos*. The pope and the king of France confronted each other again in 1301 over the Saisset affair. The pope called a council in Rome but Philippe le Bel prevented the French bishops from attending. Through a bull in November 1302, *Unam sanctam*, Boniface VIII reaffirmed the pope's supremacy over kings but died a month later after the Anagni attack, fomented against him on September 7, 1303, by the jurist Guillaume of Nogaret, Philippe le Bel's man, a native of Saint Felix in the Lauragais. In 1305, the king had his pope, Clement V, elected and settled in Avignon. Always short of money, in 1306 the king confiscated the property of Jews and Lombards before taking on the Templars. Clement V suppressed their Order in 1312 and in 1314 their Master, Jacques de Molay, died at the stake, calling on Philippe le Bel, the damned king, and Clement V, to appear before the court of God. Which they did a few months later.

Boniface VIII's Palace in Anagni

BERNARD SAISSET

On July 23, 1295, Pope Boniface VIII created the bishopric of Pamiers, cutting the southern part off the bishopric of Toulouse, and named Bernard Saisset at its head. When Jean of Picquigny, Vidame of Amiens, and Richard Neveu, Archdeacon of Auge from the Church of Lisieux, came to Languedoc in 1301, it was to investigate the rather irreverent, if not seditious, behaviour of this bishop. Once the investigation was over, Bernard Saisset was taken *manu militari* to Senlis where, on October 24, an assembly presided over by Philippe le Bel and composed of barons, knights, prelates and clerics studied his case. The bishop, who claimed lineage from the Saint Gilles, was reproached with loving his Occitan land too much and saying out loud that it had been despoiled by the French, of not sufficiently appreciating the French King whom he willingly called a bastard, and, especially, for fomenting a revolt against him. Despite the archbishop of Narbonne's support of his suffragan, Philippe le Bel wanted the former abbot of Saint Antonin removed from his post, even though the latter denied everything. But the pope kept his trust in Bernard Saisset, whose spirited character he shared.

on June 7, 1298, the pope promulgated a constitution that made it everyone's duty to join the struggle against heresy. Philippe le Bel asked his officers and his vassals to apply it. The Carcassonnais were then isolated and carefully negotiated peace with the inquisitor, using their consuls as intermediaries. It was signed on October 8 at the Dominican convent. Certainly, they were all absolved, or nearly all since twelve people including Aymeric Castel were excluded from the measure. But Nicolas of Abbeville had demanded that the consuls abjure heresy for themselves and in the name of all the inhabitants. Were they authorized to do so?

As soon as calm was restored in Carcassonne, Nicolas of Abbeville went to Albi to meet Foulque of Saint Georges and help Bernard of Castanet, who was preparing a great trial. The trial, which took place from December 2, 1299 until the month of March 1300, was a continuation of the trial in 1287 that had supplied information for numerous new inquiries. Thirty-five people, including twenty-five inhabitants of Albi, were heard during the sixty-one hearings, which ended with twenty-four sentences and as many condemnations to *murus strictus*, or life imprisonment. Nicolas of Abbeville was back in Carcassonne in the month of June and, within the framework of the Castel Fabre affair, convoked Bernard Délicieux on July 4. The Franciscan had been charged by his Order to defend the seneschalsy's former tax collector and the first time he arrived at the House of the Inquisition the inquisitor refused to hear him. When he returned, the door was closed to him and he quickly put a notice on it, in which he said that he defended Castel Fabre's memory and announced his intention of appealing to the pope. Nicolas of Abbeville, fearing a confrontation with the Friars Minor, suspended his investigation. It would be resumed later on by another inquisitor, Jean of Beaune. In 1318, the sentence called for exhumation. But Castel Fabre's corpse remained in the ground since his bones had been mixed with those of other deceased. The bones of his wife Rixende were exhumed and burnt after her *post mortem* condemnation on September 8, 1329.

Fresco of the Last Judgement, St Cecile's Cathedral, Albi

Perhaps it was an attempt to calm things down, but after his feat Bernard Délicieux was sent to the Franciscan convent in Narbonne as a lector and, at the end of September 1300, Foulque of Saint Georges was named inquisitor at the Toulouse tribunal. The beginning of 1301 saw the arrival of two royal investigators, one of whom was Jean of Picquigny, Vidame of Amiens. Their mission was to conduct inquiries for the trial of Bernard Saisset and to control the royal officers. Bernard Délicieux, accompanied by inhabitants of Albi, met them and denounced the intrigues of Bernard of Castanet and Foulque. It was agreed that Bernard Délicieux was to go and present his complaints directly to the king. This was done in the autumn of 1301. The Franciscan set off for Senlis accompanied by delegations from Albi and Carcassonne. He explained his grievances to Philippe le Bel who also received Nicolas of Abbeville and Foulque of Saint Georges a few days later. In December, the King of France asked the prior of the Preaching Friars in Paris to remove Foulque from his position as inquisitor. In fact, the inquisitor would remain in his post until April 1302. Noting the Dominicans' lack of cooperation, from Lorris on December 17 Philippe le Bel sent orders to his seneschals in Toulouse, Carcassonne and Agen telling them to prevent Foulque from conducting his procedures and to take the Inquisition's prisons under their control. As for Bernard of Castanet, the two investigators sequestered his possessions and had the Berbie Palace occupied. On February 11, 1302, the Bishop of Albi met them in Toulouse to complain about these measures. When he returned to his bishopric, he was met by a riot which he faced rather courageously. Bernard Délicieux had another opportunity to meet with the King of France when he was convoked to Paris by the sovereign at Easter 1302 to an assembly charged with dealing with the case of Bernard Saisset. At this assembly, Délicieux was the representative of the Friars Minor and was accompanied by several inhabitants of Albi whose relatives had suffered from the excesses of the Holy Office and had been imprisoned. Once again, he described his point of view about the inquisitors to Philippe le Bel. The king continued to work to re-establish calm and, in June, relaxed the anti-heretical edict of April 1229 by modifying the article that severely sanctioned those who had been excommunicated for more than a year. Even if they had been reconciled with the Church, they were not allowed to recover their properties that had been confiscated. It was also in June that Bernard of Castanet was condemned to pay a fine of two thousand *livres*. And in July, considering that he had sufficiently restrained the Preachers' actions, the king returned their prisons to them. Bernard Délicieux returned to Albi. He organized a widespread movement against the Preachers, which soon numbered five hundred members. It would be impossible not to see his handiwork behind the uprising of Advent Sunday 1302. The Dominicans were forcibly expelled from churches and pursued into their convents where they were surrounded.

In January 1303, at the court in Carcassonne, Nicolas of Abbeville was replaced by Geoffroy of Ablis, who enjoyed the confidence and support of Philippe le Bel. In the month of May, the new inquisitor received a visit from Jean of Picquigny. The two men had to analyze

Senlis Cathedral

VOLTAIRE'S JUDGEMENT

In the 18th century, the man of Ferney wrote in a pamphlet entitled *Cathars, On the Crusade against the Albigensians*, "You often hear that it is the summit of brutal and absurd barbarity to maintain, through informers and torturers, the religion of a God who died at the hands of executioners."

St Cecile's Cathedral, Albi

the situation of the residents of the Inquisition's prison. On his return to Carcassonne, Bernard Délicieux gave the investigator his opinion when he accompanied him to Cordes, where new detentions had stirred things up. Back in Carcassonne, Jean of Picquigny requested that the inhabitants' Act of Absolution dated October 8, 1294 be handed over to him. The reticent consuls finally accepted to provide him with the document. The investigator and the Franciscan discovered that the consuls of the time had abjured heresy in their names and in the name of their fellow citizens. Which meant, on the one hand, that they had been heretics and, on the other hand, it implied that each of them, if he were to be considered as relapsed, risked death at the stake. On August 3, Délicieux revealed this clause in the cloister of the Franciscan convent to an indignant Carcassonne crowd. Two of the act's signatories rushed to Toulouse to warn Geoffroy of Ablis. On August 10, the latter gathered together the inhabitants of Carcassonne and tried to calm them down. But the Carcassonnais did not agree and attacked the properties of those they considered had misled them. One of them, Élie Patrice, even created a militia which received reinforcements from Albi. These men were preparing to attack the inquisitorial prison but Jean of Picquigny took back the initiative by transferring the prisoners, the "immured", from the inquisitorial *muros* to the royal prison. Bernard Délicieux, who could then question them about their prison conditions, was soon able to strengthen his movement by creating a confederation joining the cities of Albi, Cordes and Carcassonne. And in his inflammatory sermons he consistently praised the attitude of Jean of Picquigny, who was convoked by Geoffroy of Ablis on September 22. When the investigator did not respect the summons, the inquisitor immediately excommunicated him as an abettor of heresy. At the end of the year, he met the King of France at Narbonnais Castle. The king was getting ready to ride through Languedoc from Toulouse to Nîmes. The investigator's report was rather unfavourable to the Inquisition. Philippe le Bel simply recommended moderation, to the great displeasure of his Occitan subjects. In his edict dated January 13, 1304, he forbade arbitrary arrests and requested that prisoners be treated properly.

To welcome the King of France, who was then at the end of his journey through Languedoc, James of Majorca had left his palace in Perpignan in February to go to Montpellier. He was accompanied by his third son, the Infant Ferrand. Bernard Délicieux, a native of Montpellier, was therefore his subject. In the company of notables from Albi and Carcassonne, Bernard went to see James. Was it at this time that rallying part of Languedoc to the Infant in return for his promise to free the land from the Inquisition's hold was considered? In any case, while a Carcassonnais embassy went to Rome to plead the city's cause before the Supreme Pontiff, the consuls of Carcassonne invited Albi and Limoux to participate in the insurrection. Although Albi refused, Limoux accepted. At the beginning of April, the Franciscan, accompanied by a young friar called Raymond Étienne, went to Perpignan carrying a document describing the Carcassonne plans. But the court had moved to Saint Jean Pla de Corts, on the banks of the Tech River, at the entrance to the

CORDES

I t was in 1222 that Raymond VII of Toulouse founded the bastide of Cordes on the summit of the hill (*puech*) of Mordagne, with the Cérou flowing at its foot. Many artisans settled there, including weavers and shoemakers. Like in Cordoba, these artisans who worked with leather could be at the origin of the town's name. A legend with no basis in fact tells that, at the end of the 13th century, the population, furious with the inquisitors' behaviour, threw three of them into a well. It was located near the market. Today the place is marked with a wrought iron cross and has a marble plaque commemorating the event. On June 29, 1321, through mediation by the inquisitors Bernard Gui and Jean of Beaune, Cordes received absolution from the Catholic Church. The town, today called Cordes-sur-Ciel, has retained its medieval appearance with its gates called La Jeanne, Les Ormes and Le Planal, a barbican, a wall walk, and Saint Michael's Church, dating from the 13th century. Rue Droite is lined with Gothic houses from the 13th and 14th centuries, such as Grand Fauconnier, Grand Écuyer or Grand Veneur. On the façade of the latter, on the third floor, a high-relief sculpted frieze presents hunting scenes. Here, a hunter aims his spear at a boar pursued by a dog; there, a hunter blows his horn while another shoots an arrow at a hare driven by a dog.

Detail of Grand Veneur House

Cordes

"TELL FRIAR DOLCINO…"

In 1300, Dolcino of Novara succeeded Gherardo Segarelli as head of the Apostolic Movement. In three letters, he developed a doctrine inspired by his master's spiritual inheritance. He stigmatized a Church and a pope who betrayed the faithful and announced a time of universal peace and the coming of a pope worthy of assuming the inheritance of Saint Peter. He preached in Bologna, Padua, Riva de Garda, Piacenza, Vicenza and Trento. At the end of 1304, Dolcino was in Novara, his native city in Lombardy. He and his followers were pursued and took refuge further north, at Serravalle, in the Sesia valley. In 1305, Clement V called for a crusade against them. Hounded, the Dolcinians followed the course of the Sesia to its confluence with the Sorba. In June 1305, they set up camp at the summit of Parete Calva, at 1,600 m. The next winter was harsh. They were cold and hungry. In order to survive they stole and killed. The situation became intolerable and Dolcino and his people had to flee. On March 9, 1306, leaving the weakest among them behind for certain death, they moved southwards, crossing the snow-covered Monte Barone range in terrible conditions, and reached Monte Rubello, at 1,400 m. The Bishop of Vercelli, Raniero Avogrado, Dante's *Navarrese*, besieged this Dolcinian Montségur. The winter was hellish for the defenders. They survived eating the flesh of their dead. The attack was launched on March 23, 1307. Many heretics were killed; 40 were captured and taken to Biella. There was a quick trial. On June 1, Dolcino and his companion, Marguerite, were cut into pieces. Their remains were burnt at the stake. In Umberto Eco's *The Name of the Rose*, two Dolcinians are condemned to the stake by Bernard Gui. The latter's *Inquisitor's Manual* provides precious information about those he described as "pseudo-apostles".

Vallespir. Bernard Délicieux followed it there. Before entering the castle of the King of Majorca, conscious of the importance of his action and the threat posed to its writers by the document's very existence, he destroyed it. He described the project of Carcassonne's consuls to the Infant orally. James of Majorca suspected a stab in the back and questioned Délicieux and then his son, Ferrand, who disclosed everything. A year later, the King of Majorca informed the King of France about it. In the month of August 1305, a delegation of consuls from Carcassonne, Albi, Castres and Cordes went to Philippe le Bel to ask for clemency. In vain. On orders from the pope, Bernard was confined to house arrest in Paris. On August 24, obeying the king, the seneschal of Carcassonne, Jean of Aunay, carried out numerous arrests. On September 28, 1305, fifteen Carcassonnais were hanged, including Élie Patrice. But Aymeric Castel managed to escape. On November 29, 1305, forty inhabitants of Limoux were killed in their turn. The consulate of Carcassonne was abolished and the city had to pay a fine of sixty thousand *livres*. Albi was spared. The *muros* prisoners returned to the prison of the Inquisition. As for Bernard Délicieux, he was handed over to the successor of Benedict XI, the new Pope Clement V, who was then in Lyon, before continuing with him to Mâcon, Nevers, Bourges, Limoges, Périgueux, Bordeaux and Poitiers. In 1308, he went with the pope to Avignon. In the course of those three years, he was in a state of partial liberty.

Before the new pope, the former Archbishop of Bordeaux Bernard of Got, had assumed his new position, complaints had been submitted to the Curia. Some of them came from representatives of the cities of Albi, Carcassonne and Cordes and were directed at the inquisitors and Bernard of Castanet himself, implicated by the abbot of Gaillac and the chapters of Saint Cecile Cathedral and Saint Salvi Church, both in Albi. In January 1306, ten consuls, four jurists and forty-five inhabitants of Albi named eight people to begin legal proceedings before the pope. They were directed against Bernard of Castanet, who hired his own lawyer. On March 13, Pope Clement V asked the Bishop of Béziers, Berenger Frézoul, and the Bishop of Toulouse, Pierre de la Chapelle-Taillefer, who had recently been given cardinals' red hats, to make a report on the Inquisition's prisons. Two Preachers, Bernard Blanc and François Aymeric, surrounded by representatives of Albi, Cordes and Carcassonne, were to investigate the complaints lodged with the Curia. While waiting for their conclusions, the Bishop of Albi and the inquisitors were supposed to stop bringing actions against any suspected heretics. The Bishop of Albi was even removed from his post, which was temporarily filled by Arnaud Nouvel, the abbot of Fontfroide. During the month of April, after visiting the Inquisition's prison in Carcassonne, the committee denounced the conditions under which the forty prisoners were held, some for over twenty years. At the beginning of May, Pierre de la Chapelle-Taillefer went to the prison of Albi, where he found comparable conditions. It was in Bordeaux, on June 25, 1307, that the pope received the complaints from the inhabitants of Cordes, Albi and Carcassonne, heard the defenders of the inquisitors and Bernard of Castanet, and the description of the report on the prison enquiry. Although the Supreme Pontiff nonsuited the plaintiffs, he nevertheless ordered an enquiry into Bernard of Castanet who was called into question for his morals and behaviour by two canons from Albi. One hundred and fourteen people were heard in the spring of 1308 by the abbots of Fontfroide and Saint Papoul. On July 27, Clement V cleared Bernard of Castanet of all suspicion but, on July 30, named him Bishop in Le Puy, judging that his return to Albi might be problematic. The fate of the Inquisition's prisoners had still not been resolved. Raymond Desbordes, Castanet's successor on the bishop's throne in Albi, was aware that ten individuals from his diocese were still mouldering inside the walls of Carcassonne's prison, waiting until the legal proceedings concerning them reach a conclusion. In February 1310, even though the pope transferred them to Albi, the bishop did nothing. Not until 1319 did Bernard Gui take things in hand. But by then it was too late, three of the prisoners having died in the meantime. They were condemned posthumously and their property confiscated. In Carcassonne, Guillaume Garric was still imprisoned. Clement V interceded with Philippe le Bel to have the law professor freed and his castle returned to him. His confiscated mansion had been sold at auction, but his wife was able to buy it back. In 1321, Guillaume Garric was once again pursued by the Inquisition. Condemned to exile in the Holy Land, this time he would not see his mansion again, as it had been bought at a very low price by the chapter of Saint Nazaire Cathedral.

MULTORUM QUERELLA

On April 30, 1312, the final day of the Council of Vienne in the Dauphiné, Pope Clement V promulgated the constitution *Multorum querella*. The investigative reports that had reached him and the complaints he had received since he donned the papal crown provided information about the Inquisition's excesses and abuses. Through this constitution, he placed bishops and the Office's inquisitors on the same level. Both were allowed to search for, summon and imprison suspected heretics. But subjecting them to torture and the final sentence was to be a decision taken in common. Despite this text, which they contested strongly, the Office's inquisitors kept the upper hand over inquisitorial procedures, with the notable exception of the bishopric of Pamiers, run by Jacques Fournier.

BERNARD DÉLICIEUX'S LAST BATTLE

Starting in 1308, Bernard Délicieux was allowed to move about freely once again. He stayed in Toulouse and then in Carcassonne. In 1315, he became a simple friar in the Franciscan convent in Béziers. The Order of Friars Minor was then torn between the Community and the Spirituals. The former wanted to exclude the latter, whose defence was taken by Bernard. From Béziers, he led a delegation of sixty-four Spirituals to Pope John XXII in Avignon. The pope received them on May 23, 1318, but the meeting went badly. Several of Bernard's companions were arrested and four of them were burnt as heretics in Marseille on May 7, 1319. Bernard Délicieux, who had some enemies at the Curia, was placed in detention. The pope asked Guillaume Méchin, Bishop of Troyes, and Pierre Letessier, Abbot of Saint Sernin, to conduct the investigation for his trial. He was accused with having struggled against the Inquisition for years, conspiring against the King of France, and having poisoned Pope Benedict XI, who died in 1304 from indigestion. According to the accusation, Bernard had supplied harmful potions and powders to Arnaud of Villeneuve, one of his friends and the pope's doctor. The investigation was completed in 1319. The trial took place in Toulouse, Castelnaudary and Carcassonne from September to December 1319, presided over by the Bishop of Pamiers, Jacques Fournier, and the Bishop of Saint Papoul, Raymond of Mostuéjouls. Bernard Gui and Bernard of Castanet, then Cardinal-Bishop of Porto, supported the prosecution. The judges had recourse to the question. The sentence was handed down on December 8. Although Bernard was cleared of the poisoning accusation, he was condemned for the others, as well as for practicing sorcery. He was sentenced to life imprisonment, shackled and fed with water and dry bread. He was stripped of his ecclesiastical dignity. Two civil magistrates appealed the verdict, which they considered too lenient. On February 25, 1320, the pope wrote to the presidents of the court that Bernard Délicieux should be stripped of his religious habit. This was too much for this man of faith. Taking away his Franciscan habit was to deprive him of his reason for living. He died a short time later at the *muros* in Carcassonne, which he had so badly wanted to knock down.

The Notary and the Theologian

In 1296 Pierre Authié was nearly fifty years old. As a notary in Ax les Thermes, he had drawn up documents for the Count of Foix. He was a wealthy man, possessing huge properties and a large library with several books, such as *An Anonymous Treatise on Catharism*, that would certainly not have pleased some narrow-minded thinkers or some inquisitors. He was perhaps the descendant of another Pierre Authié, who had also lived in Ax and who, in 1233, had received the perfect Bertrand Marty, then the future bishop of the Toulouse Cathar Church. The second Pierre Authié and his brother Guillaume decided to leave for Lombardy to be ordained perfects. They passed through Cuneo, where they met Pons-Arnaud of Châteauverdun, and tried to come into contact with the exiled Cathar Church, or what remained of it after the stake at Verona. The Church no longer had a bishop and the highest known Occitan Cathar dignitary was a deacon, Raymond Isarn. With two perfects, he was in Sicily, an island under Aragonese control since the Sicilian Vespers of 1282 and, hence, not very favourable to the papacy. The two brothers went to Visone, near Acqui in southern Piedmont, south of Montferrat. After Sirmione, this was the refuge of a group of Occitan Cathars, among whom were two perfects, Bernard Audouy, a native of the Lauragais, and his *socius*, Pierre-Raymond of Saint Papoul. Early in the year 1300, after having been ordained, the Authié brothers returned home, accompanied by Pierre-Raymond and two other perfects, Mathieu German and Prades Tavernier, who had also been ordained in Lombardy. On their road home they went through Toulouse, where Pierre Authié left money at the money changer's Raymond Ysalguier. Before Easter they were back in Ax, where Pierre and Guillaume's brother hid them in his cellar. During their stay in Ax, the two brothers were spotted by a Beguin from Pamiers, who wanted to denounce them to the Inquisition, but friends of the family made the informer disappear somewhere on Larnat mountain. Meanwhile, another perfect, Amiel of Perles, had joined them. Pierre and his five companions began to preach in the narrow valleys of the Sabarthès and on the Aillou plateau but in the autumn the group divided up after Pierre had ordained as perfects his own son Jacques, Pons Bayle, the son of a notary from Tarascon, and Pons of Na Rica, a native of Avignonet. Several of them, including Guillaume Authié and Prades Tavernier, went off to preach in the lands of Aillou and Sault, then in the High Corbières. The others, with Pierre Authié and his son Jacques, went to the Toulousain. In 1301, all of these perfects first met in Ax, then in Limoux from where they sent Philippe of Alayrac to be ordained by Raymond Isarn in Sicily. Philippe returned accompanied by a female perfect, Aude Bourrel. This renewed Cathar Church affected circles of notables, like the notaries of the Count of Foix, but also people of more modest condition: artisans, shepherds and peasants. The nobility also remained open to heretical ideas. In March 1302, Count Roger-Bernard of Foix was allegedly consoled at the time of his death by Pierre Authié. On September 8, 1305, Jacques Authié and Prades Tavernier were captured in Limoux after being denounced and

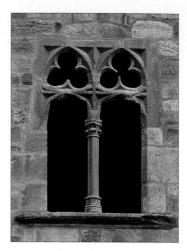

Window in Arques Castle

ARQUES

At the beginning of the 11th century, Arques was part of Lagrasse Abbey's worldly belongings. A century later, this *castrum* became a possession of the lords of Termes. In 1231, its lord was Pierre of Voisins, a former companion-at-arms of Simon de Montfort. Olivier of Termes submitted to the king of France definitively in 1246, and recovered part of the domains of his forefathers, including Arques, which he ceded in 1260 to its temporary occupant, Pierre of Voisins. In 1268, Pierre's son, Gilles I, had the village reorganized into a bastide and undertook construction of the castle and its keep, three storeys and twenty metres high. Work was completed in about 1316 by Pierre's grandson, Gilles II. Arques was the native village of Déodat Roché (1877-1978), one of the first historians of Catharism and founder of *Cahiers d'études cathares*. His house is the setting for an exhibition dedicated to *Catharism Today* and also contains a multi-media library.

The keep at Arques Castle

Vestiges of Montaillou Castle

Castle of Clement V, Villandraut

were detained at the *muros* in Carcassone, from which they were able to escape. Fear descended on the land once again and ten inhabitants of Arques, upon hearing of the arrest of the two perfects who had converted them, rushed off to Lyon to see Pope Clement V to abjure their heresy and obtain his forgiveness. In November, a raid was carried out in Verdun en Lauragais and many inhabitants were arrested. The repression spread to other villages in the valley of the Tarn River which had welcomed Pierre and Jacques Authié, such as Villemur, as well as Monclar de Quercy and Verlhac-Tescou, east of Montauban. Despite these events, Pierre Authié preached and consoled and even, at the end of the year 1306, ordained two new perfects, Pierre Sans and Raymond Fabre.

In January 1307, Bernard Gui entered the Inquisition's tribunal in Toulouse. On Lent Sunday 1308, he gave his first general sermon in Saint Stephen's Cathedral and pronounced several sentences: three condemnations to the stake and two exhumations. On May 25, 1309, during his second general sermon, ninety-one sentences were pronounced, of which fifty were condemnations to strict *muros* and six exhumations. A few months earlier, Philippe of Alayrac had been arrested and imprisoned in Carcassonne, but had managed to escape. On August 10, Bernard Gui put out a wanted notice for Pierre Authié. He was arrested near Beaupuy, a village in Lomagne not far from Belleperche Abbey, and locked up in the *muros* of Toulouse where he found Amiel of Perles, whom Bernard Gui had handed over to the secular arm on October 23. The old perfect started a hunger strike and died. On September 8, Montaillou, in the lands of Aillou, was surrounded by armed troops and Geoffroy of Ablis settled in the house of Clergue the rector to interrogate the inhabitants who, while awaiting their turn, were held at the castle by Jacques of Polignac, the *muros* warden from Carcassonne. The villagers remained free but were invited to come to Carcassonne as soon as they were summoned. Most of them were sentenced to light penalties. Others, like Raymond Maury, were placed in the *muros*. Several, including Alazaïs Azéma, appeared again before Jacques Fournier twelve years later.

On January 2, 1310, men-at-arms came to arrest Pierre Sans in Tarabel, in the Lauragais, but he managed to escape. On April 9, Pierre Authié heard Bernard Gui delivering one hundred and thirteen sentences, including six exhumations and sixty-two prison terms. Seventeen persons were handed over to the secular arm, including Pierre Authié and the Hugoux couple who had lodged Pierre Sans in Tarabel. Pierre Authié was burnt at the stake raised on the square in front of Saint Stephen's Cathedral. His brother Guillaume, his son Jacques, and Arnaud Marty suffered the same fate in Carcassonne, as did Prades Tavernier. Traces of the other perfects faded away. In 1309, Philippe of Alayrac escaped from Carcassonne with Guillaume Bélibaste, whom he had ordained a perfect and who accompanied him in his flight through the Fenouillèdes, Roussillon and Catalonia. He returned to Donezan in 1310. Arrested at Roquefort de Sault, he also died at the stake. As for Bernard Gui, he took no rest; on April 23, 1312, he dictated no less than two hundred and twenty-five sentences.

BERNARD GUI

Bernard Gui was born in the Limousin about 1261-1262. He made his profession of the faith on September 16, 1280 at the Preaching Friars and on January 16, 1307 was named inquisitor at the tribunal of Toulouse. During the years 1317-1318, while retaining this position, he went on a mission to northern Italy and Flanders at the request of Pope John XXII. The pope sent him to be head of the bishopric of Tuy, in Galicia, on August 26, 1323. On July 20, 1324, he became Bishop of Lodève and on the 24, he was replaced at the Toulouse Inquisition tribunal by Pierre Brun. He died on December 30, 1331, at Lauroux Castle in Bas Languedoc. This scholar left many writings. His *Inquisitor's Manual*, written between 1321 and 1324, was a synthesis of his experience. The document consists of five parts, the first four being practical facts or advice for inquisitors' use. In the fifth part, the author describes the doctrines and rites of different heretics: Waldensians, Cathars, Apostolics, Beguins, as well as models of interrogations to which they could be subjected. His manual also mentions the case of Jews. On December 29, 1319, Bernard Gui had had a public burning, in Toulouse, of two wagonloads of Talmuds, seized from the city's Jews.

Jacques Fournier, Belpech church

JACQUES FOURNIER

J acques Fournier was born in1285 in Saverdun. This nephew of the abbot of Fontfroide Abbey, Arnaud Nouvel, entered Boulbonne Cistercian Abbey as a youth and there showed his intelligence and rigour. He continued his theological studies at Saint Bernard's College in Paris. In 1305, he was welcomed to Fontfroide by his uncle, whom he succeeded as abbot in 1311. In March 1317, Pope John XXII named him Bishop of Pamiers. He asked to be charged with the Inquisition in his diocese, by delegation of the inquisitor from Carcassonne. He conducted investigations into the trials of heretics in Sabarthès and, in 1319, directed the trial of Bernard Délicieux. In 1326, the pope transferred him to the bishopric of Mirepoix. In 1328, he named him Cardinal-Priest of Sainte Prisque, a post that his uncle had also held. In 1330, he entered the Curia, and received the papal tiara under the name Benedict XII in 1335. He began the construction of the Palace of the Popes in Avignon. He tried to annul the commendam system that had been put in place by his predecessor which undermined the monastic orders, including Citeaux. Before his death in 1342, he donated to Fontfroide Abbey his books, among which were his register of the Inquisition, now kept at the Vatican.

An Occitan Village

Prades is a village in the land of Aillou. Prades Tavernier was a weaver there. Around 1294, he used to go frequently to Châteauverdun, where the chatelaine Stephanie taught him the understanding of Good. He accompanied her and her son to Barcelona and then to Lombardy to meet Occitan perfects. In Lombardy, Prades Tavernier received Cathar ordination and met the Authié brothers. Returning home, he and Guillaume Authié regularly stayed in Prades and in Montaillou, the *Occitan Village* described by the historian Emmanuel Le Roy Ladurie, less than half a league away. In Montaillou, the two hundred inhabitants listened to their preaching all the more since the representatives of spiritual and temporal powers, the Clergue brothers, were won over by heresy. Bernard Clergue was the Count of Foix's bailiff; his brother Pierre was the parish's rector. Most of the families –the Benet, Belot, Maury, Marty– were believers and the others were tolerantly neutral towards their heretical neighbours. By 1209, this reputation began to attract the Inquisition's attention and an expedition was organized to Montaillou. The sole and precious source on the Cathar Church of Pierre Authié and its establishment in Montaillou is Jacques Fournier's Inquisition register. From July 15, 1318 to November 9, 1324, the Bishop of Pamiers interrogated no fewer than ninety-five people; inhabitants of Montaillou, but also of Quié, Tarascon, Arques, Caussou, Ax, etc. On June 19, 1320, Beatrice of Planissoles, the mistress of Pierre Clergue, appeared before Jacques Fournier. On August 19, it was the turn of Grazide Lizier, another of the rector's conquests, who could not be auditioned since she had died in prison. Condemned *post mortem*, her remains were exhumed and burnt on January 13, 1329. Arnaud Teysseire of Lordat, Pierre Authié's son-in-law, appeared on September 22, 1320. Raymond Authié, the brother of Pierre and Guillaume, was forced to testify about him on January 30, 1321. He told the bishop that, on his return from Lombardy, his brother Pierre had asked him to go and inform Arnaud Teysseire of his presence in Ax and to ask him to return the book he had lent him before leaving. Arnaud Teysseire, ill, died on May 29, 1323, in Allemans Prison in Pamiers where the accused were incarcerated. On May 22, 1321, it was Bernard Clergue's turn to be interrogated. He died at the strict *muros* to which he had been sentenced. The detailed inquiries by Jacques Fournier in Pamiers were not limited to those suspected of heresy. He also interrogated four Waldensians, including the deacon Raymond of Sainte Foy, who were condemned to the stake. Other accused were Baruch, a Jew suspected of returning to Judaism after having been baptized, and Guillaume Agasse, the commander of the leper-house in Pamiers, guilty of having participated in an *international* plot of lepers against Christians. Their aim was nothing less than poisoning them all to get hold of their property. Upon his arrival in Pamiers, Jacques Fournier had had Gaillarde Cuq arrested, a witch he did not judge but who supplied him before the hearings with precious information about Montaillou and its population.

I, BEATRICE

On June 19, 1320, two inhabitants of Dalou in the canton of Varilhes, Guillaume Roussel and Guillaume of Montaut, testified against Beatrice of Planissoles, the widow of Othon of Lagleize. They had allegedly heard heretical words ten years earlier. Among other things, she allegedly asked, "If God was in the sacrament of the altar, how would he let himself be eaten by priests?" She was convoked on July 23, 1320, by the Bishop of Pamiers before whom, without swearing an oath, she denied everything. She was summoned to appear on July 29 to testify under oath. She did not turn up. She was finally spotted and arrested by the bishop's men at Mas Saintes Puelles. Beatrice was auditioned in Pamiers on August 7, 8, 9, 12, 13, 22 and 25. Her testimony, like that of many other inhabitants of Montaillou, provides more colour to the picture of heresy in the land of Aillou, but against a background of love affairs. Indeed, Beatrice was eventually condemned for having been the concubine of two priests. In 1294, she had just married Berenger of Roquefort, Lord of Montaillou. Their steward, Raymond Roussel from Prades, invited her to accompany him to Lombardy to meet with the Good Christians. He educated her about the fine points of their religion. "The souls of men and women who have not been Good Christians, come out of their bodies and enter the bodies of other men and women up to as many as nine bodies." But he left after trying to seduce her. Another man of Montaillou took her by force one day. This was Raymond Clergue, the cousin of the village's rector, Pierre Clergue, who made advances

to Beatrice after the death of her husband, Berenger. She refused because "a woman who has carnally known a priest cannot see the face of God." But she finally gave in to the priest who, between two embraces, completed her education about Catharism. They loved each other on Christmas Eve before the mass, the time mattered little; they loved each other in Saint Peter's Church in Prades, the place mattered little. This union was not fruitful because the heretical priest had an apparently infallible contraceptive method: before intercourse, he placed herbs wrapped in linen cloth between his partner's breasts. After she married Othon of Lagleize in Crampagna on August 15, 1301, their relationship was interrupted. But Pierre Clergue joined her in Dalou to talk to her about Good but also about love in the cellar of the family house. A few years later, in 1308, the priest of Montaillou went for a last visit to a Beatrice weakened by illness. In the meantime, in 1305, Beatrice had confessed to a Minor Friar of the Limoux convent in Notre Dame Church in

Marceille. For her final interrogation on August 25, 1320, Beatrice was ill and bed-ridden. Jacques Fournier asked her why she had fled. She related that she had done so out of fear of his court, despite recommendations by Barthelemy Amilhac, a priest in Lladros and one of her former lovers. She was also questioned about some small objects that were in her possession at the time of her arrest. Among other things were two babies' umbilical cords in a bag and clothes soiled with what appeared to be menstrual blood. The first belonged to her grandsons, the second were a souvenir of her daughter Philippa's first period. She had kept everything on the advice of a converted Jewess. The clever Jacques Fournier saw these exhibits more as remedies of this woman who loved Bons Hommes too much than as evidence of witchcraft. Beatrice was sentenced to the *muros* on March 8, 1321, by the inquisitor Jean of Beaune in the Preaching Friars convent in Pamiers. But her sentence was commuted on July 4, 1322. Barthelemy Amilhac was to have the same fate.

Notre Dame Church in Merceille, between Limoux and Pieusse

Morella Castle

MORE STAKES

....

About 1315, while Guillaume Bélibaste was in Catalonia, Beguins settled in the ecclesiastical provinces of Narbonne and Provence. Those who called themselves *The Poor Friars of Penitence of the Third Order of Saint Francis* took their doctrine from books, and in particular from the *Commentary on the Apocalypse of St John* by the Franciscan Pierre-Jean Olieu (1248-1298), a native of Sérignan near Béziers. They believed that they should possess nothing and that Saint Francis was the man who had best understood and respected the teachings of the Gospels. Any distortion of these teachings constituted real heresy. They denounced the Franciscan Order's drift away from them, saying that only the Spirituals were worthy heirs of its founder. They condemned even the Italian Fraticelli. They assimilated the Roman Catholic Church, which they called carnal, with the Babylon of the Apocalypse, the great prostitute, and contested pontifical power. The bull *Sancta Romana* promulgated by John XXII on December 30, 1317, declared their doctrine heretical and announced their persecution. Beguins of both sexes were led to the stake in Narbonne, Béziers, Lunel, Pézenas, Toulouse and Carcassonne. As for the four Spirituals, companions of Bernard Délicieux, who were burnt in Marseille on May 7, 1319, the Beguins considered them to be martyrs.

The Gentleman of Tortosa

At Pentecost of the year 1306, a shepherd from Montaillou, Pierre Maury, went to the fair of Laroque d'Olmes to buy rams. While in town, he went to visit his young sister, Guillemette, married to the cooper Bernard Piquier who used to beat her. He also used the opportunity to meet the perfect Philippe of Alayrac, who made his living as a shepherd, and a man from Cubières, Bernard Bélibaste. Around a table at the inn, Pierre told them about Guillemette's distress. The perfect advised him to steal her away from her husband. They made an appointment in Rabastens for the day of Saint John the Baptist. On the said date, Pierre Maury, accompanied by Guillemette, waited on the banks of the Tarn. Although Philippe of Alayrac was not there, Bernard Bélibaste was waiting for him, in the company of his brother Guillaume. The two brothers promised to take care of Guillemette but they were on the run. During a fight, Guillaume had killed a shepherd from Villerouge-Termenès. Three years later, in 1309, Pierre Maury was summoned to Saint Paul de Fenouillet by the prosecutor of the Archbishop of Narbonne. He was suspected of having provided shelter for Philippe of Alayrac and Guillaume Bélibaste, ordained a perfect by Philippe in the meantime, who had just escaped from the *muros* of Carcassonne. Pierre Maury remained free because of a lack of evidence. Less lucky, his father, his mother and his three brothers were taken to prison after a raid in Montaillou on September 8. He decided to go into exile in Catalonia. He was accompanied by Bernard, Guillaume's brother, who was ill and died on the way, in Puigcerdà.

After his escape with Philippe of Alayrac, Bélibaste crossed the Pyrenees and in Torroella met a believer from Junac, in Sabarthès, Raymonde Piquier, who was with her daughter Guillemette. They were travelling together to allay suspicion but quickly Raymonde became Guillaume's companion. After the departure of Philippe, Bélibaste arrived in Berga, where he was joined by Pierre Maury. From there, he set off on a journey that took him to the edges of the lands of Valencia. He was able to meet small colonies of believers from Sabarthès who had emigrated to escape the Inquisition. He went to Lerida, and then to Granadelle and to Flix, on the Ebro River. It was in Flix at the beginning of 1314 that Bélibaste met another perfect, Raymond of Castelnau, probably a *filius* from the Cathar Church of the Agenais, who died in Granadella at the end of 1316, thereby making Bélibaste the last known living Occitan perfect. Until the end of 1317, Bélibaste stayed in Tortosa several times, before settling in Morella, from where he made frequent visits to San Mateo, five leagues away. The Maury family from Montaillou had taken refuge in the latter village: Pierre, Guillemette, her sons Jean and Arnaud. Bélibaste was still sharing the life of Raymonde, who became pregnant in 1319. To keep up appearances, he had her marry Pierre Maury. But he soon regretted it and Raymonde returned to his side. One day, a certain Arnaud Sicre arrived in San Mateo where he found work at a shoemaker's, Jacques Vital. His mother, Sibille Bayle, a Cathar believer, had refused to abjure at her arrest and had died at the stake. His brother, Pons Bayle, a Cathar

Tortosa

The ramparts of San Mateo

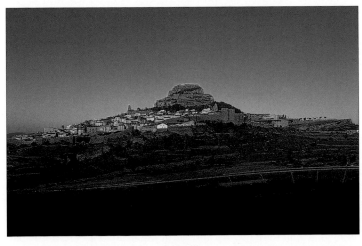

Morella

A VIPER IN HIS BREAST

It was Guillemette Maury who invited Arnaud Sicre to meet Guillaume Bélibaste. "And if we showed you Good?" she asked him, shortly after her arrival in San Mateo. At the Maury's houses both in San Mateo and Morella, Arnaud Sicre had the opportunity to be in close contact with Guillaume. When the latter came to San Mateo, the two men shared a bed and the perfect got up six times in the night to say his Hours. Before meals, Guillaume blessed the bread and cut it. Although he ate no meat, he ate fish. Bélibaste preached within the discretion and warmth of these narrow family circles, even though for one of Guillemette's cousins, also named Pierre Maury, "the gentleman of Morella doesn't know how to preach". Bélibaste confided to Sicre that, at Raymond of Castelnau's burial at Granadella, he had pretended to bless the body of the deceased. Before Arnaud joined his aunt, Guillaume had sent him to a Saracen soothsayer in Calanda, twelve leagues from San Mateo, to find out where she was staying. When Guillaume Bélibaste, Arnaud and Pierre Maury, and Arnaud Sicre left to go and get her, they stopped over in Ascó. Sicre's three companions, who had some doubts about him, tried to get him drunk in order to loosen his tongue, but in vain. After their capture, Sicre and Bélibaste shared the same jail cell. Bélibaste told his denouncer that he had noticed that he had not greeted him properly at their first meeting. After receiving the price of his betrayal, Arnaud Sicre was congratulated by Jacques Fournier on October 21, 1321. And on January 14, 1322, the inquisitors Bernard Gui and Jean of Beaune, after taking down his testimony, absolved him completely for having keeping company with heretics. It had been in a good cause…

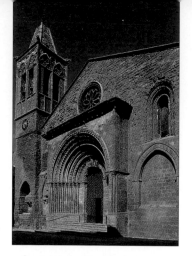

Santa Maria Church, Agramunt

VIGILANCE

J acques Duèse, a native of Cahors, became Pope in 1316 under the name John XXII. He was seventy-one years old and succeeded Clement V after a two year vacancy of pontifical power. While the last centres of Catharism were dying out in Languedoc, the papacy remained very careful about possible deviant eruptions and in 1329 John XXII condemned twenty-eight propositions by Johánnes Eckhart as being dangerous if not heretical. The man in question, known as Master Eckhart, had died two years before. He had been a Dominican, a master of theology at the *studium generale* in Cologne founded by his Order, and where two other Preaching Friars, his intellectual guides Albert the Great and Thomas Aquinas, had preceded him seventy-five years earlier. The success and contents of Master Eckhart's teachings had worried the Archbishop of Cologne, who ordered a committee, mainly composed of Franciscans, to analyze his doctrine before taking the matter before the papacy. A philosopher and theologian, marked with mysticism, Master Eckhart was an independent spirit. He had distanced himself from the Church as an institution, which could only worry the man who was in charge of maintaining its unity.

perfect, had been the companion of Pierre Authié. Arnaud was welcomed at the Maury's. It was in their house that he met Bélibaste two weeks later. Given the family's references, everyone believed that Sicre was a real believer, especially since he declared that he had known the Authié brothers well. He said he was going home to see his old aunt, Alazais, and his young sister who was living in the Pallars to convince them to come and live in San Mateo. He said his aunt was very rich and his sister very pretty and would be a good match for the young Arnaud Maury. He therefore left and returned shortly before the Christmas holiday of 1320. His aunt, who was very old and suffering from gout, could not travel and his sister had stayed with her. But the old lady who had given some money to her nephew to celebrate Christmas at San Mateo would really like to see a Bon Homme. In 1320, at the time of Lent, Sicre left again with Bélibaste, Arnaud and Pierre Maury. Their road took them to Beceite, Ascó, Flix, Sarroca, Lerida, Agramunt, Trago, Castelbon and Tirvia, where they were arrested. Sicre and Bélibaste were imprisoned in a tower; at Sicre's request, the two others were freed. Sicre was a double agent. When he had returned north of the Pyrenees in 1320, he had met Jacques Fournier, who had supplied him with money for the Christmas celebrations in San Mateo. He hoped to receive a bonus for his part in the capture of the last Occitan perfect and to recover his mother's belongings. At the end of August 1321, Guillaume was taken to the Carcassonne *muros* before being handed over to the Archbishop of Narbonne, his temporal lord. He died shortly afterwards at the stake in Villerouge-Termenès.

Once the last perfect had disappeared, no *consolament* was possible, and there was no hope for the few remaining believers. But inquisitorial action continued. As since there were no more known heretics and few of the others, the inquisitors used their energy to exhume corpses to burn them. Pope John XXII, who wished to prevent macabre excesses, set up *inquisitorial consultations*, necessary before any condemnation. Nevertheless, in 1325 the inquisitor Duprat delivered four posthumous condemnations, including one for Arnaud Morlane, the parish priest of Pennautier, and sent a woman believer from Tarascon to the stake. In November 1328, Henri Chamayou, inquisitor in Carcassonne, and Pierre Bru, inquisitor in Toulouse, pronounced fifteen sentences of exhumation. They concerned the lords of Lastours and members of their families as well as Blanche, the wife of the former consul of Carcassonne, Guillaume Serre. In September 1329, the Carcassonne inquisitorial commission examined forty cases; the corpse of Rixende, wife of Castel Fabre, was exhumed and burnt and four people were sentenced as relapsed heretics: Raymonde Arrufat, from Narbonne; Isarn Raymond, of Albi; Adam Baudet, of Conques; and the old Guillaume Serre, who had spent forty years in the *muros*. All died at a stake raised on the banks of the Aude. In 1330, the insatiable Chamayou and Bru wanted to investigate eighteen new posthumous trials. John XXII declared the cases inadmissible. Nonetheless, the infernal machine of the Inquisition, had it been allowed, would have dug up and burnt the dead of an entire people, who had already suffered greatly for over a century.

The castle at Villerouge-Termenès

HISTORIOGRAPHY OF CATHARISM

The slow taking into consideration, within the field of historical research, of the issues of Catharism in particular –like medieval heresies in general– is a complex process and is still not perfectly understood. First of all a victim of its status as a dissident minority eliminated from history, hence essentially known from the point of view of the victors, but also of the overly great wealth and diversity of medieval sources documenting it, meaning that too few historians could claim to study a really representative range. Today, paradoxically, Catharism is not a well-known historical phenomenon, if not totally unknown, especially in France. Denounced in its time as a doctrinal, neo-Manichaean heresy, through the medieval, controversial, anti-heretical texts, later on Catharism was traditionally studied on this same foundation by scholars who were themselves theologians, and that until the beginning of the 20th century. Following Bossuet, one can also cite Mgr von Döllinger, Mgr Douais, Mgr Vidal, but also the Lutheran Charles Schmidt who, in 1848, with his *History and Doctrine of the Sect of the Cathars* provided a basic work that was relatively serene and objective. In parallel, at the end of the 19th century, the lyrical enthusiasm of the Pastor Napoléon Peyrat (*History of the Albigensians in three volumes, 1871*) popularized the subject and drew lasting attention to Montségur, while at the same time esotericism was besieging the theme with dangerous speculations. Relayed and amplified during the first half of the 20th century in works by historians of comparative religions (Söderberg, Runciman), this "theologian's" vision of Catharism defined by its dualism culminated with the thesis of the German historian Arno Borst –*Die Katharer*– who, in 1953, defined the heresy, he believed definitively, as a doubtful, Oriental, non-Christian doctrine that was fated to natural extinction by its internal deficiency. However, the middle of the 20th century saw a profound upheaval of perspectives of research into Catharism, with the discovery or the taking into account of new kinds of documents, from then on seen as likely to complete, support or redefine – but in any case readjust in favour of the heretics – the theses of the medieval anti-heretical controversy. I have in mind the inquisitorial archives and texts of Cathar origin. Henceforth, the heretics come to life and speak for themselves. From the publication of the voluminous *Register of the Inquisition of Jacques Fournier* by Jean Duvernoy (three volumes in Latin in 1965, three

Ramparts of the Cité of Carcassonne

volumes translated into French in 1976-1978) and then other registers of the Inquisition, other sociological works appeared, at their head the brilliant *Montaillou, Occitan Village* by Emmanuel Le Roy Ladurie (1975). Following work by the Dominican scholar Antoine Dondaine – the discovery and publication of *The Book of Two Principles*, the *Anonymous Cathar Treatise* and the *Latin Cathar Ritual*, many publications followed. Two treatises and three Cathar rituals are known at present. In 1959, René Nelli placed at the disposal of the public the first edition of *Cathar Writings* – all the Cathar texts translated and commented. Next came a process of critical reconstruction of Catharism and its internal realities, beginning with the general survey, *Catharism* by Jean Duvernoy, in two volumes: *History of the Cathars* (1976) and *The Cathars' Religion* (1978), which took all the sources into account for the first time. Work was underway for about fifteen years by the international team at the Centre d'Études Cathares and the review *Heresis* (1983-1999). A series of annual colloquia in Carcassonne took place:

Montségur Hill

Mouvements dissidents et novateurs, under the direction of André Vauchez (1989); *La persecution du catharisme*, under the direction of Robert Moore (1993) or else, to follow up (and bring down) the paths of romantic or esoteric mythologizing of Catharism: *L'édifice imaginaire* (1994). This generation of works helps to replace the heresy into its purely Christian context and to its exercise as a Church intended to care for souls. At the same time, contributions of medieval archaeology refute the near-myth of "Cathar castles" and replace the sociology of Catharism into the framework of southern towns and castra. The work of the British medieval historian Robert Moore –*Persecution, Its Birth in Europe*– marked a new start for the issue of heresy, considered as one of the bitter fruits of a persecuting society. Militant and coercive, the reforming Church of Rome and Citeaux denounced heresy at the same time as it forged the ideologies of holy war and pontifical theocracy. A collective work that appeared in 1998 under the direction of Monique Zerner –*Inventer l'hérésie?*– questioned the very reality of heresy. Casting doubt on the existence of medieval Christian dissidence, whose corollary is to minimize the impact of religious persecution, is nonetheless a historical postulate that is difficult to maintain if one takes the trouble to scientifically compare all the medieval sources. This remains to be done in this perspective. The collective undertaking of the historiography of Catharism still has work ahead of it.

Verfeil

Anne Brenon

REFERENCE POINTS

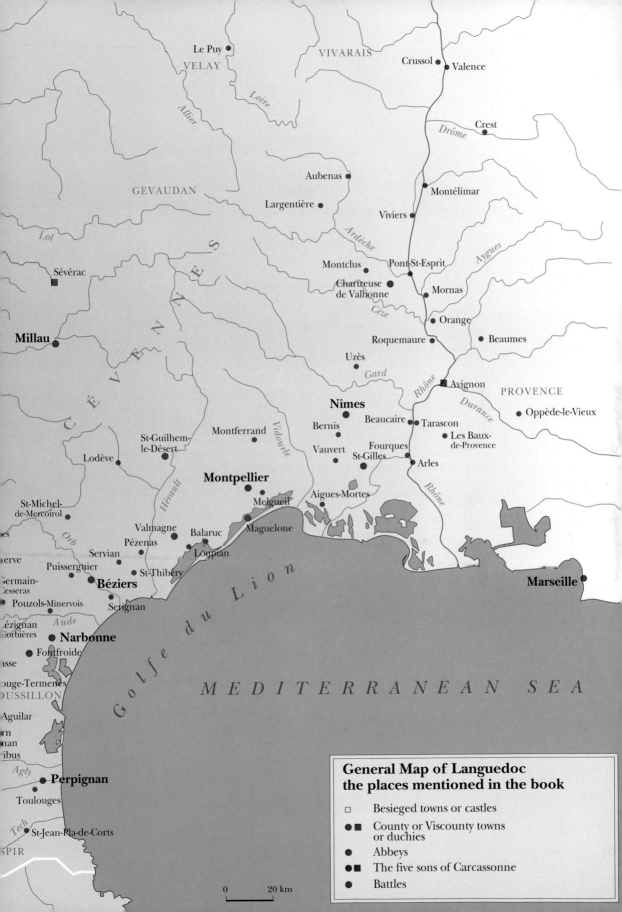

INDEX

BIBLIOGRAPHY

ALBARET (L.): *L'Inquisition - Rempart de la foi ?* Gallimard, 1998

BARTHÉLEMY (D.): *L'an mil et la paix de Dieu. La France chrétienne et féodale 980-1060*, Fayard, 1999

BENAZZI (N.) ET D'AMICO (M.): *Le livre noir de l'Inquisition*, Bayard, 2000

BENNASSAR (B.): *Brève histoire de l'Inquisition*, Fragile, 1999

BERLIOZ (J.): *Tuez-les tous, Dieu reconnaîtra les siens*, Loubatières, 1994

BONNASSIE (P.) ET LANDES (R.): « *Une nouvelle hérésie est née en ce monde* » in *Sociétés méridionales autour de l'An Mil*, CNRS, 1992

BONNASSIE (P.) ET PRADALIÉ (G.): *La capitulation de Raymond VII et la fondation de l'université de Toulouse, 1229-1279*, Université de Toulouse-Le Mirail, 1979

BOZÓKY (E.): *Le Livre Secret des Cathares, Interrogatio Johannis*, Beauchesne, Paris, 1980

BRENON (A.): *Le vrai visage du catharisme*, Loubatières, 1988/ *Les Archipels cathares. Dissidence chrétienne dans l'Europe médiévale*, Dire, 2000/ *Les cathares. Vie et mort d'une Église chrétienne*, J. Grancher, 1996/ *Les cathares, une Église chrétienne au bûcher*, Milan, 1998/ *Les cathares, Pauvres du Christ ou Apôtres de Satan ?* Gallimard, 1997/ *Les femmes cathares*, Perrin, 1992/ *Petit Précis de catharisme*, Loubatières, 1996

Cahiers de Fanjeaux: n° 1, *Saint Dominique en Languedoc*/n° 3, *Cathares en Languedoc*/n° 4, *Paix de Dieu et guerre sainte en Languedoc au XIIIᵉ siècle*/n° 14, *Historiographie du catharisme*/n° 20, *Effacement du catharisme*, Privat

COLLARD (F.): *Pouvoirs et culture politique dans la France médiévale*, Hachette, 1999

DÉJEAN (J.-L.): *Les comtes de Toulouse 1050-1250*, Fayard, 1988

DES VAUX-DE-CERNAY (P.): *Historia Albigensis*, J. Vrin, 1951

Dictionnaire encyclopédique du christianisme ancien, 2 t., Cerf, 1990

Dictionnaire encyclopédique du Moyen Âge, Cerf, 1997

DOM DE VIC (G.) ET DOM VAISSÈTE (J.): *Histoire générale de Languedoc*, 10 t., J.-B. Paya, 1840-1846

DUBY (G.): *Le dimanche de Bouvines*, Gallimard, 1973

DUVERNOY (J.): *Dissidents du Pays d'Oc*, Privat, 1994/ *Inquisition à Pamiers*, Privat, 1986/ *Le catharisme*, 2 t., Privat, 1976 et 1979/ *Le dossier de Montségur. Interrogatoires d'Inquisition, 1242-1247*, Le Pérégrinateur, 1998/ *Le registre d'Inquisition de Jacques Fournier*, 3 t., Moutou, 1978

Europe et Occitanie, les pays Cathares, (collectif), 5ᵉ session d'Histoire médiévale, Heresis, 1992

GARDEL (M.-É.) (sous la direction de): *Cabaret. Histoire et archéologie d'un castrum*, Heresis, 1999

GLABER (R.): *Histoires*, trad. et prés. de Mathieu Arnoux, Brepols, 1996

GOUGUENHEIM (S.): *Les fausses terreurs de l'an mil*, Picard, 1999

Montségur, 13 ans de recherche archéologique, 1964-1976, (collectif), Grame, 1981

GUI (B.): *Manuel de l'inquisiteur*, Les Belles Lettres, 1964

HAURÉAU (B.): *Bernard Délicieux et l'Inquisition Albigeoise 1300-1310*, Loubatières, 1992

Heresis, Revue internationale d'hérésiologie médiévale, édition de texte, recherche, Centre d'Études cathares, depuis 1983

Histoire en Pays de Sault, A.C.C.E.S. Roquefeuil, 1998

Encyclopédie des Religions, Bayard, 1997

IOGNA-PRAT (D.): *Ordonner et exclure. Cluny et la société chrétienne face à l'hérésie, au judaïsme et à l'islam (1000-1150)*, Aubier, 1998

La Chanson de la Croisade Albigeoise, 3 t., Les Belles Lettres

LE ROY LADURIE (E.): *Montaillou, village occitan*, Gallimard, 1976

Les articles *Dante* et *Inquisition*, Encyclopedia Universalis

Les Capétiens, Histoire et dictionnaire, 987-1328, (collectif), coll. Bouquin, Laffont, 1999

Les Cathares en Occitanie, (collectif), Fayard, 1982

Les Troubadours et l'État toulousain avant la Croisade, (collectif), Celo/William Blake & co. Édit, 1994

MÂLE (E.): *La cathédrale d'Albi*, Zodiaque, 1974

MOORE (R.) (sous la direction): *La persécution du catharisme. Actes de la 6ᵉ session du C.E.C.*, Heresis, 1996/ *La persécution, sa formation en Europe, 950-1250*, coll. 10/18, 1997

NELLI (R.): *Écritures cathares*, nouvelle édition actualisée par Anne Brenon, Le Rocher, 1995/ *La vie quotidienne des Cathares du Languedoc au XIIIᵉ siècle*, Hachette, 1969/ *Raimon de Miraval. Du jeu subtil à l'amour fou*, Verdier, 1979

PAILHÈS (C.): *L'Ariège des comtes et des cathares*, Milan, 1992

PANOUILLÉ (J.-P.): *Carcassonne, le temps des sièges*, CNRS, 1992

PELHISSON (G): *Chronique (1229-1244)*, CNRS, 1994

PRIN (M.) ET ROCACHER (J.): *Les Jacobins*, Le Tournefeuille, 1996

PUYLAURENS (G. DE): *Chronique*, Le Pérégrinateur, 1996

QUEHEN (R) ET DIELTIENS (D): *Les châteaux cathares... et les autres*, René Quehen, 1983

ROQUEBERT (M): *L'épopée cathare*, 4 t., Privat, 1971-1989/ *Les cathares: de la chute de Montségur aux derniers bûchers, 1229-1279*, Perrin, 1998

SIMON (M.) - BENOÎT (A.): *Le Judaïsme et le christianisme antique, d'Antiochus Épiphane à Constantin*, PUF, Nouvelle Clio, 1994

THOUZELLIER (C.): *Livre des deux principes. Introduction, texte critique, traduction, notes et index*, Cerf, 1973

TOUATI (F.-O.) (sous la direction de): *Vocabulaire historique du Moyen Âge (Occident, byzance, Islam)*, La boutique de l'Histoire, 1994

VAUCHEZ (A.): *La spiritualité du Moyen Âge occidental (VIIIᵉ -XIIᵉ siècle)*, P.U.F., 1975/ (sous la direction de): *Mouvements dissidents et novateurs du christianisme médiéval*, Actes de la 2ᵉ session du C.E.C. Heresis, 1990

ZODIAQUE, coll. La nuit des temps: n° 10, *Quercy roman*/ n° 43, *Languedoc roman*

ILLUSTRATIONS

This table presents details of some illustrations and their origins where space in the individual caption was insufficient.

Front Cover:
Seal of Raymond VII of Toulouse, Archives nationales, Paris; bishop's head, J. Vaylet Museum in Espalion; A Dominican teaching, illumination, late 14th or early 15th century, Municipal Library, Toulouse; detail of Scaligers' Tomb, Verona; Horseman, 13th century, Civic Medieval Museum, Bologna; Expulsion of the Albigensians from Carcassonne, illumination, Grandes Chroniques de France, British Library; Quéribus; Castle of the Counts of Carcassonne.

Back cover:
Oil lamp, Montségur Museum; Old man of the Apocalypse, 14th century, painting in Saint Antonin's Chapel, Jacobins Convent, Toulouse; Baptismal font, Museum of Religious and Mosan Art, Liège; Baptism of Christ, Baptistry of the Arians, Ravenna; Cross of Toulouse, keystone in St Stephen's Cathedral, Toulouse; Orant Stele in Cassès.

Pages 4-5: Carcassonne
Page 6: Disbelief of St Thomas, Cloister of Santo Domingo of Silos
Page 7: Ruins of Saint Cyprian's Basilica in Carthage
Page 50: Pentecost, Cloister of Santo Domingo of Silo
Page 51: Lauragais landscapes
Page 63: Detail of tympanum on Strasbourg Cathedral
Page 96-97: The Hole of the City at the foot of Lastours Castle
Page 98: Peyrepertuse
Page 99: Fresco in the Knights' Room, Castle of the Counts of Carcassonne
Page 127: Bishop, Façade of Saint John of Lateran, Rome
Page 133: Crusader, Avignonet
Page 134: Crusader, Naples Cathedral
Page 143: Knight, detail of the Battle of Las Navas de Tolosa, Versailles
Page 173: Saint Dominic, Fresco in Santa Maria Novella, Florence
Page 219: Heretic delivered to the flames, about 1254, Register of Alfaro of France, National Archives, Paris
Page 230: Morella
Page 231: Puilaurens
Page 269: Saint James, Portico of Glory, Compostela Cathedral
Page 312: Aguilar
Page 313: Quéribus and Canigou